LIKE EVERYONE ELSE BUT DIFFERENT

Like Everyone Else but Different

The Paradoxical Success of Canadian Jews

SECOND EDITION

MORTON WEINFELD

with RANDAL F. SCHNOOR and MICHELLE SHAMES

Carleton Library Series 245

McGill-Queen's University Press
Montreal & Kingston • London • Chicago

© McGill-Queen's University Press 2018

ISBN 978-0-7735-5280-7 (cloth)
ISBN 978-0-7735-5281-4 (paper)
ISBN 978-0-7735-5308-8 (ePDF)
ISBN 978-0-7735-5309-5 (ePUB)

Legal deposit first quarter 2018
Bibliothèque nationale du Québec

First edition 2001

Printed in Canada on acid-free paper that is 100% ancient forest free
(100% post-consumer recycled), processed chlorine free

Funded by the   Financé par le   Canada Council   Conseil des arts
Government   gouvernement   for the Arts   du Canada
of Canada   du Canada

We acknowledge the support of the Canada Council for the Arts, which
last year invested $153 million to bring the arts to Canadians throughout
the country.

Nous remercions le Conseil des arts du Canada de son soutien. L'an dernier,
le Conseil a investi 153 millions de dollars pour mettre de l'art dans la vie
des Canadiennes et des Canadiens de tout le pays.

Library and Archives Canada Cataloguing in Publication

Weinfeld, Morton
[Like everyone else – but different]
Like everyone else but different: the paradoxical success of Canadian
Jews/Morton Weinfeld with Randal F. Schnoor and Michelle Shames. –
Second edition.

(Carleton library series; 245)
Revision of: Like everyone else – but different : the paradoxical success
of Canadian Jews/Morton Weinfeld. – Toronto: McClelland & Stewart,
©2001.
Includes bibliographical references and index.
Issued in print and electronic formats.
ISBN 978-0-7735-5280-7 (cloth). – ISBN 978-0-7735-5281-4 (paper). –
ISBN 978-0-7735-5308-8 (ePDF). – ISBN 978-0-7735-5309-5 (ePUB)

1. Jews – Canada – Social conditions. 2. Judaism – Canada. I. Schnoor,
Randal F., author II. Shames, Michelle, author III. Title. IV. Title: Like
everyone else – but different V. Series: Carleton library series; 245

FC106.J5W43 2018   305.892'4071   C2017-906843-1

This book was typeset by Marquis Interscript in 10.5/13 Sabon.

Contents

Preface to the Second Edition

When first published, this book was well received and well reviewed. It went out of print, and later the publisher went out of business. In the meantime, many students in my McGill courses over the years enjoyed the book, which remained the only social-scientific overview of contemporary Canadian Jewish life. The book was also selected for *One Hundred Great Jewish Books: Three Millennia of Jewish Conversation*, edited by Rabbi Lawrence A. Hoffman (BlueBridge 2011). When I received the 2013 Marshall Sklare Prize from the Association for the Social Scientific Study of Jewry, it was largely in recognition of my research and writing on Canadian Jewish topics. It seemed time, therefore, to prepare a revised and updated second edition, which should appeal to scholars interested in diversity, Canadian studies, and modern Jewish studies, as well as to general readers. So here it is.

Much of the text remains unchanged. The book retains its original core and structure as well as its accessible style, variety of sources, jokes, and personal observations and experiences. Data and studies and events from the earlier period have been retained so that updates can better illustrate trends over time. Historical sections necessary to understand the current scene have also been retained. But much has been changed. I have updated statistical data from surveys and the census, and scholarly and other more popular sources, to reflect the past two decades. Canadian Jewish studies has begun to emerge as a more distinctive academic field. But more important have been a series of changes on the ground which have impacted the situation facing Canadian Jews.

Certain trends were unforeseen and others have gathered steam since the first publication. Canadian multiculturalism continues to be tested in the aftermath of the events of September 11, 2001, and following anti-immigrant trends in Europe and the election of President Trump. The drives for gender equality and more LGBTQ space have increased. Conventional norms, and indeed religious denominations, have been challenged by rising intermarriage rates, which bring a new fluidity and hybridity to Canadian Jewish life. The role of Israel, both within the Jewish community and in the broader Canadian society, has also become problematic. Canadian Jewish politics and policies have been largely reshaped through the Stephen Harper and into the Justin Trudeau years. Finally, anti-Semitism has re-emerged in different real or perceived forms as an important item on the communal Jewish agenda.

I still feel that the Jewish experience – and specifically the Canadian variant – is a valuable case study for people seeking to understand the limits of and possibilities for minority groups in liberal-democratic societies. But I wonder to what extent this experience can be reproduced by other groups. I remain an optimist about the Canadian Jewish future, but to a more tempered degree than in the past.

I would like to thank my two excellent collaborators. Dr Randal F. Schnoor is a sociologist who has been teaching Canadian Jewish studies for over a decade at the Koschitzky Centre for Jewish Studies at York University, Toronto. Ms Michelle Shames has both a BA and an MA in sociology and has worked as a researcher looking at criminal justice reform in the United States. Each has contributed in their own way, through ideas and research abilities, to making this edition more valuable and current. Charles Shahar and Harold Troper provided valued input. I would also like to thank McGill-Queen's University Press, and specifically Philip Cercone, Kathleen Kearns, Jacqueline Mason, and copy editor Susan Glickman. The stipend associated with my Chair in Canadian Ethnic Studies helped defray the expenses associated with this project. In addition, I would like to thank the McGill Institute for the Study of Canada, and the Professional Development Fund at McGill, for their support.

Since the first edition my family has expanded, so that our three children are now joined by three lovely partners, and as of this writing, two grandchildren. This edition is dedicated to my wife and to all members of my family.

Preface to the First Edition

Writing this book has been a true labour of love. I wrote it over more than four years, but its gestation period has been much longer, dating back at least to the late 1970s, when I began teaching a course on the sociology of North American Jewry at McGill. I am deeply involved, personally and professionally, in the subject.

The book grapples with all the major themes of modern Jewish life in Canada. Jews have always been interested in their own saga, and, as I shall argue, with very good reason. Canadian Jews are no different. Regardless of how involved or well-versed they are in Canadian Jewish life, they should find much in this book that is informative, engaging, and provocative. But this book is also written for those who are not Jewish. I have found a sincere fascination among Canadian non-Jews concerning this strange people. This has been my happy experience for many years with my eclectic band of (mainly non-Jewish) lunchtime regulars at the McGill Faculty Club. In subtle ways they, too, have contributed to this book. No subject has been off limits. Often a Jewish topic would arise, not from my own prompting. Whatever the issue – the latest turn in Israeli politics, a movie with a Jewish theme, free speech and Holocaust denial, the mysterious behaviours of Hasidic Jews, the latest Jewish joke – I would find collegial interest and fresh perspectives. This general curiosity is growing with increasing contact between Jews and non-Jews, not least through the rising rates of intermarriage. I hope this book helps.

I base my assertions, at least most of them, on evidence. But I have also cut down on the jargon of social science, provided basic information, and explained Jewish and technical terms. The book is for anyone interested in the modern Jewish experience, in Canada, in the challenges of cultural diversity, and in the intersection of all three. I offer my own interpretations, and some of these are controversial. In the face of a Jewish community which feeds on crises and pessimism, I argue for a different vision of the Jewish future. In my own view, to be a Jew is to be an optimist.

I owe many people a debt of gratitude. Mordechai Ben-Dat, Desmond Morton, Harold Troper, and Gerald Tulchinsky read the manuscript and offered valuable comments, suggestions, criticisms, and facts. I spoke to many people, most in person, but others by phone or email. They helped me as formal interview subjects and as sources for specific bits of information or assistance. Several students helped as researchers. To (without titles and honorifics) Ron Aigen, Murray Baron, Tzila Baum, Ian Beitel, Cathie Best, Franklin Bialystok, Myer Bick, Irv Binik, Jay Brodbar, Shari Brotman, Robert Brym, Mervin Butovsky, Warren Clark, Harvey Cohen, Sergio DellaPergola, Paula Draper, Honey Dresher, Celia Economides, Daniel Elazar, Ronald Finegold, Tzipie Freedman, Baruch Frydman-Kohl, Robert Fulford, Linda Glustein, Yechiel Glustein, Hy Goldman, Michael Goldman, Howard Goldstein, Sid Gotfrid, Allan Gotlieb, Charles Gradinger, Frank Guttman, Gershon Hundert, Howard Joseph, Norma Joseph, Joe Kislowicz, Linda Kislowicz, Bobby Kleinman, Penny Krowitz, Jean-Claude Lasry, Susan Le Pan, Malcolm Lester, Ho Hon Leung, Bob Luck, Peyton Lyon, Sheldon Maerov, Herbert Marx, Norman May, Richard Menkis, Joel Miller, Lionel Moses, Doug Norris, Gunther Plaut, Carol Polter, Reuben Poupko, Manuel Prutschi, Anita Rappaport, Janice Rosen, Anna Rubalsky, Jonathan Sarna, Diane Sasson, Randal Schnoor, Stuart Schoenfeld, William Shaffir, Charles Shahar, Moshe Shulman, Rob Singer, Ted Sokolsky, Norman Spector, Stephen Speisman, Heidi Stober, David Taras, Harriet Tobman, Marion Van Horn, Joel Wardinger, Bryna Wasserman, Martine Whitaker, and to several others who wished to remain anonymous, my sincere thanks. I apologize to any whom I have omitted. Many others not listed here have shaped my understanding of Canadian Jewry through countless informal encounters and conversations over the years. This is certainly true of many academic colleagues in the fields of ethnic relations and modern Jewish studies.

I would like to thank several people at McClelland and Stewart: Doug Gibson for recognizing the need to tell this story, Alex Schultz for helping to shape the manuscript and guide it home, and Adam Levin for his careful copyediting and attention to detail. I thank my agent, Beverley Slopen, for her continuing support. Special thanks to all the office staff at McGill, both in the McGill Institute for the Study of Canada and in the Department of Sociology, who helped in so many ways. Lynne Darroch and Natalie Zenga were there to help me with computer challenges as they arose. Several sources contributed financially. I would like to thank the Multiculturalism Branch of the Department of Canadian Heritage, the Department of Citizenship and Immigration, and the Social Sciences and Humanities Research Council through their funding of the Metropolis Project and the Montreal consortium Immigration et Métropoles, and McGill University through its support for the Chair in Canadian Ethnic Studies and its sabbatic leave policy.

Most important of all, I thank my family. Much of this book has been shaped by my experiences first with my wife, Phyllis, and later with my three wonderful children, Rebecca, David, and Joanna. They were an inspiration, a source of encouragement, and tolerated absences and long nights at the computer. But family also means generations past, specifically my parents and my wife's parents, now all deceased, who came to Canada. To all of them, I dedicate this book.

LIKE EVERYONE ELSE BUT DIFFERENT

INTRODUCTION

A Paradoxical People

Diversity and Success

Can they all be Canadian Jews? A devout Orthodox man who has *payess* (sidelocks) and prays three times a day; a Modern Orthodox man who wears a knitted *yarmulka* (skullcap) at home and at work; a Conservative Jew who drives to synagogue every Sabbath; a Reform Jew in a mixed marriage who celebrates both Hanukkah and Christmas; a European Ashkenazi; a North African Sephardi; a recent immigrant from Russia, Israel, South Africa, or Ethiopia; a fourth-generation Canadian; an atheist; a left-wing Zionist supporting Peace Now; a right-wing Zionist who supports Likud; a dentist, stockbroker, business executive, teacher, psychotherapist, cab driver, or secretary; a knee-jerk liberal or a neo-conservative; a native speaker of English, French, Polish, Russian, Spanish, German, Yiddish, or Hebrew? Yes, they are all Canadian Jews. This book tells their story. Their diversity provides the context and an explanation for the paradoxical successes of Canadian Jewish life.

Jewish life in Canada today is perhaps as good as it has been anywhere since the Golden Age of Spain. Indeed, as I write these words the Centre for Jewish Studies at York University has organized an academic conference for October of 2017 entitled "No Better Home for the Jews ... than Canada?" In an atmosphere of relative security, Jews are able to fulfil the twin promises of Canadian multiculturalism: they participate fully in the life of their society, and at the same time maintain a vibrant Jewish culture. Jews have stumbled onto a magical equilibrium. For most minority groups, these two objectives stand in sharp opposition. Usually, the more that members of a minority group participate in the majority society and culture, the less they succeed at preserving their own. They will join a different church and set of organizations, harmonize their social and political values with those of the majority, lose interest in their ancestral language and culture, socialize and even marry outside the group. Canadian Jews do this as well, but so far, less than non-Jews. The relative Jewish success at combining both objectives is remarkable, and this is the core theme of this study. For Jews, the trade-off is not nearly as severe; they can have their honey cake and eat it, too.

Jews are full of contradiction, diversity, conflict, irony, and, yes, mystery. In this, Jews are not unique; paradox is a feature of the human condition. But what is special is the extent and the outcome of paradox. Jews in the diaspora – as much by luck as by design – have created a workable synthesis of opposites. This success has at times proved elusive or fleeting. But nowhere does its prospect shine brighter than in Canada today. Jews are at once Biblical and post-modern, religious and ethnic, devout and secular, admired and reviled, conservative and liberal, prosperous and insecure. Jewish communal and cultural institutions are ubiquitous, even as evidence of assimilation mounts. Jews are relatively affluent and accepted every-where, yet legitimately insecure about an apparent revival of anti-Semitism in modern forms. Jews are generally among the haves and societal insiders, but their socio-political attitudes often empathize with more marginal groups.

Beginning in the late 1800s, Jews in the West have been overrepre-sented on the liberal end of the political and socio-cultural spectrum. They have passionately embraced civil liberties and support for the welfare state. They have achieved the highest levels of educational and occupational success, often in the most modern fields. Some have gained fame as scientific or artistic geniuses. Others have earned great wealth. They have been the first group to achieve zero popula-tion growth in the United States, and have low fertility rates in Canada as well. A secular Jewish culture involving elements of lan-guage, music, art, politics, and lifestyle has emerged. All these are hallmarks of modernity.

Yet at the same time, most identified Jews retain ties to their his-tory and traditions and even non-religious Jews cling tenaciously to some religious rituals and holidays. While many Jews have embraced newer and more progressive forms of worship, others adhere to older religious principles, revere the same ancient land, and use essen-tially the same language as did King David. Many study the same texts as the commentators in and the commentators on the Talmud.

They practise rituals going back centuries, even millennia. The traditional Jewish family remains a powerful ideal. The Holocaust has confirmed the Jewish status as an archetypal victim and pariah, continuing a tradition going back for centuries. Orthodox and ultra-Orthodox Judaism have managed to survive and thrive in North America, defying earlier scholarly predictions.

Canadian Jews also differ by region across the country, by religious denomination, by social class, by culture, by ethnic and national origin, even by ideology. The old joke, "For every two Jews, there are three organizations," captures this profusion. For some analysts these differences, and the fractious conflicts that arise from them, are a source of weakness, or of danger. My own view is that these differences and the paradoxes that spring from them are a source of strength. This diversity is a key to Jewish success. There are Jewish eggs in many baskets. There is no one formula that applies to each Jew. Not every group of Jews needs to maximize both multicultural goals, that of external participation and that of internal solidarity.

This study analyzes how this paradoxical balance operates in the day-to-day lives of Canadian Jews and the Canadian Jewish community. Some chapters will focus on participation in the broader society: how Jews earn a living; their relations with non-Jews; their encounters with the older and newer forms of anti-Semitism; their involvement in Canadian politics. Others will focus on issues of internal Jewish concern: the nature of Jewish marriages, families, and sexual relations; how and why Jews pray; the many varieties of Jewish culture; how Jews educate their children and participate in Jewish organizations. Every part of the story is revealing; together they help us understand the enigma of Jewish survival. Moreover, they may illuminate challenges facing other minority groups not only in Canada but in other liberal-democratic societies as well.

American authors have written many books pondering the present and future of American Jewry. Their recent mood has been pessimistic, but it was not always so. In 1985, Charles Silberman's *A Certain People* hailed the American Jewish experience as an unmitigated success story.[1] American Jews then, like Canadian Jews today, enjoyed full participation and acceptance in American society while retaining a seemingly strong Jewish cultural identity. In 1986, Calvin Goldscheider's *Jewish Continuity and Change* argued boldly that American Jewish life would continue despite transformations and declines in religious observance.[2] Then, with the publication of the results of the National Jewish Population Survey (NJPS) of 1990, the roof fell in. The NJPS offered American Jews the first statistical portrait of their community in twenty years. While experts debated whether the recent mixed-marriage rate was 52 per cent or 41 per cent, the trend seemed clear. Through cultural assimilation or by marrying out, American Jews were disappearing. And those who remained were becoming an increasingly fractious group, torn apart by a growing religious *Kulturkampf*, or culture war, over the issue of "who is a Jew?" Panic set in among communal leaders. Jews needed a religious or cultural revival, as well as a new unity, to prevent the unthinkable. The titles of some relevant books capture the pessimism: Alan Dershowitz's *The Vanishing American Jew*, Elliott Abrams's *Faith or Fear*, Jack Wertheimer's *A People Divided,* Samuel Freedman's *Jew vs Jew*. More recently, the 2013 Pew survey of American Jewish life, *A Portrait of Jewish Americans*, accentuated this pessimistic perspective, largely due to an estimated intermarriage rate, with no conversion, of 71 per cent for non-Orthodox recently married American Jews.[3]

The debate between the optimists and pessimists continues in Canada as well as in the United States. The organized Jewish community has in general embraced the pessimistic view. And the worries are not only about assimilation. Recall that the Golden Age of Spain was followed by the Inquisition and the Expulsion in 1492. The varied and vibrant Jewish culture which emerged later in Eastern and Central Europe was destroyed during the Holocaust. And today, the "Golden Age of Canada" presents new challenges and contradictions. The security of North American Jewry is not immediately threatened by traditional anti-Semitism. But new forms of victimization facing Jews have emerged, reflected in efforts to isolate and delegitimize the state of Israel. And many see even greater dangers in assimilation, intermarriage, and divisions within the Jewish fold. As the old lament puts it: "If everything is so good, why are things so bad?" This idea is at the core of the following quip:

> If Jews want to feel good, they should read the anti-Semitic press: Jews are in control, Jews are powerful … If Jews want to feel bad, they should read the Jewish press: Jews are disappearing, Jews are weak, anti-Semitism is rampant, Jews are not united.

I do not share the prevailing pessimism, though I recognize there are real challenges ahead. Historian Simon Rawidowicz rejected the image of Jews as "an ever-dying people," arguing that almost every generation has felt that it was the last link in the chain. The current generation is no different.[4] But the problems of continuity and unity are neither new nor daunting. Innovative responses to these challenges are already underway as part of the new "continuity agenda." In addition, no one should assume that present trends establish the blueprint for the future; the only guarantee about the Jewish future is that the unpredictable will happen. And I am even less pessimistic about the future of Jews in Canada, where the inroads of assimilation are not as severe.

But my optimism is sustained by another, broader, understanding. Given the broad sweep of Jewish history, I see no reason why the current conditions in North America must sound the death knell of (non-Orthodox) Jewish life. Things are not so bad. To be sure, anti-Semitism persists, expressed in old and newer Israel-linked themes. But if Auschwitz was not the end of the line neither will be debates about Israeli policies nor Madonna or Justin Bieber dabbling in Kabbalah. Jewish survival has resulted from an unintended but fortuitous blend of diverse, indeed contradictory, demographic and cultural strategies that can adapt to changing circumstances. Jews, as we shall see, maintain an uneasy equilibrium of opposing forces pulling them both outward and inward. This has been the case throughout the modern period. They struggle – like a fiddler on the roof – to maintain their balance.

THE CANADIAN DIMENSION

The story of Canadian Jews today has its own particular interest and importance. Given English-Canadian insecurity vis-à-vis the Americans, and Québécois insecurity vis-à-vis the English language, Jews are the ideal Canadians. Jews are chronically insecure, like Canadians or Québécois, and love to take their collective pulse. No one should be surprised. It is just three generations since the death camps, and now the new threats of cultural extinction and demographic attrition have appeared. The discourse of survival so common to both English- and French-speaking Canadian writers and thinkers also describes the Jewish experience for two thousand years.

Despite the increased visibility of Jews in Canadian life, few social scientific books analyze their daily lives and communities. The exceptions are edited collections of academic articles, memoirs, or research monographs focused on specific topics. (See the Bibliographic Essay.) These important books add to our academic knowledge but are insufficient for scholars or general readers who seek one integrated overview and interpretation of the complexities of contemporary Canadian Jewish life.

Understanding Canadian Jews is of importance to three intersecting areas of contemporary scholarship. First is the area of modern Jewish studies. The Jewish community in Canada has become an increasingly significant member of the diaspora. The demographic future of Jewish life in Western and Central Europe is bleak.[5] Anti-Semitism remains a significant and perhaps growing problem in most European communities, nurtured in an increasingly xenophobic environment which has culminated in murders in France and Belgium. The exodus to Israel and to the West from Eastern Europe, specifically the former Soviet Union, has led to both a demographic and cultural depletion. Despite heroic attempts at communal revival, ongoing economic, political, and social instability makes it unlikely that Eastern Europe will reproduce strong Jewish communities. The communities in Latin America and South Africa continue to atrophy. Even the American Jewish population is relatively stagnant. Among all diaspora communities, only in Canada and Germany have there been significant recent increases. Canada, with over 385,000 Jews in 2011, has the fourth largest Jewish population after Israel at 6.1 million, the United States at about 5.7 million (though some estimates with wider definitions or using different methodologies are larger), and France at 475,000. The United Kingdom has 290,000 Jews and Russia has 186,000 Jews.[6]

The second research area is the field of Canadian Studies. A reasonable assumption is that the experience of Canadian Jews can teach us something about the limits and possibilities of multiculturalism in Canada. The idea of multiculturalism embraced by Canadians in the 1970s did not emerge out of nowhere. American Jewish writer Horace Kallen popularized the idea of "cultural pluralism" early in the twentieth century to symbolize what he saw as the impact of mass migration on American life. Kallen later described the term in his famous metaphor of an orchestra:

The American way is the way of orchestration. As in an orchestra the different instruments, each with its own characteristic timbre and theme, contribute distinct and recognizable parts to the composition, so in the life and culture of a nation, the different regional, ethnic, occupational, religious and other communities compound their different activities to make up the national spirit. The national spirit is constituted by this union of the different.[7]

Cultural pluralism, of course, fits the Canadian reality perfectly. Canada was settled by the First Nations, then the French and the English, and waves of later immigrant groups. Despite the historic and ongoing inequalities faced by Canada's First Nations and visible minority groups, for many people a tolerance for and appreciation of diversity is the essence of being Canadian. Well before Kallen's writing, Prime Minister Wilfrid Laurier, at the dawn of the twentieth century, anticipated future multicultural sentiments in his famous comparison of Canada to a cathedral:

The cathedral is made of marble, oak and granite. It is the image of the nation I would like to see Canada become. For here I want the marble to remain the marble; the granite to remain the granite; the oak to remain the oak; and out of all these elements I would build a nation great among the nations of the world.[8]

This was music to the ears of diasporic Jews, who had for generations been living within yet apart from host communities. Indeed, some minority communities see Jews as a model for what they can accomplish in this country. Perhaps this is accurate. But the fact that Canadian Jews are doing well is not due mainly to the official policy or rhetoric of Canadian multiculturalism so much as to those features of Canadian law and society which reflect the values of liberal democracy. Neither is it due to any intrinsic merit or talent on the part of Canadian Jews themselves. It likely derives from their inherited cultural characteristics and their long history as a product of diverse diaspora communities.

Third, the case of Canadian Jews can interest scholars in the general field of the sociology of minority groups, studies of transnationalism and diasporas, sociology of religion, and those interested in immigrant integration, ethnic inequality, and issues of diversity generally. The experience of struggling in many different diasporic settings for close to two thousand years helped Jews develop resourceful strategies and flexible institutions. Jews were well placed to take advantage of what multiculturalism had to offer. The Jewish experience has been that of the "other" in Christian and Muslim societies. Other minority groups, including some currently being "othered" in Western societies, may be experiencing similar processes.

These three areas can intersect in the emerging field of modern Canadian Jewish studies. That sub-field was launched in *Canada's Jews*, a pioneering book by demographer Louis Rosenberg which was the last attempt to provide a comprehensive contemporary overview.[9] First published in 1939, the classic volume was statistical and relied largely on analysis of the 1931 census data. Nothing as thorough has been done since. Although this study is partly inspired by Rosenberg's work, it is not a compendium of demographic statistics. Rather, it seeks to capture the textures of daily life of Jews and their communities using a variety of disciplinary traditions and data sources. These will include census data, community surveys, social scientific studies, news reports and op-eds, the odd joke, and my own experiences, observations, and reflections. Since this study is aimed at three distinct scholarly communities, as well as an interested public, I have had to minimize the use of disciplinary jargon. Information that is familiar to one set of scholars will not be to another. The footnotes link to scholarly sources, as well as journalistic articles, websites, and other sources.

Jews remain a source of curiosity, admiration, and fear among many in the non-Jewish world, and this is also true for Canada. I have found it in casual conversation with a range of non-Jews, from blue-collar workers to academics. Scholars have tried to pinpoint exactly what makes Jews so unusual. Non-Jewish writer Ernest van den Haag accepted generally flattering but largely racial stereotypes held about Jews.[10] He implied that Jews are smarter than other people, have a distinctive character, and make better doctors and more aggressive lawyers. Anthropologist Raphael Patai has argued that Jews are indeed a unique people not because they have remained separate, but because they have over the centuries absorbed significant cultural influences from the outside world.[11] Combining these two perspectives, we can conclude that Jews are the same as everyone else, but also very different.

PERSONAL BIASES

No researcher comes to a topic with a clean slate. And no analysis of a topic is based on a neutral set of facts and a self-evident interpretation of their meaning. There is always selectivity at work, based either on the writer's biography or on an intellectual predisposition.

Some years ago, the Bata Shoe Company sent two sales representatives to Africa to check out the potential market. The pessimist returned and said, "It's terrible! No one is wearing shoes! There's no market at all." The optimist returned and said, "It's terrific! No one is wearing shoes! The market is enormous."

In the interests of full disclosure, it is now common for scholars to reveal personal background and biases. So where am I coming from? Obviously, I am an insider. This means I may have certain insights, but must carefully avoid cheerleading. I am a committed Jew who is optimistic about the future of Canadian Jewry. I was born in 1949 in Montreal to Polish Jewish Holocaust survivors. My parents sent me to Jewish day school until the end of high school, and for ten summers to a Hebrew-speaking camp in the Laurentian Mountains. I graduated from McGill University with a BA and later earned a doctorate at Harvard. I am married to a Jewish woman, and my three children attended a mix of Jewish schools and camps. We belong to a liberal, Reconstructionist synagogue. My father lived in Israel from 1975 until his death in 1990, and I have visited many times. I cherish Israel – as I do Canada – many warts and all. I appreciate the full spectrum of Jewish life, from ultra-Orthodox to Jewish secularist, from Likud to Labour. Not for one second do I think that my brand of Jewishness has a monopoly on virtue. It just happens to suit me.

My Jewishness also embodies all sorts of inconsistencies. Take my approach to keeping kosher. Jews are forbidden to eat certain foods, like pork and seafood, and to mix dairy products with meat. So what do I do? At our home we cook only kosher products and have separate meat and dairy dishes, but we also keep paper plates and plastic cutlery so we can eat Chinese food at home. Our dishes are kosher, but not our stomachs. We eat at any sort of restaurant. I eat cheeseburgers, as well as bacon and pork spareribs, but refuse to eat ham, shrimp, and lobster, and gag at the thought of a glass of milk with a salami sandwich. On Passover, we use a separate set of dairy and meat Passover dishes, empty out the kitchen cupboards, and eat only special kosher-for-Passover products. I have brought a box of matzo to the McGill Faculty Club so I can have it during Passover along with the unkosher lunch I buy there. Of course all this makes no sense and is thoroughly illogical. But I am not alone. Many Jews have their own idiosyncratic kosher habits. Modern Jewish life is one big cafeteria, where Jews pick and choose.

As an academic and sociologist, I have been teaching about contemporary Jewish life for four decades. I began as a teaching assistant at Harvard, working for my advisor, the eminent sociologist Nathan Glazer, who taught a course on American Judaism. Since 1977, I have been a professor of sociology at McGill, specializing in ethnic and race relations. And since that year I have given an annual course on the sociology of North American Jews, the first of its kind in Canada. My reflections and interpretations have been shaped by my teaching and research over the years. Let me borrow a rabbinical dictum: I have learned much from my teachers, more from my colleagues, but most of all from my students.

As a sociologist, I have a behaviourist bias. When evaluating social phenomena, I prefer to know what people actually do, not just what they say or claim to believe. While it is interesting to know about people's attitudes, talk is cheap. Sociologists who are seeking here the latest esoteric theoretical fads will also be disappointed. My sociological work and this book are resolutely empirical; wherever possible, I deal in facts.

> An old Jew wants to join the navy. The recruiter asks him if he can swim. He replies, "Don't worry, I know the theory."

Lastly, Canada has been and remains a very imperfect country (which country is not?), yet the amount of overt bigotry today is far less than in the past.[12] The historic and ongoing mistreatment of First Nations by the European colonizers is crushing. So too is the inequality facing racialized immigrant minorities. Still, in 2013, Canada ranked ninth in the world on the Human Development Index and the OECD ranked Canada as the third best place to live according to the Better Life Index.[13] Perhaps those studies overstate the case. But clearly Canada's treatment of non-White and other minorities compares well even with other Western liberal democracies. Many European countries, for example, have seen the creation of openly anti-immigrant, xenophobic, and intolerant political parties. Rightly or wrongly, Canada has appeared to many observers as uniquely resistant to these trends.

COMPARATIVE METHODS

A comparative perspective is one way to minimize biases that may flow from my positon as an insider – as a Canadian Jew. To determine whether there is anything distinctive about Canadian Jews, I will compare them frequently to Jews in the United States. How could I not? Most of the modern challenges of Jewish life exist on both sides of the border. For Jews already deeply committed to certain forms of Jewish life, the religious and cultural opportunities in places like New York are unmatched by anything Canada has to offer. But that is a poor basis for comparing the two countries. On most measures ranging from knowledge of Hebrew or Yiddish to ritual observance, Canadian Jews are on average "more Jewish" than their American cousins. The differences, as we shall see, are remarkable.

Jewish scholars and communal leaders on both sides of the border recognize the greater Jewishness of Canadian over American Jews but disagree as to the reasons. Some claim the greater Canadian Jewishness is due to circumstances relating to immigration and demography. Jews in large numbers came earlier to the United States, so they have had more time to assimilate. Recently, Canada has had relatively far more Jewish immigrants, who presumably have stronger ties to Jewish tradition. In 2013, 14 per cent of American Jews and in 2011, close to 30 per cent of Canadian Jews were foreign born.[14] In this view, it is immigration, not Canadian multiculturalism, that gives Canadian Jews their edge. Others feel that the greater Jewishness is due to the much vaunted difference between the Canadian multicultural "mosaic" versus the American "melting pot." In other words, Canada was and is more nurturing of minority groups than the United States, regardless of the proportions of immigrants, and such tolerance could retard Jewish assimilation.[15] As a sociologist, I favour the interpretation that highlights Jewish immigration patterns rather than specific features of the Canadian environment, despite recognizing that this suggests that Canadian Jews will eventually become more "American" and assimilated.

In this book I will also compare Jews to other ethnic or religious minority groups. (Think of the many jokes that start, "A rabbi, a priest, and a minister ...") Recent research in the fields of modern Jewish studies and Canadian ethnic studies has consisted largely of in-depth case studies. Detailed comparisons are sadly lacking.[16] In a sense this volume, too, is a singular case study, since it is essentially about Canadian Jews. But I have long agreed with sociologist Seymour Martin Lipset that one of the best ways to study Jews is to study Gentiles.[17] Any statement describing Jewish behaviour – for example, "Jews on average look after their own" – relies on an explicit or implicit comparative framework. So I began this book espousing the analytical value of comparing Jews to other groups. If I will end with the same view is another question. I will also compare groups of Jews with each other. (Think of jokes that start, "An Orthodox, a Conservative, and a Reform rabbi ...") This is a natural outgrowth of the emphasis on diversity as a cornerstone of the Jewish paradox and as an asset that sustains Jewish life.

Since regional variations loom large in Canadian life, I will also compare one Canadian Jewish community to another. Many of the vignettes and interviews are taken from Montreal, where I grew up and have worked and raised my family. Many others come from Toronto, a city I know very well. This volume will also rely heavily on recent demographic surveys from these two cities. Montreal and Toronto are different from each other and both differ from smaller Canadian cities. A comprehensive treatment of the regional varia-tions in all the issues discussed here would require several additional books. But unless specified otherwise, I will assume that most events or experiences drawn from one setting are generic, and apply to all others. My stress is on commonalities. The broad meaning of denom-inational boundaries, relevance of religious rituals, dilemmas facing LGBTQ Jews and Jews in mixed marriages, encounters with anti-Semitism and anti-Zionism, foibles of Jewish schools and organiza-tions are familiar to Jews throughout Canada.

Where we find differences between Jews and non-Jews, I will try to suggest which of two broad reasons apply. The first is cultural. Accordingly, Canadian Jews differ from non-Jews because elements of traditional Jewish or Judaic *culture* shape their behaviour. These factors can include religious laws and precepts rooted in the Torah and Talmud, as well as other forms of Jewish cultural practice. This line of argument dates back to the work of German social theorist

Max Weber. In his classic work, *The Protestant Ethic and the Spirit of Capitalism*, Weber raised the possibility that religious doctrines, like other ideas, could have an influence on seemingly non-spiritual things like economic behaviour.[18] Extending this approach means that many mundane aspects of Jewish life – how Jews earn a living, or their political positions – are rooted in Jewish religious and cultural traditions.

The second explanation for differences in Jewish and non-Jewish behaviour relates to social structure. This argument owes much to the thought of Karl Marx and more liberal social theorists. In this view people's social position, specifically their economic class or the discrimination they face, determines their behaviour and thought in many non-economic areas. Socio-demographic characteristics also play a role. The urban history of Jews, their relative concentration in middle-class and lately upper-middle-class occupations, their historical and ongoing confrontation with anti-Semitism, and features of their immigrant experience are examples of social structural reasons that could account for such differences. I happen to be agnostic about the relative importance of cultural or social structural explanations for most features of the North American Jewish population. It depends on the issue at hand. But I am confident that both play a role.

Before turning our attention to the specifics of Canadian Jewry, we begin with two introductory chapters. The first reviews the full spectrum of Jewish diversity and Jewish identity. The second outlines contrasting qualitative and quantitative approaches to the understanding of Jewish survival.

1

Who Are the Jews?

The Elements of Jewish Diversity

"So the people of Israel did everything the Lord had commanded Moses. They camped, each under his own banner, each with his own ancestral house."

Numbers 2:34

"A Jew is a Jew and finished."
David Ben Gurion

THE ORIGINS OF JEWISH DIVERSITY

The story of Canadian Jews, like that of all Jews, begins in the ancient Middle East. (Note that in this study I will make periodic references to Biblical narratives. The historicity of these accounts is of course unsettled, and I do not accept them as fact. Rather, these myths have shaped the self-perceptions of Jewish people for millennia, and as a result have significant importance for understanding the Jewish experience past and present.) The Bible tells us the Israelites who left Egypt and settled in the Holy Land were a people composed of twelve tribes. The word "Jew," or *yehudi* in Hebrew, comes from the tribe of Judah, and later their kingdom of Judea, but was used popularly only after the end of the first Babylonian Exile. An independent sovereign Jewish existence as one or more kingdoms in the area ceased with the Roman conquest in 70 AD and the subsequent exile of most of the Jewish population. While diaspora Jews today are an urbanized, cosmopolitan lot, the foundations of their religious thought were laid in that early period when Jews were an agricultural people living on their own territory. The holidays of *Sukkoth*,

Pesach, and *Shavuot* are all tied to the agricultural cycle, and much of the Talmud – that great compendium of rabbinical debates and decisions on matters of Jewish law – concerns issues around rural, agricultural life. Part of the secret of Jewish success has been the ability to reconstruct their origins and rituals and adapt them to the exigencies of the modern, urbanized world.

While a continuous if fragile Jewish presence remained in Israel after the Roman Exile, the major centres of Jewish life and culture developed in the diaspora. It is only since the Holocaust that North America has replaced Europe as the major centre of Jewish life outside Israel, which now has the largest Jewish community in the world. The tension – in my view a creative tension – between the Israeli core and the diasporic periphery is a major feature of Jewish diversity.

Jews have never – ever – been a unified people. Internal conflict is a dominant theme of the Bible, beginning with the non-Jewish Cain and Abel. Even wandering in the desert, and after settling in the land of Israel, the Hebrews maintained their identities and loyalties to the twelve tribes. While no minority group is truly homogeneous, Jews have been spread far and wide with a recorded history which has spanned four millennia and five continents. The diversity described below has been instrumental in Jewish survival. The Canadian Jewish community of the twenty-first century, while an important part of the Jewish diaspora, is itself a microcosm of the Jewish world. Most Canadian Jews are of Eastern European origin. But we also find Jews from other European countries, from the Middle East, North Africa and Ethiopia, from Latin America, South Africa, and Israel. To this geographic, racial, and cultural mix must be added a wide spectrum of religious and cultural diversity, from various ultra-Orthodox sects to liberal Reform and secular Jews.

This diversity is nothing new. In the Canada of 1900 or even 1950, there were also great distinctions between *Litvaks* (Lithuanians), *Galicianers* (Eastern Polish), Hungarians, Romanians, *Yekkes* (German Jews), and Anglo-Saxons; between uptowners and downtowners; between old-timers and greeners; between left-wing Zionists and right-wing Zionists and non-Zionists and anti-Zionists; between communists and socialists and capitalists; between Hebraists and Yiddishists; between workers and bosses. The political and social tensions at the time were probably greater than those today, and it was more misleading back then to speak of a single Jewish community. It simply was not applicable.[1]

Today, there is a new element of Jewish diversity: the increasing proportion of those who see themselves as "partly" Jewish, whether as a result of intermarriage or simply because they embrace multiple identities. A growing number identify as part Jewish and part Christian; others as part Canadian and part Jewish. Some Jews blend their Jewish identity with one based on gender, or sexual orientation, or a profession. Some may tilt more to the Jewish and others to the non-Jewish pole. For others, their identity is an ever-changing postmodern and hybrid mish-mash. In this chapter I present three core elements – ethnicity, race, and Israel – in some detail. I then briefly outline several others. I will return to all of these topics in greater detail in later chapters.

ETHNICITY: DIFFERENCES WITHIN DIFFERENCES

Jews are a people, *am Yisrael* (the nation of Israel), an ethnic group defined by a common descent, a sense of history, and other cultural attributes. The expulsion of 70 AD sent Jews from the current areas of Israel and Palestine into the Roman Empire's European territory, north through the Italian Peninsula, westward to the Iberian Peninsula, and then into Northern, Central, and eventually Eastern Europe. In addition, Jewish communities developed throughout the Middle East and North Africa, even predating the Roman expulsion. By the eve of the Spanish Expulsion in 1492, there were three major population and cultural concentrations of Jews.[2]

Oriental Jews, the first group, came from communities throughout the Middle East and North Africa which preceded the rise of Sephardi Jewry and the Inquisition. For example, the Jewish communities in Iraq date back over 2,500 years.

Sephardi Jews (the word "*Sepharad*" means "Spain" in Hebrew) were those originally from Spain and Portugal. After the expulsions from both these countries at the end of the fifteenth century, many moved elsewhere in Europe as well as into the Middle East, North Africa, and the Americas. The European-centred Sephardi tradition moved to countries like Holland, Greece, Turkey, and Bulgaria. At times, in popular discourse, Sephardi and Oriental Jews are collapsed into one category, particularly in the Israeli context, where they are often termed "groups from the east." Thus, many Oriental Jews could loosely be considered Sephardi.

The third group are Ashkenazi Jews ("*Ashkenaz*" is the older Hebrew word for Germany). This group refers to the Jews whose origins are in Central and Eastern Europe dating back to the Middle Ages, associated with Yiddish language and culture, and influenced by Christianity and European civilization.

Until the destruction of European Jewry during the Second World War, Ashkenazi Jews comprised perhaps nine-tenths of the Jewish world. In 1931, the world Jewish population was estimated at 15.5 million, of which 30 per cent were in America, 60 per cent in Europe, and the remainder in Asia, Africa, and Australasia.[3] Roughly six million European Jews were lost during the Holocaust. After the war, fertility rates declined and intermarriage rates increased among Westernized Ashkenazi Jews as compared to Sephardi Jews, most newly concentrated in Israel. As a result, the world demographic balance shifted somewhat, though Ashkenazi Jews remain in the majority. In Israel, about half of the Jewish population is Sephardi; that proportion was even higher before the massive migration of Jews from the former Soviet Union in the 1990s. If intermarriage rates increase between Ashkenazim and Sephardim in Israel, the distinctions between and social relevance of these categories may well decline, even as they continue to be used periodically to rally political parties.

Ashkenazi Jews today comprise about three-quarters or four-fifths of the world Jewish population. They were shaped first by an environment of European Christianity, and later by the various ideological currents of liberalism, secularism, political Zionism, socialism, and communism. Yiddish was the language of Ashkenazi Jews. It emerged as a form of Judeo-German, which borrowed extensively from Hebrew, German, and other European languages. From its beginnings in Germany, it spread to Poland and Russia. Ashkenazi Jews today tend to be lighter skinned; Sephardim are in general darker. This means that racialization can also play a role in current differences and inequalities within the Jewish group. Canadian Jews are overwhelmingly of Ashkenazi origin and most Canadians reflexively identify Jews with Europe. In its publications of census results, Statistics Canada lists the ethnic origin figures for Jews under the heading "Other European." Ashkenazi Jews developed a pluralistic, institutionalized form of Judaism, from ultra-Orthodox to Orthodox to Conservative to Reform and highly liberal denominations or movements.

Sephardi Jews and Oriental Jews, particularly the larger communities in North Africa and the Middle East, were shaped by Arab cultures and Islam, as well as colonial powers such as France or England, and were relatively less influenced by the modernizing trends and secular ideologies of Europe. Ladino, a form of Judeo-Spanish, was the classical language of the Sephardi Jews of Europe. Sephardi Judaism was highly traditional and the Sephardi love of Zion was more likely to flow from religious passion than political ideology. Sephardi Judaism tends to be more traditional, and Orthodoxy is the benchmark even for those who are in practice less observant. There is little or no Sephardi Reform Judaism. But even where both communities profess orthodoxy, a Sephardi religious service will have distinctive liturgical melodies and minor differences in some prayers from an Ashkenazi one. Prayer books are often in Hebrew only, and little English or French is likely to be part of the actual prayer service.

While both Ashkenazi and Sephardi traditions in Canada are now diluted, as shall be discussed in later chapters, their cultural legacy should not be ignored. The culture of Eastern European Jewry, particularly Yiddish language, literature, and music epitomized by the klezmer musical revival, exerts a powerful nostalgic appeal. Hundreds of Jews have participated in a klezmer camp retreat in the Laurentian Mountains outside Montreal. And thousands of Jews have attended Ashkenaz: A Festival of New Yiddish Culture in Toronto, which features literature, music, dance, theatre, and films reflecting Yiddish culture. In Montreal, Sephardi identity is strong. The major communal organization is Communauté Sépharade Unifiée de Québec and the primary language is French. The Sephardic community has sponsored the Quinzaine Sépharade Festival which celebrates the many facets of Sephardi culture.

Historically, there were not only differences between Ashkenazi and Sephardi Jews, but among Ashkenazim themselves. The major division was that between Jews of Germany and those of Eastern Europe. The former were more likely to be Westernized, speak German, and embrace Reform Judaism, which itself was founded in Germany. Arriving earlier in the New World, they became wealthier and more established. Eastern European Ashkenazi Jews were more traditional, more devout, and committed to Yiddish language and culture. At the same time, they were more likely to be skilled workers, union members, and sympathetic to socialist and other left-wing ideologies. More stereotypically, German Jews were seen as excessively formal, timid, stiff, snobbish, prone to assimilation, and wealthy. The term *Yekke*, for German Jew, comes from the German word for "jacket," which the supposedly stuffy and strait-laced German Jews reputedly never took off.

A Yekke comes home with a headache, complaining that on the train he had to sit facing the rear. His wife asks, "Why didn't you ask the person sitting across from you if he would mind changing seats?" He replies, "I wanted to ask someone, but I couldn't; there was no one there!"

Eastern European Jews were seen by Germans as uncouth, less civilized, and potentially embarrassing to the more established "uptown" Jews. But even among Eastern European Jews, there were group differences. Jewish origins in Lithuania, Russia, Galicia, and Romania were associated with stereotypes and character traits – usually negative – which helped set social boundaries.[4] And among religious Eastern European Jews, there were historic differences, and clashes, between Hasidim and Mitnagdim. The Hasidim were Jewish sects led by a *rebbe*, and emphasized spirituality and joy. By contrast the Mitnagdim – mainly from Lithuania – emphasized learning and strict piety. And there were even conflicts among the competing Hasidic *rebbes* and their followers. In addition, there are today clear demarcations between Hasidim as a whole and the *yeshiva* crowd, legatees of the Mitnagdim, who look to a *rosh yeshiva*, a leader of the *yeshiva*, rather than a charismatic *rebbe* as their leader. But despite all these internal and seemingly microscopic variations, the major distinction today is that between the Orthodox and the non-Orthodox.

How important are these ethnic differences? Those between Germans and Russians, and between *Litvaks* (from Lithuania) and *Galicianers* (from Eastern Poland/Western Ukraine) have disappeared. But not long ago, marriages across these boundaries were rare, and greeted by parents with dismay. The Sephardi-Ashkenazi distinction, with its racist baggage, continues to sour Israeli social and political life, though it is more muted lately than in the twentieth century. In Montreal, Sephardi-Ashkenazi relations have been complicated by French-English tensions. A study in the late 1960s found high intermarriage rates between Sephardim and French Québécois, reflecting in part the hostility of anglophone Ashkenazi Jews toward the newly arrived francophone Sephardim. Some of these prejudices, while reduced, still persist.[5] The term "Moroccans" has been at times used pejoratively in Canada, just as it is in Israel.

These ethnic differences have cultural dimensions in language, music, ritual, and cuisine but should not be overstated. All Ashkenazi and Sephardi Jews share basic religious elements: the centrality of the Torah and Talmud, and the observance of the Sabbath, dietary laws, and major holidays such as Rosh Hashanah, Yom Kippur, and Passover. Most key prayers are identical. Both groups are committed to Jewish survival and the security and well-being of the State of Israel. Jews are not a unified, homogeneous community (neither are most ethnic groups), but the common religious core and early history sustain their idea of themselves as a people.

GENETICS: RACE AND BIOLOGY

Many people may think of Jews as a race, or at least in racial categories. But Jews are not a race. In general, most social scientists and geneticists think the concept of race is bogus. And even if there were "pure" races, it is unlikely that Jews would qualify. The Bible reminds us of the very diverse ancestral origins of the Israelites. The house of David, for example, is descended from a Moabite woman, Ruth. And the prophet Ezekiel describes his fellow Judeans as follows: "Your mother was a Hittite and your father an Amorite" (Ezekiel 16:45). This "racial" diversity is obvious to anyone who has visited Israel, since among Jews there is a wide array of skin colours and shades, and physical characteristics.

> Two Ethiopian Jews are airlifted to Israel, and as they walk off the plane they see a Yemenite. Says one: "Look, a Swedish Jew!"

It is not only among Ethiopians that we find authentically Black Jews. They also exist in the United States, tracing their origins in part from Jewish slaveholders.[6] Up to the early twentieth century – by which time their descendants had been thoroughly assimilated – there were even Chinese Jews who looked just like non-Jewish Chinese. In general, Jews throughout the diaspora approximated some of the physical characteristics of the host populations, including not only skin colour but variations in fingerprint patterns and other traits.[7] Despite what Jewish parents preach to their children, historically it is clear that sexual contact took place between Jews and non-Jews.[8]

Yet in their genes, as in much else, Jews are like everyone else, but different. Though not a "race," they do represent a distinctive group within population genetics. What this means is that while Jews, over the generations, certainly did absorb genes from other peoples, their experience of forced or voluntary segregation also reproduced distinctive genetic patterns. One result is that many Jews share certain physical and character traits which set them apart. These reflect environmental factors, but also, as we shall see, recent research suggests a role for genetic/biological sources. Ashley Montagu, a Jewish anthropologist who played a key role in attacking the concept of race, particularly as it was used to demean non-Whites, nevertheless wrote:

> There undoubtedly exists a certain quality of looking Jewish, but this quality is not due so much to any inherited characters of the person in question, as to certain culturally acquired habits of expression, facial, vocal, muscular, and mental. Such habits do to a very impressive extent influence the appearance of the individual and determine the impression which he makes on others ... It is possible to distinguish many Jews from members of other cultural groups for the same reason that it is possible to distinguish Englishmen from such groups, or Americans, Frenchmen, Italians, and Germans ... Members of one cultural group do not readily fit into the pattern of another.[9]

Many Jews may claim they can recognize some Jews by looks, gesture, or accent. For the longest period, Jewish in-marriage patterns have produced identifiable results. There may be a presumed Ashkenazi Jewish look – though many Ashkenazi Jews do not have it – that others could identify. Combined with cultural clues like first and last names, speech patterns, body language, and mannerisms, it helps Jews recognize other Jews at social gatherings. But with increasing intermarriage, people will have to be more careful at cocktail parties. There are more and more non-Jews with thoroughly Jewish-sounding names, Jews who look and act like stereotypical non-Jews, and vice versa.

Despite this growing physical diversity, Jews can still be traced back to a common ancestral gene pool originating in the Middle East and Eastern Mediterranean, which has spread even farther. The Lemba, an African Bantu-speaking tribe from northern South Africa, claim to be descended from Jews and maintain some practices like circumcision and abstention from pork. A scientific study of the Y chromosome profiles of male populations found greater genetic correlations between Russian and Moroccan Jews than between those Jews and their immediate non-Jewish countrymen. Even the Lemba pattern matched the Jewish one more closely than other sub-Saharan groups. The fact that Jewish patterns correlated closely with non-Jewish Palestinian and Syrian populations also confirms the Middle Eastern origin of world Jewry. Jewish genetic ancestry is a blend of distinctive Jewish traits and infusions from surrounding populations.

Fingerprint patterns are one indicator that has shown both local variations among Jews throughout the world and core similarities to other Eastern Mediterranean groups, indicating a possible common genetic origin. Jews also have distinctive patterns of blood types. The biological basis of Jewish identity may even extend to smaller subgroups of Jews. *Cohanim,* those male Jews who claim descent from Moses's brother Aaron and the Biblical priestly caste, show a higher transmission of certain genetic markers or variations in the Y chromosome than do other Jews. This suggests a multigenerational pattern of father-son inheritance and the possibility of a common genetic ancestor – presumably the biblical Aaron![10]

Any group with a history of geographic isolation or separation with relatively low rates of intermarriage will demonstrate distinctive patterns of disease, some genetically based. There are many conditions or illnesses peculiar to Ashkenazi Jews, the most famous being Tay-Sachs, a fatal disease of the central nervous system, and others specific to Oriental and Sephardi Jews. Some, like lactose intolerance, are found in all groups of Jews. More recently, evidence has emerged about increased genetic mutations among Ashkenazi Jews that predispose them to higher rates of breast, ovarian, colon, and prostate cancer.[11] The American Jewish newspaper *The Forward* publishes an annual supplement devoted to "Jewish Genetic Diseases." This supplement includes updates on the current status of about twenty "Ashkenazi" diseases. Other research addresses Jews and mental illness. While the experts cited claimed that Jews were no more likely than any other group to suffer from mental illness in general, Jews were more likely than others to suffer from some specific conditions.[12]

But Jews should not panic. Their common ancestral gene pool has not condemned them to ill health. Far from it. Jews enjoy on average better health than non-Jews despite these genetically based diseases. This was true even early in the twentieth century. Looking at the years 1926 to 1936, demographer Louis Rosenberg found that the crude death rate for Jews was half that of the Canadian rates, and their infant mortality rate was less than half.[13] This was also true for the immigrant Jews in the United States.[14] Those advantages did not likely result from any common genetic heritage. Most researchers emphasize cultural attitudes toward health, ranging from religiously mandated hand-washing and cleanliness, to greater readiness to consult physicians and to worry – perhaps excessively – about the health of children.[15] In other words, Jewish health advantages more likely flow from non-genetic factors such as higher income and educational levels, while any health disadvantage may have a genetic basis. Nevertheless, the attention given to the increased risk of some diseases with a genetic/hereditary component has raised Jewish anxieties and made genetic screening a hot button issue in the Jewish community.[16]

Historically, Jewish intelligence or "cleverness" was seen as an innate Jewish racial or biological characteristic, certainly among anti-Semites. Even the philo-Semite Ernest van den Haag speculated that Jews gained intellectual benefits from their tradition of marrying the brightest males to the daughters of the wealthiest families. This quasi-Darwinian process guaranteed two things. First, the genes of the brightest males would be passed on to succeeding generations, which was less likely in the Catholic tradition of priestly celibacy. Second, the children of these arranged Jewish unions would be more likely to survive because of better nutrition, sanitation, housing, and medical care, financed by the wealthy parents of the daughter. This marriage pattern, along with the positive health effects of urbanization on Jews, could explain high levels of Jewish intelligence.[17]

The social and cultural environment of Jews has also played a role. Writing at the end of the First World War, the American economist and social critic Thorstein Veblen argued against the Zionist idea because the process of "normalizing" the Jews would rob them of a creative spark that benefited all humanity.[18] Veblen was afraid of losing the Jewish scientists, writers, musicians, and artists who flourished a century ago. In his view, "renegade Jews" in the diaspora rebelling against the strictures of Orthodoxy and conventional morality were the source of Jewish genius and creativity, not any advantageous genetic endowment. Tilling the soil and fighting the British or the Arabs in Palestine would deprive Jews of that creative tension. European nations would enjoy fewer scientific and artistic breakthroughs.

The assumed link between Jews and intelligence or creativity predates the modern period. Any image of Jews in earlier periods as being devout and insular is misleading. One study identified 626 "outstanding" scientists alive between 1150 and 1300 AD, and found that ninety-five were Jewish. This was an estimated thirty times greater than their population proportion in countries which practised science. Those tendencies anticipated the achievements in the modern period. Between 1901 and 2014, Jews won an estimated 23 per cent of Nobel Prizes, proportionately more in the sciences and fewer in literature and peace.[19] This reflects the more objective, meritocratic, and non-discriminatory world of science where a discovery is a discovery regardless of who makes it. In the world of "high culture," Jews could be subjectively judged as unwelcome interlopers. Still, in countries where residents won ten or more prizes, an earlier study found Jews won 19 per cent. Again, a high degree of overrepresentation.[20] Another study noted that of the fifteen world chess champions from 1851 into the 1980s, seven – Steinitz, Botvinnik, Smyslov, Tal, Spassky, Fischer, and Kasparov – could claim Jewish ancestry.[21]

More provocative than counts of Jewish geniuses are above-average Jewish scores on IQ and other intelligence tests. (There is an ongoing debate as to what IQ tests actually measure. They do not exhaust the possible measures or types of intelligence, but they do measure something probably worth having.) It was not always so. American studies of standardized intelligence measures in the early 1900s found that Jews – usually the children of Yiddish-speaking Russian immigrants – did poorly. One of those early studies labelled Jews, along with other immigrant children, as "feeble-minded." A 1921 study showed that Jews had more certificates of mental defect than any other immigrant group. Another test of American soldiers drafted in the First World War found that only 19 per cent of those of "Russian" origin – mostly Jews – exceeded American national norms, compared to 49 per cent of soldiers of German origin and 67 per cent of soldiers of English origin. The conclusion was that Russian-Jewish immigrants were of inferior racial stock.[22] In fact, many of the Jewish children taking the tests likely had poor English language skills. Moreover, the test content at the time was possibly far more culturally biased than such tests today. There was no biological or genetic basis for their lower scores.

Following the Second World War, Jewish scores began to improve. One nationwide study of American high-school students in the 1960s found that Jewish boys and girls outperformed their non-Jewish counterparts in math and verbal tests. On the other hand, there were no differences in tests of visual-motor coordination, and Jewish students did worse on tests of spatial reasoning.[23] Some of the findings about higher Jewish scores in intelligence tests, or greater levels of education, flow from the fact that the Jews involved in these comparisons are more urban and more likely to come from middle-class homes with educated parents. Still, noted American sociologist Christopher Jencks concluded bluntly that "Jewish children ... do better on IQ tests than Christians at the same socio-economic level."[24] These advantages were not only concentrated among those Jews who were more secular, and more focused on secular educational achievement. Orthodox children in the United States have also shown similar high IQ scores.[25]

These patterns of Jewish intelligence do not stop at the border. A Canadian study compared over 100 eleven-year-old Jewish boys to boys from four other Canadian groups. The study found Jewish advantages in the area of verbal and mathematical reasoning, but not in perceptual, motor, or spatial skill abilities. Perhaps it is not surprising that Jews are overrepresented in law, medicine, math, and science, compared to architecture, engineering, and design. An amateurish Darwinian hypothesis might suggest that generations of Talmudic study might favour certain verbal and cognitive traits over perceptual ones. In any event, there is no one convincing explanation – genetic, social structural, or cultural – for this particular pattern of Jewish intellectual ability.[26]

It is far easier to describe than to account for the greater Jewish performance on intelligence tests. If it is "nature," Jews somehow have acquired over the years more of the genetic endowment needed for success in these tests. If it is "nurture," something in Jewish culture, family and demographic patterns, or in the surrounding

environment – maybe even the threat of persecution – enhances
Jewish intelligence. While we cannot know precisely, there are solid
grounds for caution in overstating the case for a biological or genetic
basis. First, the relatively high degree of Jewish in-marriage and
inbreeding – though far from complete – poses genetic risks regarding intelligence. Moreover, the studies cited above involved Ashkenazi
rather than Sephardi Jews. Studies in Israel have found gaps in intelligence test scores between Ashkenazi and Sephardi students. The
poorer socio-economic environment of many of the Sephardi immigrants in Israel – reflecting conditions in their countries of origin as
well as discrimination in Israel – is clearly decisive. Moreover, for
several earlier centuries the dominant centres of Judaic learning and
civilization were found among Sephardi Jewry in Spain and North
Africa. Had intelligence tests been taken back then, they would
surely have favoured Sephardi over Ashkenazi Jews. As historical
currents shifted in favour of Christian Europe, Jews in those countries, despite significant episodes of persecution, reaped the benefits
compared to Jewish communities within the declining orbit of Islam.

A number of esoteric non-genetic arguments have since been made
for the strong intellectual performance of Jewish children. These
include the benefits of the type of infant swaddling found among
Eastern European Jews, of styles of "hyper-verbal" communication
between Jewish parents and children, and of early literacy instruction for Jewish children.[27] What is important here is to note that
Jews in North America have performed very well in verbal and
mathematical intelligence tests through most of the twentieth century. For Jews and non-Jews alike, intelligence is a trait, perhaps
stereotypical, often associated with Jewishness.

But the intellectual future for Jews may not be as bright as the
present. My impression – there are no definitive studies – is that Jews
are no longer so concentrated among the highest ranks of educational, professional, and scientific achievers in North America. They
are being supplanted – as are Whites generally – by Asians. This
seems certainly true in math and the sciences, where Jews once dominated. The drive and intellectual curiosity found in many children
of Jewish immigrants led them to dominate in academic honour
rolls, but no longer. Affluence and conformity have dulled the Jewish
edge, as Asians, poor or wealthy, foreign or Canadian-born, take
their place. Again, environment over heredity.

The discussion of Jews, race, and genetics has sometimes been used for more twisted reasons than the explanation of commonalities of health/disease or intelligence. In one case, it has been employed to challenge the link between European Jews and Israel. In the mid-1970s, the Hungarian-Jewish intellectual Arthur Koestler recycled theories published in Hebrew decades earlier regarding a non-Semitic racial origin of the Jews. In his controversial book *The Thirteenth Tribe*, he challenged the conventional view that lighter-skinned and lighter-haired Ashkenazi Jews were the result of generations of sexual encounters between European Gentiles and the Jews exiled from Israel after the destruction of the Second Temple. Instead, he focused on the wholesale conversion of the Khazars – a tribe of Turkish or Finnish origin which flourished in the lower Volga region of Russia – to Judaism in the ninth century AD. That event introduced an entirely new population into the gene pool of European Jewry. For reasons which are not clear, the Khazars apparently adopted Judaism as their state religion, and several thousand nobles converted. (One theory is that adoption of Judaism offered a tactical escape from the more dangerous choice of either Islam or Christianity, the two dominant and contending faiths in the region.)[28]

Koestler argued that the numbers and impact of Jewish Khazars were far greater than previously thought. As this tribe moved west, and as Jews from Central Europe moved east, a fusion occurred which produced the non-Semitic features, including a good deal of fair skin and light hair that we have come to associate with many Ashkenazi Jews. This argument not only solved a genetic puzzle of the source of the fair-skinned Jews; it also posed a political challenge to Zionist theory. It suggested that most European Jews were not descended from the original inhabitants of Israel. This weakened the Zionist claim of a "return" to their Biblical homeland, so the Koestler argument was used in extreme anti-Zionist, anti-Israel, and at times anti-Semitic polemics, where it reappears today.

Most historians do not accept Koestler's maverick theory. The accuracy of the entire Khazar episode is not firmly established, while the eastward migration of Jews from Central Europe, notably Germany, is well documented. The genetic mixing that has undoubtedly taken place could just as easily have occurred over the centuries as Jews, following the Exile, were dispersed up through the Italian Peninsula and throughout the Roman Empire, into Central and later

Eastern Europe. Moreover, genetic commonalities in both Ashkenazi and Sephardi Jews, and between Jews and other Middle Eastern peoples, also refute Koestler's contention that Jews experienced a sharp racial and genetic break with their Semitic ancestors. It is therefore clear that Jews trace their genetic ancestry to the Middle East. They are descendants, like Arabs, of a mythic Abraham. Still, there are plenty of non-Semitic-looking European Jews. Genetic mixing with European peoples through illicit sexual encounters may explain it only in part. It is also possible that there was a greater variation in the physical appearance, or "phenotypes," among Middle Eastern peoples thousands of years ago than is generally assumed. The ancient Israelites may have had less Semitic features even then. In any event, the genetic/historical origins of the Jews, and thus their ties to Israel, remain a recurrent feature of debates on Zionism, including those among Jewish and/or Israeli scholars.[29]

The racial theme has been prominent in the history of anti-Semitism, even in its theological form. Beginning in the late 1300s, Jews in Spain and Portugal began to convert to Christianity in order to escape heightened waves of persecution which marked the Inquisition and culminated in the expulsions of 1492 and 1497. These Jewish converts to Christianity, sometimes called the *Marranos, Conversos,* or *Anusim* in Hebrew, perplexed Christian authorities. Despite being exposed to the teachings of the Church, they and their descendants often continued to practise Judaism in secret. Only some non-human force could explain this stubborn trait of Jews (first encountered in the early Christian period). Jews, the anti-Semites reasoned, must not be fully human, they must be a biologically distinct species, linked to the Devil, and replete with horns and tails.[30] The foundations of modern racial anti-Semitism can thus be found in the Middle Ages, and have theological roots.

In later periods, racial stereotypes of Jews as Semites with dark skin, curly black hair, and aquiline noses were common in anti-Semitic cartoons and publications throughout Europe, regardless of the wide range of actual Jewish facial and physical characteristics. The Nazis pushed this to an extreme in the cartoons of their newspaper, *Der Sturmer.* They also warned of the infectious power of Jewish blood, arguing that even those with only one Jewish grandparent were to be considered Jews, requiring extermination. The image found in Hitler's *Mein Kampf* of the Jew as non-human, as a parasite or a bacillus, builds on the earlier foundations of racial anti-Semitism.

But racial thinking about Jews did not always lead to genocide. The racializing of religious or national groups was a common discourse through the first half of the twentieth century, and at times benign. The term "race" was used loosely throughout the West to denote national or ethnic groups. Jews, along with Poles, Italians, English, French, and other ethnic groups were designated as *racial origin* groups in the Canadian census up to and including that of 1941. After the horrors of the Second World War, racial classification was discredited, and the census terminology was changed to "ethnic origin" in 1951.

The issue of race, Jewishness, and the census may yet re-emerge in the new context of affirmative action or employment equity programs. Many Sephardi Jews are from the Middle East, and some are certainly dark-skinned. Ethiopian Jews even more so. The 2011 Canadian Census (more precisely, the National Household Survey), which contains information on both the religion and ethnicity of respondents, enables us to get a sense of racial diversity within Canadian Jewry. Looking at those who are Jewish by religion, roughly 2.2 per cent are classified by the census as "visible minorities" – likely Black, Asian, or Hispanic. But Jews as a group – rightly – are not, at least not by Statistics Canada and other government agencies, active in the designing of employment equity target groups. Perhaps Ethiopian Jews or other darker-skinned Jews would be eligible for preferential treatment if and when such programs arrive in full force in Canada.

Any discussion of "typical" Jewish looks evokes the historic legacy of racist, anti-Semitic caricature. Nonetheless, much of Woody Allen's comedy draws on his physical appearance and personality traits as a "New York Jew." Historically, Judaism, as well as Jewish powerlessness in the diaspora, led to an image of Jews as weak and uncomfortable with male aggression and physicality, quite the opposite of the Hellenistic tradition. Only in the modern period do counter-images appear, in which Jewish athletes, soldiers, and even criminals emerge to a sort of contentious hero-worship in some Jewish circles.[31] I cherish my dog-eared copy of *Great Jews in Sports* – alas, not the world's thickest book and with too much fencing and table tennis for my liking – but still a Jewish pantheon of sorts.[32] One can see fading photos of muscular old-time Jewish wrestlers, boxers, basketball players, and gymnasts adorning the walls of the YM-YWHA. Despite the image of the brainy Jew, sports played an important role in the socialization of the children of Jewish immigrants.[33] Zionism and the Israeli army also helped develop the newer "macho" images of tough Jews in North America. Today, many Jews, like other North Americans, seem to have become obsessed with their bodies. They are not only the people of the book; they are now equally the people of the health club. Many Canadian Jews sweating on their treadmills may not know of the track and field star Fanny ("Bobbie") Rosenfeld, chosen by sportswriters in 1950 as Canada's female athlete of the half-century.

Biological definitions of Jewishness raise ethical problems. Many Jews feel that Jews are born, and not made. But does this mean converts must remain permanently second-class? Despite increases in intermarriage and formal conversions to Judaism, some Canadian Jews – primarily older immigrants – may still feel suspicious about converts. Conversely, Jewish religious folklore has it that every Jew, no matter how estranged from the tradition, still retains some Jewish essence which cannot be extinguished. This ascribed quasi-biological origin is reinforced by *halacha* (the term means "way" in Hebrew, and denotes the rules and regulations of Jewish conduct accepted by Orthodox Rabbinic Judaism). Accordingly, a Jew is anyone born to a Jewish mother, regardless of circumstance or upbringing or even belief, or converted to Judaism by an Orthodox rabbi.

This emphasis on matrilineal descent dates back to Biblical days. It made sense; it is easier to identify a child's mother than its father. The Orthodox rabbinate – unlike Conservative, Reform, and more liberal denominations – has championed this biological and legalistic basis of Jewish identification. This contrasts with more voluntaristic and non-biological approaches, in which a Jew is anyone who identifies as a Jew. According to the Orthodox, someone born of a Jewish mother and Gentile father, and who does not embrace another faith officially, remains Jewish no matter how secular or irreligious their conduct. And no conversion of the father is required. However, someone born of a Gentile mother and Jewish father remains a non-Jew from the Orthodox perspective, no matter how involved or committed to Jewish life that person may be. These people, and their descendants, are not counted by the Orthodox as Jews unless they undergo a conversion supervised by an Orthodox rabbi. There are tens of thousands of Jews in Canada today who are not considered Jewish according to Orthodox Jewish law. They include people who converted to Judaism with non-Orthodox rabbis, people who

embrace Judaism voluntarily without any formal conversion procedure, and their children with a non-Jewish mother.

A final irony is that while the vast majority of Jews are White, this
offers scant protection from Canadian racists. After all, Jews were
the twentieth century's major victims of racist genocide. Even now,
Jews rank with Black and Aboriginal Canadians and other racialized
minorities as potential victims of active hate groups, who usually
target Jews and non-Whites together in their propaganda.[34] In this,
Jews differ from other European ethnic groups, who today face far
milder forms of prejudice, and very little that we might classify as
hate speech.

ISRAEL: THE JEWISH HOMELAND

For many Canadian Jews, Israel is an indispensable element of their
identity. For some this results from embracing a formal Zionist ideology. For others it flows from a reaction to the Holocaust or admiration of Israel's achievements. Others support it because it is a place
where many Jews live. Emotions range from blind love to very critical support, with the exception of firm anti-Zionists among left-
wingers and the ultra-Orthodox. Canadian Jews are not unique in
having a special tie to a piece of land. Think of Hutterite farm colonies in the West, First Nations reserves and territories, and the
Québécois attachment to their province. For some immigrant groups,
the role of land is that of a homeland – the place from which they
or parents emigrated, the fondly remembered "old country" where
generations of ancestors lived and struggled, and the place which
continues to nurture ethnic culture and traditions. But for other
immigrant groups there is a different sense of diaspora, one associated with a homeland that remains unfree, and thus a kind of "imagined community."[35] I recall a young Armenian-Canadian student
many years ago arguing that Armenia might one day be free, and
invoking the example of Zionism. I sagely pointed out to him the
differences between Israel, which had to oppose the ostensibly civilized British empire, and poor Armenia, which had to defeat the
Soviet Union's "Evil Empire." I am happy to say that I failed to
convince him to give up hope ... and history ultimately proved
him right. Palestinians, Kurds, Tibetans, as well as the many captive
nations of the Eastern Bloc, all have had a similar sense of loyalty to
an idealized homeland.

None of these examples fully recapitulates the role of Israel, as state and as territory, in defining recent Canadian Jewish identity. The Jewish diaspora is older than that of most other groups. If Jews can be thought of as a people or a nation, then Israel is the territory where that people first emerged as a historical entity. Israel has both a symbolic and real meaning for Canadian Jews. Accordingly, Israel is a holy land – *the* Holy Land – promised by God to the Jewish people. It is not by coincidence that one of the key moments of the Passover seder is the call, "Next Year in Jerusalem!" The Torah (meaning "knowledge), the central text of Judaism, is described in a key prayer as "going forth from Zion" (*key mi'tzion tey'tzey torah*). The theme of exile, or *galut*, is one core element of traditional Judaic thought. Accordingly, the Jews were exiled from the Promised Land two thousand years ago because of their sins. Redemption in the Messianic Age will also include the return to Zion and the re-establishment of the Kingdom of Israel, and the process of the "ingathering of the exiles," or *kibbutz galuyot*. The Zionist pioneers have hastened this day, to the dismay of some ultra-Orthodox traditionalists who prefer to wait for the Messiah.

In the second half of the twentieth century, Israel assumed mythic, quasi-religious proportions for other reasons. The Israeli experiment has been, and remains, a source of pride for most Jews, despite more recent serious fractures to be discussed below. In the aftermath of the Holocaust, the success of Israel, whether in pioneering, farming, fighting, immigrant absorption, scientific achievement, or basic economic development, has helped reshape the image of bookish, nerdy Jews. Despite these successes, most Jews still worry about Israel's security and welfare, which in turn strengthens the identification. A terrorist bomb in Jerusalem is experienced by many like a bomb on their street. When Israelis are killed in terrorist attacks, many Canadian Jews feel bereaved in a way they do not for innocent victims in other countries. This tie should not be confused with unwavering support for policies of any particular government. But neither should sharp criticism of specific Israeli policies by Canadian supporters of Labour or Likud be misconstrued as a lack of basic support. Many Jews also worry about the quality of Israeli democracy or Israeli Jewishness, and all these worries reinforce the tie to Israel.

Christians and Muslims also have an attachment to the Holy Land. Christians make pilgrimages to visit the holy places. But in practice Israel, and certainly Jerusalem, is simply not as central in the theology of the other monotheistic faiths as it is in Judaism. Indeed, some religious Jews seek to be buried there, to make permanent their attachment to Zion. Christians do not have this intense attachment, though some Protestant fundamentalists are very strong supporters of Israel. Catholics can invest as much centrality in the Vatican as in the Holy Land. Muslims have their prior attachment to Mecca and Medina. Israel is the only religious homeland of the Jews.

The Jewish connection to Israel as their homeland differs from their attachment to their "old country," be it Poland, Germany, or Iraq. And it certainly differs from the way Chinese-Canadians or Italian-Canadians might feel about their homelands. The Canadian Jewish experience with their ancestral homeland was at best bittersweet, with the accent on the bitter. For Jews, the real homeland is Israel. That is the place to visit relatives or to send children to reinforce their identity; indeed, two-thirds of adult Canadian Jews had visited Israel by 1990. A Toronto survey from 2005 and a Montreal survey from 2010 found that roughly three-quarters of adult Jews have visited Israel.[36] More are now going as a result of the Birthright Israel project (Taglit), which sends thousands of North American youth to Israel on free ten-day trips. Since Birthright started in 2000, over 18,000 Canadian youth have visited Israel through the program.[37]

In recent years it has become fashionable for Jews to visit cities or towns – de facto shrines – in Eastern Europe. They seek to explore the places where their parents or grandparents were raised or buried. In some cases, these visits become macabre rites, focusing on death camps. The popular March of the Living program aimed at Jewish teenagers combines one-week visits to Eastern Europe, including death camps, with one week in Israel, to coincide with Israel's Independence Day. It is an orchestrated, draining, yet exhilarating encapsulation of the transition from the despair of the Holocaust to the triumph represented by the rebirth of Israel. It is a form of cultural engineering, designed to cement a link between the horrors of the Holocaust and rebirth in Israel. Several hundred teens from Canada attend the event annually. In short, Jews do not visit the "homelands" of Eastern Europe to visit relatives. They visit graves, if they can find them.

Despite minimal Jewish attachment to the old countries as political entities, there are cultural bonds, which may well linger in Canada. The klezmer and Yiddish revivals, as well as the Sephardi celebrations mentioned earlier, represent a continuing attachment to the cultures which flourished in those source countries, as well as among the immigrant generations in the New World. For example, many recent Russian Jewish immigrants seem more Russian than Jewish and remain quite attached to Russian culture, from ballet to chess. Moroccan Jewish immigrants retained a surprising affection for King Hassan until his death in 1999. But in general, none of these cultural affinities overshadow their ties to Israel. In a later chapter, we will discuss a growing political disenchantment with or distancing from Israel among some Canadian Jews.

OTHER BASES OF JEWISH IDENTITY

Religion: For many people, Jews and non-Jews alike, religion is the core element of Jewish identity. Jews are a religious group and Judaism is their religion. Jews can be religious through a belief in God and basic Judaic tenets or through observance of Jewish rituals and commandments. There are, however, many Judaisms. Sephardi religious Judaism is Orthodox in spirit and tradition, if more flexible than many forms of Ashkenazi Orthodoxy. The Judaism of Canadian Ashkenazi Jews can be divided into four major formal denominations: Orthodoxy, Conservatism, Reform, and Reconstructionism, very roughly from the more traditional to the less traditional. There are also more liberal variants, such as the Jewish Renewal Movement or secular Humanist Judaism. This ordering roughly reflects the degree of religious observance followed by congregants; the Orthodox are more likely to observe more of the precepts of traditional religious Judaism, followed by the other denominations in descending order, with possible overlap between Reform and Reconstructionist Judaism. Yet each of these denominations is in turn diverse, none more so than the Orthodox. And none is static. Many groups of Jews are uncomfortable within denominational boundaries and define their own brand of Judaism. The growing diversity between and within denominations, the constant change, even the frictions, all are signs of vitality.

The Jewish religion interacts with all the other elements of Jewish identity. The very notion of a Jewish people – an amalgam of ethno-racial, national, and biological concepts – is paradoxically rooted in a sense of religious obligation. Jews in the Bible are a "chosen people," chosen by God as well as by themselves and by others, to fulfil a religious destiny. Not chosen as superior, but different; chosen to bear the burden, the yoke, of Jewish religious observance.

Immigration: The immigrant saga is an indelible part of the identity of North American Jews, even though a minority are in fact immigrants. No matter. The image of the "wandering Jew" is ingrained in Jewish history and folklore and in the Canadian Jewish reality, where immigrants are far more present than in the United States. And many Canadian-born adult Jews have parents, grandparents, or other relatives who were immigrants, and who in one way or another brought to life the struggles of the epic immigrant generation. The legacy of this experience is that many Jews – like other migrant groups – feel like eternal strangers, "others" still hoping for full acceptance. All the civic equality and economic success in the world does not eradicate the feeling. Nor does the fact that Jews love and appreciate the Canada of today.

This identification with the stranger is reinforced by the continuing influx of Jews to Canada in significant numbers. This identification likely has played a role in individual and communal Jewish support for recent refugees, from the Vietnamese boat people of 1979–80 to Syrian refugees in 2016 and 2017. Advocating for Jewish immigrants and integrating them into the established Jewish community are major preoccupations. At the same time, the new groups of immigrant Jews add to the diversity – and tensions – within Canadian Jewry, even as they reshape and reinvigorate the community.

Culture: Jews are also a cultural group, and many prefer to construct their identity in cultural terms. For every Jewish subgroup, there is a high culture of elite artistic creation, a popular or folkloric culture, and a culture of everyday life. Jewish culture is expressed in every type of artistry, and conveyed in virtually all entertainment media. A perennial question is whether Jewish art is any artistic expression created by someone who happens to be Jewish. The Yiddish theatre is probably Jewish art; but what about Jerry Seinfeld, Larry David, or Mordecai Richler?[38] Whether there are distinctive Jewish artistic styles, or more precisely Canadian Jewish styles, is a difficult question to resolve.

A specific language is crucial to most cultures. The central linguistic element of Jewish identity comprises classical ethnic languages such as Yiddish, Ladino, Aramaic (the language of the Talmud), other minor dialects, and of course Hebrew, which has a dual role for Canadian Jews. On the one hand, Hebrew is the ancient language of prayer and the Bible, of the Mishnah and other commentaries. It is practically impossible to be an actively religious Jew of any kind without knowing some minimal amount of Hebrew. But the religious culture of Christianity makes do without. Methodists or Episcopalians do not have a specific language. Catholics used to have the Latin Mass in all its awe and majesty, but no longer.

On the other hand, Hebrew is the language of modern Israel and Israeli culture, a living language. In this sense, Hebrew and Yiddish are somewhat like Italian or Chinese for Italian or Chinese Canadians. A minority among the Canadian-born are fluent, but Hebrew is useful for singing Israeli songs, or visiting Israel. And even as Yiddish shrinks as a language of daily use, it persists as a language that functions as a kind of Jewish badge. Many Yiddish words have infiltrated English. While Gentiles may well use them, for Jews they often serve as a secret code. Moreover, Jews, like many other ethnic groups – Italians come to mind – are a kind of "audible minority" whose blended languages combining English and the mother tongue are called "ethnolects."[39] Apart from Jewish vocabulary, whether Yiddish or Hebrew, there are specific cadences, rhythms, accents, and speech habits which are common and intelligible among Jews, particularly if they are immigrants or second-generation. For instance: "*Why do Jews always answer a question with a question?*" "*Why not?*" Or: "*How are you?*" "*How should I be?*" Many Canadian Jews recognize this type of "Yinglish." Other examples: "This weekend I have a wedding" means "I have to go to a wedding"; "Give me a dozen bagel" needs no plural. And Montreal Jews are notorious for saying "I have to make an order" when they go to the supermarket.

Culture is more than art or language. Jewish culture can also include distinctive values or lifestyle habits, though we can debate whether they are specifically Jewish. I had a Jewish student who assured me in the late 1970s that a key cultural difference between Jewish and Gentile teens was that the former were into cocaine and the latter were into beer or pot. Jewish food, whether kosher or kosher style, is central to modern Jewish culture, though some intellectuals might criticize "bagels and lox" Judaism. Even more slippery than food are middle- and upper-class lifestyle traits, mannerisms, and consumption patterns.

Family: For some Jews, the Jewish family is the source of their identity. Most of our life is lived in families, where we were raised or where we now raise our own children. Relations with parents, spouses or partners, and children, or our gender, or sexual orientation, are fundamental determinants of identity for all people. Stereotypes and myths about Jewish families and patterns of Jewish intimacy abound, from Jewish American Princess jokes to the images of the devoted *Yiddishe mameh*, or Jewish mother.

The Community: Jewish identities are acquired not only through family. For some Jews, their identity is constructed through belonging to a tightly knit community. For many the nature of community is spatial. For others the community consists of ties of kin and friendship and broader personal networks both real or now virtual. And for others, a more formal type of community is a kind of polity, with organizations for every type of need. Jews are probably the most institutionally complete minority group in Canada.[40] For Jews, the range of such institutions spans cradle to grave (Jewish daycare centres and schools to old-age homes and cemeteries) and all manner of cultural, social, fraternal, recreational, and political interests. Nothing is left to chance.

Jews have had lots of practice at forming these structured communities. They can draw upon 2,000 years of experience as a diaspora community faced with the task of surviving as best it could within an often hostile environment. Diaspora communities were embryonic forms of self-government, and the Jewish polity, like any polity, required organizations to accomplish its tasks. Absence of ingrained anti-Semitism, prosperity, and a general tolerance made all this easier in North America. Large European cultural groups have far briefer historical experience as immigrant minorities needing to set up their own communal organizations. It is only since the major migrations at the end of the nineteenth century funneled masses of immigrants to the New World that these groups have been building organized diasporic communities. They are still learning the ropes. And the same would apply to the more recent postwar waves of non-European immigrants.

Liberalism: For many non-Orthodox Jews, the essence of their Jewish identity is social and political liberalism. Give them a progressive cause, an injustice, a social movement, often one not centred on the Jewish community but linked to another oppressed group, and they come alive. Jewish liberalism remains stronger in the United States than in Canada, and may receive a boost depending on the final contours and direction of the Trump administration. In Canada, Stephen Harper's Conservative government appealed strongly to Jewish voters concerned mainly about Israel; it is not yet clear how Jewish voters are relating to the Justin Trudeau Liberal government. For many progressive Jews their politics are an expression of their understanding of Jewish tradition or Jewish issues. For others, their Jewishness is coincidental. But there is no escaping the role that political expression plays in their lives.

Anti-Semitism: The persisting pressure of anti-Semitism in all its forms – real, perceived, or anticipated – paradoxically reinforces many people's Jewish identification and therefore their support of organizations that defend Jewish interests and rights. A swastika daubed on a Jewish building, an anti-Semitic slur or tweet by a public official or personality, a polemic or protest directed at Israel, can worry even the most assimilated Jews. This is an argument that Jean-Paul Sartre made in extreme, reductionist form in his book *Anti-Semite and Jew*.[41] Sartre went too far; obviously, Jews are far more than just the people anti-Semites love to hate. Still, an old Jewish saying echoes Sartre's point, comparing Jews to eggs: the longer you boil them, the harder they get. By seeing themselves as victims, many Jews also identify with visible-minority Canadians as a part of a brotherhood of the oppressed. But others go further. The terrible uniqueness of the Holocaust stands at the core of their being. Many Jews feel that regardless of how well things are going in Canada, they can always turn sour.

There are obviously many dimensions of Jewish identity. There is no one answer to the question of who is a Jew. Jews are not an easy people to understand, and challenge many of the accepted truths about how minority groups can and do function. Each of the elements of Jewish identity listed above contributes to the unique, paradoxical blend of inward- and outward-looking forces that defines Jewish success in Canada. In later chapters I will review them in detail, drawing on current empirical data and social scientific research. But first, in the next chapter, I offer a brief discussion of two competing demographic approaches to Jewish survival.

2

Quality, Quantity, and Conflict

The Socio-demographic Context
of Jewish Survival

"Who has counted the dust of Jacob or numbered the stock of Israel?"

Numbers 23:10

"What is happening in the Western world may be termed a 'self-inflicted Holocaust.'"

Rabbi Adin Steinsaltz, in *The Jerusalem Post*,
International edition, 6 November 1993

DEMOGRAPHIC FOUNDATIONS

Any discussion of diaspora Jewish life in the twenty-first century is part of an ongoing conversation about Jewish survival.[1] On the table are the twin challenges of continuity and unity, with the Jewish future hanging in the balance. In the 1990s, a double consensus emerged. First, American Jews (with Canadian Jews not far behind) were facing a demographic disaster because of rising rates of mixed marriage and low fertility, fuelled by a general assimilation. Second, unassimilated Jews were locked in an increasingly fratricidal conflict, fought mainly along religious lines because of the dominance of Orthodoxy among those resisting mixed marriages, but exacerbated by disagreements about support for Israel. The bleak prognosis was a shrinking Jewish population increasingly at war with itself.

The two issues were linked. The Orthodox Jews were having more babies and fewer mixed marriages than the non-Orthodox. The religious polarization was not based simply on doctrinal differences, but on which Jews were helping and which hindering the cause of Jewish continuity.

I challenge both elements of this gloomy consensus. What some people see as demographic threats or as dysfunctional divisions are part of a successful balancing act, an equilibrium that actually maximizes current and future possibilities. There are both quantitative and qualitative demographic approaches to minority group survival. Most people, especially Jews, assume that they operate at cross-purposes. But they do not. As I shall illustrate, different Jewish groups use both approaches successfully.

But many Jews just do not see it that way. Differences in demographic patterns and their corresponding cultural characteristics have led to polarized feelings. An angry letter some years ago to *The Jerusalem Report* illustrated this conflict:

> Why is it that the defenders of the ultra-Orthodox life style invariably quote their higher birth rate as being one of their major achievements?
>
> Humankind as a whole derives little, if any, benefit from yet more *yeshiva* students whose undoubted intellectual energy might better be applied to seeking solutions for some of the world's problems.
>
> Perhaps the ultra-Orthodox should ponder the suggestion that, in human terms, one Jonas Salk has done more good and brought more "light to the nations" than all the rabbis in their yeshivot.[2]

The letter is a sample of the undercurrent of hostility between the Orthodox and non-Orthodox. It interweaves cultural and demographic themes. It also assumes there can be no possible link between Jonas Salk's polio vaccine and ultra-Orthodox rabbis. To the letter-writer, the religious and secular dimensions of Jewish life exist in a clear zero-sum relation. Of course, many Orthodox and ultra-Orthodox Jews share that view, but from the opposite starting point. I argue that such views are historically and analytically wrongheaded.

The fact is, numbers alone cannot be a decisive barometer of Jewish survival. Much of the alarm about the Jewish future is based on dire demographic projections, most recently the Pew survey of American Jews in 2013 mentioned earlier and to be cited often in this study. I am skeptical about these despairing forecasts: recall the important distinction between prediction and projection. The basic strength of demography, the science of human population, is projection. It is the ability to describe a current population, make some assumptions about trends in fertility, mortality, and net migration, and then project alternate population sizes and compositions into the future. To estimate future Jewish populations, demographers also make assumptions about future mixed-marriage rates. The most common assumption is to extrapolate current trends. These assumptions yield a range of projections, some higher and some lower, in a mechanical fashion.

Even projection is not problem-free. We assume demographers know what they are counting. This is easy for national population counts, or subgroups clearly defined by place of birth or age. There is generally no confusion about what we mean by "people aged sixty-five and over," or "years of education." It is much less clear when dealing with ethnic, racial, religious, or gender (as gender fluidity is increasingly accepted) groups. Different ways of defining Jews – or Latinos, Chinese, or Italians – will yield different counts and population projections. Estimates of any Jewish population will vary depending on whether we are counting Jews by religious conviction, Jews by full or partial ethnic origin, or variations in between. But if we can solve the problem of definition and choose various sets of assumptions, we can easily compute a range of projections.

Prediction is a different story, and it represents the major limitation of demography. Making a prediction is making an educated guess, not applying an arithmetic formula. Usually a prediction is the most likely of a set of projections and while a projection assumes that all variables outside the stated assumptions remain constant, they never do. Demographers, and indeed all social scientists, have a dismal record predicting major changes in social and political life, and new cultural trends. Demographers did not predict the post-Second World War baby boom nor the movement towards zero population growth in the past two decades in North America and Western Europe. They did not predict the dramatic changes and demographic consequences brought on by the women's movement, the sexual revolution, the increased use of birth control, or the rise in divorce rates and out-of-wedlock births.

Jewish history in the twentieth century is an extreme example of unpredictability. In the early 1900s, who would have predicted the genocide of the Holocaust and the role that Germany – as opposed to France (remember Dreyfus) or Russia – would play as its engine? (Recall that Germany at the time was perhaps the epitome of Western civilization and high culture.) Who, except for a handful of Zionist writers, would have predicted the emergence of a strong modern Israel as a centre of world Jewry? Or the total eclipse of Europe, North Africa, Iraq, and Iran as centres of Judaic culture? Or the collapse of Yiddish secular culture, or the rise of modern Jewish studies in the academy, both in North America? And no one predicted the resilience of Orthodoxy in North America – certainly not pioneering American Jewish sociologists like Louis Wirth or Marshall Sklare – and the surprising strength of ultra-Orthodoxy in particular in both Israel and North America.

Pessimistic forecasts about the Jewish demographic future are not new. In 1964 *Look* magazine featured its famous cover story on "The Vanishing American Jew." By the new century, American Jews were still around but *Look* magazine had vanished. In the late 1970s, I co-authored one of my first articles in the American Jewish magazine *Midstream*.[3] It was a response to a pessimistic projection made by a demographer who looked at some data from the first National Jewish Population Survey (NJPS) in 1970 and projected that in one hundred years, all or most American Jews would have disappeared. He may yet be right since we still haven't reached 2070, but I was not apprehensive. I offered a perhaps overly optimistic interpretation of the trends, including those on intermarriage, and was taken to task by at least one critic for seeming to advocate intermarriage. He was partially right; while I do not advocate it, I do feel Jews have no choice but to live with it.[4] Still, to date, Jews have not disappeared in the United States. Those dire predictions were wrong.

It is possible to take a less pessimistic view of the evidence. A much discussed 52 per cent mixed-marriage rate for American Jews marrying between 1985 and 1990, derived from the 1990 NJPS, set off alarm bells. Perhaps as those most at risk for intermarriage leave the group, the rate of intermarriage might level off for the more committed Jews who remain. Moreover that infamous figure of 52 per cent was computed for an American sample that included large numbers of respondents who had "some" Jewish ancestry but who did not necessarily identify as Jewish. Many respondents were not really Jews to start with and would have had no problem marrying a non-Jew. Focusing only on those Jews who actually identified themselves as Jews yielded a lower intermarriage rate of 41 per cent. Still high, but less ominous. According to the 2013 Pew report, *A Portrait of Jewish Americans*, 44 per cent of married American Jews had a non-Jewish spouse. Moreover, among non-Orthodox Jews, of those who married within the previous five years, 71 per cent were married to a non-Jew.[5] Most children of mixed marriage engaged in few Jewish behaviours, though many continued to "identify" as Jews. The short-term trend for the American Jewish population therefore, is likely to be stability, or modest growth, helped with more expansive and inclusive definitions of who is a Jew ... But then again, even this prediction is risky.

TWO DEMOGRAPHIC APPROACHES

Minority groups concerned with survival and continuity can develop two demographic strategies – quantitative and qualitative – to achieve those goals.[6] A quantitative strategy fostered by high rates of fertility and no intermarriage is not the only option. Jewish history, dating back to the Bible, contains examples of massive demographic loss and assimilation. The Jews in the desert embraced the golden calf en masse. As further evidence, recall that of the twelve tribes of Israel, ten were lost. Yet Jews overcame that blow, that "assimilation" of 83 per cent of the total group, and survived.

What is a quantitative strategy? The more, the better. Think of the Hutterites, the Amish, or if you will, Hasidim. Social scientists are fascinated by the Hutterites of Western Canada because of their demographic uniqueness and their geographic isolation in agricultural colonies.[7] The Hutterites have been evolving over the decades in terms of their approach to retaining members. But they still have very little intermarriage and very high rates of fertility. This is a quantitative, survivalist demographic strategy, and Hutterite culture meshes well with it. In theory, there is no partial or plural or varied mode of Hutterite identity. Either you are 100 per cent Hutterite, living on a Hutterite colony, faithful to the basic Hutterite values and way of life, or you cease being a Hutterite. This firm boundary is changing but there are still relatively few urban Hutterites, secular Hutterites, or Hutterite physicians or philosophers or Nobel Prize winners.

But the pattern of Jewish demographic behaviour is puzzling. Jews are considered a survivalist group par excellence, a model for other minorities. Yet overall, Jewish intermarriage rates have risen and Jewish fertility rates have fallen. The finding of lower rates of fertility for Jews compared to other groups is not new. In the modern period in the United States, Jews were the first to attain zero population growth. Of course, family size among the early waves of immigrant East European Jews to North America was much larger than at present. But it was still not as large as that of other (mainly Catholic) European groups. Data from the 1931 Canadian census confirm that pattern among the still largely immigrant Jews. Both the fertility rate and the birth rate for married Jewish women aged fifteen to forty-four were about one-half the national rates.[8]

Jews as a whole have much lower fertility and higher intermarriage rates than do Hutterites. Could we therefore say that Hutterites are committed to survival and Jews are not? Of course not. Both groups are committed to survival but have different demographic behaviours because of different cultural features. It is not possible to maximize both the qualitative and the quantitative for an entire group. There are trade-offs between the two approaches as some sort of equilibrium emerges. What, then, is a qualitative demographic approach? It is one which maximizes the attributes of each individual member of the minority group so as to compete successfully within the wider society. Small is beautiful. Children in smaller families tend to do better in school, which may help explain the relative educational success of the children of Jewish immigrants. This success goes along with high levels of participation, and may involve forging contacts with the majority group that can further the interests of the minority. For Jews, different subgroups display identifiably different demographic patterns, some quantitative, some qualitative. The blend of strategies is linked indelibly to the culture, and indeed the collective agenda of North American Jews, a whole which is indeed the sum of different parts. Some Jews are medical researchers, others master the Talmud.

For most committed Jews, low fertility rates and mixed marriage are dangerous, sapping the quantitative base of Jewish life. But aspects of these specific demographic patterns can be understood paradoxically as contributing to collective group needs. Anthropologists have long argued that intermarriage can help to cement alliances between tribes, as a sign of friendship and acceptance. On the other hand, high rates of outmarriage can threaten the group. If all Jews married out and retained no ties to Judaism, Jews would disappear.

There is no doubt that at the individual level, intermarriage is a cause and an effect of assimilation. Yet the relation is more nuanced at the group level, where demographic patterns shape and reflect the varied cultural characteristics of Jews. Increasing rates of intermarriage are more than simply a flight of Jews from their heritage and an attack on Jewish interests. There are actually potential benefits. The more friendships with non-Jews are cultivated, the greater will be sympathetic understanding of Jewish concerns by non-Jews.[9] Jews who engage with the non-Jewish world take risks which others avoid, and serve as scouts at the frontier of the external world. While this may reflect or weaken their specific brand of Jewishness, their actions promote the broader interests of the group.[10] As long as Jews wish to win Nobel Prizes or send effective lobbyists to defend Jewish interests before government, there will be a risk of intermarriage.

HUTTERITES, QUÉBÉCOIS, AND JEWS

Consider again the behaviour of the Hutterites. We can make sense of that behaviour only within the context of a specific culture and its corresponding agenda. Hutterites live a devout, agricultural life. Work, worship, and Bible study are their major preoccupations, and for older Hutterites their Germanic dialect serves a protective function. Hutterites try to minimize contact with the outside world. There is no political agenda relating to a homeland that requires political lobbying or effective advocacy. No Hutterites have won, or wish to win, a Nobel Prize. As a result, the traditional Hutterite religious model of no intermarriage, the limited status of women within the family, and a large number of children makes sense.

To illustrate again the link between demographic patterns, collective group survival, and cultural characteristics, consider the Québécois. After the Second World War their fertility rates plummeted. Would we therefore conclude that the French in Quebec had given up on *la survivance*? Certainly, some Québécois leaders thought so, bemoaning the quantitative threat posed by the drop in fertility, sounding much like Jewish leaders condemning intermarriage and small family size. Quebec policy-makers periodically tried to encourage Québécois (basically women) to have larger families through baby bonus programs, much to the consternation of feminist critics. But they were misguided. The postwar drop in Quebec family size did not indicate a rush to collective suicide. The political and cultural context was changing as Quebec society modernized rapidly, invested in education, and abandoned church control over social institutions. The flight from rural life, which had begun before the war, continued. The commitment to survival remained just as intense, but it was pursued with a qualitative rather than quantitative approach, to match an evolving cultural and political agenda. This was a move to embrace modernity, including higher education and science, which even included and offered a proactive immigration and francization policy to make up for the demographic shortfall. There is a correspondence between demographic behaviour and the social, political, and cultural agenda of the Québécois. And the same logic applies to Jews.

In the Jewish case, smaller families among the non-Orthodox have had positive impacts on long-term qualitative characteristics of the Jewish community. Smaller family size leads to more nurturing per child, greater educational attainment, and later occupational success. Smaller family size provides more opportunities for Jewish women to make contributions to communal life and to the general society, given the still prevailing unequal division of household duties between men and women. Women can fulfil their own career aspirations while also raising children. Fewer children lead to the possibility of greater familial and communal investments per child. This in turn leads to greater contributions from each member towards material or secular objectives, as well as successful competition with the non-Jewish world.

Of course, not all Jews adhere to the same demographic pattern. A growing religious minority embraces a quantitative strategy. And some Orthodox – but not ultra-Orthodox – Jews are found today studying at top universities, working as scientists, lawyers, or business executives, or like Joe Lieberman, running for American vice-president.

If all North American Jews were Hasidim, with high fertility rates and almost no mixed marriage, of course the Jewish population would grow. Jewish families would be highly observant and each (male) Jew would have an in-depth knowledge of Torah. But at the same time, the nature of Jewish life as we know it would be dramatically different. There would be few academic conferences held to discuss the nature of Jewish life in the future. There would be few Jews like me. There would be no Jewish studies curricula on any campus, no art exhibits or symposia. There would be no non-Orthodox Jewish cultural life as we understand it. No scientists, no professors, no Nobel prizes. The capacity to organize effective lobbying or public relations efforts might be highly constrained. Of course, this is one extreme.

Now suppose all Jews were resolutely secular. They could still identify as Jews. Some could be interested in Jewish literature, Jewish philosophy, the security of Israel, Jewish communal institutions, Jewish culture. Some could speak Hebrew and Yiddish. (In fact, the American evidence suggests they would score less favourably on all these sorts of measures than religious Jews.) They could talk the language of bureaucrats. But chances are they would rarely darken the door of any synagogue, which might all disappear in any case, and never fulfil a religious ritual of any kind. They would intermarry in droves. Under those conditions, I think there would be very few Jews left in three generations.

What Jews have evolved more than other minority groups is an equilibrium. Some Jews have larger families, do not intermarry, and live very traditional, relatively insular Jewish lives. Others lie at the other end of the spectrum, with multiple contacts with the non-Jewish world. And many others fall in the middle. They all contribute, directly and through their interactions, to the organic whole which is modern Jewish life.

PLURALISM AND CONFLICT

And what is the result? We have a Jewish community that is highly pluralistic. Many fear that this pluralism has gone too far, leading to conflict and disunity – which it often does. In the modern era, we have seen sharp ideological and group differences mark Jewish life. Let's review the current list: Orthodoxy, Conservatism, Reform, Reconstructionism, New Age Judaism; religious and secular; Hasidic and other ultra-Orthodox; Hebraist and Yiddishist; Zionist and non-Zionist and anti-Zionist; left-wing or right-wing Zionist; traditional and avant-garde. These groups have different cultures and agendas. In fact, modern Jewish pluralism has been very fractious indeed; disunity has been the rule. A remarkable exception was the brief period after the Holocaust and the creation of Israel, when Jews fashioned a communal consensus that lasted perhaps into the late 1970s. But that idyll is over. Jews remain a "stiff-necked," cantankerous people.

In the wake of Yitzhak Rabin's murder in 1995, and again after the intifadas and clashes with Hamas and Hezbollah on Israel's borders with Gaza and Lebanon, and a perceived nuclear threat from Iran, there have been understandable calls for Jewish unity. But unity can lead to sameness and stifle creativity. There has also been growing opposition in some Jewish quarters to Israel's actions in these matters, in the general Palestinian issue, and in Israeli domestic issues. For example, in June 2017, the Netanyahu government decided to delay implementing a decision to broaden access to the *kotel* (Wailing Wall), and to restrict access to non-Orthodox conversions in Israel. This exacerbated tensions between Israel and the diaspora in Canada. In the words of Linda Kislowicz, president of the Jewish Federations of Canada, "The damage is deep but I hope temporary. I think that we shouldn't underestimate the fragmentation, the fracture, the disappointment, the anger even."[11] Discord on these, and other issues, impacts Jewish communal relations within Canada. But still, a respectful pluralism is far preferable to an inflexible, suffocating homogeneity. Let us recall that in the ghettos, and even in the concentration camps, rivalries persisted. Difference, dissent, and debate are part of Jewish identity today as in the past.

But there is more. This fractious pluralism is not simply a cross (pardon me) which Jews must bear. It is ironically a source of Jewish strength. There are so many ways to be a Jew. Some decades ago Lewis Coser published a major work with the paradoxical title *The Functions of Social Conflict*.[12] In his study, Coser outlined a variety of scenarios in which conflict can benefit both the competing groups and the society as a whole. In the Jewish case, this would mean both Jewish sub-groups and Jewry writ large. Conflict among the denominations has the unanticipated benefit of forcing each to sharpen and deepen both their commitments to the community and their self-understanding.

Moreover, actual intra-group conflicts in the daily lives of Canadian Jews are minimal. This is because so much of Jewish life is organized on a pattern of voluntary self-segregation. For most matters, Jews associate with similar Jews in their neighbourhoods, their synagogues, their children's Jewish schools or summer camps, in Jewish organizations, and in their private socializing. The conflict that people worry about is found mainly in public pronouncements. Some fear it could grow into a complete schism between, say, the

Orthodox and the non-Orthodox. But let us take a deep breath in the face of such a worst-case scenario. For example, it is not clear if Christianity is stronger or weaker today because of the split into Catholicism and Protestantism several centuries ago.

Conflict within the Jewish world is not a problem that Jews have to solve with the creation of a unified mode of Jewish life, replete with a single demographic pattern and a single dominant cultural orientation. Conflict is a permanent, intrinsic feature of Jewish life, part of its vital diversity. In fact, the various poles of Jewish life today complement each other rather well. The sub-groups within the Jewish world perform different strategic and collective functions, which together help achieve the diverse goals of the communal Jewish agenda. Jewish survival owes much today to this blend of quantitative and qualitative demographic strategies.

COUNTING JEWS

How many Jews are there in Canada? The answer depends on whom we decide to count. As we have seen, Judaism is a faith, but Jews are also a people with common ancestry. The Canadian census addresses this dualism head on. For many people, the census is a dry, uninteresting set of numbers. Not true for Canada, and not true for anyone interested in Canadian Jews.

In the United States, estimating the number of Jews has been a challenge, since their census collects no data on religion – the American Constitution as interpreted forbids it. Questions on nationality in the American census also leave Jews out as a category. That is why, for a long time, analysts trying to say something quantitative about American Jews were forced to use the census numbers for "Russians" as a proxy for Jews, or rely on cumbersome and expensive special national surveys. Canadians are more fortunate. The Canadian census is a wonderful if still imperfect tool for understanding an enigmatic group like the Jews. The Conservative government of Stephen Harper decided to make a controversial change in advance of the 2011 census. Instead of the mandatory long form census, which included questions on ethnic origin and religion, the government instituted an optional National Household Survey. This decision, apparently motivated by "privacy" concerns, provoked a great deal of debate. Concerns were expressed that smaller and economically vulnerable minority groups might be undercounted. Since

Jews are a fair-sized group and on average economically secure, any Jewish undercount would be minimal. So in estimating the current Canadian Jewish population we use data from the NHS of 2011. In 2011 there were an estimated 309,650 Jews by ethnic origin, and 329,500 Jews by religion. Some of these "ethnic origin" Jews no longer feel affiliated. The question on religion asks simply "What is your religion?" The question on ethnic origin asks "To which ethnic or cultural group(s) did this person's ancestors belong?" While one can choose up to four ethnic origins, only one religion is recorded. That may well have to change, as interfaith marriages increase, and more Jews (and other Canadians) identify as hybrid or hyphenated in terms of religious identification.[13]

There is clearly no one-to-one correspondence between these two definitions. Many Jews by religion might not claim Jewish ethnic origin. Known as "Jews by choice," they could be formal converts into Judaism or technical non-Jews who call themselves Jewish. (Ivanka, daughter of US president Donald Trump, became an Orthodox Jew through conversion.) They can also be Jews who for some reason picked another ethnic origin as their census answer, such as Polish, or English. On the other hand, there are many Jews by ethnic origin who might claim another religion. Either they themselves, or some ancestors, converted out of Judaism. They are truly lost to the Jewish community.

But even these non-Jews can have a tough time escaping fully from their Jewish background, as former American secretary of state Madeleine Albright can confirm. Once the media found out that her parents were Czech Jews who had escaped the Holocaust and converted to Christianity, she was forced to acknowledge her background in public. Many Jews – including me – found it hard to believe that she had not known about her Jewish ancestry. In Canada there are comparable examples of "Christian" Canadians of European background who, deliberately or not, have kept their Jewish ancestry hidden in their closet. A rich vein of Jewish humour emphasizes the difficulty such people face in escaping their Jewishness by conversion; it manages to bubble to the surface.

A Jew converts in order to join an exclusive country club. On his first day as a member he accidentally falls into the swimming pool fully clothed. Climbing out soaking wet and embarrassed, he groans, "Oy gevalt ... whatever that means!"

There are also many who claim Jewish ethnic origin but insist that they have no religion. A non-Jew with a Jewish grandparent or great-grandparent may decide, depending on their mood during a particular census-taking, to claim a Jewish ethnic origin. Others in this group might be thoroughly assimilated, with no ties to or feelings for Jewish life, and unable to distinguish an *aleph* from a *bet*. Still others could have a strong Jewish cultural sense and identity, perhaps anchored in the local community, in Yiddish, or in a bond with Israel. They might even attend the odd synagogue service and be able to follow the prayers. Here, too, Jewish humour has long stereotyped the difficulty of being a Jewish atheist or agnostic.

Two Jewish atheists in the *shtetl* are arguing over who is the greater non-believer. One is a devotee of Spinoza, the other of Marx. In the midst of their heated argument one suddenly stops and says, "Moishe, it's getting late, we have to hurry to the synagogue in time for the evening prayers!"

Many Canadian Jews wrestle with the distinction between being "ethnically" and "religiously" Jewish. The gap in census counts has historically been greatest in Vancouver, part of the new western "frontier" for Canadian Jewry. Vancouver has many Jews of mixed ancestry who no longer identify their religion as Jewish, as well as many secular Jews. This leads to very fluid conceptions of identity. Consider the following quotations from an earlier Vancouver study.[14]

I was born Jewish and will pass on the traditions as I know them, e.g. Pesach, Hanukkah, etc. However, being an agnostic, to go further than that would be impractical. I did not circumcise my son because I felt it to be hypocritical and also since the latest medical literature says it is barbaric and unnecessary.

Up to college I only had Jewish friends. In college I started meeting non-Jewish people and found a whole different lifestyle in them. Two of my best friends are Christian and I celebrate Christmas. I consider myself Canadian first, then Jewish. I found the Jewish community in Montreal too close, too stifling. I understand how important it is for the Jewish people here in

Vancouver to get close and get a better sense of identity, but it's not important to me. However, my heritage is Jewish and ethnically I will always be a Jew.

As a convert or Jew by choice, I feel strongly that I converted to a religion. There is an ethnic component but the religion is the centre of Judaism.

To get the best estimate of the number of Jews in Canada in 2011, we use the "standard definition" which adds secular Jews – those with Jewish ethnic origin and no religion – to those who are Jewish by religion, for a total of 385,345 Jews or 1.17 per cent of the Canadian population. (See Table 1 in the Appendix. Table 2 presents a newer estimate which includes respondents with combinations of Israeli ethnic origins or birthplace, etc., and that raises the total to about 391,000.) Between 1981 and 1991, the Canadian Jewish population increased by 14.2 per cent, slightly greater than the increase of 13.4 per cent for Canada. The Jewish population increased by an estimated 4.2 per cent between 1991 and 2001, and 4.7 per cent from 2001 to 2011.[15] This differs from the American case, where the 2013 Pew data show that the Jewish population according to conventional definitions has increased slightly or been static.[16] (The 2013 Pew data yields an estimate of 5.3 million American Jews; other estimates with more expansive definitions reach between 6 and 7 million Jews, or around 2 per cent of the American population.)

A major problem emerged in the 2016 census. Ethnic-origin Jews fell from 309,650 in 2011 to 143,665 in 2016. Many likely chose Canadian, Russian, or Israeli instead; Canadian Jewry did not decline by more than half. In 2011, "Jewish" was included as one of twenty-four possible responses. The list is based on the largest groups from the previous census, and the Jewish group did not make the cut-off in 2016. Thus many "ethnic" Canadian Jews who might not choose "Jewish" as their religion may be lost to the total count. If this issue is not resolved for the 2021 census, its use for Jewish demographic analysis will be seriously compromised.[17]

As of 2011 there were few clear demographic signs of the "vanishing Canadian Jew." Much of this Canadian advantage in identity and population growth – which is not guaranteed in perpetuity – comes from the greater proportion of foreign-born Jews. We therefore turn to a discussion of the growth of the Canadian Jewish community through waves of immigration, and its distribution throughout the country.

3

Building a Community

Migration and Regional Settlement

"Get thee out of thy country ..."
Genesis 12:1

"Love ye therefore the stranger for ye were strangers in the land of Egypt."
Deuteronomy 10:19

FOUNDATIONS

Many people think of Jewish immigration to Canada as a topic best studied by historians. After all, the great mass migrations at the end of the nineteenth century are over. But from the time of Abraham, Jews have been on the move. The immigrant saga occupies a mythic place in the identity of Canadian Jewry, as it does in the United States. And this despite the fact that Jewish immigrants, from the early Eastern Europeans to the more recent Holocaust survivors, North Africans, Russians, and Israelis, often were met with ambivalent receptions by the established Jewish organizations as well as Canadian-born Jews.

The profile of Canadian Jews mirrors that of Canada itself. As immigration and regionalism are two defining characteristics of the Canadian reality, so too do they mark the life of Canadian Jews. Part of the vaunted uniqueness of Canada's "mosaic" compared to the American "melting pot" stems from the higher general levels of immigration to Canada. In the second decade of the twenty-first century, 17 per cent of all Americans were foreign-born, compared with 20.6 per cent of Canadians.[1] Immigrants help all minority communities, including Jews, retain their culture.

Thus the greater level of contemporary Jewish immigration in Canada helps explain the differences between the two Jewish communities. Immigration continues to add to the diversity, and tensions, within the Canadian Jewish community. Yet paradoxically it adds to its strength and vitality.

Jewish migration to Canada, like that of other groups, is the story of different waves of immigrants, from different backgrounds, motivated by different concerns. The first Jews arrived in Canada as individuals, their stories the stuff of high drama. Joseph de la Penha was a Jewish trader from Rotterdam who in the 1670s was driven by a storm onto the coast of Labrador. While King William III of Orange and England granted de la Penha title over Labrador some twenty years later, the family never acted on the offer.[2] In 1738, a teenaged French Jew named Esther Brandeau arrived disguised as a young man; she was sent back after one year.

The first organized migration was that of European merchant families, who settled first in Halifax and later in Montreal, Trois-Rivières, and Quebec City following the British conquest. This population of traders and merchants grew slowly, reaching 154 souls by 1841. All were of British or Central European origin, some having arrived via the United States.[3] They were mainly Sephardi, and founded the oldest continuing synagogue in Canada, the Spanish and Portuguese Congregation of Montreal, in 1768. The legacy of that first Sephardi immigration largely disappeared, as did that of the first Sephardi immigrants to the United States.[4] But the post-Second World War North African immigration to Montreal has revitalized the Sephardi influence in a way not felt in most American cities.

The first large wave of Jewish migration to Canada was from Central Europe, arriving between 1840 and the 1880s. This wave included some Eastern European Jews who migrated to Germany, and later to the New World, for a variety of economic and political motives. Some were tradesmen and artisans whose livelihood was threatened by large-scale industrialization. The failure of the European Revolution of 1848 added to Jewish insecurities. While tens of thousands of Jews emigrated from Central Europe at that time, the large majority went to the United States. By 1877 there were an estimated 280,000 Jews in the United States, the vast majority the product of German migration.[5] In Canada, the total Jewish population as of 1881 numbered only 2,456.[6]

Perhaps because these early numbers were so small, a Germanic/ Reform stamp on the nascent Canadian Jewish community was far weaker than in the United States. Reform Judaism never achieved the dominance in Canada that it established early in the United States.[7] Stephen Birmingham's *Our Crowd*, a chronicle of the nineteenth- and early twentieth-century German Jewish "aristocracy" in America, could not have been written about Canada.[8] The German Jewish migration to the United States established niches in banking (Loeb, Kuhn, Goldman), journalism (Sulzberger, Pulitzer), and retail trade (Saks, Nieman-Marcus, Bloomingdale, Sears) in a way that did not take place in Canada. By 1871, Jews represented a minuscule .03 per cent of the Canadian population. But slowly and surely, Jews began to spread throughout British North America.[9]

The second large wave of Jewish migration was from Eastern Europe: Russia, Poland, Lithuania, Ukraine, and Romania. This phase began in the late 1870s, and was given added impetus by the Russian pogroms of 1881. As a result of the partitions of Poland and the Napoleonic Wars, Polish Jews came largely under Russian control. Jews were confined to an area along the western borders of Russia, known as the Pale of Settlement, set up by Catherine the Great in 1791.[10] Conditions for the Jews in the Pale worsened in the second half of the nineteenth century. Following the emancipation of the serfs in the 1860s, Jews faced increased competition from non-Jewish artisans, workers, and traders. Mobility restrictions and other laws and regulations limited Jewish opportunities. In addition, climbing fertility and declining mortality rates increased the Jewish population faster than the growth of economic opportunities. Russia underwent a period of political and ideological foment at the turn of the century, which saw increases in anti-Semitism as well. Migration was the solution. Millions of Eastern European Jews left for North America between the 1880s and 1920s.

Precise records of the ethnic origin of immigrants to Canada prior to 1900 are unavailable. In addition, we have no numbers about immigrants to Canada via the United States.[11] During the years 1900 to 1920, government statistics report a total of 3,246,051 immigrants who came to Canada, of whom an estimated 138,467 or 4.3 per cent were Jews.[12] The total Canadian Jewish population increased from 2,456 in 1881 to 126,201 in 1921, much of that by immigration. By comparison, in the United States the Jewish population increased from 280,000 in 1877 to an estimated 4.5 million in 1925.[13] The peak year of migration to Canada was in 1913–14, with 18,000 Jews out of a total influx of 400,000. The migration of Eastern European Jews also coincided with the expansion of the Canadian population westward. While Jewish life was indeed centred in the cities of Montreal, Toronto, and Winnipeg, there were also many Jews living in rural areas and smaller cities and towns.

The story of Jewish immigration is one of travail, and eventual triumph. The forces that propelled Jews to come to Canada were economic deprivation and persecution. The early Central and Western European immigrants to Canada laid the foundations for many welfare institutions that served later waves of immigrants. This included Montreal's Young Men's Hebrew Benevolent Society, founded in 1863, and the Baron de Hirsch Institute, founded in 1902. In Toronto, welfare in the late nineteenth century was concentrated in the (male) Toronto Hebrew Benevolent Association, in the (female) Ladies Montefiore, associated with the Holy Blossom Synagogue, and in the Toronto chapter of the Anglo-Jewish Association.[14]

The occupational structure of the Eastern European Jews differed from that of the earlier Jewish migrants, where merchants, traders, and professionals had predominated. Between 1870 and 1900, the majority were artisans, unskilled labourers, small-scale merchants, clerical workers, and people in unspecified occupations. By 1920, over 70 per cent were skilled labourers and artisans, a much higher proportion than found among the general immigrant population to the United States and Canada.[15] Relatively few Jews were farmers and unskilled labourers. Efforts to set up Jewish agricultural colonies in the Prairie Provinces in the 1930s under the patronage of the Baron de Hirsch eventually came to naught. But those agricultural efforts grew to assume a mythic status in the history of Canadian Jews.[16] The descendants of Jewish farmers in Western Canada enjoy a kind of *yichus*, or respect for their lineage, normally reserved for bluebloods.

Compared to the migration of other European groups to Canada or the United States, Jewish migration was more likely to be a one-way move. While some Jews returned to Europe, this was less common than among other European immigrants, who would return to the homeland after they saved enough money to buy some land. Anti-Semitism made a return less attractive for Jews, and as a result Jews immigrated as families. Men were more likely to send home for a spouse than to return to re-establish ties in the old country. Jews knew they were in Canada to stay, and had to plan for the economic future of their children. This meant acting responsibly and energetically in their own jobs, and encouraging their children to do well in school.

We should neither understate nor overstate the extent of early Jewish economic success. The streets of Canada, like those in the United States, were not paved with gold. The Eastern European Jewish migrants and most of their children were overwhelmingly working-class, a condition which lasted well into the 1930s. Mordecai Richler's hustling Duddy Kravitz is a typical character of the 1940s, a Canadian-born Jew trying to move up. Nevertheless, compared to other urban immigrant groups, the Jewish climb up the occupational ladder was rapid. This was also true for New York in the early twentieth century.[17] But it was not until the postwar period that a large and stable Canadian Jewish middle class began to emerge.

Compared to the United States, the Canadian government's motives were more economic than racist. The United States effectively restricted immigration in 1924 as a result of anti-immigrant pressures, typified by the newly remobilized Ku Klux Klan, even though the American economy was still strong. Jewish migration to Canada persisted in substantial numbers up to 1931. The onset of the Depression was the catalyst for the change. Economic insecurities fed into existing anti-Semitic prejudice and closed the doors to desperate Jewish refugees from Nazi Germany.[18] While Jewish immigration throughout the 1920s averaged several thousand per year, for the dangerous 1930s the number was only several hundred. Jewish immigration to Canada resumed, albeit slowly, only after the end of the war.

The next Jewish immigrants to arrive were the Holocaust survivors. The first group arrived from 1947 to 1952. A total of about 34,000 came to Canada, of whom some 11,000 were official Jewish DPs, or displaced persons. Of a total of about 98,000 DPs of all origins coming to Canada, Jews ranked third, after Poles and Ukrainians.[19] The survivors strengthened the ties of Canadian Jewry to Eastern European Jewish life. While many, probably most, were not strictly Orthodox, they were steeped in the rituals and lore of traditional Judaism. Though many were broken in body or spirit, they made major contributions to organized Jewish life. They were active in Jewish education and culture, playing key roles as teachers in day schools, as contributors to and readers of Yiddish newspapers, and as volunteers, staffers, and patrons of cultural organizations. Not surprisingly, the survivors also played a role, hesitantly at first, in raising communal awareness about the Holocaust.[20]

The impact of Holocaust survivors in Canada was greater than in the United States, where the relative demographic weight of survivors was much less. By 1953 about 140,000 Jewish survivors had emigrated to the United States.[21] If we estimate about five million Jews in the United States in 1950, and about 204,000 in Canada in 1951, the difference in the relative proportions of postwar survivor migrants is truly striking.[22] They comprised only 3 per cent of the American but 16 per cent of the Canadian Jewish population. In time, the survivors became an active political force and a prod to a timid Jewish establishment, particularly when it came to the militant defence of Israel or of Jewish rights in the face of perceived anti-Semitism. Toronto's Rabbi Gunther Plaut recalled: "Survivors of the *Shoah* have played a great part in Canada and made a stronger impact on our community than in the United States. I remember a 1961 Canadian Jewry that was hesitant to speak out publicly, let alone march in the streets. The survivors helped to change that."[23]

MORE RECENT WAVES

An important wave of immigrants from North Africa began to arrive in the late 1950s, settling mainly in Montreal. These immigrants, most from Morocco, were francophone and Sephardi in cultural orientation. They added a unique dimension of pluralism to Jewish life in Montreal. There remains some confusion as to their precise number, since not all French-speaking Jews are North African or Sephardi, and not all Sephardi Jews are francophone or from North Africa. One estimate of the North African population in 1972 ranged from 10,000 to 13,000. By the late 1990s, other estimates ranged from 25,000 to 30,000.[24] A 1996 survey of Montreal Jews found 18 per cent of respondents to be Sephardi, and 21 per cent claimed they spoke French at home, exclusively or with English; that suggested a lower total of around 21,000 Sephardi Jews. By 2011, census estimates for the Sephardic population in Montreal were over 22,000, comprising almost one-quarter of the Montreal Jewish population. About 17 per cent of Montreal Jews spoke French at home, as did 73 per cent of Sephardim.[25]

The North African Jews were, like the largely Eastern European Holocaust survivors before them, rooted in an "Old World" Judaism far removed from influences of secularism. At the same time, their preference for French complicated their integration into the larger, more established anglophone Jewish community of Montreal; a process not without its frictions.[26] Over one-third of Sephardi respondents in one study asserted that the relationship between them and Ashkenazim was "not harmonious."[27] In one sense, these immigrants helped to create valuable bridges for Jews to the Québécois, just as Quebec nationalism was emerging full-blown. But in another, they made concerted pro-federalist action difficult, since some of their leaders were seen as "soft" and not as viscerally federalist as the Anglophone Jews. I recall attending a meeting of Jewish communal representatives preparing a tripartite brief for the Bélanger-Campeau Commission on the future of Quebec in 1990. In exasperation at the seemingly tough pro-federalist stance of most of the anglophone Jewish leaders, one francophone leader yelled, "What are you afraid of? What are you afraid of?" Not surprisingly, data from the same 1996 survey show Ashkenazim were more than twice as likely as Sephardim to feel "pessimistic" about life in Quebec.

All this was not lost upon sovereigntist leaders in Quebec, who favoured francophone Jews and their organizations as they tried to demonstrate an absence of anti-Semitic bias. This "divide and conquer" approach yielded only a marginal payoff for Parti Québécois strategists. According to the 1996 survey, only 6 per cent of Sephardim supported either sovereignty-association or independence, compared to just under 1 per cent for Ashkenazim. And surprisingly, Sephardi respondents had a slightly higher inclination to leave Quebec. In fact, the Sephardi community of Toronto grew rapidly in the 1980s and 1990s. Over the years, the Sephardi-Ashkenazi divide within the context of Quebec sovereignty has become less of an issue as support for sovereignty has stabilized or decreased. With few exceptions, Sephardim in Québec have tended to shy away from politics.[28]

Along with the Sephardi immigrants, and following the first wave of Holocaust survivors, came other European immigrants. Over 6,000 Jews arrived in 1957, many from Hungary following the failure of the 1956 Revolution. A few managed to arrive from Poland in 1968–70, following reformist tensions and civil unrest. These wavelets of Jewish migration included large numbers of Holocaust survivors as well.

Soviet Jews – as they were called then – began arriving in the 1970s. The Soviet authorities manipulated the numbers of visas granted, depending on their needs of the moment. Jews were pawns in the *Realpolitik* of the Cold War. These immigrants posed a new challenge for the Canadian Jewish communities. As a group, they were highly educated, perhaps more educated than any other refugee group. But whereas previous immigrants had usually been steeped in traditional Judaism, the opposite was the case here. Russian Jews were largely unfamiliar with Judaism and Judaic culture. They had been subjected to decades of anti-Jewish and anti-Zionist propaganda by the officially atheist Soviet state. Rampant anti-Semitism in Russia added a further incentive to encourage them to reject Jewish ties. A study of a small sample of Russian Jews in Toronto found that two-thirds said they had "negligible" or "weak" exposure to things Jewish in the USSR. Half "never or hardly ever" attended a synagogue, and only one-quarter were affiliated with a Jewish organization, usually the Association of Soviet Jews in Canada. Eighty-seven per cent said that three or four of their closest friends in Canada were other Soviet Jewish immigrants. Here, as in the case of Israeli migrants, there seems to be a case of an emergent "community within a community."[29]

Estimates of the size of new immigrant groups always vary, as we have seen with the Sephardi community in Montreal. At times, it is hard to define the group for statistical purposes. Their size may also be overstated by group leaders competing for communal dollars or to establish influence within their own community or with government. Consider the case of the Soviet or Russian Jews. Published estimates of their numbers were at 8,000 in 1983 and 20,000 by 1993.[30] The 1991 census revealed only 11,280 Canadian Jews who had been born in the USSR. The estimates continue to grow. By 2011, 14,795 Canadian Jews were born in Russia, and an additional 11,275 were born in Ukraine, 2,560 in Belarus, and 6,420 in other countries formerly part of the USSR. But these figures do not include Canadian-born children of Russian immigrants.[31] According to the Pew report, in 2013, 5 per cent of American Jews were born in the former Soviet Union, and up to 11 per cent were either born or had one parent born in the former Soviet Union.[32]

Jewish community leaders were torn during the 1970s and most of the 1980s about how important it was to get Soviet Jews to Israel, as opposed to elsewhere in the democratic West and Canada in particular. Most Soviet Jews were able to leave with exit visas to Israel, but increasingly large numbers changed their plans en route in Vienna and sought refuge in the West. Western Jewish communities did not want to appear to be stealing potential immigrants to Israel; thus the interests of Israel, the Soviet Jews, and diaspora Jewish leaders did not always coincide. In the post-Soviet 1990s, Russian Jews seeking to leave could no longer qualify as refugees under the 1951 Geneva Convention, though some would continue to stretch the rules. As Russian Jews poured out in the 1990s, there were enough to go around to populate both Israel and, to a much lesser extent, North American Jewish communities. From 1989 to 1997, over 700,000 of these Jews immigrated to Israel.[33] In 1990 and 1991 alone, over 300,000 immigrated to Israel from the Former Soviet Union (FSU). From 1992 to 2000, between 46 and 68,000 people moved from the FSU to Israel annually, which accounted for nearly three-quarters of Israeli immigration during that time period. FSU immigration to Israel dropped below the 10,000 mark in 2005 with between 6,000 and 9,000 immigrants annually between 2005 and 2012. The proportion of Israeli immigrants coming from the FSU returned to around the 50 per cent mark. In 2012 they accounted for 43 per cent of Israeli immigrants.[34]

Israelis are yet another, and in some ways the most problematic, immigrant wave. (The Israelis used to be called *yordim*, a pejorative term from the Hebrew word *yored*, which means "one who goes down." This contrasts with the Hebrew term *oleh* for an immigrant to Israel, meaning "one who goes up" as if to a better place.) Here, too, no one knows how many have come. One activist in the Israeli Canadian community estimated the number at between 12,000 and 15,000 at the end of the twentieth century.[35] In any event, other earlier estimates were much higher. One study mentions an estimate of 30,000 just for the Toronto Israeli community, but with no direct source. Another asserts a range between 20,000 and 50,000 for Canada as a whole.[36] The 2011 census reveals that 21,155 Canadian Jews were born in Israel, of which 4,460 reside in Montreal and 11,465 in Toronto.[37] Often these discrepancies result from different definitions of who is an Israeli. Israelis need not have been born in Israel. Many Israeli immigrants to Canada were born elsewhere, moved to Israel, then migrated to Canada. According to the 2013 Pew report, 4 per cent of the net US Jewish population were either born or had at least one parent born in Israel. This is an undercount since, as mentioned, many Israelis may not have actually been born in Israel.[38] A recent estimate from the CEO of the Israeli American Council, also likely an exaggeration, reported that there are between 500,000 and 800,000 "Israelis" living in the US.[39]

The Israeli immigrants posed a different set of challenges for the host Jewish communities, one laced with a bittersweet irony. In one sense they were ideal Jewish immigrants. They were highly knowledgeable about Jewish culture, fluent in Hebrew, and knew Jewish history, the Bible, and a fair bit about Jewish holidays. But many, perhaps most, were not at all observant. On the High Holidays in Israel, they were as likely to go to the beach as to go to pray. They had no experience with the variety of North American synagogues. Religion in Israel meant *dati* or Orthodox, and was tainted by associations with religious political parties. Some Israelis assumed positions as teachers in Jewish schools and as staffers in a variety of Jewish communal organizations – replacing in some cases the earlier generation of Holocaust survivors – but others were resolutely secular and had trouble developing a diaspora-based Jewish identity.

There was an even more profound problem. The Israelis were travelling in the wrong direction. North American Israelis wrestled with residual feelings of having betrayed the Jewish state. Their presence in Canada challenged a basic premise of Canadian Jewish life, and the community was unsure of the proper response. Canadian Jewry had long been highly Zionist, committed to building up Israel and espousing the value of *aliyah*, immigration to Israel. Too much of a welcome to the Israelis raised awkward questions for Canadian Jews and Zionists. If it encouraged even more Israeli migration, it might weaken Israel's demographic base. Yet a tepid reception would do a disservice to a possibly needy group and violate the tradition of immigrant aid so central to Canadian Jewish life. So the ambivalent Israelis were met with ambivalence on the part of the host community.

Most had minimal contact with the organized Jewish community, and for some time many Israelis maintained a "myth of return," or *chazara*, with which they convinced themselves, and others, that their stay in Canada was temporary.[40] That desire to return, or the need for some such justification, has waned in recent years. Both diaspora Jewish communities and the Israeli government now have a more nuanced attitude towards Israeli ex-pats. Canadian Jewish leaders and organizations now welcome involvement by Israeli immigrants. Israel recognizes that some of their ex-pats might be lured back home, and may also see the Israeli community as forming a bridge between the diaspora and Israel.[41]

This signals another difference between Canadian Israelis and other immigrant groups. Neither Italians nor Poles nor Jamaicans nor Chinese violate a cardinal national or religious myth in leaving Europe or the Caribbean or Asia and coming to North America. The only immigrant groups where such ambivalence might exist are those with a struggling homeland, like those in Africa, the Middle East, and South Asia. They keep one eye fixed on the travails of the mother country fighting against external or internal oppression. But most of those migrants, despite their ideological commitments, are unlikely to return. Life in Canada is just too good. Those with an opportunity to do so – Eastern Europeans since the collapse of communism, or Black South Africans since the end of apartheid – have not flocked back. Israelis are no different. Their question is the same: to sink roots in Canada, or to return? The answer is, increasingly, to stay.

Migration from Israel soon brought an unexpected policy problem. In the 1990s, to the consternation of Canadian Jews, hundreds of Israelis successfully claimed refugee status.[42] These claimants were Jews – and some non-Jews – from the former Soviet Union who alleged they were victims of religious discrimination in Israel – in jobs, housing, the army, by the rabbinate – and that the Israeli government offered them no protection. To many Canadian Jews, the whole thing seemed Kafkaesque. Israel, a state created as a haven for those who had suffered religious persecution, was now labelled before the world as a violator of the human rights of the very immigrants who sought freedom there. More to the point, few Canadian Jews believed that these Russians had in fact experienced the kind of state-sponsored persecution that was supposed to trigger refugee protection. That these acceptances came disproportionately from Immigration and Refugee Board hearings in Quebec added to the suspicions, since it was feared that some of the board's decisions in the province were motivated by anti-Israel sentiment. The numbers were significant. Between 1990 and 2009, 11,000 claims from Israel were made, 1,600 of which were accepted.[43]

Not surprisingly, the issue led to friction between the Israeli and Canadian governments. The story broke in July 1994, when the Israeli newspaper *Ha'aretz* reported that Canada had accepted about 160 Israeli refugees the previous year. The Israeli deputy foreign minister, Yossi Beilin, was furious, claiming that "the situation in which the Canadian government grants refugee status to Israeli citizens is really ridiculous." Replying to Beilin's comments, Canadian immigration minister Sergio Marchi, in what one Israeli journalist called the "sharpest riposte ever heard from a Canadian Minister in the forty-six years of Israel's existence," responded, "I don't think it is the business of another country to dictate to Canada who can and who cannot be considered a refugee. Israel should deal with her own problems and not try to dictate rules of behaviour to others."[44] Eventually, matters were smoothed out. After strenuous representations on the part of Canadian Jewish organizations, the acceptance rate of these alleged refugees from Israeli persecution declined to just to twenty-four in 1998 and twenty-nine in 1999.[45]

Jewish migration has not ended with Israelis. Others continue to come from South Africa, Ethiopia, Latin America, the United States, indeed, the four corners of the earth. The 2011 census revealed 33,495 foreign-born Jews had immigrated just in the previous ten years. Of these, 40 per cent were born in the Soviet Union; 24 per cent in Israel; 15 per cent in the United States; 6 per cent in Western Europe, and the remainder in places like Latin America, Eastern Europe, the Middle East and North Africa.[46] As with Canada as a whole, large, sustained immigration has been a part of the Canadian Jewish experience since the 1880s. Immigration continues to shape the identities of Canada and Canadian Jews alike.

IMMIGRANT INTEGRATION: AN OXYMORON?

All these Jewish immigrants need to be integrated – a process that transforms Canada just as it transforms the established Jewish community. But what kind of integration? Social scientists speak of economic, social, political, and cultural integration; others talk of adaptation, absorption, settlement, or incorporation. Behind these terms, which all mean somewhat similar things, lies a basic question. How much integration is needed for immigration to be considered a success? Some observers perceive failures or even crises of immigrant integration in Canada in the early twenty-first century. Perhaps they have unrealistic expectations. I take a minimalist approach. An immigrant who supports himself or herself and a family and obeys the law is, in my view, successfully integrated. I do not expect most immigrants to Canada to earn very high incomes or to appreciate fully the novels of Margaret Atwood or the plays of Michel Tremblay, or even to master English and/or French quickly – though of course all that would be nice.

The term "immigrant integration" is almost an oxymoron. Integration into what? Into their smaller-sized communities of origin, not into Canada as a whole. These intermediate groups buffer what is a difficult, at times traumatic, process of adjustment in a new environment. Adult immigrants have one foot in the old country, and most *never* fully integrate into Canada. Their children and grandchildren are the ones who do that. Adult immigrants retain ties of language, culture, and kin to the old country. They integrate first into an extended family, if there is one in Canada, then into an ethnic sub-community and place of worship, and then into a larger ethnic community, replete with its own culturally specific institutions. Most remain hyphenated Canadians in a real, sociological sense. This is not a tragedy. Rather, this process of "nested" integration eases traumas associated with immigration into a new society.

This is also the pattern of Jewish immigrant integration. My parents illustrated this process when they arrived in Canada in 1948. They integrated – quite happily, I might add – into a particular subgroup of Polish Jewish Holocaust survivors. Though they learned English, they spoke Polish or Yiddish with their friends. A similar pattern is true for most Jewish immigrants to Canada, and, indeed, for most immigrants of any kind. I recall a conversation in Toronto with a Black cab driver who spoke with an African accent. He identified himself not as Black, not as an African, not as Nigerian, but as a Yoruba, one of the major tribes of Nigeria. And he congregated with other Yoruba, and belonged to Yoruba associations. For Jews or Africans, these patterns are not tragedies, not "failures" of integration. Just life being lived.

The Jewish community maintains one key organization devoted to the integration of Jewish immigrants: The Jewish Immigrant Aid Services. (This agency is now part of a larger agency called Ometz, in Montreal.) It offers help of all sorts to Jewish immigrants during the first three years of their arrival. Other immigrant communities have sought to develop comparable services, though these often rely on governmental as opposed to communal funding. But JIAS is not the whole story; all Jewish immigrant groups have their own organizations, which adds to both the diversity and fragmentation of the community. Some are largely autonomous, others are part of mainstream agencies. The YMHA has programs aimed at specific groups of immigrants, such as Soviet or Ethiopian Jews. Jewish schools and social service agencies are sensitized to the specific cultural needs of immigrants. These various organizations are marked by the distinctive languages these groups speak. The survivors speak Yiddish and other European languages, the North Africans speak French, the Soviet Jews speak Russian, and the Israelis speak Hebrew.[47]

Consider the Israeli case. Israelis in Toronto have had their own literary clubs, a short-lived school, a weekly Hebrew radio broadcast, a Hebrew community newspaper, a Scouts organization, two senior citizen's clubs, Hebrew-speaking chapters in pro-Israel organizations such as Hadassah, Na'amat (Pioneer Women), the Organization for Education Resources and Technological Training, and congregations for Israelis organized by Sephardim and Chabad-Lubavitch. In addition, we find organizations and events such as Kachol Lavan (The Centre for Hebrew and Israel Studies), Israeli folk-dancing festivals, the *Israel Today* radio show, Israeli Source, a store which sells Jewish and Israeli books and religious articles, a Friday night community dinner for Israeli families with children, Hebrew clubs such as Etrog Israeli Club, and the Jewish Israeli *Yellow Pages*. In Montreal, an organization named Betzavta, founded in 1986, began to sponsor cultural and Hebrew-language programs. Part of this greater acceptance by Canadian Jewry reflects a more accommodating attitude by Israel towards its expatriates. The city also hosts events such as the annual Montreal Israeli Film Festival, and an annual rally celebrating Israel's Independence Day.

The Russian Jewish migration also has had its own organizations. The Association of Soviet Jewry in Canada, based in Toronto, has provided medical, legal, educational, and cultural programs and direct assistance. The Russian Jewish Program at Montreal's YMHA is another example. Founded in 1982, it offered a variety of cultural and service programs, many of which accentuate Russian as much as Jewish cultural traditions.[48] Children's classes in art, math, ballet, drama, chess, and the Russian language inculcate Russian cultural traditions. The Jewish Public Library in Montreal has a program offering free children's books in Russian. One of the traits of the Russian Jewish migration is that many community members are not Jewish according to *halacha*, and indeed, many non-Jews participate in these programs. This includes attending synagogue services. According to one observer, "Many *Goyim* are there; they like it, they get vodka at the *kiddush*."

The Russian and Israeli organizations may not be as permanent as those serving Sephardim. The former are devoted to immigrant integration, and they will fade like the earlier *landsmanschaften* as the second and third generations get established. The Sephardim, however, rightly see themselves as preserving a permanent and distinctive Judaic tradition. Their organizations will last well after the passing of the immigrant generation.

These ethno-specific organizations particular to immigrant subgroups have various purposes. In one sense, they may prevent integration into the broader Canadian society and into the mainstream Jewish community. Yet in another sense they facilitate eventual integration by providing a warm, familiar environment in which the immigrant can feel at home. This Jewish mini-tribalism is an indispensable asset. Moreover, the task of integrating immigrants provides native-born Jews with a unifying mission and sense of purpose.

Because Toronto and Montreal have the largest and oldest Jewish communities, we might assume that they also have exceptionally high proportions of immigrants. Not so. Foreign-born Jews have been moving to and settling in the West. In 1997, a survey of Calgary's Jewish community found that over seven per cent spoke Russian at home and that one-quarter of Calgary's Jews were raised outside Canada.[49] In 2011, roughly 28 per cent of Calgary's Jews were foreign-born. Jewish immigrants are found in all regions of Canada. In 2011, the lowest concentration of immigrants was in Manitoba, with 24 per cent of the Jewish population. In Atlantic Canada, 27 per cent of Jews are immigrants, as are 34 per cent in Quebec and 33 per cent in Ontario. Perhaps most surprising are the high percentages found further west: 35 per cent in Saskatchewan, 32 per cent in Alberta, and 34 per cent in British Columbia.[50] The welcoming and integrating of Jewish immigrants is a challenge throughout the country.

The Jewish community is concerned not only with Jewish immigrants, but with immigration policy in general. Jews as individuals and through the now defunct Canadian Jewish Congress or the League for Human Rights of B'nai Brith were traditionally strong advocates of generous immigration and refugee levels. Immigration is for Jews a political litmus test; despite security concerns after 9/11, it is hard to imagine Jews en masse supporting candidates calling for major cutbacks in immigrant numbers. Jewish Immigrant Aid Services has lobbied against measures seen as restrictive, such as bills C-55 and C-84, passed in the late 1980s. The former bill dealt with the refugee determination process in Canada, while the latter provided sanctions to deter illegal immigrants from trying to enter Canada, and smugglers and carriers from transporting them.[51]

However, more recently, a fracture developed within the community regarding Bill C-31, legislation passed by the Stephen Harper government in 2012 which revised the criteria for treatment of refugee claimants in Canada. While advocating "small but significant improvements," the Centre for Israel and Jewish Affairs (CIJA), the de facto replacement of the Canadian Jewish Congress, outlined a position broadly supportive of the government: "In our assessment, the recent changes to Canada's immigration and refugee system offer significant improvements towards protecting the safety and security of Canadians, deterring human smuggling and dispensing with unsubstantiated refugee claims fairly and quickly." In opposition to this view, an organization called the Jewish Refugee Action Network was created, featuring prominent progressive Canadian Jews, to challenge the legislation. J-RAN, whose honourary co-chairs were Stephen Lewis, former Canadian ambassador to the United Nations, and his wife, journalist Michele Landsberg, was sharply critical. In the words of J-RAN co-founder Rabbi Arthur Bielfeld, "Some of us feel the changes are draconian and very much at odds with what we consider the essence of Canadian culture." Liberal sentiments nevertheless prevailed. Beginning in 2015, several Jewish synagogues throughout Canada organized to support and sponsor Syrian Jewish refugee families.[52]

Canadian Jews have been soft on immigration and more likely to give refugee claimants the benefit of the doubt. How could it be otherwise for the "wandering Jews?" The ancestors of many North American Jews probably lied to immigration officers. Some of those claiming to be tailors had likely never sewn on a button. The Canadian government has recognized the expertise of the Jewish Immigrant Aid Services (JIAS) and has consulted regularly with JIAS senior staff. Provinces also now play direct roles in Jewish immigration. Since the 1960s, Quebec has assumed greater control of immigration and the province and JIAS have undertaken several successful projects since the early 1990s, each one recruiting and settling 100 Russian Jewish families. The government of Manitoba pursued a similar plan with the Winnipeg Jewish community aimed at bringing Argentinian Jewish families to Winnipeg. In fact, this effort produced a large influx of immigrants from Israel rather than South America.[53] All this is a far, far cry from the dark days of the 1930s, when government bureaucrats worked to keep Jews out.

Jewish organizations are right to take an interest in immigration, since immigration has been such a defining feature of Canadian Jewish life. Back in 1911, during the period of mass migration, fully two-thirds of Canadian Jews were foreign-born. Well into the twenty-first century, the proportion has remained close to one-third – still very high.[54] This is much higher than the general Canadian figure of one-fifth foreign-born. So while many in Canada think of Jews as an established native-born group, the truth is more nuanced.

The picture is dramatically different in the United States. There, immigrants make up 14 per cent of the Jewish population, and analysts of American Jewish life pay them relatively little heed. A case in point: in the 2013 Pew report of 118 pages, only one page and one table discuss foreign-born Jews.[55] For American Jews, immigration is something that affected their grandparents or great-grandparents; for Canadian Jews, it is more of an ongoing reality.

BITTERSWEET ENCOUNTERS

It is a paradox of Jewish life that a community that has been so dependent on immigration, and has dedicated resources and energy to help Jewish immigrants integrate and to support liberal immigration policies, has a record of a lukewarm acceptance of Jewish immigrants. In terms of interpersonal contacts and attitudes, prejudice and tension have been the rule. This is a continuing theme in the history of Jewish immigration to North America. The conventional account stresses the elitism, perhaps prompted by insecurity, of the established affluent and educated Jews, influenced by Germanic, Sephardi, or British cultural elements. The masses of Eastern European immigrants brought with them the culture of the *shtetl*, the small Jewish towns and villages popularized in the fiction of Sholom Aleichem. These Jews were working-class, spoke Yiddish, worshipped in Orthodox synagogues, and were often socialist and/or Zionist. Many of the established Jews viewed these newcomers with alarm. They feared they would rock the boat and stimulate anti-Semitism. They were, in a word, an embarrassment.

So there was mutual antipathy. Eastern European immigrants through the 1930s resented their alleged benefactors as inauthentically Jewish and opposed to working-class values. The reaction of Canadian-born Jews ranged from ambivalence to condescension to hostility. Rarely did they express enthusiasm. This was also the case much later for the Holocaust survivor migration, or "the *greeners*." This is one of the most dramatic tales of the Canadian Jewish experience, and it is bittersweet at best.[56] This antipathy was not only cultural, as after all both the old-timers and the newcomers were of European Ashkenazi background. Another factor may have been involved: the guilt felt by Jewish Canadians at not having done enough to pry open the gates before the war, or to pressure their government to rescue more people during the war. Many realized that if they hadn't come earlier, they could have found themselves among the survivors, or worse.

My father's story captures the element of chance and distance in contacts with Canadian-born Jews. He was born in Poland in 1902, but his uncle had already struck out for Canada in the late nineteenth century. Part of that uncle's family stayed in Montreal, another part moved out West. My father had two siblings. His older brother left Poland and arrived in the United States in 1922. His sister escaped from Europe in the late 1930s, and arrived in the United States in 1939, one of the few. My father felt he could not leave his parents even as the storm clouds gathered, and was trapped in the whirlwind of the Holocaust. His first cousins and their children were safe in Canada. He survived, married my mother – who had no family left – and immigrated to Canada, settling in Montreal.

The reaction of his now very established and affluent Montreal relatives to his arrival after the war was, to say the least, restrained, and no connections were ever made. No great loss. My parents established a rich social life without them. But the insecurities in that postwar period ran deep. My father remained close to his brother and sister, who had settled near Washington, DC. But he once confided to me that he sensed – it is not clear if he had any evidence for this feeling – that they were pleased he had settled far away in Canada. My uncle had married an American-born Jew and spoke English with no European accent at all. My aunt worked for the Library of Congress and was a profound American patriot. Both were highly Americanized. I doubt they made valiant efforts to sponsor my father into the United States.

It would be easy to harp on the moral failings of my relatives, or of the Canadian-born Jews who received the survivors in the postwar period. But that would miss the point. We tend to overlook the overwhelming social insecurity which those Jews felt. Beneath the facade of acculturation and material success, Jews were threatened, or felt threatened, by a palpable anti-Semitism. A Gallup Poll taken in Canada just after the war found Jews ranked as the second-least desirable of any prospective immigrants to Canada, just ahead of the Japanese.[57] Major institutions, like corporations, universities, and the public service, still closed their highest ranks to Jews. So it is not surprising that those who were established looked at the newcomers with trepidation.

In any event, the survivors managed to rebuild their lives and overcome the physical and psychological horrors they had to endure. They made great contributions to the fields of Jewish education and Yiddish culture, as well as to Canadian society in general. While some lived modestly, others prospered. Indeed, in the 1990s, a *National Post* article listed the fifty wealthiest Canadian; of the ten Jews listed, five – Marcel Adams, David Azrieli, Leslie Dan, Saul Feldberg, and Paul Reichmann – could be identified as Holocaust survivors or refugees.[58]

The ambivalence to immigrants did not stop with survivors. North African migrants of the 1950s and 1960s encountered perhaps greater hostility. Here, the issue was less insecurity and more the greater cultural differences between the host English-Ashkenazi Jewish community and the French-speaking Sephardi immigrants. One survey of Montreal North African immigrants in 1972 found they were three times more likely to prefer to work with French Canadians than with Canadian-born Jews. The intra-communal tensions were real and, in private, some Ashkenazim routinely expressed condescending attitudes. Doubtless, this rejection played a role in the high degree of social interaction the North Africans established with the French-Canadian population.[59] These Canadian Jewish sentiments echoed similar prejudices in Israel against Sephardic immigrants and later, the Ethiopians. Earlier, established communities in France and Germany looked down on the *Ostjuden* from Eastern Europe who had arrived prior to the Second World War.

By the end of the 1990s, marriages between Ashkenazi and Sephardi Jews were still rare in Canada. One Montreal study released in 2000 estimated that 13 to 14 per cent of married Sephardim had an Ashkenazi spouse, and that a slightly higher percentage were married to people not born Jewish.[60] (Exactly half of those spouses who were not born Jewish had later converted to Judaism, which is extremely high by North American standards.) There are still educated Ashkenazi Jews in Canada who recount horror stories and negative impressions about "the Moroccans." These individuals would deny strongly that they are creating or perpetuating racist stereotypes. In the late 1990s, a physician told me stories about such Jews refusing to wait their turn in a waiting room. A social-service worker told me that Moroccan Jewish clients are unreliable, ask for welfare when they do not really need it, and are more likely to be those involved in spousal and child abuse. A retailer claimed "they" are dishonest. This is racism, pure and simple. These feelings may also reflect the insecurities of anglophone Ashkenazi Jews faced with their ongoing loss of power, and the increasingly key role played by francophone Jews in Quebec. By the third decade of the twenty-first century it is likely these views have declined, but not been fully eliminated.

Through the 1990s, most of the major Jewish communal organizations had few Sephardi members on their boards. According to insiders, this was due both to lack of interest by Sephardim, and their reluctance to be token members and perhaps endure subtle prejudice. In the twenty-first century, the involvement of Sephardi Jews in broader community organizations has increased significantly.[61]

North Africans were not alone. The Russian Jewish immigrants have also had problems. It is true that Canadian Jews, like other diaspora communities, fought mightily to help pry open the gates of the Soviet Union. But even that success did not eliminate prejudice. Much as in Israel, there is a tribal shorthand that at times has disparaged "the Russians." Some are labelled as criminals, tarred by the emergence of organized Russian crime syndicates. Others are considered inauthentically Jewish, or inadequately committed to Jewish life. And in response, some Russians decry Canadian Jews as materialistic, uncultured, and cold.

But these resentments are not the whole story. As important is the high degree of communal help extended to poor immigrants in the past, and even more is available now. Although this help may have been accompanied by patronizing attitudes and most immigrants remained within their own sub-communities, Jewish immigrants did not and do not stand alone. Organized communal and financial support for recent Jewish immigrants tends to be greater than that of other Canadian ethnic groups for their arrivals. It parallels, though of course lags far behind, the extensive support Israel offers.

THE COMMUNAL AND CULTURAL LIFE OF IMMIGRANTS

By many criteria, Jewish life was more "authentic" in the early immigrant era. Yiddish was the common language of most Jews. Contact with non-Jews was minimal. Not being wealthy, the immigrants focused on spiritual, social, and cultural activities. However, we should not over-romanticize the warmth and idyllic nature of their lives. Mordecai Richler's depictions of the sleazier side of immigrant Jewish life offer a counterpoint to this idyllic view, even if exaggerated. Religious observance among the immigrants rapidly gave way to the requirements for economic success, such as working on the Sabbath. Immigrant Jewish neighbourhoods also saw high rates of poverty, family disintegration, and crime. For example, in 1933 the crude (unadjusted) crime rate for Canadian Jews, many of them immigrants, was almost 386 per 100,00 population compared to 317 for the Canadian population at large.[62] Cases of desertion and marital discord were not rare, and neither were out-of-wedlock births and juvenile delinquency. The children of immigrants felt the beckoning tugs of even an anti-Semitic Canada very strongly. Some resented parental restrictions, or felt embarrassed at their parents' Yiddish or accented English or Old World ways. Anti-Semitism also was common in employment, social and educational discrimination, and in street brawls with Gentile toughs.[63]

The impact of immigration remains greater on Canadian than on American Jewry. In part this is because immigrant Jews are relatively more numerous in Canada. But there is also a more nuanced historical reason. The Eastern European Jewish immigrants to Canada differed from their counterparts who went to the United States in an important respect. The bulk of the American Jewish mass migration began in the period between 1880 and 1900. In the case of Canada, the migration was more concentrated between 1900 and 1920. This twenty-year gap made a difference. The Yiddish culture established by the Americans was more "assimilationist." The

Canadian migration, arriving somewhat later, had more time to be influenced by the more nationalist ideologies of Zionism and Bundism. Both Herzl's Zionist Organization and the Bund were founded in 1897. They flourished in the early twentieth century and competed successfully against purely class-based left-wing ideologies, which leaned towards universalist, non-Jewish identities. From the socialist perspective, why be a Jew when you could be a member of the revolutionary working class? In contrast, left-wing Zionism offered a way to link progressive politics to the ancestral homeland of the Jews through the ideal of building a workers' state in Palestine. The ideology of the Bund celebrated Yiddish culture, socialist politics, and a territorial solution to the "Jewish Question" in Eastern Europe. Both these ideological currents, stronger in Canada, reinforced a sense of Jewish peoplehood and were resistant to assimilation.[64]

At the time of the mass migration in the early 1900s, the culture of English Canada had little respect for the culture of new immigrants. All immigrants faced varying combinations of occupational discrimination and social prejudice, and Jews were no different. Nevertheless, Jewish immigrants, like others, fashioned a dynamic communal life.[65] They did this without government grants or the support of departments of multiculturalism. But eventually the immigrant culture led to creativity that was recognized by all of Canadian society – the example of Leonard Cohen comes to mind.

While Jewish immigration remains strong, Jews – like other Canadians – have also been moving from Canada to the United States. There are no precise figures, but beginning in the 1970s my impression is that more and more Jewish Canadians have moved south. Perhaps increasing numbers of Canadian Jews are going to American universities for undergraduate and graduate studies. Fewer are returning. Jewish graduates of leading law, medical, and other professional schools are starting their careers in the United States or moving there later. Perhaps unease with the Trump administration might slow this movement. It seems increasingly common to find a Canadian Jewish family with siblings or children in the United States, due either to recent emigration from Canada or older patterns of migrations to North America which produced split families. The recent pattern is a *Yiddishe kop* drain which deprives Canadian Jewry of valuable talent. As with any general Canadian brain drain, it bears watching.

SPREADING OUT

Canadian Jews are not spread evenly throughout the country, and they are almost exclusively urban. In 1871, almost all lived in Central and Eastern Canada, 48 per cent in Ontario and 42 per cent in Quebec, with about 7 per cent in Western Canada. By 1931, as the mass migration wave came to an end, 80 per cent were in Ontario and Quebec and almost 20 per cent out West. Jews quickly moved to the cities. The proportion living in rural areas declined from one-third in 1871 to only 4 per cent – about 5,500 people – in 1931. These rural proportions were highest in the West, notably in Saskatchewan, where over one-fifth of Jews were rural.[66]

Jews are the ultimate urbanites. As far back as 1931, almost four-fifths of Canadian Jews lived in Canada's three largest cities, a ratio that has remained fairly constant ever since. This metropolitan concentration means that Jews are where the action is. In every city where Jews and other immigrants have arrived, they have helped create a cosmopolitan atmosphere. Jews can make their presence felt in the cultural, social, political, and economic domains of North American life in a way that leverages their relatively small proportion of the population. This explains why surveys have found that the American public overestimates the Jewish percentage of the population. A 1998 survey by the American Anti-Defamation League found that 23 per cent of the American population felt that Jews comprised one-quarter of the United States population. Another 43 per cent felt that Jews comprised between 10 and 25 per cent. A 2015 survey conducted by the same organization found that 40 per cent of Americans thought that over 10 per cent of the world population was Jewish.[67]

Commentators on early Canadian Jewish history are often faced with a dilemma. On the one hand, most immigrants were urban. On the other hand, emphasizing the urban roots of Canadian Jewry might reinforce negative stereotypes. It can weaken the claim that Jews played an early role in all the rugged varieties of the Canadian experience. From this perspective, extolling the contributions of the minority of Jews who were involved in the fur trade, in farming, in rural peddling, or even as merchants, shopkeepers, or professionals in small-town Canada meets a strategic need. It sustains a heroic and more "Canadian" version of the Jewish experience.

Thus, there are two themes to the pattern of Jewish settlement. The dominant story is that of heavy concentration in Montreal and

Toronto, creating a dense, quintessentially urban Jewish community and culture similar to that found in New York and other American cities. The occupational profile and rhythms of Jewish life were urban and industrial. Jews clustered in clearly identified neighbourhoods. In Montreal, this was defined by streets like St-Laurent ("the Main"), St-Urbain, or Park Avenue (Avenue du Parc), stretching from Mount Royal and parts of Outremont down to the waterfront. The greatest Jewish concentrations were found in the wards of St-Louis and Laurier, in which just over half of the population was Jewish in 1931. This is where the immigrant Jews concentrated in the "downtown" area of Montreal, with the wealthier, anglicized, Canadian-born Jews in the "uptown" areas, such as Westmount.[68]

In Toronto, the area of Eastern European Jewish concentration was The Ward, bounded by Queen, Yonge, and Gerrard streets and University Avenue. Jews eventually moved to Kensington Market and Spadina to the west. In the 1930s, these concentrations were somewhat less than in Montreal, with less than a third of the area being Jewish. Winnipeg by 1931 was home to over 17,000 Jews, concentrated largely in the West End along Selkirk. Winnipeg's Ward Three was the area of early Jewish concentration, with one-fifth of its population Jewish.[69]

These neighbourhoods symbolize the historic immigrant Jewish experience. In many ways, they recreated *shtetls*. Yiddish was heard on the streets and seen on signs in shop windows, and Jewish schools and synagogues were everywhere. Jewish butchers, bakers, and grocers supplied goods to a largely Jewish clientele. These Jews were mainly working-class, though eager to escape upward through commerce or education as the opportunities arose. Among many older Canadian Jews, the "old neighbourhood" remains a fiercely held element of their Jewish identity, even after they have moved out to the suburbs.

Two Montreal Jews meet on the street. "Hello Rosenberg!" says one. Rosenberg replies, "My name is no longer Rosenberg. I read that people are changing their names to represent their roots, so I changed my name to C.D. St-Urbain." His friend: "C.D. St-Urbain? I understand the St-Urbain, because you used to live on St-Urbain Street. But why the C.D.?" Rosenberg: "Easy. Corner Duluth!"

From time to time, I have heard Canadians, including senior government officials, complaining about "Chinese malls" in Toronto and Vancouver. Almost all the storeowners, personnel, and customers are of Chinese origin, and Chinese languages are spoken and seen on store signs. The officials fear that these malls will prevent Chinese immigrants from integrating into Canadian life, and will provoke a major backlash against all recent immigrants. But memories are short. These commercial concentrations are not very different from those that existed on New York's Lower East Side, on the Main, or around Kensington Market generations ago. Then, it was Yiddish that was ubiquitous, yet the children and grandchildren of the immigrants integrated.

Today there is a distinctively tribal character to Jewish life in Toronto and Montreal. Toronto Jewry is enormously diverse, made of separate entities. There are the old-time Toronto Jews, Russian Jews, Israeli Jews, Sephardi Jews, South African Jews, religious Jews of various persuasions blended with newer sub-communities of ex-Montrealers and other Jewish migrants from small-town Ontario or elsewhere in Canada. All have created formal and informal sub-communities. In Montreal the two major tribes are the Ashkenazim and Sephardim, the latter gaining in size and clout, with a host of much smaller groupings that parallel those in Toronto. The notion of one homogeneous mainstream community does not hold.

The second theme, as mentioned above, is that Jews were never exclusively urban, and not only eastern Canadian. Jewish electoral politics in Canada has traditionally been linked to heavy concentrations of the "Jewish vote" in key ridings in Montreal and Toronto, but the opposite pattern has also been found. From earliest times, Jews spread westward. In 1860, Selim Franklin was the first Jew to be elected to a seat in any Canadian legislative body, not in Ontario or Quebec but in British Columbia. The first Jew to sit in the House of Commons was Henry Nathan in 1871, representing Victoria. Moreover, for three decades and into the twenty-first century, Herb Gray was re-elected repeatedly in his Windsor riding, with no Jewish vote to speak of. British Columbia's Dave Barrett, the first and only Jewish provincial premier, did not rely on any Jewish bloc.

The early movement of Jews to the West was, in large part, orchestrated by the established community. Many of the leaders in Montreal, faced with the mass migration of Russian Jews after the pogroms of 1881, developed plans to direct the migration past Montreal and Toronto. Several early attempts were made to establish Jewish farm colonies on the prairies. After an initial failure, a Jewish farm colony was established in 1888 in Wapella, Saskatchewan, which was reasonably successful (among the new arrivals to Wapella was one Ekiel Bronfman). In the meantime, Montreal Jewish leaders were able to persuade the Baron de Hirsch, a wealthy philanthropist, and his Jewish Colonization Association to underwrite some farm settlements in western Canada. In 1892, the colony of Hirsch was established. Over a dozen farm colonies and settlements were established on the prairies from 1882 to 1911. None survived past the mid-1940s. With the change in immigration policy under Prime Minister Laurier in 1896, even more opportunities were available for Jewish migrants to the West.

Not all Jews west of Winnipeg were farmers; many were traders and peddlers.[70] Winnipeg emerged quickly as the third centre for Canadian Jewry. Winnipeg Jews, mainly of Russian origin, were more rooted in Yiddish culture, more progressive in outlook and politics, and more integrated into mainstream social and political life than their counterparts in Toronto and Montreal. According to historian Abraham Arnold, there was a "mystique of western Jewry," and Winnipeg acquired a reputation as a new *Yerushalayim*. Allan Gotlieb, Winnipeg native and former Canadian ambassador to Washington, was once asked at a social gathering to account for the singular achievements of Winnipeggers, Jewish and non-Jewish alike. To the query, "Why Winnipeg?" he replied, "Why Athens?"

Certainly the geographic isolation from the power centres farther east incubated a populist Jewish culture that sought "an equal place in Canadian Jewish leadership."[71] Jews have been prominent in the Liberals, Conservatives, and CCF/NDP in Manitoba. Western Canada had a weaker anglo-centric tradition and weaker established elites, whether anglophone or francophone, so Jewish communities there did not face those barriers to the same extent.[72] At the same, Jewish life in the Prairies, particularly given the large number of Ukrainian and other European immigrant groups, most closely approximated Eastern European conditions, where Jews mingled with the same set of groups.

Toronto and Montreal remain the dominant centres of population, with nearly 190,000 and just over 90,000 Jews respectively in 2011. But more Jews are moving west. A central element of that move is the exodus from Quebec. One of the newest Jewish sub-communities in Toronto consists of ex-Montrealers. And while many Montrealers stop at Toronto, others travel further west, approximating the general flow of the population. In the face of the exodus, one peculiar source of Jewish immigration to Montreal has been Hasidim from New York and elsewhere. These Jews have been attracted by Quebec's financial support for private religious schools, and by a now-dismantled Quebec baby bonus program worth several thousand dollars per child. That migration, which has levelled off, helped stabilize Montreal's declining Jewish school-age population. More recently, Jewish immigrants from France have arrived in Quebec as a result of an increase in anti-Semitism in that country.[73]

In 2011, approximately 1 per cent of Canadian Jews lived in Atlantic Canada, 23.9 in Quebec, 57.9 in Ontario 8.2 in the Prairie Provinces, and 8.9 in British Columbia. In fact, it makes more sense to analyze Canada's Jewish population growth by city than by province. Between 1991 and 2011, in major Canadian cities, growth rates varied. In descending order, Vancouver and Victoria both grew by 33 per cent, Ottawa by 20 per cent, Halifax by 19 per cent, Toronto by 15 per cent, and Calgary by 13 per cent. The Jewish populations in Edmonton, London and Hamilton remained roughly the same, give or take one per cent. Only three large Canadian cities experienced a decline during this period; Winnipeg and Montreal of 10 per cent, and Windsor of 16 per cent.[74]

It is also important to look at differences in the proportions of each city comprised by Jews. Clearly, the greater the absolute and relative number of Jews, the greater the potential for Jewish life. There is no Canadian equivalent of New York City, teeming with Jews and called "Jew York" by anti-Semites.[75] Nonetheless, Jews are prominent in business, the professions, higher education, the media, and culture in both Toronto and in English Montreal, so their presence feels greater than their actual numbers, which are modest. Jews made up 3.4 per cent of the Toronto metropolitan population, 2.4 per cent of Montreal, 1.9 per cent of Winnipeg, 1.5 per cent of Ottawa-Hull, 1.2 per cent of Vancouver, and less than 1 per cent of all other major Canadian cities, according to the 2011 census.[76] These numbers mean that Jewish life in Toronto and Montreal has a different dynamic than that in the other Canadian cities.

Two regional fault lines have divided the Canadian Jewish community. One is between Toronto and Montreal, nurtured by a

Montreal chauvinism that ranges from bagels and smoked meat to a perception of a warmer, more tightly knit community. Part of this may be sour grapes in the face of Toronto's economic and demographic ascendance, as well as a stereotype of Toronto as colder, at least in terms of its pre-war Anglo heritage. "Toronto the Good" is not "Toronto the *heimish*." A 1998 letter to the *Canadian Jewish News* was a lament by a transplanted Montrealer now living in Toronto.

> … Did someone say that Jews take on the attributes of their environment? Perhaps they have to.
>
> My wife and I came to Toronto 20 years ago, after she retired from a successful teaching career at McGill University …
>
> Knowing only former Montrealers, we tried to get acquainted with Toronto people. To this end we would from time to time invite people we had met, for dinner and a pleasant evening …
>
> The invitees were a mix of Jew and gentile. Over the years we thus entertained probably more than sixty or seventy such couples, separately or in a small group. Everyone said they had a lovely dinner, a most enjoyable evening, and left. We never saw one of them again, although one woman did come back to retrieve an umbrella she had left behind.
>
> Now I may be traducing Torontonians, but during our many years in Montreal, whenever we invited people for an evening, everyone, without exception, would sooner or later invite us back, whether for dinner or otherwise. We thus formed many good and lasting friendships that lasted even after we left Montreal.
>
> Does this mean that Montrealers are different from Torontonians, perhaps more warm blooded, perhaps less shy to get close to strangers? The answer is beyond me. More than once I have heard from recently arrived South Africans of the impossibility for them to break into Toronto circles.

Traits like "warmth" are obviously hard to quantify, and as a Montrealer, I should resist the temptation to disparage Toronto. The much larger Toronto Jewish community is more geographically dispersed than is the case in Montreal. On a per capita basis, Jewish Montreal used to outperform Toronto in terms of philanthropy and the greater variety and vibrancy of its institutions. But there are other subtle differences in the character of the two communities. Montreal Jews, despite shrinking numbers, may still have a more confident sense of Jewish identity. In the words of Gershon Hundert, a Torontonian teaching Jewish history at McGill, "The difference has to do with the 'Orangeness' of Toronto. Toronto Jews seemed to act with a certain discretion about their Jewishness, which is not the case in Montreal. In Montreal, Jews had their place in the social landscape."[77] Isolated as a "third solitude" between the contending anglophone and francophone communities, the Montreal Jewish community for a long time set a high standard for creativity and leadership. In the colourful words of Toronto historian Frank Bialystock, Toronto's Jews and their communal leaders have been chronic underachievers, "180,000 people sitting on their ass."[78]

LIFE IN THE OUTLYING REGIONS

The second regional fault line in Canadian Jewish life lies between the centre – Toronto, Ottawa, and Montreal – and the regions, notably other Ontario cities, the West, and Atlantic Canada. It is often asserted that the regions have been neglected by the "national" Jewish community, which should be a familiar plaint to Canadians. The presidency of the now defunct Canadian Jewish Congress generally rotated between Toronto and Montreal. The same applied to the CJC conventions held every three years, until 1998, when the convention was held for the first time in Winnipeg. Toronto and Montreal have large, deeply rooted Jewish communities. Jews from these two cities are by many measures – but not all – more "Jewish" than those in other cities, particularly in Western Canada.

The special texture of Jewish life in smaller cities and towns has been captured in Canadian fiction.[79] Sheldon Maerov, a community worker in Toronto, was raised in Calgary and then worked in Edmonton before moving east. He reflected on his Western experiences:

Everyone knew everyone. And not just in Calgary. When you grew up in Western Canada, you knew everyone from Vancouver to Winnipeg. Between BBYO [B'nai Brith Youth Organization] and Young Judea, you touched a lot of bases, whether you were involved in Jewish life or just on the periphery. We also knew everyone from Saskatchewan, because twice a year there were

conventions. In the West there was not this great range, mainly
BBYO and Young Judea.

In my time, every kid in Calgary went to the Talmud Torah.
I didn't know a Jewish kid who didn't go to the Talmud Torah
or the Peretz School. It was expected, and assumed.

But Maerov contends that by the next generation things had
changed. His children growing up in Edmonton attended a Jewish
school, but many Jewish children did not, and his children knew
non-Jews in a way he did not. Are his reflections particular to the
West, or do they describe the conditions of life in small Jewish
communities everywhere? Maerov suggests that one characteristic
specific to the West is distance. "In the West, you're isolated. In
London or Kingston, you're a few hours by car from Toronto.
In the West, a few hours by car and you're still in the middle of
nowhere. Your world really is much smaller, and you have to
become more self-sufficient."[80]
Jewish identity in Canada varies by region, but in no consistent
pattern. On some measures, Jews in Montreal and Toronto score
higher than those from the other areas; on some lower. For example,
Jews from smaller cities in Ontario and cities in western Canada are
more likely to belong to a synagogue or to a Jewish organization,
though less likely to light Sabbath candles. Even the small Jewish
communities of Atlantic Canada contain more Jewish vitality than
is commonly anticipated. While some communities have been hit
by population declines, the major centre, Halifax, saw its Jewish
community increase by one-fifth between 1981 and 1991, another
10.9 per cent by 2001 and another 7.1 per cent by 2011. Part of this
increase was the result of Russian Jewish migration to Canada.[81] In
the words of sociologist Sheva Medjuck, "There are out there in all
these scattered centres, active Jewish communities which despite
obstacles are maintaining their Jewish identity and in many cases
thriving." Recent social surveys of Jewish life in Atlantic Canada are
lacking. In her survey of Jewish life in Atlantic Canada in the 1970s,
Medjuck found that 69 per cent kept kosher to some degree – often
harder to do without local kosher butchers, 58 per cent reported
some form of Sabbath home ritual observance, 85 per cent attended
Passover seders, and 75 per cent lit Hanukkah candles.[82] The point
is that in Atlantic Canada and other smaller communities, Jewish life
does indeed exist, though it is being weakened by the steady drain of

younger Jews to larger centres.[83] There, they look for either professional opportunities, or Jewish husbands and wives.

Can Jewish life in the smaller centres continue, and even thrive? Perhaps modern technology can come to the rescue. Online resources offer educational and cultural programming. A laptop can try to replace a Jewish school, and online resources may substitute for a Jewish deli or bakery or a large communal rally. But software may not be a substitute for a fresh *challah* or the locker room of a JCC. It would seem that for Jews, "life is with people." Still, a virtual online Jewish community is better than no Jewish community at all.

What will happen to Canadian Jewish life if more of the population moves west of the Ontario-Manitoba border? Intermarriage rates suggest that Jews who move out west are less committed to Jewish tradition and that their communities do not yet provide the same quality of Jewish life as that found back further east. Either new waves of Jewish migrants will invigorate western Canadian Jewish life, or laid-back, West Coast, New Age attitudes, combined with some rugged individualism, will transform the Jewishness of new arrivals. A more practical issue has to do with philanthropy. In the west, there may not yet be enough wealthy families to bankroll all the Jewish institutions needed to sustain a vibrant communal life. Some wealthy western Canadian Jews, like the Belzberg and Asper families, among others, have made huge contributions, but they represent older generations.

So Canadian Jews are renewing themselves through continuing waves and wavelets of immigration. And the community is also on the move, to Toronto as well as to points west. These immigrants to Canada are a microcosm of world Jewry, and enhance the pluralism – and yes, the divisions – within Canadian Jewish life.

4

Earning a Living

From Work to Wealth

"The more property, the more worry ... the more Torah, the more life."
Pirkei Avot 2:8

"I have been poor and I have been rich. Believe me, honey, rich is better."
Sophie Tucker

MAKING IT

To borrow the phrase popularized by writer Norman Podhoretz, Jews have "made it" in Canada. Any doubters are welcome to inspect the high-end cars parked outside any YMHA or JCC. Canadian Jews have exceptionally high levels of education, occupational status, and income. This is not new. Indeed, it is part of a great paradox of modern Jewish life, in North America as well as most other diaspora communities. Everywhere, Jews have had to contend with legal discrimination and/or popular prejudice. And yet everywhere, from Montreal to Moscow, from Toronto to Tunis, Jews have done relatively well economically.

The roots of Jewish economic achievement in Canada are old and deep. They go back to the earliest periods of Jewish settlement. Even when the masses of Jews were working-class, in the first years of the twentieth century, Jews were overrepresented among the professions and in business. And those who were workers brought with them a drive to succeed which they passed on to the next generations. Their commitment to the working class was fleeting; all wanted something better for their children. Of course, not all Jews are doing well. A fair percentage among immigrants, the elderly, single mothers, and others are struggling below or near the official poverty line. But the central story is that of success.

And in Canada today there is more. Not only are Jewish incomes high; that is true for other Canadian minority groups, like the Japanese. Jews are now statistically overrepresented among the most affluent, the movers and shakers in Canada's elite economic circles. This *is* new. For a long time, conventional wisdom held that even if Jews as a group were doing well educationally and economically, they were still largely shut out from the bastions of Canadian corporate power by a WASP establishment. In his 1965 classic, *The Vertical Mosaic*, sociologist John Porter found that Jews made up less than 1 per cent of the economic elite, far below their population percentage. (The economic elite was defined as comprising the 985 people holding directorships in 170 dominant Canadian corporations.) Moreover, even the few Jews that made it were a group apart: they did not belong to the same clubs or associations, and their philanthropic activities rarely overlapped.[1]

In 1975, Wallace Clement published a follow-up analysis of the Canadian corporate elite that addressed Jewish representation. Clement studied the origins of 775 directors and senior executives of Canada's top 113 corporations in 1972 and found thirty-two Jews, or 4 per cent. This was a dramatic increase over Porter's data from the 1950s. But the social isolation persisted. Clement noted that twenty-five of the thirty-two stemmed from only six families, involved in family firms often one generation old. Jews were much less visible as directors of banks or insurance companies, 2.4 per cent and 1.2 per cent respectively. So the historic pattern of exclusion of Jews from centres of financial power continued. Significantly, only two belonged to one of the six exclusive Canadian men's clubs.[2] Instead, they tended to belong to Jewish clubs, like the Montefiore or the Elmridge Golf Club in Montreal, founded in the days when Jews were excluded from Anglo-Saxon institutions. Though rich, perhaps the source of their wealth set them apart. Historically, Jewish fortunes were made in areas like retail trade or real estate, not the traditional sources of wealth or power of the Canadian establishment at the time.

Of the 171 members of the Canadian business establishment identified by Peter C. Newman in 1975 – mainly men of wealth, CEOs and company presidents, as well others who were well connected – ten, or 6 per cent, were Jews.[3] Even as Porter, Clement, and Newman were documenting the entrenchment of WASP economic power at the expense of Jews and others, change was underway. Some Jews become uncomfortable at any mention of Jewish success, thinking it stirs up resentment and anti-Semitism. Maybe it does. But Jewish economic achievement is the foundation for so much cultural and communal development. This is likely the meaning of the rabbinic adage: "If there is no bread, there is no Torah."

FROM EARLY ELITE TO ROOTS IN THE WORKING CLASS

The early Jewish community in Canada before the mass migration of the 1880s to 1920s was relatively affluent. Moreover, Jews made disproportionate contributions to the economic development of the new country. In the late 1700s, Jewish entrepreneurs and pioneer traders, such as Ezekiel Solomon and Jacob Franks, helped develop commercial trade along the St Lawrence and Great Lakes routes. By the mid-nineteenth century, the small Jewish community included bankers, merchants, lawyers, and doctors. The Joseph family of Montreal was a case in point. Abraham Joseph helped found the Banque Nationale; Jacob Henry Joseph was a founding partner of the Union Bank and the Bank of British North America; Jesse Joseph served as the head of the Montreal Gas Company.[4] To the extent there was a definable economic or corporate elite in Canada at the time, Jews were well represented. They seemed to face little or none of the discrimination which was soon to colour their experience in Canada.

Things began to change with the influx of Eastern European Jews in the late nineteenth century. These Jews were mainly workers or small traders and peddlers. Many were involved in the early union movements as members or organizers. Certainly, their Eastern European experience had made them open to socialism and working-class solidarity. The conditions of these immigrants Jews, many of whom found work in the garment industry's sweatshops or doing piecework at home, were exploitative. Mackenzie King, in a series of newspaper articles on the subject, described their hellish working conditions. King found that sixty-hour work weeks were the norm; one contractor worked his employees thirteen hours a day, seven days a week.[5] Often, Jewish workers were locked in fierce disputes with Jewish employers, who needed to keep labour costs low to sustain any reasonable profit margin in a fledgling industry. The conflict was exacerbated by the cultural gulf between the anglicized owners and their Yiddish-speaking workers.

By 1900, some of the major firms were Jewish-owned and subject to strikes. In 1912, Jewish workers in Montreal struck against the clothing industry, and while they did not achieve union recognition, they managed to wring concessions in a compromise resolution. In 1916 and 1917, a second fierce strike organized by the Amalgamated Clothing Workers of America took place.[6] A different conflict erupted in 1917, when Jewish bakers in Toronto decided to raise the price of their bread to keep pace with inflation due to wartime shortages. Militant Jewish women organized boycotts and at times violent protests against the bakeries, while also baking their own bread. In the postwar slump of 1920–22, bread prices were lowered and the dispute faded away, leaving much bitterness in the community.[7] Conflict between labout and owners persisted into the 1930s, even as the Depression made most workers wary of striking. The International Ladies Garment Workers Union, a product of socialist and Labour Zionist effort, faced a challenge from the communist-inspired Industrial Union of Needle Trades Workers. To meet the communist threat, the mainstream unions entered a militant phase, successfully raising wages. The Toronto Jewish Bakers' Union succeeding in organizing most of the Jewish bakeries in Toronto.[8]

Why did immigrant Jews take to the garment industry? For many, it was the only area for which they had any training. In addition, there were cultural factors that made the needle trade attractive. Jews could expect not to have to work on the Sabbath or major Jewish holidays when working for Jewish employers. They could also expect not to encounter anti-Semitism from Jewish co-workers. Then, as now, Jewish economic activity could be seen as part of a "Jewish sub-economy" linking employers, employees, consumers, and suppliers in one network. This kind of economic network provided some initial opportunities for Jewish immigrants in the same way that other new immigrants found jobs through contacts in their ethnic communities.[9] The common origins also set limits for the friction among workers, and between workers and bosses. Some of the smaller employers led lives not all that different from their employees; in some cases they lived near each other and even frequented the same kosher butcher, synagogue, or cultural or fraternal association. Moreover, anti-Semitism at home and abroad served to unite Jews, cutting across gulfs of wealth and social class. Indeed, it was during the turn-of-the-century migrations that we see the beginning of classical economic anti-Semitism in Canada. In 1898, the Montreal Chamber of Commerce for the first time denied an applicant membership explicitly because of his Jewish origin.[10]

Like many ethnic groups, from their earliest days Jews in Canada had a distinctive occupational and industrial profile. Concentrated in cities, they wanted up and out of the working class, at least for their children. They were "in" the working class, but for the most part never fully "of" it. This impression is sustained by the subsequent rapid occupational mobility among Canadian Jews. Between 1880 and 1920, as more recent immigrants replenished the Jewish working class, a few others assumed the lower rungs of the middle class. And within the working class, whether in New York, Montreal, or Toronto, Jews were concentrated in the ranks of skilled as opposed to unskilled labour. We forget that tailors and most of the workers in the garment industry at the time were considered skilled workers.[11]

Census data reveal the working-class character of Canadian Jewry on the eve of the Depression, but also their footholds in the middle class. While figures for Jewish and non-Jewish men are similar, Jewish women had higher rates of paid employment than other women because they were largely urban and not part of farm families. The major differences lay in the choice of occupations and industrial sectors. Close to a third of all Canadians were in primary industries – farming, mining, or logging – compared to just over 1 per cent for Jews. Other differences in occupations were equally pronounced. Jews were far more likely to work as merchants, clerks, skilled, and semi-skilled workers; non-Jews as unskilled workers. Half of Jewish women worked as clerks or in sales, compared to the Canadian figure of 28 per cent.[12]

If we designate "professionals" and all the categories of "proprietors, managers, and officials" as a middle or capitalist class, we arrive at a figure for the 1930s of 30 per cent. Then we can say with some confidence that more than two-thirds of the Canadian Jewish population was working-class. This figure is practically identical with that for Canada as a whole. But for non-Jews, more than half of this "capitalist" class were farmers and only 1 per cent were wholesale and retail merchants; for Jews, the pattern was essentially reversed. So the foundations for the rise into the middle class were set as far back as the 1920s and 1930s.

The relative rarity of Jewish unskilled workers cannot be explained entirely by Jewish concentration in cities. Close to one-half of Italians – who were also a relatively urban immigrant group in 1931 – were unskilled workers. Unlike Italians, who were largely of peasant or rural stock and became "urban villagers" in North America, Jewish immigrants included large numbers who had lived in cities or towns in Europe.

Jews, like immigrant groups past and present, developed certain economic niches to call their own. In 1931, one-fifth of Canadian Jews and over two-fifths of Jewish immigrant women were working in the textile industry. Jews were twelve times more likely than all Canadians to work in textiles, and twenty-one times more likely to work in the fur industry.[13] But the peculiar occupational characteristics of Jews did not stop at workers' choice of industry. We find as early as 1931 that Jews were more than twice as likely as non-Jews to be lawyers, notaries, physicians, and surgeons. This advantage was reduced substantially, but still persisted, within Canada's largest cities. Jews were also seven times more likely to be working in recreational services, notably as "owners and managers of theatres and theatrical agencies." So here the census confirms the anecdotes about the role of Jews in the fledgling entertainment industry. These patterns have persisted over the decades. By contrast, Jews in 1931 were less likely to be working as public servants and in finance. Indeed, for every Jew employed in finance, there were six employed in agriculture.[14] That has changed.

Although immigrant Jews and their children were slowly moving up, there was little room for them at the very top. In the 1930s, systematic overt as well as covert anti-Semitism restricted Jewish economic opportunities in senior positions with dominant Canadian corporations. This type of exclusion of Jews was documented by demographer and socialist Louis Rosenberg. Under the pen name Watt Hugh McCollum (say it quickly) in his popular booklet *Who Owns Canada?* Rosenberg compiled a list of fifty corporate "big shots" and found not a single Jew among them.[15] Even as Jews began to penetrate slowly into the economic elite in the 1950s and 1960s, they were still shut out of old-money firms in banking, insurance, and heavy manufacturing.[16] In addition, qualified Jews faced restrictions in the senior public service, the judiciary, and in senior positions in universities.[17] Jews were a socially insecure group, afraid to rock the boat or to assert demands for equal rights even as they moved up the economic ladder.

ECONOMIC MOBILITY, JEWISH STYLE

After the Second World War, Jews began to leave the Canadian working class in droves. Much of the success of the children and grandchildren of immigrants was fuelled by education. Many became professionals, while among the business classes children often inherited the family firm. During the postwar economic boom, Jewish incomes rose above the national average. But these high incomes were surprisingly not related to leaving the Jewish economic enclave. For most minorities in North America, moving up has meant moving out and breaking economic ties. Not so for Jews. In one way or another, Jewish "connections" proved valuable in earning a living. Or at least, they certainly were not a liability.

In 1979, I surveyed a sample of Jewish household heads in Montreal and found that 70 per cent were either self-employed or worked for mainly Jewish-owned firms, and 35 per cent had Jews as "most or all" of their business associates – all without any negative impact on incomes. Those whose economic activities were cocooned in Montreal's Jewish sub-economy did as well those who were not.[18] Moreover, participation in this sub-economy was as common among third-generation Jews as among immigrants.[19] This contradicts the conventional sociological wisdom according to which economic concentrations are pronounced for immigrants but decrease for their children and grandchildren.

I could not pinpoint the attraction of the sub-economy. It was not the fear of anti-Semitism, or the desire to work in an environment more receptive to religious requirements, as would be suggested by historic explanations for such Jewish concentrations. It was not the prospect of higher incomes; their incomes were no higher or lower than incomes of other Jews. One possibility is simply inertia. Jews born or raised in Montreal may have inherited from their parents, or from their friends, existing networks which they maintained over the years.

Jeffrey Reitz found similar patterns in Toronto in the late 1970s. Unlike other minority groups at the time, successful Jews did not abandon Jewish neighbourhoods; they recreated middle- and upper-middle-class Jewish neighbourhoods in the suburbs. Jews had distinctive occupational patterns, similar to those noted by Rosenberg for Canada in 1931. Reitz found that:

> Jewish men are [...] 8 times more likely than other men to work in textile products. They are also 6 times more likely to be physicians, 7.9 times more likely to be lawyers, and 3.5 times more likely to be university teachers. Jewish women are three or four times more likely than other women to work in sales, particularly real estate. Jewish women are also concentrated as social workers (2.7 times more likely), in commercial and fine art (2.3 times) and as lawyers and social scientists.

Reitz also found that Jews in Toronto had higher ethnic economic concentrations compared to other groups, and, as in Montreal, that these levels were just as high for third-generation Jews as for immigrants.[20] Indeed, in most cases, these proportions were even higher than for immigrant Jews. Looking at Canada as a whole, a study using 2002 data and data from the 2011 census found that Jews were represented in self-employment roughly two to two and a half times more frequently than the general labour force.[21] Yet in the modern period, as economic restrictions have all but disappeared, these concentrations linger, and with no significant harmful effects.

What is this Jewish sub-economy? One section consists of Jewish organizations, which employ staff and provide community services. A second consists of businesses which provide special services for Jews. For example, the Montreal and Toronto Jewish business directories for the year 2000 listed scores of kosher bakeries, butchers, fish markets, caterers, and supermarkets, as well as Judaica gift stores and bookstores. Toronto had thirty-six kosher restaurants or delis – including two Second Cups. A third is the sector where the business networks are Jewish but the products made or sold are not. The rag trade is the historic example. A Montreal Jewish telephone directory called the "Blue Book" listed in its 1998 edition 3,000 companies and organizations. Its message was clear. "What's the Blue Book's purpose? To help you find, within our community, companies that can supply you with the products or the services that you need."[22] By the second decade of the twenty-first century we find largely online resources, for example jewishpages.ca, jewishintoronto.com, and jewishinmontreal.com. Some of the enterprises listed on these sites are not "Jewish," but many others are. For example, in 2016, we find Montreal has thirty-six kosher restaurants, delis, and bakeries. Though the Jewish sub-economy has persisted past the immigrant generation and into the middle class, we no longer think only of shops clustered along Bathurst Street in Toronto or in the Snowdon area of Montreal. The phenomenon has become more upscale. Jewish lawyers, physicians, dentists, and accountants are often in partnerships or share offices with other Jewish professionals, and will often have more Jewish clients than would be likely by chance. Consider the following anecdotal examples.

A Toronto Jewish businessman involved in a high-tech service industry, who had worked for and had dealings with both Jewish and non-Jewish businesses, distinguished between his personal comfort and business relations. He admitted feeling more comfortable with Jews. He could relate better to them and they to him, particularly in the social interactions that accompany business meetings. But that did not translate into "dollars and cents. I would not be swayed if a person was a Jew, I want to get the best price no matter." Moreover, he never experienced any direct anti-Semitism. He actually preferred to deal with non-Jews when it came to prompt payment of bills. And within the Jewish fold, ethnic stereotypes were alive and well. "The Israelis and Moroccans are the worst, they're slow and will try to kill you." He much preferred to deal with (non-Jewish) Lebanese, who "keep their word." So, whatever comfort level drew him to prefer working with Jews, it did not extend to uniform business judgments in favour of all types of Jews.

A successful Jewish lawyer with a prominent "Jewish" firm claimed that Jews are drawn to law historically because of the affinity with the legalistic nature of the Talmud. (Easy to assert, harder to prove.) He also suggested that there is a distinctive culture in Jewish law firms. For example, in a "WASP" law firm, he said, there will be a lock on the liquor cabinet while in his law firm, they lock up the cookies. (Comedian Jackie Mason would understand.) He believed that Anglo Protestant firms have more decorum than Jewish firms, with more "yelling" in Jewish firms. But wait, there are subcultural differences by region. He also asserted that Jewish lawyers in Quebec yell more than those in Ontario, who will try to "out-WASP the WASPs." Moreover, he felt that Jewish clients preferred Jewish lawyers because, on the one hand, they were more comfortable confiding in them and, on the other, it would be easier to "give them shit." And what of the substance of the law, rather than its style? His view was that the American liberal tradition was not as strong in Canada, despite the record of outstanding progressive lawyers and judges like Rosalie Abella, Alan Borovoy, Maxwell Cohen, Irwin Cotler, Bora Laskin, and Clayton Ruby. Among the younger Jewish lawyers he has met, financial rewards are looming larger as a motive to practise law. "They can do well."[23]

A doctor who worked in a "Jewish" hospital insisted that he didn't choose medicine because he is Jewish. Still, he recalled that the Jews in his medical class tended to socialize together. The atmosphere in the hospital is close-knit and friendly, and "when things happen in Israel, people in the hospital want to fly off." And what of the medicine itself? He observed no obvious differences in the medical practice of Jewish physicians versus non-Jews – though he felt Jewish patients tend to be more demanding.

There is likely an effect of referral networks at work here. Jewish doctors, for example, might be more likely to refer patients to other Jewish doctors, people whom they already know. Jews in business and the professions, especially in Toronto and Montreal, have interacted very disproportionately – and in some cases differently – with other Jews. What is not clear is the degree to which this kind of in-group networking persists well into the twenty-first century.

INTO THE MIDDLE CLASS

Jews are solidly entrenched in the middle and upper classes. A few statistics on education, occupation, and income make the case. Among Canadians aged twenty-five to thirty-four who identified as Jewish by religion in 2011, 56 per cent of men and 67 per cent of women had at least a bachelor's degree; the corresponding national percentages for all Canadians were 25.5 per cent for men and 37 per cent for women.[24] This young cohort of Jews is well placed to succeed in the future. High Jewish educational achievement is not limited to diasporic Jewish communities. In fact, according to a 2010 OECD study reported in *Time Magazine*, Israel ranked second in the world in the proportion of adults with university degrees, after Canada.[25]

In North America, educational achievement of the sort described here marched along with intellectual accomplishments. For example, Jews made up one-half of a list of the top American intellectuals compiled in 1971.[26] Jews comprised between 30 and 40 per cent of

American Nobel Prize winners in science and economics through the 1970s, and 20 per cent of the professors in the leading American universities as early as 1975.[27] Since Jews make up roughly 2 per cent of the American population, these figures are impressive. In general, Jews continue to be overrepresented as Nobel Prize winners. For example, by 2007, they represented 19 per cent of chemistry winners, 26 per cent in physics, 41 per cent in economics and 28 per cent in medicine.[28] More generally, top American universities have large statistical over-representations of Jewish students and faculty, leading some other universities to actively recruit Jewish students.[29]

In Canada, the pace of change was somewhat slower. Relying on data from the late 1950s and early 1960s, sociologist John Porter described a dismal picture regarding Jewish representation in Canada's intellectual elite. He used as a measure membership in Section II of the Royal Society of Canada, dealing with English literature and civilization. Finding only one Jew out of 104, he concluded, "What is striking is the absence of Jews in the higher levels of the intellectual community."[30] But things have improved. One study of the Royal Society of Canada's Section II membership in 1987 identified about 5 per cent as of Jewish background.[31] This marks a significant increase, and is well above the Jewish share in the population. Still, the percentage is well below the levels found in the United States. These figures "raise concerns about the possibility of ethnic, gender, and religious discrimination in a significant Canadian institution."[32] My own very rough estimate based mainly on name recognition and other data sources of a sample of the 2015 list of RSC Fellows suggests that about 10 to 15 per cent were of Jewish origin, which compares well to the 1.2 per cent of the Canadian population who are Jewish. So there has been a steady increase. Moreover, Jews are now found as deans, principals, and chancellors at major Canadian universities.

These advantages in education are not simply a result of Jews living in cities, where educational levels are higher. Within the populations of Montreal, Toronto, and Vancouver, we find a similar pattern. In 2011, the proportion of Canadians aged twenty-five to sixty-four who identified as Jewish by religion and were either in university or had completed at least a bachelor's degree was roughly 51 per cent in Montreal, 62 per cent in Toronto, and 62 per cent in Vancouver. In each case, this is roughly twice the percentage of non-Jews. The differences among the three cities result from different demographic profiles, notably the higher proportions of aged Jews in Montreal and the younger, more mobile population in Toronto and Vancouver.[33]

One result of this high level of education is economic achievement. Jews have significantly lower rates of unemployment than non-Jews.[34] Jews also have higher-status occupations. Jokes about Jewish doctors and lawyers are rooted in reality. Jews have retained and expanded their 1931 statistical overrepresentation in law, medicine, and business, as well as in newer fields like university teaching. There has been a steady movement out of small business, wholesale, and retail, and into professional and service occupations. Jews are statistically overrepresented in medicine, law, and accounting, as well as service professions like teaching and social work. In 2011, approximately three in ten Jews held managerial and professional positions compared to one in five other Canadians. In Toronto, approximately four of ten doctors and dentists are Jewish. Overall in Canada, 25 per cent of Jewish households earn more than $150,000 per year, compared to 5 per cent of non-Jewish households. They have begun slowly to penetrate economic sectors hitherto closed to them as they are building up wealth in family-owned firms and creating their own family foundations. The 2011 Forbes list of the world's billionaires listed twenty-four Canadians, of whom six are Jewish.[35]

INTO THE BOARDROOM

Today, Jews are among the richest and most influential North Americans, both in sectors which had hitherto been closed, and through their family-owned firms. In these days of multinational and global networks, the old Anglo-Canadian establishment is no longer as dominant. Their monopoly power is sharply reduced. The initial wave of wealthy Jewish families, beginning with the Bronfmans, represented just the tip of a growing and extremely affluent segment of Jewish society. But even as wealthy Jews – and their money – become accepted in Gentile high society, they retain strong loyalties to and status within the Jewish community. They remember, or are not allowed to forget, their roots. These commitments, often typified by gala fundraising dinners for Israel Bonds or Israeli universities, are routinely chronicled in Canadian Jewish publications.

In the United States it is easy to monitor the ups and downs of Jewish wealth. *Forbes Magazine* produces an annual list of the

400 wealthiest Americans. While it is fairly easy to estimate wealth based on publicly traded shares, *Forbes* also estimates assets from privately held companies. A detailed study of the magazine's 2009 list suggests that 35 per cent of the Forbes 400 were Jewish or of Jewish origin.[36] Of course, wealth is not identical to corporate power, as reflected in CEOs who make key business decisions but are not among the very wealthiest themselves. In 2014, approximately 30 per cent of the 100 top-paid American CEOs were Jewish.[37] American Jews are wealthy, but still far from dominant controllers of the levers of corporate power.

And what of Jewish wealth in Canada?[38] The second volume of Peter Newman's *The Canadian Establishment, The Acquisitors*, focuses on new movers and shakers at the top of Canadian corporate power. Though published in 1981, just six years after Newman's first volume, this study of the newer generation of wealthy Canadians reports a greater presence of Jews. For example, while families like the Belzbergs and Reichmanns get only passing mention in the first volume, by the second their stories are detailed over many pages. Diane Francis's *Controlling Interest: Who Owns Canada?* published in 1986, reveals even further penetration of Jews into the corporate elite. She lists thirty-two "dynasties" of great family wealth and corporate power. Of those, ten – a *minyan* – are identifiably Jewish. (Some wealthy Canadian families may have partial Jewish ancestry. The Bentleys of British Columbia are descended from Austrian Jews who escaped to Canada in 1938 and then became Anglicans.)[39] Francis's tally certainly compares well with that in the United States.

Different lists, with different counting procedures, will come up with slightly different numbers. In what follows, I rely mainly on name recognition, supplemented on occasion by consulting of other websites. But the percentages are all estimates or orders of magnitude; the point is not absolute precision but to demonstrate the opening up of the Canadian economic elite to Jews in the postwar period. The *Financial Post* published a list of the fifty richest Canadians in January of 1996. I estimate that seven of the families were Jewish, or 14 per cent.[40] But this list does not include personal assets and has to rely on guesstimates for privately held firms. The fiftieth place on the *Financial Post* list is nailed down at $145 million. According to one source familiar with the contours of Jewish wealth, a significant number of Jewish families – another five to seven – ought to have been on the list. That would have yielded a figure of roughly 25 per cent, similar to Francis's list, and to the American ratio. The *National Post* published a list of the wealthiest Canadians as of April 2000, and I estimate that approximately ten of the fifty names are Jewish, again not far from the American percentage.[41] Another list published in August 2000 by *Canadian Business* contained at least seventeen Jewish entries among the one hundred richest Canadians.[42] More recently, in a list of Canada's richest people in 2015, I estimate based mainly on name recognition and other information that 20 to 25 per cent are Jewish.[43] These percentages are actually more impressive than the American ones, because Canadian Jews comprise only 1.2 per cent of the Canadian population, compared to over 2 per cent in the United States. It is not clear how the national pattern varies by province, but one study of wealth in Quebec is revealing. According to a list of the sixteen wealthiest Quebecers in 2011, an estimated five are Jewish.[44] This is interesting, if only as a factoid that can be related to debates about Jewish marginality in Quebec.

So far we have been discussing wealth – where Jews do very well – not actual corporate power. For that, we need another type of list, such as the one compiled by the *Financial Post* for November 1995. Canada's corporate elite is defined by the newspaper as the top executives of Canada's 125 largest companies, as well as CEOs of the fifteen largest subsidiaries, the fifteen largest financial institutions, the largest life, property, and casualty insurers, the country's most profitable companies, and the CEOs of the largest companies in each of Canada's primary industrial sectors. I estimate that sixteen of the 200 elite members, or 8 per cent, are Jewish, surprisingly similar to the 7.6 per cent figure for American senior executives in 1986. More recently, from a 2012 list of the highest paid – a different metric – Canadian CEOs, I estimate that 6 per cent were of Jewish background.[45]

There is an interesting divergence between the American and Canadian patterns. In the United States, the percentage of Jews among the wealthiest Americans, between 25 to 35 per cent, is similar to the percentage among the highest paid CEOs, 30 per cent. In Canada there is greater divergence, 27 per cent to only 6 per cent. Jews are more concentrated among the wealthiest Canadians than among major CEOs. It seems that it remains easier for Canadian Jews to amass wealth than to rise to the top of a major public corporation. Is this a result of anti-Semitism, or simply an indirect exclusion resulting from an old boys' network? Perhaps residual anti-Semitism plays a role in the publicly traded corporations, and in the more established banking, insurance, or heavy-manufacturing firms. Perhaps Jews with business talent prefer to pursue careers in their own private firms, as investors, or in areas such as real estate. The CEOs counted above are drawn from companies which are traded publicly, and thus many large and powerful private Jewish firms may be omitted. True, the 6 per cent of Jews on that CEO list is far greater than the percentage of Jews in the Canadian population. But it is perhaps not greater than the Jewish proportion among lawyers or accountants or MBAs, which are better groups for comparison.

Still, by the early twenty-first century, the issue of Jewish access into the Canadian business establishment seems largely resolved. As described in Peter Newman's *Titans*, the new establishment includes Jews, francophones, other Europeans, and Asians.[46] The private clubs that safeguarded the old Anglo establishment have become mausoleums, more likely to be boarded up than used as bastions of privilege. Jewish wealth and influence are now mobilized to assist in all manner of non-Jewish causes. Newman describes as the epitome of this the role played by investment advisors Ira Gluskin and Gary Scheff in helping launch the Barnes exhibit of French Impressionists at the Art Gallery of Ontario in 1994. Not only did they donate one million dollars to help meet the exhibit costs, they also sponsored an exquisite opening-night dinner – not kosher – for over 3,000 guests. The menu itself was four pages long. My favourite item is "Buckwheat Blinis with Red Caviar (with sour cream chive)." *Toronto Life* described the event as the most lavish black-tie party in Toronto history. According to critic Robert Fulford, "the evening illustrated one of the most significant changes in the history of the city, the absorption of a remarkable number of Jews by the late twentieth century equivalent of the Family Compact."[47]

Jews today are benefactors and board members of universities, hospitals, and cultural organizations in most Canadian cities. They are pleased to mingle with the scions of English and French elite families, and are generally well received. At times, individuals have played a crucial role. The decision of Sandra Kolber, the wife of Senator Leo Kolber, to get involved with the Montreal Symphony Orchestra allegedly coincided with an increase in Jewish financial support for the orchestra. People bring their networks with them.

Universities also benefit from Jewish largesse. Take the case of the University of Toronto. As reported by Peter Newman, the executive team of the University of Toronto's fundraising campaign in the fall of 1997 included at least six Jews among the twenty-seven top movers and shakers.[48] The University of Toronto's National Report for 1997 identified seventy-eight non-corporate donors of $100,000, of whom I estimate sixteen were Jewish, or just over 20 per cent. A University of Toronto 2015 "Boundless" list named cumulative campaign donors. Among personally identifiable gifts totalling over one million dollars, I estimate that 25–30 per cent of such gifts were made by Jewish individuals.[49]

The process through which Jews become involved in mainstream philanthropic endeavours is not random. In the case of medical charities, there are some causes – diseases or hospitals – which become more identified with Jewish involvement than do others. This reflects the key roles of Jewish physicians in certain hospitals or of Jewish fundraisers who call upon their networks in the community. According to one insider, some medical fundraisers become de facto Jewish in terms of people organizing and attending, even though the events are non-denominational and prominent non-Jews attend as well. Jewish organizers may use these formally non-Jewish charities to develop contacts – Jewish and non-Jewish – to solicit funds for specific Jewish charities. Of course, there are galas which are exclusively Jewish, such as Israel Bond evenings or Combined Jewish Appeal dinners. They are an important part of the establishment social scene for the organized Jewish community. Yet even here, a pattern has emerged in which prominent non-Jews are featured as honourees. This cross-fertilization expands the scope of Jewish networks into the affluent non-Jewish sectors.

Jewish philanthropists shoulder a dual burden. They give generously to Centraide in Montreal, the United Way in Toronto, and to their equivalents in every Canadian city. But these services flow disproportionately to non-Jews, who are more likely to require social assistance. Jews also support a parallel set of Jewish welfare institutions to which fewer non-Jews contribute, and where the costs are high. Jewish campaigns, notably the annual Federation Appeals, are almost totally funded by Jews. Jewish support for mainstream charities and welfare is part of a general socio-political liberalism and is considered a simple civic duty. But there is a clear if unstated strategic consideration at work. Jews are grateful to Canada. No matter how successful, many carry a historical baggage of insecurity and marginality. As a result, this mainstream giving offers Jews benefits apart from the intrinsic rewards of good citizenship. It confirms their social acceptance. It persuades non-Jews to value, if not support financially, the Jewish community's own welfare charities. Finally, it is a kind of insurance policy. Perhaps ameliorating the conditions of the worst-off Canadians will mitigate feelings of resentment towards Jewish wealth.

This business success and philanthropic prominence entrenches Jews in Canadian "high society." Over the years, there has clearly been a blurring of the Jewish-non-Jewish boundaries with regard to organizing and attending Canada's major fundraising balls, as guests at private dinner parties, or as good friends. Wives of wealthy Canadians play a key role in this world. In *The Glitter Girls*, her volume about affluent women in the 1990s, society journalist Rosemary Sexton described Toronto socialite Catherine Nugent thus: "Nor is Catherine a bigot. She was perhaps the first to give parties bridging the WASP and Jewish worlds. She mingled the Grafsteins, Kofflers, Kayes, and Cohons with the Scriveners, Irvines, and Kilgours, and still does."[50] Still, social functions covered in the society pages of major Canadian newspapers can often be categorized as being basically Jewish or non-Jewish. No one should assume that the Canadian establishment has become blind to ethnicity, race, and religion. As one insider told me, "People still know who is who."

They may know, but the boundaries are now more permeable. About one-quarter of the Toronto socialites profiled by Sexton are Jewish. Moreover, the affluent lifestyles which wealthy Canadian Jews and non-Jews enjoy – condos in Florida, magnificent homes, the fanciest cars, European vacations – are also converging. There is no longer much point in counting the numbers of Jews in the establishment lists that Peter Newman or others provide – for two reasons. First, as the new establishment becomes more diffuse, it becomes increasingly difficult to derive the best list of measures to determine what constitutes status: it could be wealth, corporate power, philanthropy, or social clout. And second, whatever list one picks, Jews are likely to be well represented.

JEWISH POVERTY

But the economic picture is not uniform. A high average level of Jewish income masks the paradox of persisting Jewish poverty.

Many of my students are made uncomfortable by the high average incomes and profiles of Jewish wealth, so to them, poor Jews mean that not all Jews are rich exploiters. Indeed, due to the widespread perception among Jews and Gentiles alike that all Jews are well off, poor Jews have been called "invisible." How extensive is Jewish poverty? Using data from 1981, one analyst concluded that almost 16 per cent of Jews were poor or near poor; for Canada as a whole the figure was 25 per cent.[51] By 1991 the gap had narrowed. 16 per cent of Canadian Jews were still poor or near poor, but the figure for all Canadians was down to 19 per cent. In 1996, the Jewish and non-Jewish poverty rates were each pegged at 17 per cent. By 2011, 14.6 per cent of Jews were poor compared with 14.8 per cent of the non-Jewish population. The convergence persists as the overall Canadian poverty rate has declined.[52]

Jewish poverty has become more concentrated among the ever-increasing elderly population. More surprising is the finding that the poverty rates, measured by annual income, among the elderly who identify as Jewish by religion were higher than among the elderly population as a whole, at 15.7 per cent compared to 13.4 per cent in 2011.[53] Perhaps some elderly immigrants are understating incomes to the census out of an Old World distrust of state authorities. Many may also own their own homes or condos or have other assets, and manage to make do on a limited annual income.

In some ways, the Jewish poor resemble the bulk of the Canadian poor, but in others they differ. Like the general poor population, poor Jews are concentrated among the elderly, immigrants, the working class, and single-parent families. But there are differences. Some of the Jewish poor may be graduate students, whose incomes will increase. Among Jewish immigrants a high proportion are elderly. In 2011, the poverty rate for Canadian-born Jews was approximately 13 per cent, but it was significantly higher for foreign-born Jews, depending on the place of birth.[54] Jewish poverty is more likely to be a transient, one-generation phenomenon. There are relatively fewer Jews whose poverty results from a multi-generational cycle of poverty intersected with chronic unemployment and under-employment, poor education, single parenthood, homelessness, criminality, drug and alcohol abuse, and dysfunctional or abusive families. Jewish poverty, like Canadian poverty, also varies by region. Poverty rates are greater in Montreal than in Toronto. In 2011, 20 per cent of Montreal Jews were poor, compared with 12.9 per cent of Jews in Toronto.[55] In Toronto, Jewish poverty falls below the city level, whereas in Montreal, the Jewish poverty rate lies above it.[56] This reflects the generally worse economic conditions in Montreal, and the higher proportion of Jewish elderly living there.

Perhaps the distinguishing characteristic for the Jewish poor in Canada is the shadow cast by the relative affluence of the community as a whole. It is hard enough to be solidly working-class or in the "struggling" middle class, given the cost of supporting a Jewish lifestyle (see later section in this chapter). Even worse to be poor. But with so many affluent Jews, there is a greater sense of self-blame and failure that translates into a reluctance to admit need or to use available Jewish welfare resources. And at the same time, the image of Jewish affluence has tended to bump poverty off the communal agenda. Hence the term "invisible poor."

Some of the pockets of poverty are linked to specific sub-groups of Jews. In a 1997 Montreal study of ultra-Orthodox groups, the Belz and Satmar Hasidim in Outremont as well as a grouping of *yeshiva*-oriented Jews further west, I and my colleagues found that 41 per cent fell below the poverty line: roughly double the rate for Montreal. Their poverty was a product of three factors. Many married men were committed not to full-time work, but to religious study. Second, those who were working lacked the training needed for high-paying employment. Finally, almost all families had many children, which pushed them below the poverty line despite nominally adequate wages.[57] The ultra-Orthodox population is the fastest-growing segment of Canadian Jewry. Despite the threat of growing poverty, it is still a mystery as to how others in these ultra-Orthodox communities are able to afford what seem to be, from the outside, decent – if crowded – homes, some expensive clothing, and large vans for their large families. In the past, philanthropy from a few wealthy patrons like the Reichmanns kept these communities afloat. But that seems no longer sufficient. If ways are not found to integrate their men into the modern labour force, the economic burden on the mainstream Jewish community will increase. It is a paradox that in this "most Jewish" of sub-communities, there is here the greatest danger of deep-seated structural poverty that can persist over many generations.[58]

THE MYSTERY OF JEWISH SUCCESS

How to explain the above-average Jewish incomes? One answer is straightforward. High incomes are obviously related to high levels of education. Jews are more educated, hold better-paying jobs, and therefore earn more money than the average Canadian. Jewish workers are also middle-aged or older and live in Canada's largest cities, both factors associated with higher incomes. Perhaps they work more hours per week. These factors are easy to measure, and serve to demystify those high Jewish incomes. And some studies have found that these factors alone can explain the income advantage.

Sociologist Jeffrey Reitz conducted a study that found Jewish men in Toronto were earning higher incomes largely as a result of their education and occupation. "The high incomes of Jewish men do not appear so high after adjustment for higher qualifications."[59] On the other hand, this study found the incomes of Jewish women to be below average, and I have no idea why. Perhaps some Jewish women had husbands with high incomes and therefore less incentive to maximize their own earnings. A highly technical national study based on 1991 census data found that Jews earned about 34 per cent more than the Canadian average, and Jews with a university degree still earned about 18.5 per cent more than similar Canadians. The analysis then took into account the distributions by gender, age, marital status (marriage tends to boost earnings), province of residence, metropolitan or non-metropolitan residence (incomes are higher in large cities), geographic mobility, period of immigration, knowledge of official languages, occupation, industrial sector, weeks worked and full-time versus part-time work. The earnings of Jews were then compared to British-origin Canadians, for similar levels of education. And lo and behold, the extent of the Jewish income advantage disappeared.[60]

But other studies reach different conclusions. They have found that education, occupation, and other background variables could not fully explain Jewish income advantages. Sociologist Peter Li's detailed study based on the 1981 census found Jews earned $3,230 above average – quite a bit in those days – even after controlling for the usual background factors. This was like an unexplained bonus for being Jewish. Not all minority groups fared equally well. For example, Blacks and Chinese earned $1,626 and $821 less than might be expected based on their backgrounds, a net penalty.[61]

Studies using the data from the 1986 census found similar patterns. One found only 40 per cent of the income advantage of Jewish men could be accounted for by these other socio-demographic factors.[62] Of course that left 60 per cent unexplained. Another found that a gross income advantage of Jewish men of roughly $11,000 was reduced to about $7,000 or $9,000 when other background variables were considered.[63] Another study by Peter Li, using 1991 census data, found that Jewish earnings from employment were almost $5,400 above the average after taking into account educational, occupational, and other beneficial characteristics. Still a large unexplained income advantage for Jews.[64]

More recently, research looking at annual incomes for 2005 found somewhat different results. When compared specifically with Canadians of British origin, Jewish men did not have any statistically significant advantage in income once controlling for education, and Jewish women earned less than expected, given their levels of education. However, this particular study did not control for occupational characteristics.[65] Nevertheless, when compared with the total Canadian population, Jews on balance still appear to experience an advantage, including higher returns on education.

These higher Jewish incomes are perhaps not that mysterious. A study using 2002 data found that Jews had a higher income return for years worked than other religious groups in Canada.[66] Perhaps Jews work "harder" if not longer because of a fear of real or latent anti-Semitism, or because of the need to earn more to support a Jewish lifestyle as I shall describe below. Jews drink less, and so their productivity may be higher. Maybe Jews have better interpersonal skills – play golf or squash, tell better jokes – which can translate into higher incomes. Most important, they may work "better," as a result of attending better schools. Li's original study also found that Jewish incomes increased more per extra year of schooling than was the case for other groups.[67] Jews in Canada may have been graduating from higher-quality (at least by reputation) Canadian universities, such as McGill or the University of Toronto or the University of British Columbia, since most Jews live in Toronto, Montreal, and Vancouver. Their credentials may, rightly or wrongly, be worth more on the job market. It is also possible that Jews may have been doing better academically at these presumably demanding universities than other Canadians. If this is true – there are no studies – then they may actually have been learning more, over and above the value – perhaps inflated – of their degree. So simply comparing Jewish and non-Jewish university graduates, as these studies do, might be misleading. Canadian census data treat every degree and every year of schooling at every level as roughly equivalent. They also offer no evidence about grade point averages. If Jews are either learning more or impressing their employers, both could translate into better jobs, better career trajectories, and more income. Finally, it may be that Jews are more able to mobilize valuable social networks – contacts and connections – which might also lead to higher incomes.

Despite their differences, all these studies agree on the important role of higher levels of education in explaining the high Jewish average incomes. So it is logical to focus on Jewish educational levels as a foundation for their general economic success.

CULTURE AND SOCIAL STRUCTURE

Why do Jews do well in school? They have the second highest average level of schooling in North America of all religious groups, following Hindus. Leaving aside the issue of intelligence, we can identify both cultural and social explanations. One view has it that traditional Judaic culture with its emphasis on the value of learning – for example, the importance attached to the rabbi, who is a teacher and not a priest, and to individual mastery of the Talmud – leads to success in secular education.[68] After all, Jews are "the people of the book." For a people with no state and no armies, as the Jews were before the founding of Israel, power is intellectual. Elements of Jewish theology and religious organization may also lead to independent thinking and a reverence and aptitude for logical debate which is conducive to rational thought. In addition, the non-hierarchical nature of organized Judaism does not stifle individual creativity. Jews have no Pope. While Orthodox Jews obey a uniform *halacha*, they also hold that "Every Jew makes his own Sabbath." This individualistic anti-hierarchical tradition may have contributed to less authoritarian child-rearing patterns, paving the way for independent thinking, problem solving, and school achievement. All these are important middle-class values with alleged pay-offs in the physics or history classroom, and the workplace

Even within Orthodoxy, rabbinic schools have routinely clashed over interpretations of the Torah, dating back over two millennia to the polarized camps of Hillel and Shammai, the Perry Mason and Hamilton Berger of Talmudic jurisprudence. These kinds of arguments which link Judaism to independent thinking do not only explain Jewish educational success. They can also account for Jewish economic innovation in the scrap business, the needle trade, show business, retailing of all sorts, or real estate and development. The study of the impact of religion on economic activity goes back well over a century to the work of Max Weber. In his view, Catholicism was an impediment. Great Britain and the Netherlands, Protestant countries, were prominent in the development of modern capitalist economies. The spirit of capitalism was at root supposedly nourished by Protestantism, though Weber's fellow German social theorist Werner Sombart suggested that Judaism played a key role in the development of capitalism. Sombart noted that Jews were early pioneers in the use of finance, of credit, and of international trade and commerce though their diasporic connections.[69]

Before we return to the Jews, a digression of good cheer for Catholics. For some decades, the average income of American Catholics has exceeded that of White Protestants. Whatever the alleged impediments associated with Catholicism, they seem to be gone. Indeed, those with more Catholic schooling are even more advantaged, compared to other Catholics and to Protestants.[70] Some studies have found that students in Catholic private schools in the United States were doing better than comparable students in public schools.[71] More recently, studies show that the American Catholic school advantage may have disappeared in the twenty-first century.[72] In 2011, 17 per cent of Canadians who claimed Italian origins, 22 per cent of those who claimed Polish origins, both groups overwhelmingly Catholic, had a bachelor's degree or above. By contrast, 16 per cent of those who claimed English origins, 17 per cent of those who claimed German origins, and 16 per cent of those who claimed Dutch origins, mainly Protestant groups, had the same qualifications.[73] And of course, the Quiet Revolution in Quebec also raised Catholic educational attainment.

Now back to the Jews. The cultural arguments for Jewish success underscore a paradox. They postulate a link between mastering religious texts and mastering scientific studies or doing well in school or in the job market. In other words, material success in the modern world owes much to values and traditions rooted in a pre-modern, pre-Western, pre-industrial, pre-secular, and pre-capitalist world. Historically, the relation between secular education and religiosity was inverse for Jews. In Europe and North America, Reform Jews were more likely to have more education and higher incomes; at the other end of the spectrum, Hasidic Jews to have low levels of secular education and low incomes.[74] To be sure, the relation is becoming more nuanced. Modern Orthodox Jews have clearly begun to succeed in educational and occupational endeavours; there are knitted *yarmulkas* all over Ivy League campuses as well as at top Canadian universities. And the example of the Reichmann family has indicated that enormous economic success can be reconciled with devotion to Orthodoxy.

Still, the basis of religious Jewish education differs from that of scientific Western thought. In traditional Judaism the truth, or rather the Truth, is known. Knowledge is deductive, created by applying the Torah's truth and basic laws and principles to specific cases. Rabbis and schools of Judaic interpretation can argue about middle-range issues, but generally not about the basics of the faith. Too much independence and questioning can lead to excommunication, as Spinoza discovered. In the Western scientific tradition, by contrast, the truth is never known. Theories are always being overturned. Knowledge is inductive, building from experiment to experiment, getting closer to – but never attaining – a final truth. There is no built-in reverence for the authority of the ancients; the new takes precedence over the old. So, while learning is valued in both traditional Judaism and modern society, the types of learning would seem to be diametrically opposed.[75] I am not completely persuaded by the cultural arguments. The Jews who are most immersed in traditional Judaic texts are not the highest achievers in secular education.

Another set of arguments for Jewish educational and occupational success is rooted in social structure. This view holds that educational success stems from the social experience of Jews, not from Judaic culture itself. Jews were usually involved in trade and commerce in villages, towns, and cities whether in Europe, North Africa, or the Middle East. They did this in part due to preference, and in part because they were excluded from owning land and from certain craft guilds. They were used to money, credit, merchandising. They had a long experience in the diaspora, often as a "middleman minority" linking other competing national or ethnic groups, holding on to specific trading niches. All this made them well suited for success in urban North America. Perhaps the insecurity of minority status also forced Jews to work harder; they had to be better than the non-Jews. It also made them used to taking the sorts of risks that entrepreneurs have to take.

Features of the early Jewish migrations also played a role. Jewish immigrant families were smaller, which permitted a more nurturing environment, and led to more material and emotional resources for each child. The early generations of Jews in Canada mainly immigrated to stay, fleeing second-class status or persecution, so they had to make good in North America and invest in the future success of their children. They also came as families, or sent home for spouses, which created a relatively stable home environment. This, too, led to greater academic and economic success for the children.[76]

Social structural arguments are also paradoxical. In part they suggest that out of adversity, out of minority status, out of persecution and migration, can come success. Being prevented from owning land in parts of Europe or having to study harder to overcome anti-Jewish quotas in the Canadian past would thereby lead to higher achievement today. Pushed to an extreme, this kind of vulgar neo-Darwinism implies that Jews owe a debt of thanks to anti-Semites past and present. Luckily, we do not have to push the argument to that extreme, and can still recognize the kernel of truth in the structural position.

In any case, most sophisticated social structural arguments would not claim that cultural values play no role in Jewish economic achievement. It is just that these allegedly Jewish values are not uniquely Judaic. Much has been made about similar "Asian" values and their link to educational success.[77] The energy, work ethic, and educational success of Asian immigrants – East Asians, South Asians, and West Asians – indeed remind me of the earlier success of the Jews. Hard-working and supportive parents committed to the welfare of their children, and involvement in a religio-cultural tradition which values learning, will yield positive outcomes for Jews – and anyone else.

CONSEQUENCES OF AFFLUENCE

These high incomes and related wealth support Jewish communal life. They are the basis for funding the rather large network of organizations that make up the Jewish polity – a kind of "public sector" for the Jewish community and sub-economy – which has included the earlier Canadian Jewish Congress and its successor the Centre for Israel and Jewish Affairs, or CIJA, B'nai Brith, and the welfare federations, as well as synagogues, schools, etc. (These organizations and the Jewish polity will be discussed in later chapters.) These organizations could not thrive to the same extent in a low-income community. It is paradoxical that the affluence which can seduce individual Jews away from their heritage is also indispensable for its preservation. The foundation of all this is a set of "big givers" who can be tapped to provide the bulk of the funding. But there is more. The public sector of the Jewish sub-economy is a form of income redistribution within the Jewish community. These organizations generate employment for a large variety of Jewish (and non-Jewish) communal workers. Jewish teachers, rabbis, social workers, administrators, youth organizers, librarians, researchers, planners, and clerical staff occupy paid positions. Financial aid is available for help with school or camp fees, and there are grants to the Jewish poor or to Jewish immigrants administered by the various agencies. In recent decades, about 80 to 90 per cent of the total amount contributed to the annual Jewish Appeal has come from 10 to 20 per cent of the donors. It is an effective form of progressive, voluntary taxation and subsequent redistribution.

Jewish affluence also sustains Jewish life in a more personal way. It helps meet the high cost of "living Jewishly." For those Canadians who seek to live a comprehensive Jewish life, the costs can be crushing. A committed middle-class Jewish family often pays for private Jewish schooling, potentially lavish bar or bat mitzvah celebrations for the children, occasional trips to Israel, Jewish summer camps, membership in a synagogue and other Jewish organizations, and an added premium for the cost of kosher food. These expenses are not luxuries, but costs related to living a complete Jewish family life, for many families. Here are some approximate blended estimates for a middle-class Jewish family of four, drawn from my own experiences, informal conversations, and fee schedules found on websites or in the Jewish press. Some items are annual, and some reflect one-time expenses. Some are eligible for tax deductions as charitable donations. The aim is to provide an "order of magnitude" rather than a precise amount.

1 Annual synagogue membership and/or purchase of High Holiday seats: $1,500 to $5,000.
2 Jewish schooling for two children of elementary and high-school age, either full day school tuition, $5,000 to $25,000, depending on the specific city and whether elementary or high school, or the less expensive afternoon school option, $1,000 to 2,000 per child.

3 Donations to the local Jewish Appeal and other Jewish communal and Israel-related charities: $2,000.

4 Membership in a YMHA or Community Centre: $500 to $1,000.

5 Premium for keeping kosher, mainly the cost of kosher meat: $800 to $2,000 (this ignores the cost of purchasing two sets of daily and two sets of Passover dishes).

6 Costs when a child becomes a bar or bat mitzvah can be staggering. These include paying for lessons and entertaining 50 to 300 people at a reception. This can mean renting a hall, printing and mailing invitations, ordering flowers, hiring a band or deejay, and last but not least, providing the food. The food often consists of hors d'oeuvres, a main course, a range of desserts or a sweet table, and an open bar (cash bars are unheard of at Jewish affairs, because they seem tacky and because Jews are moderate drinkers). Many celebrations include more than one meal or party. There is often a kiddush after synagogue Saturday morning, a Saturday evening party, and sometimes a lavish brunch on Sunday morning for the out-of-town guests, close friends, and relatives. Such affairs may also yield an income of sorts, in that most guests will bring generous gifts, usually cheques, to the bar or bat mitzvah. This income remains in the family. But the net familial cost of a modest *simcha*, or celebration, can easily run from $1000 to $25,000.

7 Trips to Israel for the children and the parents. Such trips are often taken in conjunction with Jewish school or youth programs, or as part of bar and bat mitzvahs, or as family vacations, or special missions to Israel organized by the community. While the popular Birthright-Taglit trips to Israel for students eighteen to twenty-six are free, the cost of other trips can range between $3,000 and $6,000 per person.

8 Jewish summer camps are part of Jewish life for many families. These camps range from lower-cost "Zionist movement" camps, religious camps, and Jewish community camps, to expensive private camps in Canada or the United States with mainly Jewish campers. Costs for a full summer can range from $2,500 to $10,000 per child.[78]

These amounts are often beyond the reach of families burdened with all the other expenses associated with housing, feeding, and raising children. The Jewish communal agencies try to make them affordable for those middle-class families, who often earn too much to qualify for significant financial aid, but many items are still beyond the means of single-parent families and those with low income. Interestingly, almost all these costs are related, in one way or another, to raising and socializing children. This is not selfish consumer spending by adults on their own pastimes and pleasures. Middle-class Jewish parents routinely cut corners on their own personal spending to help pay for these other "Jewish" expenses.

There is more. Apart from these "necessities" of Jewish life, there are a host of expenditures which reflect Jewish "conspicuous consumption" and add to the struggle to "keep up with the Cohens." There is a crass materialism, perhaps reflecting the nouveau riche syndrome, in some of the opulent homes and lifestyles found in the more affluent Jewish neighbourhoods. There are no definitive studies; what follows are largely impressions. But there is clearly a Jewish elite and upper-middle-class subculture. It is marked by upscale cars, designer clothes and jewelry, fancy vacations, luxury condos down south and/or a house in the country, elite health clubs and spas, high-priced summer camps, and *objets d'art*, including works by Israeli or Jewish artists. And when these affluent Jews host family *simchas*, the costs can go through the roof.

These families, whose wealth comes in equal measure from successful businesses or careers in law, medicine, dentistry, and accounting, exert strong pressures on the less affluent but still middle-class members of the Jewish community – including professors! These are not evil, or ignorant, people. Many contribute generous amounts of time and money to worthwhile Jewish and non-Jewish causes. They include many donors who sustain the organized Jewish community. They care deeply for their children and families. But they do set a tone which provides fodder for satirists, as well as angst for those struggling to keep up. The combination of wealth and a presumed tendency among Jewish families to spoil their children can be a potent mix.

The son of a wealthy Jewish matron is being carried by the chauffeur from his mother's mansion into her car. A passerby sees this and asks worriedly, "I'm sorry, is your son unable to walk?" The mother replies, "Of course he can, but thank God he doesn't have to."

For some nouveau riche Jews, it is perhaps easy to blur the lines between class and crass. There is a perception that Jewish wealth is spent too lavishly, while old WASP money is the epitome of refined understatement. On the contrary, as several of the high-society families featured in Rosemary Sexton's *The Glitter Girls* demonstrate, Jewish American Princes and Princesses need not be Jewish. And yet ... and yet ... The description of the bar mitzvahs of Dale Lastman in 1970 and his brother Blayne in 1975, sons of Toronto mayor Mel Lastman and his wife, Marilyn, reads like something penned by Mordecai Richler and delivered by Joan Rivers.

For Dale's bar mitzvah, the family rented out the entire convention floor of the Royal York Hotel – nine large rooms – and one thousand guests were invited. As Rosemary Sexton describes the event: "Marilyn made Dale King for a Day. A moonlighting CBC television crew built a stage fit for a Broadway show. Constructed for King Dale's court was a throne (a red velvet upholstered throne-like chair that Marilyn borrowed from a relative of a friend who was a monsignor in the Catholic church)." As for the tablecloths, "Draped over the top of the royal-blue, floor length tablecloths were shiny Mylar overlays made with fourteen carat gold thread. Mylar was not sold then in Canada, says Marilyn, so she brought it in from New York."[79] The good news here is that Dale managed to grow up reasonably unscathed; he has become a top securities lawyer in Toronto, as well as CEO of the prestigious law firm of Goodman, Phillips, and Vineberg.[80] For the bar mitzvah of son Blayne in 1975, according to Sexton, "$25,000 of orchids were flown in." For Blayne's wedding thirteen years later, which allegedly cost $150,000, seven hundred guests partook of a 230-kilogram cake shaped like a flying saucer, and which contained fifty-nine smaller cakes inside. This pattern of ultra-lavish bar and bat mitzvahs has continued. Celebrations in Toronto in the 2010s have included flights to Las Vegas to make a short movie with Mike Tyson and appearances by American pop-rock band Maroon 5 and Canadian superstar Justin Bieber.[81]

It is too easy for academic analysts, or satirists, to dismiss this lavish lifestyle. There is a link between affluence and Jewish achievement, whether in business, the arts, scholarship, or philanthropy. Some people would like to think that this wealthier group of Jews is thoroughly distinct from the more heart-warming Jewish prototypes: the dedicated physician, the civil-rights lawyer, the school teacher or professor, the Nobel-bound scientific researcher, the artist or poet or writer, the rabbi or Judaic scholar, the social worker, the therapist. This is wishful thinking. There are personal, familial, historical, social, and cultural links which bind these various Jewish lifestyle communities to each other.

5

The Bonds of Intimacy

Jewish Families and Relationships

"Honour thy father and thy mother ... Thou shall not commit adultery."
Exodus 20: 12, 14

"Now take my wife ... please!"
Henny Youngman

COMPETING IMAGES

Family, sex, gender, marriage, and generational issues are the emotional battlegrounds of modern Jewish life. Laughter and tears, joy and heartache, gratification and guilt, respect and resentment are the weapons of choice. These issues frame a fundamental contradiction. As a highly educated, urban, and generally cosmopolitan group, North American Jews are at the frontier of the newest trends of family life and interpersonal relations. But as a religious community with a deep sense of history, reverence for tradition, and memories of life in the old country, many Jews support conservative approaches to these issues. Some Jews solve the problem by choosing one or the other. Hasidic families and radical feminist/egalitarian families each chart their own very different courses. This range of lifestyles, from the most traditional to the avant-garde, reflects the different cultures of different groups of Jews. It is both a source of conflict and an adaptive strength. Many Jews try to integrate both competing perspectives into their personal lives and fashion a workable synthesis. It can be fulfilling as well as draining.[1]

The Jewish family is popularly thought to be, in the words of historian Paula Hyman, "warm, supportive, and ever nurturing." Not only Jews hold this somewhat idealized view. Abbé Henri Grégoire, supporter of Jewish emancipation at the time of the French revolution, wrote in a famous 1789 essay: "They [Jews] have placed strong barriers against libertinism. Nothing is more rare among them than adultery; their marital union is truly edifying; they make good spouses and good parents."[2] Linked to such views are popular contemporary stereotypes that Jewish men make good husbands since they do not drink or beat their wives, and that Jewish mothers are devoted to their children.

Why should we expect Jewish family life to differ from that of Italian-Canadian or Chinese-Canadian or Anglo-Christian families? Surely every ethnic or religious group cherishes families and so-called family values? No group openly values adultery, promiscuity, child abuse, or the neglect of the elderly. The fact that some Jews may think their family ties are special is not proof. One difference is the role of the family in the struggle for Jewish continuity, which has few parallels among other Canadian groups. The family replenishes the supply of Jews and socializes children into Jewish life and community. Any weakening in the family, and Jewish survival is threatened. Trends that might seemingly stem that generational flow – fewer marriages, more familial abuse, increasing divorce rates, falling fertility rates, and increasing rates of mixed marriage – are not just seen as problematic for those directly involved. They are also viewed with alarm by Jewish survivalists. Yet it will become increasingly difficult to find a Jewish communal leader whose nuclear or extended family is untouched by mixed marriage.

Popular perceptions of very warm and harmonious Jewish families may have been fostered by misleading interpretations like *Fiddler on the Roof*. Improved historical research has challenged the saccharine images of the old country and the immigrant generation. Life was not always idyllic and harmonious. Even in Eastern Europe, marital breakup through divorce or desertion and generational strife were far more common than assumed.[3] The letters to the editor of New York's Yiddish newspaper *The Forward* were full of tales of family conflict among the early waves of Eastern European immigrants.[4] Jewish family life in the past was, as it is today, a blend of myths, stereotypes, and reality that co-exist in an uneasy equilibrium.

The competing images of Jewish women – usually generated by men – offer one example. A blend of the *balabusteh*, or efficient homemaker and the *Yiddishe mameh* suggests a pre-feminist image of a devoted wife, mother, and grandmother. Accordingly, she is prepared to sacrifice her all for the family, cooking gargantuan helpings of food, doling out chicken soup, and demanding nothing for herself. *How many Jewish grandmothers does it take to change a light bulb? – Never mind, I'm fine, I'll sit in the dark.* Notice the manipulative undertone of self-sacrifice, another time-worn stereotype, that lurks beneath the seeming dedication. The same image can be transformed into that of a suffocating and overprotective mother. In contrast, the notorious J A P or "Jewish American Princess," another current image, is egocentric, spoiled at birth by protective parents. Accordingly, she grows up to be an emasculating, materialistic woman, whether single or married, whose self-centred preoccupations are mainly her clothing and her looks. This misogyny is typified by J A P jokes. *What does a J A P make for dinner? ... Reservations.*[5]

The stereotypes of Jewish men are less pronounced, perhaps because the comics and writers who have developed these images have been mainly men. Accordingly, Jewish men inevitably make good husbands since they are good providers, do not drink or beat their wives, and do not fool around or ask for divorces. At the same time, they may also be henpecked or unlucky or plain wimps. While the *yenta*, or gossip, is inevitably feminine, the *schlemiel* and the *schlemazel* (the former spills soup on the latter) are invariably masculine.

Stereotypes about sexuality – again largely generated by men – also loom large. According to them Jewish women, despite the erotic legacy of the Song of Songs and of the myth of the Jewess as an exotic temptress, are assumed to be generally uninterested in sex. That is, after they are married. If it was ever true that Jewish girls "didn't do it" beforehand, they do now. Monica Lewinsky's affair with President Bill Clinton has laid that to rest. (As we shall see, North American Jews in general have liberal attitudes regarding sex.) On the other hand, Jewish men are stereotypically known more for intellectual or financial success, or for neurotic issues, than for sexual prowess.

As we look at intimacy and Canadian Jewish family life, we are not concerned with such stereotypes. Jewish family and personal relations at present, particularly for those who are not among the ultra-Orthodox, are caught between two competing forces. Modernity tugs Jews towards gender equality, families that are smaller and decidedly nuclear rather than extended, and a greater possibility of marital breakup, LGBT relationships, and mixed marriage. It might seem at first glance to be a force that might threaten the Jewish future. Tradition tugs in the opposite direction. Yet somehow a balance is struck.

WOMEN AND JUDAISM

To understand Jewish intimacy and family life, we begin with the changing status of women in the religious and economic spheres. The Jewish religious tradition as inherited from the past is sexist. So what else is new? On this issue, traditional Judaism is no different from traditional Christianity and Islam. Some examples: The traditional morning prayers recited by Orthodox Jewish males include the infamous thanks to God that He – and it is apparently a He – did not make the supplicant a woman. During menstruation, women are considered unclean. Only men are counted in the *minyan* (quorum of ten people required for prayers) and only men can lead prayer services, read from the Torah, or serve as rabbis. These precepts are not followed by the other Jewish denominations, and this deep-rooted gender inequality has spawned a number of hostile reactions among contemporary Jewish women, who have challenged the confining traditional roles of wife, mother, and caregiver. But for the most part the reactions have led not to a rupture, but to a seeking of higher status for women within families and within Judaism and all other aspects of Jewish communal life.

Consider first women and organized religion. Reform Judaism, Reconstructionism, and the New Age Jewish Renewal movement have embraced gender equality in all areas. Conservative Judaism has also done so, though more slowly. The biggest dilemma is faced by the Orthodox, mainly the Modern Orthodox. Many such women are educated, versed in the doctrines of feminism, and embrace principles of equality. Some have sought to soften the harsh legacy of the Orthodox tradition, or even reinterpret its essence. They have a tough assignment. There are maverick Orthodox or observant but egalitarian *minyans* and *chavurot* (small, intimate, informal congregations), like the First Narayever Synagogue in Toronto, that modify the tradition. We also see the rise of what are called "partnership minyans" within Orthodoxy: prayer services that seek to maximize women's participation by enabling women to lead parts of service and, in some cases, count as part of a *minyan*. These prayer services, which began in 2002 in the United States and Israel, have now spread quickly.[6] But this option will not satisfy all Orthodox women seeking change.

Another approach involves "separate but equal" Talmud study groups, or religious services for women alone. Around the beginning of the 2000s, we see the proliferation of women's religious seminaries, particularly in Israel, which offer high quality *yeshiva*-like religious education. It has become quite common for North American Orthodox young women to do a year of seminary after high school. Furthermore, in 2009 an Orthodox women's *yeshiva* was established in New York City, Yeshivat Maharat, which ordained women to the Jewish clergy. This development has caused considerable controversy in the Orthodox world. With time, it may be that this phenomenon will be further normalized, at least in Modern Orthodoxy. Even more controversial are various attempts to ordain women as rabbis within Orthodoxy as part of the general engagement of feminism and Judaism.[7] Some feminists have noted that in the Bible and the Talmud there are examples of heroic women. The *eshet chayil*, or woman of valour, can be seen as the equal partner of men. Much is made of female personalities like Deborah, the judge of the Biblical period, and the learned Beruryah of the Talmudic period. Feminist leaders and scholars have argued that the exclusion of women from serious Torah study and religious leadership has been due more to custom than to clear *halachic* dictates.[8]

But for some Canadian Jews, Orthodoxy and feminism can never be reconciled. My late father, a sweet, gentle man, was raised in Orthodox synagogues in Poland. He could never make his peace with the services in my Reconstructionist synagogue, ranging from the heavy use of English to the complete gender equality. They made him uncomfortable. In Orthodoxy, according to Concordia University's Norma Joseph, "there is a real fear of the feminist challenge, and the lines are drawn."[9] A Toronto woman offers the following poignant account:

The synagogue I used to attend was the one in which my parents were married, my brothers celebrated their bar mitzvah, and I was named and married. When I was pregnant I told myself that if it were a girl I would find a more progressive synagogue because I wanted to assure my daughter greater equality in her Jewish life. My family was devastated. My grandfather, in an attempt to restore *shalom bayit* (peace in the home), concluded that it was not so terrible. Since I would stay if I had a son, he and my father would still have the pleasure of sitting with him in a synagogue, of seeing him *davening* [praying], of seeing him learn his bar mitzvah. I realized that implicit in this was that they would not really miss much if I had a daughter and left their synagogue because her participation in synagogue life was so minimal. This argument convinced me to change synagogues no matter the sex of my child. I wanted my child to understand equality.[10]

There are now many female non-Orthodox rabbis in Canada; at least twelve in the Greater Toronto Area alone. And there are hundreds of non-Orthodox female rabbis in the United States.[11] Some North American women rabbis have reported episodes of sexual harassment, and others of being paid less than male counterparts. But clearly, the Judaic status of women is in flux. Jewish women have created or reinterpreted religious rituals.[12] A young girl becoming a bat mitzvah is now *de rigueur* among non-Orthodox branches of Judaism and is emerging as normative in modified form within Modern Orthodoxy. A monthly ceremony which ties in to *rosh chodesh* (the new moon) celebrates fertility and renewal. In some feminist circles, there has even been a renewed interest in the *mikveh*, or ritual bath, used by very observant women following menstruation, albeit with a progressive gloss. In both egalitarian Orthodox or all-women *minyans*, women assume all religious functions. More and more women in non-Orthodox synagogues are found wearing a *kippa* and *a tallis* – a skullcap and prayer shawl. The *havdalah* service, which closes the Sabbath Saturday evenings, requires no *minyan*, and thus more Orthodox girls in synagogues are getting involved in the ceremony. Instead of reading from the Torah for the full congregation as part of a bat mitzvah ceremony – which they are not permitted to do – Orthodox girls experience alternatives. Some read the Torah to a female-only gathering. Some may have a *kiddush* and deliver a *d'var Torah*, a commentary on the Torah, without calling it such. One Orthodox synagogue created a ceremony for girls after Shabbat services, devised by the rabbi, but without any *talleysim* (prayer shawls).[13]

There has also been progress within the secular organizations of the community, though there is more work to do. The now defunct

Canadian Jewish Congress had two female presidents, and more recently, the president of the Toronto Board of Rabbis and the president and CEO of Jewish Federations of Canada/United Israel Appeal have been women. In general, women are becoming more visible in both professional and lay positions in Jewish federations. Organizations are scheduling more meetings at lunchtime, rather than at 5:30 p.m. when many professional women morph into mothers. The position of Jewish women in the world of work has also been changing. In many ways, it is easier for traditionalists to accept women as earners than as religious equals. After all, in many communities in Eastern Europe, it fell to women to assume many of the breadwinning functions if their husbands devoted themselves to study.

Not surprisingly, Jewish women lag behind Jewish men on most measures of educational and occupational success. But as we saw in Chapter 4, they compare very well with other Canadian women, as do Jewish men with other Canadian men. In 2011, 61 per cent of Canadian women aged thirty-four to forty-four who self-identified as Jewish by religion had a university degree, compared to 32 per cent of all Canadian women.[14] American patterns are almost identical, with 58 per cent of Jewish women having graduated from university compared with 29 per cent of all American women.[15] And in both countries, the Jewish advantage is even greater at the level of graduate degrees.[16] In Canada in 2011, 26 per cent of Canadian Jewish women aged twenty-five to sixty-four held degrees above the undergraduate level, compared to 9 per cent of all Canadian women in the same age group.[17] Part of this gap can be explained by the Jewish concentration in large cities, where higher education is common. But even there, the differences remain dramatic. In 2011 in Montreal, 51 per cent of Jewish women held a university degree compared with 30 per cent of all women; in Toronto, it was 61 per cent to 37 per cent; and in Vancouver, 62 per cent to 35 per cent. These advantages translate to other economic gains. For example, among women in the labour force in 2011, 10.3 per cent of Jewish women compared with 8.5 per cent of all Canadian women held "management occupations."[18]

But along with this greater educational and occupational success have come lower fertility rates. I remember attending meetings concerned about the demographic future where rabbis proposed a "baby bonus" paid by the organized community to get Jewish women to have more children. Traditionalists concerned with Jewish survival might blame these low fertility rates on feminist objectives (note, women are blamed rather than men).[19] But there is a more optimistic interpretation as well. Educated and working women with fewer children can contribute to Jewish life by increasing family incomes and by getting involved in leadership roles. Even as they have fewer children, Jewish mothers seem to be more committed to raising them. American research by economist Barry Chiswick finds that "Jewish women with no young children at home are more likely than other women to be in the labor market, but if they have children at home, particularly if they are preschool children, Jewish women are less likely to work, and if they do work, it is for fewer hours per year."[20] Another attempt to synthesize tradition and modernity.

Chiswick argues that this pattern of Jewish women working less than other women when they have young children optimizes their "investment" in their children, which allows the children to succeed in turn. Chiswick reports on a similar study using Canadian census data, in which married Jewish women worked less than other married women.[21] He contends that this maternal pattern is linked to the high achievement of Jewish children and Jewish adults, as well as to the maintenance of Jewish identity. Of course, among Jewish women there is variation. Generally, religious women are more likely to stay or work at home.[22] Few analysts are willing to raise the sensitive question of how increasing career commitments of women and increasing reliance on child care might affect the educational and economic performance of future generations of Jews. If, in fact, the nurturing role of the Jewish mother has been part of the explanation for Jewish economic success, the issue has ramifications beyond the change in family roles. Perhaps Jews may lose their economic advantages if their children receive less nurturing. Chiswick gingerly poses the question: "A challenge facing the Jewish family is the maintenance of high levels of achievement while supporting the evolving role of Jewish women in the labor market. There is a new challenge and a new opportunity for the Jewish community – Jewish childcare arrangements and Jewish day schools as a communal response to the evolving role of Jewish women in the labor market."[23]

In theory, paternal care or high-quality daycare can make up any slack. But children are not raised in theory. Jewish men, like all men, are more likely to assume that the primary parenting responsibility should fall to mothers. This is rather ironic. Jewish fathers in other countries and in the past were actually more involved in child-rearing and concerned about the Jewish dimensions of the home and the child's education. In North America, this male duty atrophied; the father's role became that of breadwinner.[24]

In recent years among middle-class and upper middle-class American Jewish families (and one can assume among Canadian ones as well), there has emerged a model of "dual career partnership marriages." High levels of education among American Jewish women has led to male partners assuming greater shares of domestic duties, to match female commitments to job and career. It seems that careers of American Jewish women are now facing minimal penalties of marriage and parenthood, and "multitasking" becomes more prevalent for both men and women.[25]

SEX

Equality for women whether in religious doctrine or the workplace builds on conceptions of women – and men – as more than sexual beings, and as such holds some promise for change. But men and women are also sexual beings. Without sex, there would be no Jewish continuity. Judaism can be assumed to be relatively more affirming about sexual pleasure than Christianity, though never as celebratory of beauty and the body as was Hellenism. The Song of Songs is erotic love poetry, but it is an exception in the body of Jewish religious writing. The Orthodox rabbinic tradition even claims that this erotic text refers to the love between God and the people of Israel rather than that between a man and a woman. As sex therapist Dr Ruth Westheimer has confirmed, in traditional Judaism the sex act is seen as a joyous occasion – within the bounds of marriage – where spouses are required to try to fulfil the needs of their partners.[26] The conventional wisdom, at least among Jews, is that Judaism is less ambivalent about sexual pleasure than is Christianity.

A rabbi and priest are sitting on a train. The priest asks, "Rabbi, I know you are supposed to keep kosher, but haven't you ever eaten pork?" The rabbi replies, "Father, I'll admit once when I was a student in the yeshiva I was consumed with curiosity, and I did eat some pork." The priest grins. A few minutes later the rabbi asks, "Father, I know you are supposed to be celibate, but didn't you ever have sex with a woman?" The priest replies, "Well, rabbi, when I was a seminary student, I too was curious, so I found a girl and had sex with her." The rabbi smiles, "Beats the hell out of pork, doesn't it!"

Jokes are one thing, but where do Jews rank compared to other groups in terms of sexual attitudes and behaviours? The general liberalism of North American Jews spills over into attitudes about sex and gender. American surveys have routinely found Jews to be more likely to support civil rights for the LGBTQ community, to be more tolerant of pornography, and to support gender equality, sex education in schools, the right to abortion, and the availability of contraceptives. These liberal views coalesce around the defence of rights of privacy as well as free speech. And this Jewish liberalism and tolerance is not simply a reflection of Jews being college graduates. Studies have found that at all levels of education, American Jews are more tolerant than others.[27] An American survey of high school students found that Jewish respondents had more liberal sexual attitudes and were less embarrassed about sexuality than their peers.[28] For instance, 27 per cent of Jews surveyed said they supported waiting until marriage to have sex, compared with 51 per cent of Catholics, 52 per cent of Protestants, and 77 per cent of Mormons. They were even more liberal than those professing no religion, 29 per cent of whom supported waiting until marriage.[29] Jewish communal organizations would generally support liberal positions on private behaviour and other policy issues, such as equal rights for homosexuals, access to contraception and abortion, and opposition to most censorship. The only difference is the Canadian restrictions on hate speech, to be discussed in Chapter 11.

So let us assume Jews hold more liberal attitudes than the average person. But actions speak louder than words. There are few national surveys of sexual behaviour that include enough Jews for statistical analysis. One landmark study of a sample of Americans included only fifty-four Jews. It found that 33 per cent of them claimed to have had eleven or more sexual partners, compared to 17 per cent of Catholics, 21 per cent of liberal Protestants, and 17 per cent of fundamentalist Protestants.[30] While certainly not definitive, the study at least suggests that Jews are sexually curious. A survey of students at the University of Toronto carried out in 1968, and therefore somewhat dated, found that "unmarried Jewish men have frequent sex in more than twice as many cases (31 per cent) as do unmarried Catholic or Protestant men." Interestingly, the same survey found that unmarried Jewish women had a higher virginity rate than others.[31] Perhaps some of the Jewish men were, as stereotypes suggest, pursuing non-Jewish women.

But in general, we know little about North American Jews and sex. There are certainly no recent empirical studies on these issues in Canada. A 1992 survey of CEGEP (junior college) students in Montreal included anglophone and francophone Jewish students in the sample. Respondents were asked if they had participated in any of nine different sexual acts, ranging from kissing to vaginal and anal intercourse. Here, the Jewish scores were moderate. Out of nine, the average scores ranged from 7.2 for French Canadians, 6.4 for English Canadians, 6.2 for francophone Jews, 5.8 for Haitians, 5.4 for anglophone Jews, 5.1 for Italians, and 3.5 for Greeks.[32] It is hard to know how to interpret these findings, other than to assume that young Jewish men and women are at least normally adventuresome. Sex is also present among the unmarried Orthodox, according to one Orthodox rabbi. At least into the 1980s – things may well have tightened up more recently – he claimed the concept of the "*tefillin* date" was current among students at Yeshiva University. It referred to the practice among some Orthodox young men out for a date to take along their *tefillin*, or phylacteries, should they not get home in time for prayers the next morning.

Enough titillation. Sexual pleasure, according to Jewish religious tradition, is certainly valued but is unimportant compared to the obligations of marriage and child-rearing. Sex belongs in marriage, and its highest purpose is procreation. Religious Jews have no choice in the matter. They are commanded to marry, bear children (*pru u'rvu),* and instruct them in Jewish tradition (*veshinantem levanecho*). These religious prescriptions also resonate strongly among less religious or even secular Jews. The concern for *naches* from children is strong among all Jews. Is it uniquely Jewish? There is no equivalent expression in English; the dictionary translations of "pleasure or satisfaction or pride in one's children" are just too tepid. It is the *raison d'être* of family life for many Jews, the *quid pro quo* received in exchange for continual sacrifice for the children. A child-centred preoccupation – having and raising children, and worrying about them – has also meant getting married. It is not yet clear to what extent these norms will be challenged and replaced among the Millennial Jewish generation, and beyond.

HUSBANDS, WIVES, AND CHILDREN

The Jewish family is generally pictured as a model of caring and harmony between conventional spouses and between parents and children. Delayed marriage and family formation have increased among American Jews. For example, the Pew survey of 2013 found 74 per cent of American Jewish men and 43 per cent of American Jewish women aged twenty-five to thirty-four were unmarried, up dramatically from previous years. This pattern may also be found in Canada. Between 2001 and 2011, the fastest growing Jewish groups as far as marital status is concerned were those in common-law arrangements, with a 32.5 per cent increase, and those who were divorced or separated, with a 22.1 per cent increase.[33] Marital or partnered harmony may allegedly be a guarantor of continuity, represented by succeeding generations of well-adjusted, high-achieving, and committed Jews. But there has always been conflict within Jewish families. The 1995 Canadian General Social Survey, a large national sample, included eighty-one Jewish respondents who were married or living common-law. While 74 per cent of the total sample indicated they had a "very happy" relationship with their spouse, the small sub-sample of Jewish respondents averaged 62 per cent, the lowest percentage of any religious group included in the survey. So much for greater Jewish harmony. Even more interesting is the gender breakdown. Jewish women were slightly more likely than other Canadian women to claim a very happy relationship, 77 per cent to 73 per cent. But only 51 per cent of Jewish men did so, well below the total Canadian men's average of 75 per cent.[34]

Relations with children and among siblings have never been entirely smooth. Cain killed Abel, Abraham almost sacrificed Isaac, and Jacob, with his conniving mother, tricked Isaac and stole Esau's birthright. Even Tevye's daughters rebelled against him and his "tradition." Children of Jewish immigrants, whether in the mass-migration period or more recently, would often rebel against their parents. Juvenile crime is a graphic indicator of such family problems. Rates of juvenile delinquency among Jews in the New York of the 1920s and 1930s were as high as among any immigrant group, and Jewish organizations agonized about possible solutions. In Canada in the 1920s, Louis Rosenberg reported that the crude rate of Jewish juvenile delinquents convicted of major offences was more than double the Canadian rate.[35] When adjusted for the largely urban residence of Jews the gap narrowed, since crime is higher in cities, but Jews were still above the national average. By the 1930s, rates of Jewish delinquency had dropped dramatically and stayed low. But they did not disappear. In recent years, social workers routinely encounter troubled Jewish teens, often from immigrant backgrounds.

But if youth crime is generally less of a problem, other issues now shake the idealized image of the Jewish family. The problems of spouse abuse, child abuse, and elder abuse have been recognized. Jewish agencies operate in both Canada and the United States to advocate for battered women, Jewish and non-Jewish.[36] It is not at all clear whether there has been an increase in abuse or simply more awareness of and publicity about the issue. This is true even in the ultra-Orthodox communities. No hard figures are available, but confidential conversations with social workers reveal a strong consensus that even in these communities divorce rates are rising, despite the greater availability of courses preparing religious young men and women for marriage. Over the years, these special courses in family purity have changed to include sections on relationships, though men and women attend these courses separately. Traditional match-making and courtship patterns remain alive and well in these communities, but the expectations of those getting married have changed. Often the women are more worldly than the men, which adds to the stresses in these marriages. The women often take college or post-secondary courses and seek employment while the latter generally continue to study in *yeshivas* or in *kollels*, which are institutions for adult Judaic learning.

As a community with many members trained in the helping professions, Jews are not reluctant to seek help for marital or family problems. There are many options, including Jewish social workers and Jewish agencies. There are also specific agencies aimed at the ultra-Orthodox, that either provide services or act as a conduit linking their clients to specific professionals. The issue of Jewish family violence has emerged from the closet. For example, Auberge Shalom, founded in 1989 in Montreal, was the first agency in Canada aimed mainly at abused Jewish women. Besides providing physical shelter, it also runs a support group, offers a twenty-four-hour support hotline, and can send staff into people's homes. The staff includes non-Jews and mainstream Jews, as well as ultra-Orthodox women who counsel members from their own community. The organization called Act to End Violence Against Women operates shelters in Montreal, Toronto, Vancouver, and Winnipeg, as well as provides many other services including legal information and advocacy campaigns.[37] Some ultra-Orthodox abused women will turn to rabbis, who in turn might consult with mainstream Jewish agencies or with specific social-service agencies geared to the ultra-Orthodox community.[38] In a different vein, members of these communities are even consulting with sex therapists; others are seeking out prostitutes as a source of sexual gratification.[39]

According to social workers, the Jewish family remains strong and cohesive, and less prone to severe dysfunction than other ethnic groups. Relative sobriety alone could explain this advantage, since alcohol often leads to violence and discord. And fewer economic pressures also mean fewer stresses to erode family solidarity. Of course, Jewish families have seen generational confrontation and teenage rebellion. Which families have not? In recent times, the sources of generational clashes have changed. The celebrated red-diaper babies of the 1960s, radical children, confronted their liberal parents on issues ranging from politics to pot. Now, inter-faith dating and intermarriage have emerged as key flashpoints. Most Canadian Jewish parents have heard the shrill teenage complaint: "You tell me not to be racist or prejudiced, yet you don't want me to go out with a non-Jew!"

Traditional Jewish mothers – the *Yiddishe mamehs* – are perhaps not as harmfully overprotective as stereotypes suggest. Jewish parents actually encourage independence on the part of their children. In the postwar period, suburban Jewish parents may well have shifted towards independence as a better route towards success.[40] But even the presumed overprotectiveness of the Jewish mother has been identified as a key factor in the success of Jewish children and adults.[41] Nagging children to eat properly or dress warmly can, in fact, lead to better health. Regardless of its impact, this overprotective and guilt-inducing image of Jewish mothers is common. Here is a classic joke which makes the point. The title is "Things a Jewish Mother Would Never Say." Some of the better entries:

- Be good, and for your birthday I'll buy you a motorcycle.
- How can you see the TV sitting so far back?
- Don't bother wearing a jacket – it's quite warm out.

– My meeting won't be over till later tonight. You kids don't
mind skipping dinner, do you?
– You don't have to call every week. I know how busy you are.
– Your wife knows best – forget about the advice I gave you.
– Mother's Day, shmother's day, you just go to the beach and
enjoy yourselves.

Children are central to Jewish religious and family life, which is
marked by the rituals of the life cycle. Indeed, the religious practices
most commonly observed, even by relatively assimilated Jews, are
those associated with birth, puberty, marriage, and death. Much of
the religious behaviour of average Jewish families is oriented toward
maximizing the Jewish environment of their children – a form of
"pediatric Judaism." Jewish holidays, for instance, are observed to
the extent they provide meaningful experiences for children as much
as for their intrinsic spiritual nature of the holiday. Hanukkah with
presents, dreidels, and latkes; Purim with costumes; Sukkoth with
children decorating the Sukkah; and Passover with children asking
the four questions and looking for the *afikomen*, a hidden piece of
matzo, benefit in ways that the High Holidays and Shavuot do not.
This new child-centredness is of course common to Christianity as
well. The benefits flow to the cause of continuity. They do not enhance
Jewish spirituality, which has usually been an adult enterprise.

My guess – no data – is that Jewish parents dote on their children
more than, say, Canadian-born Anglo-Christian families. They are
certainly more expressive. Health is the biggest worry of all, which
may tap into other Jewish cultural traits. One time I was an assistant
coach at a neighbourhood children's soccer game. One youngster
came off the field in great pain, limping severely. I took him over to
his mother and her friend, hoping it was not serious. The mother, of
Anglo-Protestant origin, and speaking more calmly than I was, commented to her friend, "You know, this has happened several times in
the past few days. I think it might be a good idea to take him to the
doctor." Imagine typical Jewish parents in a similar situation. At the
first suggestion of a mysterious limp, they might well be at the emer-
gency room of their local hospital while on the cellphone with their
GP trying to identify the best pediatric orthopedist in town.

This concern for children does not translate into higher fertility
rates for Jewish women. Despite the heroic efforts of the ultra-
Orthodox, aggregate Jewish fertility in the United States remains

below that for non-Jews. Jews were, for better or worse, trailblazers in the race to low, and in the United States below replacement, fertility rates. Jews were early and efficient contraceptors. One American study published in 1959 found that 83 per cent of American Jewish women who employed contraception started such use before their first pregnancy, compared to 52 per cent of Protestant women. (The question was not even posed to Catholics.)[42] The pattern of low fertility dates back to the turn of the century, when Jewish families were smaller than other immigrant families. The first birth-control clinic opened by Margaret Sanger was in the Jewish immigrant section of Brownsville in New York – unlikely a chance event.[43]

In the United States in 2013, Jewish American women aged forty to fifty-nine had an average of 1.9 children, compared to 2.2 children for the general American public. In Canada through the 1980s, there was a similar pattern.[44] My estimate for 1991 is that for one thousand women over fifteen, Jews (by religion) had given birth to 1,601 children, compared to 1,772 for non-Jews. Over time there has been a significant increase in Canadian Jewish fertility, such that by 2011, the Jewish fertility rate in Canada was estimated to be 1.99 compared to only 1.61 for the Canadian population.[45] One possible explanation for this difference between Canada and the United States is the larger share of Orthodox and ultra-Orthodox Jews in Canada. In addition, national Canadian fertility rates have been depressed significantly by drops in fertility in the province of Quebec. But there is significant variation within the Jewish community. One estimate for Hasidic women is that their fertility is four times higher than the Canadian Jewish average.[46] In both Canada and the Unites States, higher fertility and lower intermarriage among the Orthodox, and certainly the ultra-Orthodox, will reshape Jewish families and Jewish live in general.

Are Jewish marriages more stable? Judaism does not see marriage as a prison, and the Jewish attitude to divorce is of course more liberal than the Catholic. But it is doubtful that the rabbinic authorities who legitimated divorce envisioned the high rates which would come to prevail in modern societies, among Jews as well as all others. Divorce was stigmatized within folk Jewish traditions, even if it was not as rare as sometimes assumed. And of course, the Orthodox rules of divorce penalize women routinely. It is the man who must grant a divorce decree, or *get*; a wife cannot issue a *get* to her husband. On the other hand, a wife must consent to a *get* before the divorce becomes final. The potential for abuse is significant, mainly directed against women who cannot really initiate divorce proceedings. These women for whom the decree is withheld, often as blackmail, remain in a kind of limbo, unable to remarry.

The plight of these women, or *agunot*, remains a central issue on the Jewish feminist agenda. A 1987 Canadian study by B'nai Brith identified 311 cases of conflict over a *get*, with 202 arising because of the husband's refusal to grant one, and ninety-two because of the wife's refusal to accept one. Both the lawyers and rabbis involved in that study confirmed that women suffered more from the proceedings.[47] In a rare example of the state interfering in religious affairs of a community, the Canadian Parliament came to the defence of the *agunot* after lobbying from Jewish women's groups and other communal organizations. In 1990, a federal law, section 21.1 of the Divorce Act, was passed, which "allowed divorce courts to require affidavits indicating that barriers to remarriage within the deponent's religion had been removed by the applicant and empowering the courts to dismiss any application for failure to comply with this requirement."[48] So Jews who withhold a *get* or refuse to accept one can be prevented from obtaining a civil divorce. Indeed, under the law, judges would not hear the pleadings regarding the details of a divorce settlement from the party who was impeding or not accepting a *get*. A 2007 decision of the Canadian Supreme Court, Bruker v. Marcovitz, held that a husband could not ignore any agreement in a dissolution of marriage that required him to provide a *get*. More recently, efforts have been underway to deal with the problem, such as encouraging pre-nuptial agreements, or "e-shaming" husbands into granting a *get*.[49]

By 2011 the divorce and separation levels for Jews and non-Jews in Canada were similar, approximately 7 per cent.[50] American divorce rates for both men and women, Jews and non-Jews, are higher than the Canadian rates; no surprise there. America's more liberal culture makes divorce more frequent across the board, for everyone.

Jews are also less likely to have children out of wedlock or be involved in single-parent families. This is actually an old story. In the 1920s and 1930s, the Jewish percentage of illegitimate births was only one-fifth the Canadian average.[51] In 2011, 2.2 per cent of Canadian Jewish men and 7.6 per cent of Canadian Jewish women headed lone-parent families, compared to 3.3 per cent of non-Jewish men and 12.7 per cent of non-Jewish women. Of course, these figures can include both cases of divorce and out of wedlock births. How much of these gaps reflect the impact of Jewish cultural values and how much the higher socio-economic status for Jews, I do not know. Jewish marriage and family patterns vary by city. Vancouver is trendy, Montreal and Toronto are more traditional.[52]

GETTING MARRIED

Most Jews likely want to get married, and they do. A few Jews are single by choice. They are a small minority, and they pose an ideological challenge to traditional ideas about Jewish families. For most singles, the problem is finding the right mate. There have always been single-parent families in Jewish communities, usually widows, with a lesser number of divorced women. Today, Jewish singles and single-parent families challenge religious and communal institutions to accommodate their needs through innovative programming.[53] And single-parent families face daunting economic barriers to providing a Jewish life for their children,

The growth of the Jewish singles scene, and accompanying organizations, attests to the drive to get married, and to marry other Jews. The increasing numbers of divorced and single-parent women (and men) add a newer, more urgent element to the marriage market. In the Jewish singles scene joy and despair co-exist, and stereotypes of Jewish and Gentile men and women abound. The impressions below – stereotypes or not – were distilled from several members of Jewish singles organizations.

The reports I heard from the field at the turn of the century were distressing. One Montreal woman in her forties was thrust into the dating scene following a divorce. She found Jewish men were concerned "totally" with looks, while women tended to overlook the appearance of men. What matters to the Jewish women, according to a Toronto observer, is whether the man is a "doctor, dentist, or lawyer." And the men reportedly want a "princess" with looks, and who is slim. One single woman reported that many Jewish men find Gentile women attractive because they feel that those women want "me for me, not my car." Moreover, some of the Jewish men want to sow their wild oats, which adds to the attraction of Gentile women. While many Jewish women are interested in a Jewish partner, some get involved in the non-Jewish singles scene because of the shortage of Jewish men, or curiosity. Jewish women also have wild oats to sow. The non-Jewish club or party scene is allegedly looser, more relaxed, and less inhibited, perhaps because there tends to be more drinking. At a non-Jewish party, women will rarely refuse to dance, while Jewish women will only dance if they are interested in the man. And Jewish men in general "do not like to dance."

Keeping up with the times, singles registries and the more traditional matchmakers have largely given way to the internet. In some cases, after filling out a lengthy questionnaire, computer algorithms are used to make initial matches. But after the computer, a matchmaker, rather than the individual seeking a partner, is the one to sift through matches. As in the pre-internet era, matchmakers speak at length with each client, only now there is an infinitely larger pool within which to find suitable matches. For instance, the international database SawYouAtSinai.com has over 50,000 profiles visible only to the roughly 350 matchmakers on staff. The site claims to have brought over 1,000 couples together in their first ten years of operation.[54] A Canadian example is JToronto, founded in 2013, which targets singles in the GTA (Greater Toronto Area) between twenty-five and forty of all Jewish denominations.[55] At least some of the singles using these services opted for them after failed attempts at online dating, where users are argued to be "not as serious" about looking for a partner to marry. These services also provide a contemporary platform for singles who don't want their profiles visible to the public.[56]

However, the greatest change to the dating scene is the proliferation of Jewish dating websites, where one can filter potential matches by anything from Jewish denomination to level of adherence to rules regarding keeping kosher. There are even sites specifically for Orthodox Jews, as well as options for Jews of non-traditional sexual orientations. Online dating over the past decade, as one *Canadian Jewish News* article put it, has gone from being "a shameful last resort to a necessary evil."[57] The most well-known of these sites is JDate, launched in 1997. According to a 2012 report by the site's parent company, they have over 750,000 active members worldwide.[58] Another interesting example is JSwipe, which was created in 2014 as a spin-off of the popular dating application Tinder, and boasts over 165,000 users in over seventy countries.[59] This application differs from JDate in that the objectives of users are more likely to be an immediate meeting or encounter based on physical attraction. Users scroll through a databank of photos using their mobile device, swiping right on individuals they find attractive. Matches are only established when both parties have selected each other's photo.

Little research has been conducted on the phenomenon of Jewish online dating apart from a 2006 survey of JDate users.[60] Respondents' motivations for using the site included meeting a Jewish partner (78 per cent), signing up out of curiosity (41 per cent), knowing someone who met their significant other on the site (37 per cent), and feeling pressured by family to meet someone Jewish (12 per cent). In terms of respondents' success on JDate, 32 per cent experienced a relationship that lasted more than three months with someone they met on the site, and 19 per cent said they met their spouse, fiancé, or partner on the site.

And Jews aren't the only ones signing up. In 2002, only five years after JDate's debut, of the approximately 500,000 members of the site, over 5,000 selected the option "from another religious stream."[61] Some non-Jews choose to register on Jewish sites out of genuine interest in the Jewish faith, while others do so for more tactical reasons, including feeling that Jews are more "put together," and the belief that Jews make better partners because they are more family oriented and have better values. Among Gentiles, males on the site commonly report feeling more physically attracted to women of Jewish origin, and females commonly argue that Jewish men "know how to treat women."[62] These Jewish dating sites are international in scope, so there is no need for any specifically Canadian Jewish website. Canadian Jewish users can of course filter their search based on geographic location.

Matchmaking in the traditional style is still the norm in the ultra-Orthodox community, though couples now also meet through friends or relatives, and then move to the services of the *shadchan*, or matchmaker. In the *yeshiva* world, if the *shadchan* approves, the young couple may meet several times in dates where they will sit in public areas and chat, usually about direct practical concerns. Among the Hasidim, there are far fewer boy-girl meetings, but things still get talked about to avoid problems during the marriage. In one reported Toronto case, a prospective marriage within the ultra-Orthodox community fell apart because the two families could not agree on the future length of the young boy's sidecurls, or *payess*. I knew a Jewish woman who was a radical, liberated feminist in the late 1960s, but once made a surprising confession only half in jest.

She wondered if maybe she should let her mother choose her a husband. After all, nobody knew her or wanted her happiness like her mother ...

In any event, the evidence suggest that North American Jews do have a preference, all else considered, for marrying other Jews.[63] This is captured by the JDate slogan "Matzo ball recipes don't survive on their own." After all, if the Jewish population in Canada or the United States ranges between 1 and 2 per cent, it is indeed surprising that so many Jews marry within the group.

LGBTQ JEWS

Over recent decades in Canada in general, and among Canadian Jews, there has been a greater acceptance of the LGBTQ community.[64] Yet the sad truth is that for many Canadian Jews, notably among the more traditional, having a gay child may still be deeply troubling. The same could be said for non-Jews, but there are differences which make this Jewish discomfort surprising. Jews, on average, are politically liberal (as shall be discussed in a later chapter) and are generally against discrimination based on sexual orientation. While there is an Orthodox stigma against homosexuality, even here there are changes in attitude. And of course, other denominations are less hostile, even accommodating. Other factors make acceptance of homosexuality more difficult than one might expect. The major one is the extreme family- and child-centredness of Judaism: parents want grandchildren. Another is communal, and relates to continuity. Same-sex couples are less likely to reproduce, and thus on average rear fewer children than straight couples, so they may be seen as contributing less to Jewish continuity. This is clearly changing, as more and more same-sex Jews either have or adopt children. In the United States, surveys suggest 7 per cent of the Jewish population is LGBTQ, and of these 31 per cent are married or partnered, and 9 per cent are raising children. And as increasing numbers of LGBTQ Jews are becoming parents, this will pose new challenges to Jewish schools and synagogues.[65]

Jewish liberalism on homosexuality is most obvious in support for tolerance on the part of the state. Jewish teens in Canada are far more open to same-sex marriage than other Canadian teens, which means the future will look better for LGBTQ Jews seeking to marry. According to one survey, 87 per cent of Jewish teens in Canada approved of same-sex marriage. The national teen average was 73 per cent.[66] But what goes on within Jewish families and the formal Jewish community may be different. There is extensive debate among religious denominations as well as individual Jews seeking to negotiate spaces for members of the Jewish LGBTQ community.[67] Jewish liberalism may soften the antagonisms, but LGBTQ Jews have only recently been accepted by mainstream Jewish organizations, communities, and families. The change takes place mainly within synagogues and within minds and souls. The push of gay men and women for equality and dignity within the Jewish community parallels the struggle within Canada as a whole. Homosexuality tests the limits of Jewish pluralism and the adaptability of Jewish family life. And as LGBTQ Jews defend their interests, they do so in time-honoured Jewish fashion – by organizing.

The struggle of LGBTQ Jews in Canada is marked by the challenge of finding their space in two different communities, a true case of intersectionality and indeed double marginality. One option has been the creation of specifically Jewish LGBTQ organizations as safe spaces. Naches was the first formal organization representing the gay Jewish community in Montreal, and its history is revealing. It was founded in 1972–73 to provide an unthreatening environment where gay Jews could celebrate Jewish traditions. Beforehand, gay Jews found themselves having to choose between identifying as queer or as Jewish, and more often they would choose the former. By 1978, Naches was registered as a nonprofit organization and had a functioning board. The very early years were tough. Membership grew slowly, from ten to twenty people. The organization received hostile and obscene phone messages. The *Canadian Jewish News* would not accept ads, and members held meetings in private homes because no community organization would grant them space. By the 1980s, there were over one hundred members, but because so many were still concerned about anonymity, there was just a telephone list comprising first names only, with no accompanying addresses.

Things began to change in the late 1980s. Membership was approaching 200. The name was changed to Yachdav, meaning "together." Under the leadership of Harvey Cohen, who was visible in both the gay and Jewish communities, Yachdav approached the YM-YWHA for affiliation. That process took about eighteen months, and was possibly helped by the fact that one of Cohen's relatives was very active in the Y. Cohen recalls that following a meeting after the positive decision was made, the executive director of the Y commented, "They really are nice people."[68] After the breakthrough with the Y, there were other outreach efforts to become more involved with the established Jewish community. One major stride came about over the organized participation of Yachdav in a Combined Jewish Appeal Super Sunday fund-raising effort. At first there was resistance to allowing Yachdav to participate as a group, but eventually that changed. One member who volunteered was a teacher at a local Jewish school, who claimed, "I was so nervous I could lose my job."

By the 1990s, things had changed even further. Yachdav had a newsletter, close to 400 members, of whom about 60 per cent were men, and charged dues of $54, or $90 for a family membership. They received a grant from the Jewish Community Foundation and also started a support group for Jewish parents of gay men and women. Only the rabbinate, understandably, was slow to welcome the group. At one point, an invitation to meet with Montreal's Rabbinical Council was rescinded due to opposition. Yachdav did not evolve into a "gay shul" as is the case in Toronto, so the direct religious challenge is minimal. Since that time, LGBTQ life in Montreal has evolved with the formation of the latest group called Ga'ava (which means "pride" in Hebrew). This organization continues in the tradition of sponsoring social and cultural events.[69] There is also a support group in Montreal for Jewish families with gay children.[70]

Organized queer life in Toronto dates back at least to the mid-1970s, when a group with the name Ha-Mishpacha emerged. Through the 1980s, the small group encountered a cold reception from the Bloor JCC and the established community. Over time it changed its name (B'nai Kehillah, Chutzpah) and emphasis, and eventually opted to become a congregation, taking the name Keshet Shalom in 1992. In its first years, it went through many acute debates on Jewish ritual, though it never grew to be a full-fledged gay congregation as found in some American cities. Keshet Shalom closed in 2001. But at the same time, the organized Toronto Jewish community has begun to subsidize – how times have changed – a newer Jewish group aimed at university students and young adults called JLGBT, or Jewish Lesbian Gay Bisexual Transgendered students and young adults. This group was formed in March 2000 and evolved into the very successful Kulanu Toronto, Toronto's main Jewish LGBTQ organization. Kulanu offers a variety of programs and marches annually in the Toronto Pride Parade in a float sponsored by the Holy Blossom synagogue. There are several other queer-positive congregations in Toronto, including the Danforth Jewish Circle, the Reconstructionist Darchei Noam, and Shir Libeynu. Some established synagogues in Toronto, such as the First Narayever Congregation, perform same-sex marriages. There are now prospects for growth and other signs of acceptance in the city.[71] There have been AIDS support groups at Holy Blossom and Beth Tzedec congregations, and a congregation aimed at Jewish lesbians holds High Holiday services every year. But in general, the trend seems to be to include LGBTQ Jews in regular synagogues rather than focus on exclusive safe spaces. And as mainstream congregations change with the times and become more inclusive, the future of specifically LGBTQ congregations is uncertain.[72] With regard to Conservative synagogues, LGBTQ Jews are welcome, but the boundary is still typically drawn at marriage.[73]

LGBTQ Jews also confront interfaith relationships, and tend to be more tolerant than straight Jews. Yachdav did not allow non-Jews to join directly, but they could be invited to events by a member or may be part of a family membership. The issue has to be treated with care. Once, a non-Jewish woman joined Yachdav, became active, and was made president. But some members became suspicious during an Oneg Shabbat when she was handed a *siddur* (prayer book) and began to leaf through it in the wrong direction. She was exposed, and impeached.

There is no uniform policy on the part of denominations concerning openly gay members of synagogues. Gay members of Orthodox synagogues are not thrown out. There is a growing tolerance among some Modern Orthodox synagogues.[74] There is still more openness and acceptance in Canadian Conservative, Reform, and Reconstructionist congregations. The official Reform and Reconstructionist movements have essentially embraced full acceptance. The Jewish religious community across all denominations will have to confront the challenges of openly gay members, same-sex marriages, and gay rabbis. Some synagogues seem comfortable with a "don't ask, don't tell" policy, but this will not satisfy the LGBTQ community.

The dynamics of LGBTQ interfaith partnerships are interesting. Obviously, if there are no children being raised by the couple, these mixed marriages or partnerships are less likely a major source of assimilationist guilt. The non-Jews in these relationships are by all accounts very supportive of their partner's Jewish commitments. Research reports anecdotal evidence that suggests gay Jewish women are coupled more often with Jews than are gay Jewish men. Gay Jewish men often express interest in finding a Jewish partner but have difficulty due to a lack of potential partners, the fact that some are not openly gay, and issues around internalized anti-Semitism.[75] Some gay Jews have felt resentment towards the Jewish community for a perceived lack of acceptance. As time goes on these obstacles are lessening. While same-sex sexual activity is not condoned, there is a growing acceptance within the Modern Orthodox community. An online "Statement of Principles on the Place of Jews with a Homosexual Orientation in Our Community" that circulated in 2010 insisted that gay Jews deserve the same respect as any other Jew. This statement signed by dozens of Orthodox rabbis has signalled a significant change in the level of awareness and sympathy towards LGBTQ individuals in the Orthodox community.

The number of same-sex couples in which at least one partner is Jewish is rising.[76] Tension between identification with the LGBTQ and the Jewish community is likely decreasing. Changes in the Jewish community have allowed much more space for LGBTQ Jews to remain proud Jews. This may be best typified by the success of the television series *Transparent*. The show portrays the life of an elderly Jewish man who transitions into female status, and members of his family, his children and former wife, who are all Jewishly identified in one way or another.

In sum, it would seem that the formal Canadian Jewish community has evolved significantly in terms of creating space for LGBTQ Jews. This was the view expressed in 2016 by Carlos A. Godoy, president of Ga'ava, the Jewish community's LGBTQ Advisory Committee (Quebec): "CIJA, like its predecessor organizations, has stood alongside LGBTQ Jews and LGBTQ Canadians for the better part of the last decade [...] Across Canada, the organized Jewish community deserves credit for its leadership in standing with the LGBTQ community – Jewish and non-Jewish alike – against hatred and discrimination."[77]

In recent years a new challenge has emerged, perhaps unexpectedly, for Jewish members of the LGBTQ community. It is called "pinkwashing" (gay prisoners in German concentration camps had to wear pink triangles). Pinkwashing refers to the argument that Israel's general openness to gay rights, compared to the harsh restrictions and oppression against LGBTQ activity in the Arab/Muslim world, does not exonerate Israel from condemnation for misdeeds relating to the occupation in the West Bank or other forms of oppression of Palestinians in the West Bank and in Israel. Indeed, Tel Aviv is considered one of the most gay-friendly cities in the world, and in fact Tel Aviv and Haifa boast popular night life scenes in which Jewish and Palestinian gay men and women mingle in freedom and safety.[78]

This issue has been a polarizing one on North American campuses, notably within the context of general debates on the Middle East, and the emergence of BDS (Boycott, Divestment, Sanctions) campaigns aimed at academic policies ranging from divestment of Israeli endowment investments to restricting academic exchanges with Israeli universities. As one Canadian student told me recently, "It is very hard being a Jewish queer who supports Israel on campus. In fact, for much of the LGBTQ community, the debate is over, and Israel is seen only as negative." At times, these issues have emerged in the context of allowing Jewish floats in Gay Pride parades. And at times violent conflict and shouting matches have taken place. So a new challenge of intersectionality has emerged, with a vengeance. The added complexity to the conflict is that many of the Jewish or pro-Israel LGBTQ activists on campus may themselves be quite critical of specific Israeli policies, but often not to the harsh anti-Zionist degree of their opponents.[79]

Gay Jews are now carving out a space in the Jewish cultural landscape. One of the more interesting developments within the North American LGBTQ Jewish community has been the attempt to define links between homosexuality and the secular Yiddishist culture of Eastern Europe. That culture is seen as a softer one, with a less macho type of sensibility. Gay themes are identified in or with Yiddish literature and music, along with a notable blurring of gender boundaries. Barbra Streisand's "Yentl," a girl who dressed as a boy in order to study in a *yeshiva*, symbolizes the intersection of gay camp and Eastern European culture. As the community has started coming to terms with gay and lesbian Jews, it has also begun to raise awareness of and extend inclusiveness to trans Jews as well.

THE ELDERLY

All groups venerate their elderly, at least in theory. But Jews are living longer than in the past, and longer than most groups in North

America. We could describe this in positive terms, but throughout the organized Jewish community, aging has often been viewed as a policy problem or challenge because of the mounting costs associated with Golden Age Associations, seniors' residences, geriatric hospitals and chronic-care facilities, as well as a variety of home-care services. Middle-aged Jews are also more likely to be burdened for longer as a "sandwich generation," caring for aged parents and in-laws long after their children have grown up. At parties, Jewish baby-boomers may compare notes about their growing children, their own health worries, and the more serious health problems of their parents. As in many areas, like lower fertility rates or higher educational levels, Jews have been pioneers at the frontiers of modernity. So too with longevity and its consequences.

The increasing proportion of Jewish elderly is due to a combination of decreasing fertility – fewer children – as well as longer life spans. As educated and middle-class Canadians, Jews are likely to have better health and be better able to utilize existing health care than other groups.

There are other factors contributing to the increasing proportion of aged Jews in the population. One is the growing rate of mixed marriage. As younger Jews marry out, many of their children are lost to the Jewish fold. They are not part of the community, while their older parents and grandparents are. In the census, some of these children may not list their religion as "Jewish." Another is the Holocaust. The survivors, who have represented a fair chunk of Canadian Jews over sixty-five, were likely to have fewer children than other people. My parents had just one. Many survivors lost spouses and children during the war. Others' years of peak fertility occurred during wartime, when child-bearing was nearly impossible, or they simply didn't have the health or energy necessary to rebuild families after the war.

In 2011, 16.9 per cent of Canadian Jews were over sixty-five, compared to 13.8 per cent of the general population. This gap is of fairly recent vintage.[80] The aging of the early twentieth-century immigrant cohorts and the later wave of Holocaust survivors and North African immigrants has helped in widening the spread. Aging is found in all Jewish populations, with the exception of Israel. The American situation is similar. 24 per cent of American Jews are over sixty-five, compared to 18 per cent of the total American population.[81] In both Canada and the United States, age distributions vary widely by city. Looking at the proportions of the population over sixty-five in 2011, we find youthful Vancouver at 13.8 per cent, Toronto at 16.4 per cent, Montreal at 20.4 per cent, and Winnipeg at 18.8 per cent. In the United States, not surprisingly, we find Miami leading the way at 31 per cent, New York at 20 per cent, Philadelphia at 17 per cent, and Boston at 12 per cent.[82] There is nothing in Canada that compares with West Palm Beach, Florida, where 62 per cent of Jews are over sixty-five.

An aging population is not simply a policy problem for North American Jews. It is a wrenching test of Jewish family values and moral principles. This will become more acute as the Jewish elderly get even older. Among Canadian Jewish seniors, approximately 48 per cent are over seventy-five, compared with 51 per cent of all Canadian seniors.[83] The myth of a special closeness between aging Jewish parents and their children is alive and well, in anecdotes and in research. In a study of seniors in Hamilton, one respondent claimed: "Jewish families are closer. Children visit their parents. There's always a holiday or *simcha* to get together for."[84] Most Canadian Jewish seniors live in families, usually with a spouse. Because women live several years longer than men, they are more likely to be living alone; 40.2 per cent of elderly Jewish women live alone, compared with 17.7 per cent of men. But for all the mythology of warm extended Jewish families, and beloved *bubbies* and *zaydies*, when their spouses die, very few seniors live with their children.[85] In this regard, living arrangements for elderly Jews do not differ from those for Canadians as a whole. When a spouse dies, seniors are largely on their own.

Another interesting phenomenon is the proliferation of a certain type of high-rise condo building in largely Jewish areas such as Côte St Luc in Montreal or Thornhill in Toronto. These cater to a clientele over 50 per cent Jewish, who are generally middle-class or beyond. Many if not most of the Jewish residents are baby-boomers or more advanced seniors, still capable of independent living. There is a distinctively Jewish ambience in these buildings and, in at least one case, Jewish religious services are offered. In some ways, these Canadian high-rises resemble South Florida condo developments catering to a largely Canadian Jewish clientele of snowbirds. (As just one example, one can google "Century Village" in Florida. The culture of these Florida condos was satirized on *Seinfeld*, where Jerry Seinfeld's parents owned such a unit.)

If elderly Jews cannot or will not live with their children and cannot afford private options, many feel that the Jewish community, with or without government assistance, should pick up the slack. In a 2010 study of Montreal Jews, respondents identified the needs of the poor and elderly as the community's top priority.[86] The first Jewish senior citizens' home in Toronto was established in 1913. Today, the Baycrest complex is a model agency meeting the needs of the elderly. In Montreal, the Montreal Hebrew Sheltering Home was established in 1910, and evolved into the Maimonides Home for the Aged. A 2015 survey of 460 Jews aged fifty-five or older living in Ottawa found that over a quarter of respondents would definitely consider living in a Jewish retirement residence, more than half might consider doing so, and 14.8 per cent would not consider it at all. Furthermore, 23 per cent of participants said that the presence of "a Jewish environment" would be an extremely important factor in their selection of a senior's residence, whereas 12 per cent said that this would have a negative impact on their choice.[87] A 2015 survey in Vancouver similarly found extensive support for Jewish seniors' homes.[88]

How close are Jewish parents to their grown children? Even if they do not live together, there is a great deal of contact. In a survey of Jewish young adults in Montreal, John Sigal and I found that they spoke to their parents very often; the large majority at least daily.[89] The same pattern was found in a study comparing Jewish and non-Jewish senior women in Hamilton.[90] Regardless of the levels of contact, relations between the generations can be strained. The mobility of Jews, young and old, adds to the stress as parents age. Older Jews are often "abandoned" by mobile, professional children who leave their hometowns for work. As we have seen, taking in elderly widowed parents is rare, and it is unclear how harmonious these living arrangements are or would be. Many Canadian Jewish elderly in turn "abandon" their children and grandchildren by heading to Florida for part or all of the year. When seniors are healthy and still with spouses, problems are not severe. They increase when a spouse dies and health deteriorates. Remarriage is one way to solve the problem – though there are not enough Jewish men to meet the need. Often, the surviving parent still refuses to move in with the children. What is not clear is how much this craving for independence – this not wanting to "be a burden" – results from a fear that they might not really be welcome, or comfortable, living with their children's families. There is likely no solution that is ideal for seniors, their children, and the community.

INTERMARRIAGE

Last but not least: The perceived "threat" of intermarriage outweighs every other concern for Canadian Jewish continuity, including anti-Semitism and the low Jewish fertility rate. The term "intermarriage" has many meanings. I use it broadly to refer to the marriage between a Jew and someone who was born and remains non-Jewish. If the non-Jew converts to Judaism, whether before or after the marriage, then we no longer have an intermarriage. We have a marriage with two Jews. These are often called "conversionary marriages." A "mixed marriage" often refers to a marriage between a Jew and a non-Jew, where no formal conversion to Judaism has taken place, or, even "worse," the Jewish partner has embraced the non-Jewish religion. By the mid-1990s, about 30 per cent of Canadian Jews each year were marrying outside the religion. In 2011, among existing marriages involving at least one Jewish person, 26.3 per cent were cases of mixed-marriage, up from 16.8 per cent in 1991 and 20.8 per cent in 2001. The mixed marriage rate is higher for younger spouses. These increases confirm that other Canadians are now increasingly ready to marry Jews. Survey data from Angus Reid has found an increase in the percentages of Canadians who would accept that a family member would marry a Jew, from 47 per cent in 2013 to 62 per cent in 2017.[91]

The demographic impact of mixed marriage on the Jewish future can be massive. Assume one hundred adult Jews marry each other and have two children per family. This scenario leaves the population steady, generation after generation, at one hundred, based on fifty couples with two children each. A scenario with a mixed marriage rate of 50 per cent means that the next generation of Jews would be half as large: fifty Jews forming twenty-five couples having two children each, for a total of fifty Jews in the next generation.[92] But what of the other 50 per cent? First, conversion matters. Suppose all the non-Jewish spouses of these fifty outmarriages were to convert, or identify strongly as Jews and become de facto Jews. Then the total Jewish population would actually increase by 50 per cent, to 150 in the next generation: twenty-five Jewish in-marriages and fifty conversionary marriages, for seventy-five marriages with two children each. So formal conversion or a sincere commitment to a Jewish life can be crucial.

Let us say there is no formal conversion. For the Orthodox, children are Jewish if their mother is Jewish, regardless of religious observance. But let us take a sociological approach. Imagine two contrasting Jews who wind up in mixed marriages. One type is very assimilated, with minimal Jewish identity and communal ties, raised in a home where family members and friends are already in mixed marriages. In such cases, the mixed marriage is not hard to understand. It puts a finishing touch on a long-term process. It is a symptom, not a cause. The other type is far more intriguing. Here, we have people from identified Jewish homes, who may have attended synagogue regularly or had some Jewish education, yet fall in love with and marry a non-Jew. Many claim that they will continue to live a Jewish family life to some degree and, indeed, some do. Ask them, and they will identify confidently as Jews. Usually their partner is not a very devout Christian, so their children may well be exposed to some Jewish events or experiences. One may still question the future Jewish identity and commitments of these children.

What kind of Jews marry out? Not surprisingly, Jews who are third- or fourth-generation Canadians are the most likely to do so.[93] Studies have found that those whose family of origin is less religiously observant or non-Orthodox and who have less Jewish education – schools as well as Jewish camps, youth groups, and Israel programs – are more likely to marry out. Each of these factors plays an independent role; they are not simply extensions of varying Jewish family background.[94]

American sociologist Bruce Phillips moved beyond these major background factors leading to mixed marriage, finding adolescent dating patterns to be key. I suspect his findings apply equally to Canada.[95] Again, no surprises. Jews who dated mainly Jews in high school were more likely to marry a Jew. But the process is very fluid. Only half of those who in high school dated mostly Jews, or Jews and non-Jews equally, were dating mostly Jews when they met their spouse. The importance of marrying a Jew declined significantly between high school and college. Nevertheless, as Phillips pointed out, high-school dating is crucial, since "it was only those respondents who dated Jews in high school who would later be dating Jews as adults." And how do Jewish spouses meet? Out-married Jews were far more likely to meet their spouses in a neutral setting like work, school, or parties. In-married Jews were more likely to meet their spouses through a social network, such as friends, or blind dates, or through a formal Jewish group or setting. Hence the logic in those Jewish singles associations or dating websites. In fact, an unstated aim of so many Jewish youth activities, like summer camps, youth groups, Israel programs and so on, is to pair up Jewish youngsters.

The danger to continuity is only one issue relating to intermarriage. The other is that even in conversionary marriages, Orthodox Judaism does not accept conversions supervised by non-Orthodox rabbis. In the Pew survey, 3 per cent of American Jews described themselves as converts, the large majority though non-Orthodox conversion. So these people – and their children, if they are women – are not recognized as Jews according to *halacha*. The problem the Orthodox have is with the conversion process itself and the allegedly inadequate learning of the rabbi in charge. Yet conversion, any conversion, makes a difference. American research has routinely found that there are few or no differences in Judaic commitments – synagogue attendance, ritual observance, communal involvement – between conversionary marriages and Jewish in-marriages. There is no debate on the evidence.[96] Possibly, there is self-selection at work; those who convert could be more predisposed to being Jewish than those who do not, and converts may well take their new faith more seriously than born Jews. Another possibility is that the formality of the ritual adds a new dimension of commitment and perhaps eases strains with the extended Jewish family. One woman I interviewed, who converted after her marriage, was astounded to see how much closer her Jewish mother-in-law became to her, even though she had not previously pressured her to convert. The growing acceptance of converts to Judaism is ironic, given a tradition which has discouraged conversion to Judaism and been skeptical of conversions from Judaism.

A ninety-year-old Jew is dying, and asks his wife to summon a priest so he can convert before he passes on. His wife complains, "Why are you doing this? You have been a good Jew your whole life." He replies, "Better one of them should die than one of us."

The quasi-racial approach to Jewish or Gentile identity will not last as converts become more numerous. Orthodox Jews claim that

Reform classes, or the rabbis who lead them, are not up to the task. Those converts who become Reform Jews may lead less Jewish lives than converts who become Orthodox Jews. But that is not the point. I observed one Reform-sponsored class in western Canada where the rabbi was on sabbatical leave and the class was run by a woman, herself a Reform convert. She was both knowledgeable and very respectful of Orthodoxy. The books that were assigned were very informative. The notion that non-Orthodox converts ought not be considered Jews is sociological nonsense. Orthodox conversions are perhaps more demanding, but the final steps may not be as intellectually focused. A woman who underwent an Orthodox conversion in Montreal in the 1980s recalled her process for me. The classes lasted over a year, and covered a wide range of material. Her final test involved questioning by three rabbis, and the issues ranged widely: from detailed queries about the destruction of the second temple and the fast day of *Tisha Be'Av* to the steps involved in koshering liver. (I wonder if male converts get asked that question?) A visit to the *mikveh*, or ritual bath, finalized the process.

And what do we know of the "Jewishness" of the growing numbers of mixed marriages without any conversion? Bruce Phillips found great variety in these marriages in the United States, though for the most part they are minimally Jewish and their offspring will likely remain apart from the Jewish community. When asked how they were raising their children, only 18 per cent said, "Jewish only."[97] Does that mean that all the others will be lost to the tribe? Phillips identified six types of mixed marriages, depending on the degree of Jewishness. Only one-seventh were classified in the most Jewish type of mixed marriage. Canadian census data allows us to look at impact on children more directly. Among Canadian children born to parents in mixed-marriages involving a Jew, 27 per cent are identified by their parents as Jews by religion, 56 per cent as having no religious identification, and 16.6 per cent are identified as having other religions.[98] Clearly a significant drop, at least as measured by their primary religious identification. Comparisons with the United States are of interest. There, only 20 per cent of mixed-married parents say they are raising their children as Jewish by religion. And given that the mixed marriage rate for recent non-Orthodox Jews in the United States is 71 per cent, the American challenge is enormous.[99]

Mixed marriage in Canada is not (yet) as popular it is in the United States. But these numbers or types still do not capture the human variety within each mixed marriage. In Canada, about one-third of Toronto's mixed-married couples say they will provide supplementary Jewish education to their children.[100] 18 per cent in Montreal indicate that their children are attending Jewish day schools and significant numbers observe a variety of Jewish rituals.[101] This contrasts with American research which shows that even among mixed-married families raising their children as Jewish, 38 per cent still plan to have a Christmas tree.[102] To most Orthodox Jews this variation is meaningless, but it is a fact of life among the non-Orthodox. I know of one mixed marriage, dissolved after twenty-five years, where the Jew was a professor of Jewish studies and the spouse was indifferent to things Jewish. In another, the Jewish partner belongs to two synagogues, attends services on major holidays, associates mainly with his Jewish friends, while the wife attends neither church nor synagogue but participates in Jewish festivals. In yet another, a Jewish father in a mixed marriage had a very Jewish given name and surname, and two children. One child has a very Jewish given name, a second a very Anglo-Christian given name. One American Jew I know is in a mixed marriage. But he started his journey out before the marriage, becoming attracted to Ethical Culture (a form of secular humanism) first. I recall spending Hanukkah with his family, with latkes, dreidels, and candles. Yet when his twenty-year-old son visited us one Rosh Hashanah, he told us it was the first time he had ever attended any synagogue service. Despite the creative efforts of some of the Jews involved in mixed marriages, on balance most of the children – and even more likely the grandchildren – will be lost to the Jewish community according to most traditional metrics. This is now more likely in the American Jewish case, but Canadian Jewry may well catch up. All this presupposes that future processes of Jewish identification will mimic those of the past, which is unlikely. Should the community widen the definitional net, the losses would be less pronounced.

One of the looming problems in devising a communal response to mixed marriage, assuming that is even desirable or possible, is that almost no non-Orthodox Jewish family – and many Orthodox Jewish families – remains untouched. Legal scholar and Jewish communal activist Alan Dershowitz, in his book *The Vanishing American Jew*, poignantly refers to the mixed marriage of one of his own children, raised in a committed Jewish home.[103] Jewish parents like Dershowitz no longer sit *shiva* if their children marry out. They keep channels open, and still love their children. At Jewish communal meetings, people have to watch their language on intermarriage so as not to give offence. Jews also have to be careful about telling jokes about non-Jews, given the large numbers of converts and Gentiles moving in Jewish circles. Stigmatizing those who marry out just no longer works in non-Orthodox circles.

The challenge facing both Jewish communities and individuals is how to respond to the process as it unfolds, and once it becomes a *fait accompli*. How are parents to react when their son or daughter dates a non-Jew or brings one home? Attitudes of American Jews on intermarriage are now overwhelmingly liberal. The alarm first sounded by American Jewish leadership over the 1990 NJPS findings of a 52 per cent mixed-marriage rate does not reflect the recent feelings of the average Jew. The American Jewish Committee's 2000 survey of American Jewish opinion found that only 12 per cent of respondents "strongly disapproved" of mixed marriages, and almost 50 per cent thought "it is racist to oppose Jewish-Gentile marriages." This helps explain why in 2013, as mentioned, among recently married American Jews, 58 per cent had a non-Jewish spouse, and 71 per cent for the non-Orthodox.[104] Canada remains far more traditional. Despite the increasing rates of mixed marriage, Canadian Jews remain more opposed to it. For example, if told that their child was considering marrying a non-Jew, almost 60 per cent of Montreal Jews in 2010 would oppose the marriage and only 9 per cent would openly support it. If the non-Jewish spouse converted to Judaism, the proportion that would actively oppose the marriage declined dramatically to 16 per cent.[105]

But this initial opposition to intermarriage is not unique to Montreal. A 2005 Toronto survey found significant opposition to intermarriage. If their child was considering marrying a non-Jew, the majority of respondents, 51.4 per cent, would actively oppose such a marriage, and would express their opinion openly; 12.1 per cent would oppose the union but would not express their opinion; 16.7 per cent would be neutral about the matter; 10.3 per cent would support it openly; and 9.5 per cent were undecided. In short, 63.5 per cent of respondents would oppose such a marriage, and 10.9 per cent of respondents would openly oppose an intermarriage even if the person were to convert. But these survey statistics do not negate the fact that once mixed marriages occur without conversion, there has been a clear shift of the pendulum on the part of the non-Orthodox Jewish world towards outreach, and inclusion, to these families. An example would be Danforth Jewish Circle in Toronto's east end. Of the estimated 500 members, perhaps one third to one half are intermarried families. While some Reform and Reconstructionist rabbis in Canada will not perform an intermarriage, their congregations are increasingly open to such families.[106]

In these attitudes against intermarriage, Jews are clearly at odds with Canadian public opinion, which strongly favours marriage among Protestants, Catholics, and Jews, as well as between various ethnic or racial groupings. In 1995, for example, 92 per cent of Canadians approved of marriages between Protestants and Roman Catholics, 90 per cent between Protestants and Jews, and 89 per cent between Roman Catholics and Jews.[107] A 2007 poll found that 92 per cent of Canadians approved of mixed marriages.[108] Christians in Canada no longer want to persecute Jews, or convert Jews, they want to marry them ...

Most non-Orthodox parents, despite their opposition, will certainly make their peace with mixed marriage. And this may also be the case for many Orthodox, who will keep ties with intermarried children. In the non-Orthodox world, the tilt is clearly towards forms of inclusion and accommodation. Among religious denominations, liberal Reconstructionist Judaism has even affirmed that in the future, rabbis may have a non-Jewish spouse. Some policy questions remain. Should Jewish schools or synagogues refuse to hire Jews in mixed marriages as teachers? The Birthright program, which supports sending young Jewish adults on a free ten-day trip to Israel, accepts applicants with one Jewish parent, mother or father. To take a hard line, accepting only Orthodox converts, might prevent the dilution of Jewish identity but cut down on numbers. A soft line would welcome marginal Jews – and non-Jews – keeping numbers up, but perhaps weakening the average levels of commitment. An argument for the soft line recognizes that mixed marriage today is usually not a result of deliberate rebellion against parents or Judaism. Nor is it a response to societal discrimination against Jews, as was the case in the past. Usually it is just love, or the same set of factors that lead to any marriage. Keeping the doors open seems to make tactical sense.

It should be clear that this softer approach has become the subject of harsh debate among American scholars and Jewish communal leaders, in the wake of the Pew 2013 survey of American Jews. On the one hand are those who note the combined impact of trends such as non-marriage, delayed marriage, intermarriage (with no conversion), reduced child-bearing, fewer children raised as Jews, and argue that the demographic future for American Jews looks bleak. Indeed, families that are raising Jewish children score higher on all measures of Jewish identity, but there are far fewer of them. A strong Orthodox group will persist, and a large group of weakly affiliated Jews will grow, but a middle range of committed but non-Orthodox Jews will be hollowed out. And this will have impacts on the viability of many traditional Jewish institutions such as synagogues, schools, summer camps, and voluntary organizations.[109]

On the other hand, some scholars and liberal communal leaders find positive trends in these data. They note that among the Millennials in the Pew survey, one finds higher numbers who report they and their children identify as Jews and are proud to be Jewish. Accordingly, one expects that this new generation will seek to manifest forms of Jewish identity and expression which will be meaningful, but different from those of earlier generations.[110] These challenges are percolating in the Canadian scene as well, though they are not yet as acute as they are in the American case. But they are on the way.

6

The Communal Foundation of Jewish Life

People, Neighbourhoods, and Organizations

"Hillel said: Do not cut yourself off from the community."
Ethics of the Fathers, 2:5

"For every two Jews, three organizations."
Anonymous

THE CENTRALITY OF COMMUNITY

Some time ago, I attended a gathering of prominent Chinese Canadians. The talk drifted to comparisons between diasporic Jews and Chinese and one of the guests asked, "What can I do to make sure that my children retain their Chinese identity?" This question echoed the oft-repeated Jewish worry, "Are you sure your grandchildren will be Jewish?" In framing my response, I drew, rightly or wrongly, on the Jewish experience. "You, yourself, can do little. Any answer will have to come from the organized Chinese community."

It is difficult to overemphasize the communitarian basis of contemporary Jewish life. The informal community is a network of interpersonal social relationships – friends, relatives, neighbours, colleagues. It is often bounded by where we live and whom we befriend. The formal community is defined by a vast array of voluntary associations which help structure the public and private lives of Canadian Jews. For example, the website jewishinmontreal.com lists over 400 entries including seventy-nine synagogues, fifty-eight educational institutions, and ninety-six other community institutions. The website jewishtoronto.com lists a staggering total of approximately 720 Jewish organizations. These include well over

100 educational institutions, 100 synagogues, thirty-two camps, and a variety of organizations dealing with family, childcare, culture, media, and other social services.

A fascinating paradox: though individual Jewish identities seem to be threatened by assimilation and mixed marriage, the organized Jewish community perseveres. New buildings go up, money is raised, projects are being launched. To be a Jew can mean, among other things, to join, to volunteer, to make donations, to go to events, and, yes, to attend meetings. The culture of the "meeting" thrives in the Jewish world. For both community professionals and lay-leaders, meetings and activities, whether in person or in virtual form, are the coin of the realm. Reading the weekly *Canadian Jewish News*, whether in print or online at www.cjnews.com, is an excellent way to get a sense of the range of events sponsored by Jewish organizations in a typical week. Lectures, fundraisers, concerts, gala dinners, balls, raffles, and exhibitions jostle for attention along with routine activities sponsored by the myriad organizations. In fact, the *Canadian Jewish News* itself is a good indicator of the activities of the organized community. In 2013 the newspaper closed temporarily, but was revived soon after. While Jewish academics routinely disparage it as being an establishment organ, it sets a standard which few other Canadian ethnic publications can match. It really does reflect the community, for better or worse.

Of course, the Jewish community today is sharply divided. But from the 1890s to after the Second World War, the divisions were, in my view, even deeper. It made little sense, in the decades before the 1950s, to speak of a single, unified Jewish community.[1] Certainly, there was substantial division in Montreal, Toronto, and Winnipeg along lines of economic class, birthplace, ideology, religiosity, and cultural style. A major cleavage was between the anglicized wealthier Jews and the poorer East European immigrants or, in then-current parlance, the uptown and downtown Jews. These distinctions persisted into the postwar years, with tensions between the old-timers and the newcomers, or *di greeneh*.

Just as fierce were the ideological and cultural divisions within the working-class East European Jews themselves. Within the left, as well as within the more assimilated upper classes, there were also tensions between the Zionists and the non-Zionists. And, of course, there were sharp divisions between the left-wing and right-wing Zionists.[2] Some of these divisions persist today. Attitudes on Israeli politics and policies, and the peace process are still polarized. Tensions among the religious denominations have become even more fractious. But we should not overstate the degree of actual friction. In fact, there is sufficient self-segregation within the Jewish world to keep it to a minimum. For example, secular Jews and the ultra-Orthodox generally have little or nothing to do with each other, by mutual choice, so the antagonisms are minimized. And there is even an upside. As sociologist Lewis Coser has argued, one of the positive spin-offs of conflict among social groups is that it may reinforce and deepen the identities of each.[3] The differences within the Jewish world mean that there has been the potential for growth, for finding better options, and for adapting to changing or threatening realities.

Some might trace the origin of the Jewish communitarian commitment to the Biblical teachings of Judaism itself. Accordingly, it is embedded in the fundamental religious law which stipulates that prayer can only take place in the presence of a quorum of ten adult men (a *minyan*) which serves indirectly to bind the community together. Moreover, the Bible commands Jews to provide for the needy – widows, orphans, strangers, and the poor – a task best fulfilled communally. There is some truth to this cultural explanation. Unlike Eastern religions or Christianity, Judaism is somewhat more firmly grounded as a "this-worldly" religion. Belief in God is not enough to guarantee salvation. The Torah lists a total of 613 commandments, or *mitzvot*, which are obligatory acts for the very observant Jew. (Many of those 613 have been rendered moot with the passage of time.) The tradition of the mystic or the monk, or practices such as meditation/mindfulness and yoga with a Judaic gloss, are present and growing. But they have not been central to conventional Judaic conceptions of spirituality. The family and the community, and related rituals, are the agents through which holiness is expressed. Judaism's concern with this-worldly matters is captured in the iconic joke claiming that most Jewish holidays can be described in nine words: "They tried to kill us, they failed, let's eat." The Talmud is really a compendium of legal decisions and commentary, relating in part to day-to-day problems. Jews are commanded to pursue justice on this earth. The verse "*kol Yisrael arevim zeh la-zeh*" (all of Israel is bound up one to another) captures this communitarian ethos.

But culture does not tell the whole story. These cultural predispositions were reinforced for Jewish communities in the diaspora by anti-Semitism, which required Jews to look after their own and, indeed, fostered a tradition of self-governance. In the first instance, Jews would act collectively to meet religious requirements. Diaspora communities have always administered Jewish cemeteries and set up burial societies. This was important to guarantee burial – even for indigent Jews – according to traditional Jewish law. In addition, Jewish schools, orphanages, and relief organizations were established.

Moreover, Gentile rulers tended to recognize the corporate existence of Jews and to relate to Jews through designated representatives. Jews have two thousand years of experience in diasporic living and related self-government. Most of this took place not in pluralistic, liberal-democratic environments in which religious or ethnic groups had their own voluntary hierarchical organizations. It happened in pre-modern societies, where membership in the Jewish community determined one's life chances. Jews had few choices. They were faced with many restrictions and exclusions, which in turn reinforced their sense of community. Being a Jew in medieval Europe or the Middle East nurtured the fact and legitimacy of Jewish communal self-government. In Amsterdam, the formal community could excommunicate Spinoza. In Eastern Europe, the *va'ad arba aratzot*, or the Council of the Four Lands – essentially Poland including western Ukraine and Lithuania – was a model of Jewish self-government. And in 1807, Napoleon had no compunction about reconstituting a *sanhedrin* based on self-governing Jewish councils in ancient Israel during the Second Temple period to represent French Jews vis-à-vis the state. Communal organization has been second nature to Jews.

The organized Jewish community has always had two functions. One has been internal, a form of self-government reflected in the many organizations that cater to Jewish needs. This internal function is now recognized as a key weapon – and the military metaphor captures the spirit of the moment – in the battle against assimilation and for Jewish continuity. The second function has been external, representing the interests of Jews to the outside world. In an earlier period, this role often fell to key individuals. From the eleventh century on, it was filled by the *shtadlan*, or intercessor, who petitioned the king or the religious authorities on behalf of Jews, seeking to avoid persecution both physical and financial. A most delicate, and often thankless, task. Later, similar tasks were filled by *hofjude*, or "court Jews," who emerged in the German states in the seventeenth century. Unlike the *shtadlan*, the court Jew usually had a strong personal relation with a ruler, was a person of great wealth, and had wide commercial contacts. Both figures reflected the societies in which they lived, in which notions of equal citizenship for Jews were non-existent. Today, the internal and external organizations are supported through charitable giving, a kind of voluntary taxation, which has worked comparatively well.[4]

GHETTOS AND NEIGHBOURHOODS

Formal Jewish organizations rest on a foundation of informal community life sustained by Jewish neighbourhoods and friendship patterns. In the Old World, and later in Canada, these reflected social divisions based on wealth, Jewish learning, or lineage. Any sense of unity was nurtured by the ever-present danger of anti-Semitism, and made possible by the smaller scale and relative homogeneity of Jewish residential areas.[5]

Though restrictive ghettos have disappeared, where Jews choose to live within cities affects their lives. In the early periods of mass migration, Montreal, Toronto, and Winnipeg had heavily Jewish neighbourhoods. In this respect, surprisingly little has changed. As Jews have spread throughout the regions of Canada and moved out from the original areas of settlement in large cities, they have retained a high degree of residential segregation. Jews are the most residentially concentrated ethnic group in every large Canadian metropolis, most notably in Montreal and Toronto. According to one study using 2001 census data, Jews are the most geographically concentrated group in Montreal. Studies of Toronto using 2006 census data find that Jews are also the most concentrated minority group in that city. 90 per cent of Jews live in only 30 per cent of census tracts, and a "dissimilarity index" found Toronto Jews at 0.662, higher than any other ethnic group, above Chinese at 0.596 and Blacks at 0.504.[6] Some Canadians might think that the most residentially concentrated groups in Canada would be Blacks or Asians, or perhaps Italians. But they are less concentrated than are Jews. This remarkable concentration is found not only in older communities, but was even the case out West through the 1990s. While Jews, say in Vancouver, are more dispersed than their counterparts in Montreal and Toronto, they are still more concentrated than almost any other group.[7]

This Jewish togetherness is surprising. For most minority groups in Canada, those with higher levels of education or income have tended to be less residentially concentrated. They have the money and desire to move out of the ethnic enclave.[8] We associate ghetto or ethnic neighbourhoods in North America with poor or working-class immigrants. Not so for Jews. Even as Jews in the post-immigrant generation moved into the suburbs and experienced greater mixing than in the past, they have tended to cluster in disproportionate numbers in middle-class neighbourhoods. Jews have recreated their institutions – schools, synagogues, community centres, butchers, and bakeries – as they moved into the suburbs. This has been the case in Toronto, as Jews moved north along Bathurst into Thornhill and Vaughn, and in Montreal, as Jews have moved into Côte St-Luc and Hampstead, and then into the West Island.

Why do Jews continue to live together? When social scientists first began to study residential segregation, the consensus was clear: any observed clustering was due to discrimination. Jews lived near other Jews because housing markets discriminated against them or for fear that Gentile neighbours might be anti-Semitic. The bitter legacy of the ghetto hung over any ethnic or racial neighbourhood. Researchers who studied this residential clustering initially chose a word which would echo the racist sentiments of the American South: "segregation." They reflexively equated the experience of racial minorities – Blacks, Asians, Latinos – with that of European immigrant groups and Jews. Researchers tend today to prefer the term "concentration," which is more neutral. It allows for the possibility that minorities – especially those who speak a different language – might actually prefer to live in minority neighbourhoods, or that these concentrations reflected patterns of migration and settlement. In the case of Jews, residential concentrations reflect a historic legacy as well as practical responses to current realities. In the old country, Jews lived in *shtetls* (Jewish villages) or in Jewish streets or areas in towns and cities. This reflected historic restrictions but also evolved into a preference. The move to the New World changed little. Immigration is, in general, a traumatic experience, and any ethnic community or neighbourhood can provide a "psychic shelter" from an unfamiliar and perhaps hostile majority group. For the Orthodox, being within walking distance of synagogues – a necessity as they cannot drive on the Sabbath – and Jewish schools added an impetus to the formation of neighbourhoods, where kosher butchers and bakeries also proliferated. All this is understandable in the case of the mass-immigration generation of Jews. Poverty also restricted residential options of those Jews who clustered along the Main in Montreal or near Kensington Market and Spadina in Toronto. But how to explain the persisting concentrations in suburbs and among second- and third-generation Jews?

Suburban Jews in Winnipeg, Toronto, and Montreal, even more than their counterparts in many American cities, have created "gilded ghettos" for affluent Jews. Indeed, one of the pioneering works of Canadian social research dealt with the 1950s suburban community of "Crestwood Heights," actually Forest Hill in Toronto, which was at the time almost one-quarter Jewish.[9] Early Jewish residential concentration may have been due to discrimination by landlords or real-estate agents, and poverty. But today many Jews voluntarily choose to live near Jewish institutions and other Jews. When moving to new areas, Jews have been known to check for *mezuzahs* on doorposts to determine the Jewishness of new surroundings. Perhaps there is a subliminal fear of recurring anti-Semitism which leads some to seek safety by circling the wagons.

A leading Israeli-born American sociologist, Amitai Etzioni, argued in the late 1950s that the need for residential proximity among Jews and other groups would decline simply because, with telephones and cars, there would be less need for ethnic neighbourhoods.[10] In one sense, this is true. A new definition of a Jewish "neighbourhood" may be anything within ten or fifteen minutes driving distance. Many Jewish children are carpooled that long, or much longer, to Jewish schools that are not really neighbourhood schools. But technology has not eliminated the need for proximity. New Jewish neighbourhoods are recreated in the suburbs. And this does not mean that ties to the "old neighbourhood" are gone forever. Jewish families in the suburbs routinely visit the older areas of settlement for a more authentic, usually gastronomic, experience. Many suburban Jews in Montreal still trek back to the Main for smoked meat at Schwartz's, a "special" at Wilensky's, or breakfast at Beauty's. Toronto Jews may return to Kensington and Bathurst – but perhaps more for nostalgic reasons than for the food. And the same is true for other minority groups, who move away but still visit the shops and markets they knew from their youth or when they first arrived in Canada.

Jewish neighbourhoods in Toronto and Montreal, and to a lesser extent in other Canadian cities, are alive and well. A person visiting any Canadian metropolis will be able to find areas where Jews have clustered together. They are in general not far from synagogues and Jewish schools. There will often be a Jewish-style bakery or deli at hand. Find the Jewish Community Centre and you will find Jewish homes close by. Jewish areas can also be easily identified by the proportion of homes which do not have Christmas lights glowing, though many, not to be outdone, will now have *chanukiot*, or Hanukkah candelabras, in the windows. These high levels of Jewish residential concentration are no accident. People know where they live, and why.

But Jewish neighbourhoods themselves are not homogeneous. Social class separates different groups. Jews know where their wealthy live, as compared to the broad middle class. Moreover, religion also differentiates Jewish areas. Again, in Toronto and Montreal, there are well-known areas where ultra-Orthodox Jews live, and even the Orthodox tend to live close to Orthodox synagogues and institutions.

FRIENDSHIPS

Jews not only live together, they stick together. Over three-quarters of adult Canadian Jews in 1990 claimed that "most of their friends" were Jewish, compared to one half – still high – for American Jews.[11] This finding is all the more remarkable because in Montreal or Toronto, at most only 3 or 4 per cent of the metro population is Jewish. In 1996, 58 per cent of Montreal Jews indicated that "all or almost all" of their closest friends were Jewish, and another 27 per cent said "most" were Jewish. And this was likely the way they liked it. Over 70 per cent said they felt close to other Jews "to a great extent."[12] Religious Jews were more likely to have all or almost all Jewish friends: 77 per cent for the Orthodox, to 69 per cent for the Conservative, to 36 per cent for Reform or secular Jews.

For first-, second-, and third-generation Toronto Jews in the late 1970s, between 50 and 55 per cent indicated that their three closest friends were Jewish. This was much higher than for other European immigrant groups, where mixing rose dramatically after the immigrant generation. For the few third-generation Toronto Italians and Ukrainians, the figures were down to 10 and 3 per cent respectively; what you might expect by chance alone. More recent evidence from a 2005 Toronto study confirms this pattern. Almost half, 44.6 per cent, of respondents said that "all or almost all" of their close friends are Jewish, 34.2 per cent said "most" are Jewish, 15.2 per cent said "some" are Jewish, 3.7 per cent said "few" are Jewish, and 2.3 per cent said "none" are Jewish. So almost 80 per cent said that at least most of their friends are Jewish. Not surprisingly, 78 per cent of Orthodox claim that all or almost all of their close friends are Jewish.[13] These ties are found even in the smaller Jewish centres. Over 80 per cent of Calgary Jews in 1997 claimed that at least half of their close friends were Jewish even though Jews comprised less than 1 per cent of the Calgary population.[14]

So the anti-Semitic stereotype popularly held about Jews, that they are "clannish," is in a sense true. Such a clear pattern is not found for any other European immigrant group. It might be found among some visible minorities in large cities in Canada, especially if there is a high immigrant concentration. Perhaps also for First Nations, or Hutterites. But among White, middle-class, Canadian-born groups? No. A health professional in Montreal in his late fifties reminisced about the peculiar magic of growing up Jewish in Montreal. "It was a real ghetto," he sighed, approvingly.

This pattern of social self-segregation is perplexing precisely because, on so many levels, Jews and non-Jews are blurring cultural and social differences and crossing boundaries. So why does it persist? Fear of intermarriage is an obvious explanation. Jews face a religious proscription against intermarriage that is not faced by other comparable ethnic groups. The social segregation which begins in childhood and persists into young adulthood likely helps to minimize interfaith dating and eventually intermarriage. It has been common for Canadian Jewish families from rural areas or smaller cities and towns to send their children to university in Toronto or Montreal largely to meet young Jews.

Anti-Semitism is an unlikely explanation. The evidence of extensive or deep-seated contemporary anti-Semitism has been just too weak, as we shall see in Chapter 11. And the non-Jews with whom Jews are likely to come into sustained contact are mainly educated, urban, and more cosmopolitan. They are more likely to marry Jews than beat them up. Still, the fear of latent anti-Semitism may play a role. Many Jews feel, correctly, that few non-Jews share their depth of concern about the security of Israel, or Jewish assimilation, or anti-Semitism at home or abroad. This is not anti-Semitism. Gentiles may relate very openly and warmly to Jews as human beings, but

162 Like Everyone Else but Different

less effectively to Jews as Jews. Many committed Jews may therefore compartmentalize their relationships with non-Jews. They share all sorts of things – working in the office, playing tennis, going to a movie or dinner party, and even discussing family troubles – but are unable or unwilling to communicate the depth of their concerns about Jewish issues. The fact that a non-Jewish friend, or colleague, or neighbour, may be somewhat indifferent to Israel's security, or more willing to blame Israel for Middle East conflict, or reluctant to call an anti-Semite an anti-Semite, is best left unexplored. This sort of insecurity, in different form, was first described among American Jews on the new suburban frontiers of the 1950s and 1960s. Sociologist Marshall Sklare claimed that some Jews felt they must play an "ambassadorial role" in interactions with non-Jews, making a good impression on behalf of the group.[15] If that is still the case, it militates against the honest communication required for meaningful friendships. Polite small talk is preferable to making a "faux pas."

There is also a seamier side to this communications barrier, a long and still extant tradition in Jewish folk culture which essentializes Gentiles, or the *Goyim*. That undercurrent, to the extent it still exists, also impedes the formation of true friendships across the Jewish-Gentile boundary. Gentiles can be seen as, well, different. It's just easier to socialize with Jews.

Today, we find that Canadian Jews are typically middle-class and well educated. These commonalities extend into recreational activities. Jews – for whatever reason – seem to drink less than non-Jews in social situations, get drunk less often, and suffer less from alcoholism and related pathologies. This is true even though I assume – based on reports from my children – younger Jews are drinking more than my generation did. Sobriety has been a commonly assumed Jewish trait, and various esoteric or folk explanations emerged to explain it. These stressed the sacred and ritualistic role of wine in Jewish religious life, which does explain why few Jews are complete abstainers. Other arguments linked Jewish sobriety to the need to be prepared to face anti-Semitic dangers. The contrasting image of the Gentile as a drunkard, often given to acts of violence, is deeply embedded in Jewish folklore, and in the folksong and expression *shikker iz a goy*, or "a drunk is a Gentile."[16] The pattern of Jewish sobriety can be confirmed by scientific studies – including data comparing drinking in Israel with other countries – and informal observations. Interviews with experienced bartenders confirm it; they will order far less liquor for a Jewish party than for a Gentile affair. If cash bars seem to be less common than open bars at Jewish parties, this is partly because the hosts know they will not go broke. So while Jews today may be drinking more than in the past, the Jackie Mason joke still rings true: After a movie, Gentiles may be more likely to go out for a drink, and Jews to go out to eat, preferably for coffee and cake, and preferably for good-sized portions!

On another level, some Jews may be reluctant to recount Jewish jokes to Gentiles, either for fear that some of the in-group references might be lost, or worse, they might appear politically incorrect, or construed as micro-aggressions directed at a majority group. Again, as Yiddish and Jewish pop culture seep into the mainstream, this may diminish. It is not clear how much Jews differ, controlling for class and education, in other lifestyle patterns. Is it still the case that "Jews buy wholesale, and Gentiles buy retail?" If so, that might make shopping outings difficult. There is greater convergence in eating patterns between Jews and Gentiles than in the past. But even going out for a meal might still pose some problems. Some Jews are strictly kosher. Others will not eat pork, or seafood. The Jewish preference for Chinese food, or for deli, or for a brunch of bagels, cream cheese, and lox, may not be matched by Gentiles. Canadian Jews and Gentiles both winter in Florida, but often on different coasts.

There are differences in sports and recreation. While Jews today are perhaps rare among professional or elite athletes in Canada, they seem to participate enthusiastically in the fitness craze, and in all manner of racquet sports, golf, skiing, and cycling. But they are probably – we have no data – less likely to be gun owners, horseback riders, dart throwers, avid gardeners, hunters, and fishers. I may just be a nerd, but I do not own a gun, and neither do my Canadian Jewish friends. (In Israel, most Jewish households contain a weapon because of compulsory military service.) Historically, the Jewish presence in elite Canadian sports was more noticeable, because of top sports teams produced by local YMHAs, and outstanding athletes. But nowadays, as Jewish youngsters get into their later teens, they are less likely to try to become champion or professional athletes compared to Gentiles. Affluence, and alternate routes to economic success, are likely causes.

One final point. As in the case with residential patterns, Jews who socialize together do not do so randomly. Like seeks out like. In particular, ultra-Orthodox, Orthodox, non-Orthodox, and secular Jews are more likely to socialize – and marry – within their respective groups. Most of my close Jewish friends tend to be Jews like me, for better or worse. This voluntary social segregation probably minimizes frictions among Jews.

So the Jewish community is sustained by these subtle informal socio-cultural affinities. The stage is now set for us to explore the formal organizations of the community. These in turn rely on a foundation of social cohesion and interpersonal comfort among the various sub-groups that form Canadian Jewry. The organizations that comprise the Jewish polity are not simply administrative entities set up to get things done. They rest on a network of relationships, shared convictions, and bonds of intimacy.

THE JEWISH POLITY

The degree of specialization and sophistication found within the organized Jewish community is without parallel in any comparable ethnic or religious group. At times, it defies explanation. There are formal organizations for everything, and they make up a Jewish polity, a kind of self-governing quasi-state. Any polity – Canada is a polity – comprises governing institutions as well as organizations that provide services. It requires a decision-making process that links rank-and-file members to those who are chosen as leaders. An ethnic polity can be more or less "institutionally complete," a term first coined by Canadian sociologist Raymond Breton.[17] The term refers to the degree to which the organizations of a minority community can meet the various needs of its members. Jews are perhaps the most institutionally complete minority group in Canada, comparable perhaps to on-reserve First Nations and Hutterites, both of whom live apart from the general population.

A Jew can live his or her entire life within an institutionally complete Jewish community in cities like Toronto and Montreal. He or she can be born in a Jewish hospital; attend a Jewish daycare or nursery, Jewish day schools or supplementary schools, and summer camps; take Jewish studies courses on campus and socialize at a Jewish Students' Union; find work within a Jewish communal organization or Jewish-run private firm; pray within a Jewish house of worship; patronize a Jewish library and health club and play in Jewish sports leagues; get help from a Jewish social-service agency;

read Jewish papers and magazines, follow Jewish websites, listen to Jewish radio, watch Jewish TV programs; attend plays, concerts, and lectures of Jewish interest; spend his or her post-retirement years participating in programs at a Jewish Golden Age Centre; move into a Jewish old-age home or seniors' residence or hospital as needed, and be buried in a Jewish cemetery. Orthodox Jews involved in civil disputes can even go to a religious court, or *Beth Din*. The organizations that provide these cradle-to-grave services are funded by internal Jewish sources as well as in part by the government. And to this can be added the consumer goods from the private sector – kosher bakeries, restaurants, or butchers – which enhance this self-contained environment.

Political scientist Daniel Elazar outlined five spheres of communal activity: religious-congregational, educational-cultural, community relations-defence, communal-welfare, and Israel-overseas.[18] But the internal boundaries of the Jewish polity are fuzzy. Some organizations belong clearly in certain spheres: synagogues for the religious-congregational sphere and Jewish schools for educational-cultural. But other organizations are active in more than one of these spheres. This possibility of overlap, and resultant turf battles, is a constant feature of Jewish life. While many complain, in fact it is a source of strength. It reinforces the underlying pluralism of Canadian Jewish life and means that, despite formal agreements and jurisdictions, no one organization has a monopoly on a given area. For example, synagogues hold programs relating to Israel. Educational programming is found not only in Jewish schools, or university Jewish studies courses, but in synagogues, Jewish community centres, and arts centres like the Koffler Centre of the Arts in Toronto or the Segal Centre in Montreal. Some organizations, like the now defunct Canadian Jewish Congress, its successor, the Centre for Israel and Jewish Affairs, and the Jewish federations, directly and indirectly act in many spheres.

From the outside, and often from the inside, the Jewish polity can seem to be a jumble of similar or competing organizations. Here is a brief, simplified overview. The major national Jewish organization for a long time was the Canadian Jewish Congress (CJC). I found in meetings with other ethnic communal activists that it was seen as a model for their group. It was founded in 1919, lay moribund through the early 1930s, and then was revived in 1933–34 to deal with the rising tide of anti-Semitism overseas and in Canada. In its early days, the CJC was a force for democratic change and equality within the Jewish community, and a threat to the entrenched power and authority of the establishment, notably in Montreal. The CJC was seen as a "Parliament of Canadian Jewry." The Eastern European immigrants used it to challenge the authority of elite-run institutions such as the Baron de Hirsch Institute. The Labour Zionists were staunch advocates of the CJC, and were opposed initially by the establishment Federation of Zionist Societies. But by 1917, with large numbers of Jews in Europe needing aid and with the Jewish *yishuv*, or settlement, in Palestine growing, the community edged closer together. In March 1919, an estimated 25,000 Jews went to the polling booths and selected 209 delegates to the CJC: perhaps the greatest exercise of democratic governance in the history of Canadian Jewry. The second convention brought 3,800 delegates to Toronto in 1934. It was a feisty affair, with all segments of the community contesting elections.[19] It is ironic that, despite its early populism, in its later years the CJC was at times seen as the establishment, and occasionally challenged as being too timid in defending Jewish interests or as being out of touch with ordinary Jews.

The CJC effectively disbanded in July 2011. This was a watershed moment in the history of the formal organizations of the Canadian Jewish polity. Not without controversy, its duties have been subsumed under the newly formed Centre for Israel and Jewish Affairs (CIJA). The organization was founded in 2004 under the name Canadian Council for Israel and Jewish Advocacy. After nearly two years of restructuring, it was renamed CIJA in July 2011, subsuming all activities previously administered by Canadian Jewish Congress, Canada-Israel Committee, Quebec-Israel Committee, and the University Outreach Committee. Today it acts as the Israel and Jewish advocacy partner to local Jewish federations.

CIJA's organizers argued that this reorganization would improve advocacy efforts and save money, as well as better support the Jewish community and engage greater numbers at the grassroots level. But critics have questioned CIJA's accountability and representativeness. For instance, some have argued that the changes were made undemocratically, and that "CIJA has no basis to exist other than for some connected men getting together and making a decision."[20] Rabbi Philip Scheim, spiritual leader of Toronto's Beth David B'nai Israel Beth Am Synagogue and a member of the *Canadian Jewish News's* Toronto advisory board in 2011 told the paper, "It is not clear to me who CIJA represents. Unlike Congress, whose officers were elected by a body representing organizations and communities across Canada, CIJA seems to be a self-appointed body, beholden only to a very small group of extremely influential backers. This transformation is a major defeat for democracy in the Canadian Jewish community." Rabbi Scheim also took issue with the fact that a priest, but no rabbi, had been selected for the initial board.[21] In addition to a lack of representativeness, critics both within and outside the Jewish community have argued that money and power are being used within CIJA to advance specific interests, including a shift to the right, and are narrowing the dialogue with regards to Israel. There remains an ongoing debate within the Jewish community about the degree of democracy and representation within CIJA compared to the Canadian Jewish Congress.[22]

But neither the CJC or CIJA would reign unchallenged. The B'nai Brith, a national fraternal organization made up of individual lodges, has remained outside the CJC/CIJA umbrella, often bickering over jurisdiction. B'nai Brith usually petitions government on matters relating to anti-Semitism and human rights through the League for Human Rights, which it sponsors. Thus, both the CJC and B'nai Brith had standing before the Deschênes Commission on war criminals in the 1980s, and each presented separate briefs.[23]

National Zionist and Israeli-linked organizations also play a role in the polity, though specifically Zionist organizations have lost much of their importance in recent years. Zionist ideologies, like all ideologies, have lost their appeal, and most of Canadian Jewry supports Israel in general, thought there are serious disagreements about specific policy issues. The Zionist message is no longer that all Jews ought to move to Israel; it is that Israel is the focal point of the Jewish world. Zionist organizations and many Israel-linked organizations organize a variety of advocacy, educational, and cultural programs. Some organizations have a political dimension. Standing apart from these is Hadassah, the women's pro-Israel organization, which has more members than any other Jewish organization in Canada. It was founded in Canada in 1917, and today boasts tens of thousands of members. The CJC, the Canadian Zionist Federation, and the B'nai Brith jointly established the Canada-Israel Committee in 1967, the main lobby for Israel in Canada, which functioned somewhat comparably to the American Israel Political Affairs Committee, or AIPAC, in the United States. The Canada-Israel

Committee ceased to exist in 2011, its functions taken over by CIJA, which also generally supports the Israeli government's positions regardless of the party in power, and regardless of the specific issue. In addition to CIJA, the Canadian Jewish Political Affairs Committee (CJPAC) is a newer mainstream communal organization whose mandate, according to its website, is "to engage Jewish and pro-Israel Canadians in the democratic process and to foster active political participation." The official community position is generally that Israelis and not diaspora Jews are best placed to criticize their own government

But that has been changing. Public criticism by Jews of Israeli policies increased in the 1980s, though the levels were lower in the more deferential Canada than in the United States.[24] With the peace process of the 1990s, dovish Jewish groups such as Canadian Friends of Peace Now became less marginal. In 2011, a further left-of-centre political organization was created, JSpace Canada. This group describes themselves as a Jewish, progressive, pro-Israel, pro-peace voice in Canada. It is similar in many ways to J Street in the United States, or Canadian Friends of Peace Now. Moreover, as shall be discussed later, in the twenty-first century one can find clear anti-Zionist or anti-Israel Jewish organizations, such as Independent Jewish Voices, Jewish Voice for Peace, and avant-garde web resources like *Treyf*, a debatably Jewish podcast. These are seen generally as outside the conventional communal frameworks, or speaking for some younger Canadian Jews. Some are, or are seen to be, opposed to the continued existence of Israel as an independent Jewish state. They would sympathize with or support BDS (Boycott, Divestment, Sanctions) actions against Israel. It will be interesting to see if somehow space can be found within the conventional Jewish communal boundaries for groups such as these.

Other active organizations represent Israeli institutions for fundraising purposes. These are "Canadian Friends of" universities, yeshivot, and hospitals in Israel, or organizations like ORT (Organization for Education Resources and Technological Training), which runs vocational and training school programs in Israel. The Jewish National Fund is active in promoting agricultural settlement and forestation in Israel, while Israel Bonds raises funds from private and institutional investors. Other national organizations do not have an Israeli focus. The work of JIAS (Jewish Immigrant Aid Services) in the area of immigrant integration has been described earlier. The Simon Wiesenthal Centre is active in combating anti-Semitism.

It is at the local level, however, that the bulk of Jewish communal organization takes place and that the power concentrations are found. In Canada, as in the United States, the welfare federations are responsible for collecting funds and disbursing them to a variety of welfare, social, cultural, and recreational agencies. All these agencies are run by volunteer lay boards and paid professional staff. Occasionally, there is tension between the two, with power relations varying by agency and specific personalities.[25] Quite often, seasoned professionals wield more power than do elected or selected lay leaders from the community – not unlike the power wielded by senior public servants in Ottawa.

There are also health and welfare organizations indirectly affiliated with the Jewish community, such as Mount Sinai Hospital in Toronto and the Sir Mortimer B. Davis Jewish General Hospital in Montreal. These hospitals were founded initially because of the difficulties faced by Jewish doctors in securing positions, and in providing kosher food and a supportive environment for Jewish patients. But today they are funded basically by the provincial governments, and their staff and patient profile is decidedly mixed, though Jews are well represented. In theory, the state provides medical care and Jews can go anywhere. In practice, Jews are fiercely loyal to their hospitals. A community survey in Montreal in the 1970s found that most Jews listed health care as the number-one priority for the Jewish community. Recently, welfare concerns have loomed larger. In a 2010 survey of Montreal Jews, 90.7 per cent listed the Jewish poor and elderly as a top community priority. In a similar 2005 Toronto survey, 68.5 per cent listed services for the elderly, 67.4 listed the fight against anti-Semitism, and 63.3 per cent listed services for the poor as top community priorities.[26]

Other organizations were founded as alternatives to non-Jewish counterparts, such as the YM-YWHA, and continue to enjoy communal funding. Finally, private golf clubs and dining clubs were created when Jews faced exclusion from Gentile clubs. Even as access to these "Gentile" clubs is now generally open to Jews, some "Jewish" clubs continue to exist, such as Pinegrove in Montreal and Oakdale in Toronto. These clubs today are not exclusively Jewish, though they are informally known as gathering places for reasonably affluent Jews.[27]

A final element of the local community is the network of schools. Large cities have networks of private Jewish day and afternoon schools, which span the ideological range from ultra-Orthodox to liberal/secular. Historically, Jewish schools jealously guarded their autonomy, and in general were funded by fees and private donations. In recent years, federations have recognized a communal responsibility for Jewish education. They have established agencies to assist the schools, directly through educational services and indirectly by helping schools provide financial aid to needy students. I explore the issue of Jewish education in Chapter 8.

Anti-Semites at times accuse Jews of constituting a "state within a state," and of having dual – and conflicting – loyalties to their host countries. On the first part of the allegation the anti-Semites are right, with one important caveat. The Jewish polity is only *like* a state within a state (so is almost every minority polity). Jewish communal organizations have no power of compulsory membership or taxation and cannot use force. Jews can construct a meaningful, private Jewish identity while remaining detached from the Jewish polity. On the other hand, participation in the Jewish polity does not mean disloyalty or treason to Canada. In fact, there is no evidence that this high level of institutional completeness poses any conflict. Jews remain among the most loyal, patriotic Canadians. They cherish freedom (like other recent immigrant groups) more than many other majority-group Canadians, who have suffered less from its absence. That was the case for my parents. And many Canadian Jews are as active in the general Canadian community as they are in the Jewish community.

Canada and Israel have never been at war. But that does not mean that interests of Jews, or any minority group, are always identical to Canada's presumed national interest.[28] Japanese Canadians know all too well the dangers that can arise when Canadians seek to question the loyalty of a group of citizens *in extremis*. Far short of war, Israel provides litmus tests for Canadian Jewish loyalties. These questions allow of no easy answer; I will pick up the thread in Chapter 9, on Jews and politics.

CULTURAL SENSITIVITY

Jews are not forced to seek services, or live their lives, within the Jewish polity and its organizations. Since so many do, we have to assume that is what they prefer. Even if aspects of this participation come close to a kind of ghettoization – especially for the ultra-Orthodox – there is in general no coercion involved. So we wonder what Jews get out of it. The concern for "cultural sensitivity" in the provision of all manner of services in Canada has become a mantra among policy-makers in the human service area as well as for advocates of minority groups.[29] And effective ethnic polities are one way to ensure culturally sensitive – and presumably more effective – services.

There are historical roots to all of this. The expansion of the welfare state in the postwar period meant that governments began to fund or regulate the services that had sprung up to meet the needs of minority and immigrant communities. Canadians forget that most immigrant communities had thriving networks of organizations – political, recreational, social, cultural, fraternal – long before a full-blown welfare state or official multicultural grants appeared. As the public sector expanded, however, so did legitimate concerns for equal rights and equal treatment. Discriminatory, second-class treatment by mainstream institutions of the state, by design or by default, was no longer acceptable. The new assumption in the field of social services is that minority groups have specific cultures which must be considered.[30] Otherwise, they may be victimized by overt or covert racism or attacks on their self-esteem. For this reason, policies in areas like health, social service, education, law, policing, and media recognize that a diverse population requires diverse modes of service. Recognizing diversity is both fair and effective, better than offering homogeneous, one-size-fits-all services. Of course, there are limits. A liberal-democratic society like Canada does not welcome every type of ethno-specific cultural practice. The debate on wearing the *niqab* in public rituals such as trials or citizenship ceremonies is recent; the debate on female genital operations is perhaps the most dramatic case in point.[31]

One root of the concern for what we now call "cultural sensitivity" in North America can be found in the experience of Jews and Catholics at the end of the 1800s and earlier. Jewish and Catholic social service agencies and hospitals provided culturally sensitive services to the masses of Jewish and Catholic immigrants. Jewish agencies multiplied. In Montreal, the Young Men's Hebrew Benevolent Society was formed in 1863, later renamed the Baron de Hirsch Institute after a substantial donation in 1890 by the Baron. The aim was to care for the needy and elderly. The Federation of Jewish Philanthropies was set up in 1916 with twelve constituent agencies, including the precursor of the Jewish Public Library, a Yiddish library founded in 1905, the Herzl Health Clinic founded in 1907, and Mount Sinai, a tuberculosis hospital that opened in 1912 in the mountains of Ste-Agathe. In 1934, the Jewish General Hospital was created. In Toronto, the roots of the Jewish polity and the establishment of specific Jewish institutions date back to the same period. The Ladies Montefiore Benevolent Society was formed in 1878, the Jewish Mutual Benefit Society in 1896, a Jewish Old Folks Home in 1914, and the Mount Sinai Hospital in 1922. Toronto's Federation of Jewish Philanthropies was established in 1916 and became the United Jewish Welfare Fund in 1937.[32]

Well before contemporary scholars tried to analyze the meaning of culturally sensitive services for ethnic and racial minorities, Jewish social workers were wrestling with similar questions. (And not only Jews. In journals such as *Catholic Charities Review*, practitioners would seek to clarify what was essentially "Catholic" about the service in a Catholic welfare agency or hospital. Often, these debates revolved around out-of-wedlock pregnancy and adoption – issues still with us.) In publications like *The Journal of Jewish Communal Service*, professionals tried to define the "Jewish" values and principles which should inform a community centre or any other Jewish social-service agency. In recent years, Jewish federations throughout North America have renewed this concern with a vengeance. They seek to infuse more social services with a heightened Jewish consciousness linked to the continuity agenda. It is now common to begin board meetings of Jewish agencies with a *d'var Torah*, an analysis of a religious text. Another indication is the steady increase among the ranks of professional Jewish communal servants of observant, *yarmulka*-wearing Jews. Up until the early 1970s, Jewish social-service agencies were run overwhelmingly by secular or non-Orthodox progressive Jewish professionals, whose agenda was often concerned more with social justice than with Jewish survival.

The question remains: What is Jewish about these Jewish social service agencies? Do ethno-specific Jewish agencies, by definition, yield culturally sensitive services? Imagine a Jewish family in acute crisis, where a child wants to marry a non-Jew against the wishes of one or both parents and one or more grandparent. All hell is breaking loose, and they need counselling desperately. A secular state-run agency that employed non-Jewish professionals, and whose practice took no account of Jewish cultural sensibilities might not be delivering sensitive service. A situation of maximal cultural sensitivity would likely be one in which a Jewish client received help in a Jewish agency from a Jewish professional, and whose manner and content reflected knowledge of and sensitivity to Jewish culture. But even employing Jewish professionals might not guarantee culturally sensitive service. A secular Jew might not empathize with the concerns of an ultra-Orthodox Jew. A third-generation Canadian middle-class Ashkenazi Jew might not understand the culture of a struggling, immigrant Russian Jew or North African Jew or Israeli.[33]

The Jewish community is diverse. My parents' Montreal was that of Polish Jewish Holocaust survivors. Their world barely connected with that of the Canadian-born, acculturated, and affluent Jews of Westmount. Today, within the Montreal or Toronto Jewish communities, there are formal organizations representing Sephardi, Israeli, Ethiopian, and Russian Jews. These organizations are best able to meet certain needs of the sub-community not only by speaking their language, but by empathizing with their problems. Hasidic or ultra-Orthodox Jews need even more specialized services. In providing them, is the Canadian Jewish community acting responsibly, or risking further fragmentation? This is precisely the same question that Canada as a whole must ponder, regarding the limits of multiculturalism and the balance between diversity and social cohesion.

GIVING

If the range of Jewish organizations is hard to believe, so, too, is the extent of Jewish fundraising.[34] The Jewish concept of *tzedakah* (this Hebrew term has the same root as the word for "justice") differs dramatically from the Christian concept of charity. The Jewish approach sees giving as an obligation, a commandment. The Christian view sees giving more as an act of loving-kindness. Jews should rejoice when approached by a beggar, since they now have a chance to fulfil a commandment. For that reason, my father never left the house without some change for panhandlers. It is a Jewish custom to give travelers a bit of money when they are about to leave on a trip, to give to the first poor person they see when they arrive. The practice is supposed to guarantee a safe journey, since the traveler is now going not for his or her own pleasure but as a *shaliach mitzvah*, a messenger sent to commit a good deed.

Jews give to both Jewish and non-Jewish charities. According to one reported study, roughly 62 per cent of the donations made by individual American Jews to charity went to Jewish causes.[35] Jewish donations are split between domestic needs and funds for Israel. Historically, more than half the funds collected in the annual Appeal in Canadian communities were earmarked for Israel. But that percentage has been declining steadily over recent years, as Israel's economy strengthens and as Israelis recognize that supporting Jewish identity in the diaspora is, in the long run, the best support for Israel. Jewish philanthropy is prodigious, and Canadian Jews are among the most generous givers in the Jewish world. (Mormons continue to tithe, for the most part, which is a much higher rate of giving than among Jews.) But there is nevertheless a deep-seated gloom within the world of Jewish philanthropy. Annual federation campaigns have become flat, especially after the financial crisis of 2008. Fundraisers are worried about the declining loyalties of the next generation of Jews, especially the children of big givers, and the fear that Israel may lose its lustre as a target for philanthropy. In 1965, charitable donations accounted for 3.8 per cent of American Jewish personal expenditures. This declined to 2.4 per cent by 1995, increased to 3.2 per cent in 2000, then stabilized at 2.8 per cent in 2005.[36]

In general, as Jews become more accepted in mainstream North American circles, their philanthropic dollars flow to non-Jewish charities, notably universities, cultural institutions, and medical research. In fact, Jews have historically been large givers to both Jewish and non-Jewish charities. But there is a shift underway. As one Jewish communal leader put it, involvement in charities such as Centraide/United Way simply means "less money for Jewish causes."[37]

Jewish money that flows to communal bodies can be understood as in part fee-for-service and in part straight philanthropy. As indicated earlier, fee-for-service includes the purchase of memberships in synagogues or the JCC or Ys, or paying for Jewish schooling or summer camps. These fees usually are supplemented by fundraising to meet the total cost of the service; the more affluent users help support the needy. Similarly, the purchase of Israel Bonds can be understood as an investment, though an emotional one. Philanthropy, in theory, is writing a cheque for larger amounts while receiving nothing tangible in return.

In recent years, Jewish giving has been marked by three major innovations. First is the habit of directed giving to specific agencies or causes, rather than federations and appeals. An example is the

New Israel Fund, which receives donations aimed at progressive causes in Israel. Giving to specific institutions like Israeli universities or hospitals, or Jewish studies programs, or *yeshivot* in Israel or North America, has become more popular. Another example is giving to Holocaust museums, memorials, or educational centres. Yet another is the "continuity" focus of the past few decade, with its crisis atmosphere. The Birthright Israel/Taglit program is a prime example of an effort to meet this concern over assimilation. Even here, there have been competing thrusts, notably between "inreach" and "outreach" programs. The former want to strengthen the identity of Jews who are already involved; the latter to reach out to the unaffiliated or marginal. In both cases, funds are set aside for new continuity projects. (It may be arrogant for communal planners to assume that unaffiliated Jews are poor misguided souls who need information or special prodding. It is possible that most are people who have deliberately chosen a life in which Judaism plays little or no role, and are reasonably content. If they are not, most have access to Jewish friends and are bright enough to find out how to integrate back into the community. If they so decide, wonderful. But the return on the investment may not be great.)

The second innovation is the development of Jewish community foundations in the major cities. These foundations, in conjunction with federations, collect donations or bequests. The interest from these endowments supplements the money collected through the annual appeals. In this approach, the organized community retains a large degree of control through consulting with donors, though ultimately the donor can decide to target the gift. Historically, Jews have been much more comfortable with annual giving than with giving through foundations. They preferred to leave capital untouched. But this is changing. Bequests to foundations are a way of assuring that Jewish causes receive support long after the family patriarch has passed away, without leaving things up to children and grandchildren whose Jewish commitments may be diluted.

The third innovation is the thousands of private Jewish family foundations which have been created over the years in the United States and Canada. Many of these give only in part to Jewish charities. One study of Jewish American family foundations published in 2007 found that 21 per cent of total dollars went to Jewish organizations, 17 per cent to higher education, 16 per cent to health and medical, 14 per cent to arts/culture, 11 per cent to general education,

7 per cent to human services, 7 per cent to public society benefit, and 7 per cent to all other causes. In terms of the number of total grants, 24 per cent went to Jewish organizations, 17 per cent to human services, 13 per cent to arts/culture, 11 per cent to health and medical related causes, 10 per cent to public social benefits, 9 per cent to general education, 7 per cent to higher education, and 9 per cent to all other causes.[38] A similar breakdown for Canadian Jewish family foundations was not available.

Some of the family foundations are set up through community foundations; others are truly independent. The effect is to "privatize" the process of giving, and to allow individuals to set priorities which can affect the Jewish future. Many of these efforts began at the end of the twentieth century. If Steven Spielberg valued Holocaust remembrance and survivor testimony, if Charles Bronfman valued trips to Israel for every North American teen or young adult, if Ronald Lauder valued the rebuilding of Eastern European Jewish communities, and if Leslie Wexner valued training Jewish lay leaders and communal professionals, then that is what they and their foundations began to do. The explosion of activity in the entire area of Holocaust commemoration – from academic chairs to conferences to museums and monuments – has been driven more by committed donors than by communal planners. To label this as incipient anarchy in the world of major Jewish philanthropy would be an overstatement – for the time being. While these activities are all commendable, some more than others, there is certainly no master plan.

Canadian Jews generally give more than Americans. According to 1990 survey data, 41 per cent of Canadian Jews gave $100 or more to the Appeal, compared to only 21 per cent in the United States. Moreover, for those households who gave $100 or more, the average gift in Canada was $1,700, compared to $1,300 in the United States. This gap has persisted. A 2010 study of Montreal found that 62 per cent of Jews donated to the Combined Jewish Appeal and 68.7 per cent donated to other Jewish charities. A similar study of Toronto found that 78 per cent donated to the UJA in the past year or recently. These numbers are higher than in the United States. The 2013 Pew survey found that 56 per cent of American Jews made a donation to a Jewish charity or cause in the previous year.[39] But an emphasis on average or median gifts is misleading. It has been a rule of thumb in Jewish fundraising that about 5 to 10 per cent of the gifts yield 80 to 90 per cent of the dollars. An American study in 1987 found that of the $710 million raised by American federations, 60 per cent was raised from just over 1 per cent of the givers.[40] Wealthy families usually set the tone for each annual campaign by their gifts, and others follow suit. In Montreal, the Bronfman family was long the mainstay of the campaign, and established wealthy families took their cue from them. Toronto did not have a Bronfman, nor a similar large cadre of old-moneyed families, so communal giving, while extensive, was and remains somewhat less concentrated. The role of key givers has yielded its share of anecdotes. According to one possibly apocryphal story, Sam Bronfman summoned wealthy Montreal Jews to an urgent meeting just before the Six Day War in 1967. He asked those attending to take out their chequebooks and start writing. One person handed him a cheque allegedly for $250,000 – real money in those days. Mr Sam tore it up, and waited for more. What is interesting about this story is that while it may be apocryphal, no one doubts it could be true. Jews are not shy about asking other Jews to give. And in Jewish folklore, the needy are never reluctant to press their moral claim.

A beggar stops Lord Rothschild on a drive through his village, asking for charity. Rothschild gives the man ten zlotys. The beggar says, "But last year you gave me twenty zlotys." Rothschild replies, "But this year was bad for my investments." The beggar, "So just because you had a bad year, I should suffer?"

Jewish fundraisers, like beggars, are also not known for timidity.

A Protestant, Catholic, and Jew are shipwrecked on a desert island. The Protestant builds a big fire. The Catholic writes a huge "help" in the sand with a log. The Jew is lounging on the beach. They go over and ask, "Don't you want to be rescued?" He answers, "Look, before we left I made my pledge to the United Jewish Appeal but didn't pay up. Don't worry, they'll find me."

In any event, in 2014 the Toronto UJA annual campaign announced it had raised 61 million dollars; the Montreal CJA annual campaign raised 46.1 million. The Toronto United Way, which likely includes many Jewish donations as well, raised about $100 million in 2014.[41] In recent years, these Jewish figures have been increasing moderately at best, though community foundations and family foundations have become far more popular. The Montreal level is actually commendable, given the steady exodus to Toronto of potential givers, and the generally weaker economic conditions in the city. By the end of the 1990s, the Jewish Community Foundation in Montreal had collected an endowment of $104 million, Toronto an estimated $84 million, and Winnipeg an estimated $29 million.[42] By 2014 these numbers had increased to $366 million for Montreal, $530 for Toronto, and $85.8 million for the Jewish Foundation of Manitoba.[43] The interest on these amounts is still far less than the annual campaign, but the endowments are increasing significantly, and these amounts should be seen as relative orders of magnitude. The stock market run-up of the 1990s and the aging of Canadian Jewry fuelled the increase in bequests (the economic recession of 2007–09 however caused a decrease in Jewish philanthropy, which has slowly been alleviated). No other Canadian ethnic or religious group has established community foundations to the same extent.

Jewish family foundations play an even larger role than community foundations. Jews are highly represented among family foundations, to put it mildly. According to Canada's *Directory of Foundations* for 1997, then accessible to the public, there were 990 family foundations in Canada, with assets of $4.6 billion and total grants of $367.6 million (from 1993 to 1995). About 29 per cent of them made grants to Jewish causes, including Israel. These would overwhelmingly – but not entirely – be Jewish family foundations. Of these foundations, their total grants were $50.4 million (based on most recent reporting years), and of this amount $27.2 million, or almost 55 per cent, went to Jewish recipients. In other words, over 7 per cent of the actual amounts granted from all foundations went to Jewish causes.

How many foundations gave to other ethnic or religious groups? Very few indeed. Nine made donations to Ukrainian organizations, three to Chinese, two to Italian, thirty-six to Catholic churches and organizations, twenty-three to general Christian schools and education, and forty to Christian organizations in general. (There would be double counting here.) This is far below the 287 that gave to Jewish causes.[44] How does this compare with the American case? The 55 per cent Canadian figure is far higher. A dated estimate for large American Jewish foundations is that only one-third of their giving went to Jewish causes.[45] More recent information about family foundations and their possible Jewish target donations is difficult to access.

So we have established that wealthy Jews give to Jewish causes. They do so more than any comparable group, and more in Canada than in the United States. What of the broader range of giving? It is difficult to make comparisons with Christian churches, since the closest analogue would be giving simply to synagogues and direct religious organizations. According to 2010 Statistics Canada data, 33 per cent of Canadians donate to religious organizations. Just 24 per cent of Canadians under thirty-five gave to religious organizations versus 42 per cent of those aged sixty-five to seventy-four, and 49 per cent of those seventy-five and over. The average annual amount given per donor was $446 in 2010, while the median amount was $123 (for all causes, not just religion). These are below the average donations to the Jewish Appeal. Comparing levels of actual giving is difficult. One Canadian study based on a 2000 national survey of giving, volunteering, and participation included a sample of about 135 Jews and yielded different results. The average Jewish gift to all causes was $286. This was significantly more than for Catholics, comparable to liberal Protestants, yet far below conservative Protestants at $687. But only 28 per cent of Jewish giving went to "religious" causes, much less than for the other groups. It is not clear what can be inferred from such data. Jewish survey responses are one thing. A more objective measure is the total and per capita dollar amounts collected by Jewish federations and foundations, and amounts paid as synagogue fees, fees for membership in other organizations, Jewish school tuitions, and the like. And individual Jewish philanthropists make significant donations to special causes.[46]

Part of the extent of Jewish giving reflects the group's above-average incomes. But not all. Sociologist Reginald Bibby, a leading scholar of Canadian churches, has bemoaned the coming financial crisis facing churches in the wake of declining observance and memberships. This lament should not mask the profound differences between Christian and Jewish traditions of fundraising. As mentioned, Jewish fundraisers can be rough, but they are effective. Bibby described the emergence of typical "planned giving" programs in Canadian churches, and then writes, "Crass though all this might sound to some, especially those already wary of religious groups appeals' for money, it has become an extremely common practice in Canada."[47] Jewish fundraisers are perhaps less concerned with appearing crass when appealing for money. In their view, the end likely does justify the means.

PARTICIPATION AND DEMOCRACY

Jewish organizational life is full of duplication and turf battles.[48] Even the scheduling of events in the crowded Jewish communal calendar leads to days on which lectures, fundraising dinners, and other events conflict. This means there are enough leadership positions to go around, and organizations to suit everyone. To be sure, some organizations have few members. Their leaders are generals without troops, and they have inflated memberships, are poorly funded, and mainly for immigrants. This can be found among many minority groups.

Minority organizations fill a psychic and social need. Participating in them is a form of cultural identification, particularly for the leaders, who are often Canadian-born and middle-class. North America has traditionally valued joiners. Organizational involvement replaces religious observance or immersion in an ethnic culture as a way of expressing an identity. Many Jewish leaders run from meeting to meeting but are not highly religious. This kind of voluntary involvement persists long after knowledge of Yiddish is gone and keeping kosher is a distant memory. Even Jews in mixed marriages can use this organizational route as a way of expressing their Jewish identity.

For whatever reason, Jews are joiners par excellence. In 1990, 47 per cent of Canadian Jews claimed to belong to a Jewish organization, 31 per cent to do volunteer work, and 25 per cent to belong to a board or committee. By the twenty-first century, a decline set in. In 2010, 36 per cent of Montreal Jews said they belonged to a Jewish organization, fraternity, or club. About 25 per cent of Toronto Jews were similarly engaged. In 2005, of a list of twenty-three Jewish programs and organizations, the level of awareness of these organizations by Toronto Jews ranged from 17 to 91 per cent, with the highest ranking for the Bathurst Jewish Community Centre, which is the central address for Jewish services in greater Toronto.[49] My hunch is that when Canadian Jews join a Jewish organization, they are more likely to do so as Jews; when American Jews join, they are more likely to do so as Americans or volunteers.

We know a fair bit about the kinds of Canadian Jews who are involved with Jewish organizations. A 2010 survey of Montreal Jews found that 55 per cent of those who contributed at least $5,000 to CJA, 53 per cent of those living as a couple with no children, and 51 per cent of those who were sixty-five years and over also belonged to a Jewish organization. In terms of volunteering for a Jewish organization, 54 per cent of the population surveyed had done so in the past year. Respondents most likely to have volunteered were those who contributed at least $5,000 to CJA (79 per cent), those living in households earning at least $250K (70 per cent), the Orthodox (68 per cent), and couples with children at home (64 per cent).[50] In Toronto, we find that 30.6 per cent volunteered for Jewish organizations and 25 per cent claimed membership.[51] Both these numbers represent declines over the past two decades. Even though Americans, from the time of de Toqueville, have been seen as joiners, Canadian Jews match or beat American Jews in the organizational sweepstakes. In 2013, approximately 18 per cent of American Jews were members of non-synagogue Jewish organizations.[52]

And no group in Canada joins like Jews. A Toronto study found that Jews are more likely than other ethnic groups to know of communal organizations, to belong to an organization, and to express views about community affairs. And with the exception of Ukrainians – a group with long roots in Canada which was invigorated with a postwar wave of migration – the gaps between Jews and the other groups are large. On the other hand, most of those same Toronto Jews did not feel they were "close to the centre of community activities" despite their high levels of participation. Perhaps they felt that there is a core group of *machers*, or big shots, which is the real, establishment centre of the community. In any case, this perception contradicts others from the survey. Jews were most likely to claim that they knew communal leaders personally, had frequent contact with leaders, and were informed about their activities.[53] Yet they did not feel close.

There is a possible reason for this ambivalence. Jewish communal leaders carry a special burden, a legacy of the Holocaust. Jewish leaders in Germany, and in the ghettos – members of the Jewish Councils – have had to wrestle with accusations that they were not sufficiently aggressive in resisting the rise of Nazism or the actual implementation of the Final Solution. Another question is whether Jewish leaders in North America really did all they could to pry open the gates for desperate German Jewish refugees, or, later in the war, to encourage the Allies to make the rescue of Jews a top priority. In the 1960s, Jewish communal leaders began to be more assertive in defending Jewish interests and this has continued. Holocaust survivors were decisive in this move to greater militancy. An early case involved the response to a small neo-Nazi movement growing in Ontario in the 1960s. The established organizations were monitoring the group, but avoided public and violent confrontations. Many survivors felt that militant action was needed. On 30 May 1965, several hundred Jews and anti-Nazis protested violently against an attempted Nazi rally at Allan Gardens in Toronto, and several were arrested. The aftermath of the riot exposed the fault line between the militants and the more conventional communal leaders.[54] Establishment leaders no longer reflexively hold back; one thinks of World Jewish Congress president Edgar Bronfman's campaigns against Austrian president and former Nazi Kurt Waldheim, and to restore looted Jewish assets from European banks. Few leaders wish to appear timid in the defence of Jewish communal interests and security, even when they take cautionary positions.

Despite the fact that their leaders are not demographically representative of the range of the community, and despite the populist resentment of the "establishment," rank-and-file members of the community have been reasonably satisfied.[55] In fact, Canadian Jewish leaders likely are as responsive and representative as the Canadian government. Communal leadership is not a closed shop. At one level, wealthy Jewish families who comprise the "big givers" exercise power either through direct holding of office in the federations or though behind-the-scenes contacts with communal agencies. Top community professionals are in regular communication with these donors. However, through the 1970s and 1980s, positions of lay leadership slowly became more representative and meritocratic.[56] While in early years power was concentrated among elderly businessmen, this group has broadened with the infusion of other professionals (lawyers, doctors, academics, rabbis), women, the Orthodox, and younger people. In Montreal, francophone Jews have both established their own organizations, notably the Communauté Sépharade Unifiée de Québec, and begun to involve themselves as leaders in the general community. It is certainly true that the less well-off, the very old, and recent immigrants, remain underrepresented in leadership positions. (The same is true of Parliament ...)

But by and large, positions on lay boards are open to those who have the time and talent to contribute. Those who do well are generally rewarded with more responsibilities, as the demand for leaders exceeds the supply. The bias here favours the middle-class rather than an elite.

The big givers who play leadership roles are responsive to constituents, and on many issues actually reflect popular sentiment. If Jewish leaders are not socio-economically representative of their community, neither are members of the Canadian cabinet. There is probably a much better chance for a Jew to be active in Jewish communal affairs than for a typical citizen to play a meaningful role in federal, provincial, or municipal politics. It used to be said that Jewish communities were run according to the Golden Rule: whoever has the gold, rules. It is not yet clear what impact the advent of CIJA on the national scene will have on this link between Jewish wealth and Jewish communal leadership.

There is a venerable tradition within Jewish folklore that pokes fun at Jewish communal leaders and tries to keep them humble. The Talmudic sage Rabbi Gamliel, in the Ethics of the Fathers II: 2, warns: "Let those who occupy themselves with the [affairs of the] community do so only for the sake of Heaven." The message is that some leaders may line their pockets. An old joke, attributed perhaps apocryphally to Israeli Prime Minister David Ben Gurion, describes a conversation with President Eisenhower in which each leader claims he has the tougher job. Ike says, "I am the president of two hundred million people." Ben Gurion replies, "But I am the prime minister of two million presidents." And then there is the classic joke below.

A Jewish traveler arrives in town looking for a meeting with a Mr Goldberg, the head of the local Jewish community. The traveler asks for directions to his house. "Goldberg, that thief! Two rights, then a left." Getting lost again, he asks another person for directions. "Goldberg, that pig! Turn left for two blocks, and then a right." So it goes with more insults until the traveler finds Goldberg's house. As they sit down for their meeting, the traveler asks, "Mr Goldberg, being the head of the local community must take up so much of your time, meeting upon meeting. Why do you do it?" Goldberg sighs, "I know it's not easy, but I do it for the honour."

The history of all minority politics in Canada, and Jews are no exception, is a history of internal battles and divisions, of shifting coalitions and power blocs, and of changing political and communal agendas.[57] Even as most Jews recognize the efficacy of their leaders and communal institutions, they also recognize major cleavages. In one study, two-thirds of Toronto Jews felt their group is divided "very much or somewhat" between rich and poor, 29 per cent between political groups, 63 per cent between religious groups, and 43 per cent between regional groups. Moreover, 61 per cent of Jews perceived two or more divisions, far more than any other group.[58] Remember, the Bible describes how ancient Israelites were torn by division while wandering in the desert. This is nothing new.

Most of the perceived divisions are no longer dangerous. Apart from religious tensions, the community is likely more united than it has been in the past. For example, the organized Jewish left declined even before the end of the Cold War. The Workmen's Circle, long a mainstay of the immigrant progressive community, has shrunk in size and influence. The more radical United Jewish People's Order has all but disappeared. The community is united behind the basic principles of the welfare state. The problems of immigrant integration and concern for the poor remain, but without the earlier class and ethnic conflicts. Still, there have been policy issues which have challenged the organized community in the postwar period. By and large, after initial periods of resistance, the established organizations have co-opted the new groups and broadened the communal agenda to include their concerns. This has been the recurring pattern of conflict resolution in the Jewish community. There are only two litmus tests for inclusion today: support for Israel's right to exist, and for basic liberal democratic values. Thus, groups like the right-wing Jewish Defense League, which has advocated violence, and radical left-wing or ultra-Orthodox groups who are actively opposed to the very existence of a Jewish state of Israel, are to date outside the broad consensus.

The Jewish agenda has never been cast in stone, and has been surprisingly responsive to pressure from below. Among those Jews who are less conventional, or who are less deeply committed, mainstream Jewish organizations will have less impact.[59] Marginal or creative Jews generally have an aversion to formal, organizational life of any sort, whether in terms of large suburban synagogues or large-membership organizations. Smaller, grassroots, and more informal organizations will meet their needs. But if successful, these will eventually become incorporated into the Jewish mainstream.

The movements for Soviet Jewry, for Ethiopian Jewry, and for communal funding for Jewish education are examples of successful populist movements from the 1960s through the 1980s. The younger militants were eventually brought into the fold, and their agenda became the community's. Another struggle had to do with the Canadian Friends of Peace Now. For a long time, their criticism of Israeli policy, of both Likud and Labour governments, was considered too left-wing. As Montreal Peace Now activist Dr Frank Guttman recalled, in the early days the group had trouble finding a platform in the Jewish community, particularly during the Begin and Shamir years. They were unwelcome in most synagogues and communal agencies. But in recent years, once the peace process emerged in the Middle East, doors have been open to them, including in Orthodox synagogues. The group in 2000 claimed about 600 members in Toronto, 200 in Montreal, and smaller chapters in a few other cities. Today it is harder to estimate membership or support. In 2016, CFPN had close to 4,000 Facebook followers and a total of 1,100 subscribers who are contacted regularly by email or snail mail. Debates on Israeli policy continue to roil the Canadian Jewish community, as shall be discussed in chapters 9 and 11.

One early difference between Peace Now in Canada and in the United States was the policy not to take out paid ads (letters to the editor and articles were acceptable) critical of the Israeli government in the mainstream Canadian press. American Peace Now routinely sponsored such ads in the *New York Times*. All the Canadian ads have been "in-house" in the *Canadian Jewish News*. Guttman explained the difference thus: "We're Canadian."[60] The more reserved Canadian Jews keep disputes in the family. It is no longer clear if Canadian-American difference persists. In any case, the Canadian Jewish polity today tries to be an inclusive one, but fractious debates on Israel make this ever more complicated.

7

Between High Culture and Daily Life

From Literature and Art to Klezmer and Kugel

"To get away from Judaism is what most of those who began to write in German wanted, usually with the vague approval of their fathers ... this is what they wanted; but with their little back legs they were glued to the Judaism of their fathers, and their little front legs could find no new footing. Their despair over this was their inspiration."

Franz Kafka, in *Letters to Max Brod, Letters from 1902 to 1924*

"Julie, I told him, Julie – don't go!"

Wayne and Shuster, Canadian comedic legends, "Rinse the Blood off My Toga," skit about Julius Caesar and the Ides of March

THE ELEMENTS OF JEWISH CULTURE

The proof that Canadian Jews are a multicultural group is perhaps most obvious in the domain of culture. Yet this success comes with its own paradoxes. Compared to that of most other immigrants, Jewish culture is thriving, but this coincides with agonizing fears of assimilation and cultural dilution. And the contribution of Jews and Jewish styles and themes to the broader Canadian culture is large, despite – or maybe because of – a perceived cultural distinctiveness. Jews remain cultural insiders and outsiders at the same time.

What is Jewish culture? What isn't? It includes foods, rituals and customs (both religious and secular), objects displayed in Jewish homes, mannerisms, habits, and the elusive Jewish values, and music, art, and literature ranging from the iconic comedians Wayne and Shuster to Montreal's Yiddish Theatre and Toronto's Ashkenaz festival, from the novels of Mordecai Richler to the works of philosopher Emil Fackenheim and to the poetry and music of Leonard Cohen. Culture exists on different levels. It is also, in the anthropological sense, the stuff of everyday life. It is folk or popular culture. It is the high culture of an artistic elite. Religion is for some the bedrock of Jewish culture and will be explored in a later chapter. Because of the diversity of the Canadian Jewish community, there are several distinctive Jewish sub-cultures, some reflecting ethnic differences, others differences of ideology or lifestyle.

The interaction between any minority culture and the majority-group culture is often a two-way street. This has certainly been the case for Jews. Consider first that Jewish culture has been influenced by the Canadian context. Some see this influence leading to decline, others to transformation. Some see true Jewish culture only as "Judaic" culture, a unique set of religious values and traditions. Others see it as the product of social circumstances common to many European immigrant groups, or groups with a history of persecution.

Moreover, is there anything distinctively Canadian about Canadian Jewish culture, or is it the same as that originating in the United States? Philip Roth and Jerry Seinfeld are American, and have been appreciated by many Jewish Canadians. The insecurities of Canadian nationalism have few resonances among mainstream Canadian Jews, who are not generally America-bashers. Indeed, American Jews are comrades in arms. The American tie has often been a lifeline in the struggle to remain Jewish, even though Jewish culture by any per capita measure remains more vibrant in Canada. By force of numbers, American Jewry has been for the Canadian community a welcome source of creativity, personnel for Jewish institutions, and training for Jewish communal workers. In this sense, Canadian cultural nationalists and Jewish survivalists in Canada have diametrically opposed attitudes toward the United States.

Consider, as well, the impact of Judaism and Canadian Jewry on Canadian art and culture. Canadian culture, both in its popular and high forms, has been enriched, and indeed transformed, by the contributions of Jews and other immigrant groups.[1] Think of a bagel, preferably warm and fresh with some cream cheese and lox. Is it perceived as Jewish food, or is it part of the general Canadian food scene? This chapter looks at both Jewish culture in Canada, and the role of Jews in Canadian culture. Let us begin with the former.

JEWISH LANGUAGES

Language is a core foundation of culture. The two major Jewish languages in Canada are Hebrew and Yiddish.[2] In pre-war Eastern Europe, nearly every adult Jew could speak Yiddish. It was the daily language of most Jews, the exceptions being the urbanized and educated, though even those Polish or Russian speakers knew some Yiddish. Most Jewish men and some Jewish women could also read Hebrew, the language of the Bible and daily prayer. Very few could speak modern Hebrew, with the exception of some Zionists.

Yiddish has lost ground. In Canada, as in the United States, it has declined over the decades as a language of daily use, and as a mother tongue.[3] Only among certain Hasidic sects do we find Yiddish used daily, and given their large family size, there is some growth potential for Yiddish in this group. However, there has been a Yiddish revival of sorts on college campuses and through the growth of Klezmer music.[4] Hebrew is faring better. With the proliferation of Jewish school systems, and the effects of travel and links to Israel, knowledge of Hebrew has been increasing steadily. Not only do most Jews know how to read the Hebrew of the Bible and prayers, but many can now speak conversational Hebrew. Hasidim prefer not to use Hebrew, a holy language, for mundane secular purposes.

Here are the numbers, drawn in part from the tables in the appendix. Yiddish has declined as a mother tongue in Canada, from 21,400 in 1991 to 14,930 in 2011 (one must note that these numbers do not include those who claimed more than one mother tongue). It has also dropped by over 50 per cent as the language spoken at home, from 8,025 in 1991 to 3,130 in the early twenty-first century. The increasing Hasidic population, and some recent elderly immigrants from the former Soviet Union, has helped offset the loss as old-timers and older Holocaust survivors die off. More Canadians – 23,750 in 2011, down from 53,420 in 1991 – are able to converse in Yiddish than claim it as mother tongue or home language, which is a kind of good news datum. Contrarily, Hebrew is on the upswing. In the 2011 census, 18,105 claimed Hebrew as their mother tongue, up from 11,525 in 1991. These are mainly ex-Israelis. But a surprising

70,695 Canadians in 2011 claim they could hold a conversation in Hebrew, up from 52,450 in 1991. Here we see the influence of increasing levels of migration form Israel, Jewish education and travel to Israel.[5]

Hebrew is sustained mainly through Jewish education, whether in day schools and supplementary schools. Hebrew is also taught in Alberta, British Columbia, Manitoba, Ontario, and Quebec within the public-school system as part of heritage language programs.[6] The language is also promoted through the presence of Israeli immigrants in Canada. Israeli artists, singers, and dance troupes perform regularly in Canada, drawing both ex-Israelis and Canadian-born Jews to their concerts. Hebrew songs, both religious and secular, are sung at Jewish bar and bat mitzvah celebrations, and at wedding parties. Survey data confirm these census findings and interpretations. Older Jews tend to speak Yiddish and younger Jews tend to speak Hebrew.[7]

The future is brighter for Hebrew, with one possible exception. A 1997 study of adult Hasidim in the city of Outremont, Quebec, found 75 per cent claimed they were totally fluent in Yiddish, and another 12 per cent who could speak it, but not fluently.[8] And unlike other Jews, Hasidic fluency in Yiddish is not a function of age; 91 per cent of those aged seventeen to twenty-four claimed to be fluent! (A study of Sephardim in Montreal reported that one-sixth could speak "Spanish" fluently and about one-quarter somewhat. About 13 per cent – primarily elderly – said it was the language they spoke in their homes.[9] Many likely meant Ladino, or Judeo-Spanish.)

One of the great unknowns is whether the use of Yiddish in the Hasidic world – where it is spoken everywhere, taught in schools, and is the language of newspapers, magazines, and religious literature – can help revive Yiddish more generally. Could we conceive of a Hasidic/Yiddish theatre, or poetry dealing with religious themes? It sounds far-fetched (is that word English or Yiddish?) since their current cultural orientations are starkly different from those of the immigrant, secular Yiddish culture. In any case, the Hasidic milieu offers the only hope for a serious Yiddish language revival.

Yiddish has become very important in the symbolic sense, used not only for communication but also to mark specific rituals or occasions, as songs, prayers, names of food items, and curses. It often provides code words or signals among Jews, and is used to add flavour to conversations. Most Canadian Jews – and some non-Jews

– probably know some Yiddish words, like *schlep, schlemiel, goniff*, and *nebbish*; they can be found in reputable English dictionaries. It is hard to measure this symbolic significance, but I sense it is very real. Jews will twig to the use of Yiddish whether by the late Joan Rivers or President Obama. Some years ago, I was listening to a radio show dealing with auto repair, with a car mechanic as the host. She had mentioned that she was non-Jewish but married to a Jew. You can imagine my surprise when she told one caller in Yiddish, "Look, I don't want to *hack you a tchainick*" (literally, "knock you on the tea-kettle"; i.e. remind you repeatedly). This acceptance of Yiddish likely enhances Jewish self-esteem. The power of a language as a means to strengthen identity can persist well after fluency in the language is lost and it stops being a means of daily communication.[10] Television and movies have helped the spread of these Yiddishisms; from Johnny Carson's routines about the accountants H. and R. Gonniff to Mike Myers's impression of Linda Richman, the Coffee Talk *yenta* on *Saturday Night Live*. Knowledge of Yiddish can be used to measure "real" Jewishness. Most Jews know what *kvetch* (complain) means, but how many know the meaning of *kvell* (take pride in)?

But this does not foretell a Yiddish revival. Many ethnic languages become important as symbols and validating codes for members of minority groups. Used as symbols and for rituals, as well as in speech patterns and accents, ethnic languages blend with English and create "ethnolects." Italian and Caribbean Canadians perhaps come closest to Jewish Canadians in this sense.[11] These languages affect so-called "standard" English. American author Gore Vidal complained about the way in which the "Yinglish" of American Jewish writers would corrupt the English he wanted to preserve and defend.[12] In any case, Yiddish is in much better shape in Canada than in the United States. I recall many years ago the American Jewish leader Rabbi Arthur Hertzberg cheerfully beginning a lecture at Montreal's Jewish Public Library speaking in Yiddish, knowing that it would be appreciated by most of his audience. And he was right. For many observers, this greater tenacity of Yiddish – and Hebrew – could be construed as a uniquely "Canadian" aspect of Canadian Jewish culture. But it is largely a result of Canada's more recent immigration sequence. Eventually the gaps will narrow.

As for secular Yiddish culture, it is down but perhaps not out.[13] In the late 1960s during a visit to Montreal, the Yiddish author Isaac

Bashevis Singer recalled that when he arrived in New York just before the war, Jewish journalists had asked him to comment on the immanent death of Yiddish. With his trademark impish grin, he told his Montreal audience, "Fifty years later, Yiddish is still alive but those journalists are all dead." Yiddish is taught to school children in Jewish schools in Canada which trace their origins to the Yiddishist *folkshule* tradition. Yiddish is also taught in university courses. The Yiddish Theatre in Montreal, pioneered by Dora Wasserman, has continued to sponsor Yiddish-language musical productions annually, with thousands in attendance over the years. In 1998, the Quebec Theatre Guild extended a prestigious lifetime achievement award to Dora Wasserman and recognized her Yiddish theatre as an important element of Quebec's cultural scene. The highly emotional event took place at the historic Monument Theatre and was broadcast live on Radio-Canada. In Toronto, a Friends of Yiddish group promotes Yiddish language and culture, as does the Jewish Public Library in Montreal.

The surprising revival of klezmer music began in the late 1980s and 1990s. Klezmer (the term derives from the Hebrew words for musical instruments) is lively Eastern European Jewish music, traditionally played at weddings and Jewish festivals. Klezmer music is popular. In Montreal, an annual Klez Canada summer retreat, modelled on "Klez Camp" in the Catskills, has proved a huge success. These events are devoted to the study and enjoyment of klezmer music and Eastern European Jewish culture, and draw several hundred participants yearly. Canadian Jewish musicians such as the Flying Bulgar Klezmer Band, Finjan, Beyond the Pale, and others have pushed the boundaries of klezmer music in Canada beyond the Jewish community. The rapper Socalled, based in Montreal, mixes Klezmer with hip hop, while Jonno Lightstone and Brian Katz in Toronto push it towards experimental jazz. Toronto's annual Ashkenaz Festival brings thousands of people down to Harbourfront to take part in an array of concerts and other artistic productions. The emphasis at Ashkenaz extends far beyond klezmer music to fusion groups like Jaffa Road, who bring in Middle-Eastern musical forms, and includes displays of fine arts as well as literary and theatrical events. One of the high points is a spirited parade with many costumed participants that begins in Kensington Market, the old Jewish immigrant area, and wends its way down to Harbourfront.

Any discussion of klezmer music would be incomplete without acknowledging the role of queer culture in the genre's revival. Although klezmer was traditionally played at weddings and can thus be linked to more conservative aspects of Judaism, the music itself is not religious, but rather cultural in nature. Musicians and scholars alike argue that the queer affinity to klezmer (and to the Yiddish language) is rooted in the fact that both operate on the margins of Jewish society. The music therefore provides a secular avenue for LGBTQ Jews, and other progressive Jews, to express their identity while simultaneously identifying with the outsider status of Yiddish in contemporary Jewish life. It is therefore not surprising that many of the musicians active in the klezmer scene since its revival are openly gay. The Klezmatics, a group including both gay and straight members, and arguably one of the most famous klezmer bands worldwide, won a Grammy Award in 2007. Appreciation of klezmer and Yiddish among non-Jewish gays has in fact been attributed to genre's involvement in the gay rights movement starting in the late 1980s.[14] This affinity between klezmer and queer sensibilities is also true for the Canadian scene.[15]

But klezmer cannot sustain a real Yiddish revival. The days of Yiddish culture à la "Days of our Fathers" are gone. Yiddish is certainly being kept alive, but it will never again be the *mameh loshen*, or mother tongue, of Canadian Jews. Secular Yiddish culture is on life support. There are a very few non-elderly secular Jews for whom Yiddish and Yiddish culture remain central. These are Jews associated with theatre groups, or cultural groups, or klezmer music, or Yiddish as part of Jewish Studies programs. But there is no longer a stream of vibrant scholars, polemicists, writers, and poets working in Yiddish with a substantial audience for their efforts. For many years, Canada, and particularly Montreal, was home to major Yiddish poets such as Sholem Shtern, Melech Ravitch, Rachel Korn, and to a thriving Yiddish culture.[16] Even A.M. Klein, whose poetry was written in English, knew Yiddish and was deeply influenced by the immigrant Yiddish tradition. The influence of Yiddish now operates by osmosis, through sensibilities rather than language. Similarly, the Yiddish press has disappeared, though in its heyday Canada boasted three major Yiddish dailies: *Der Kenader Adler* (Canadian Eagle) in Montreal, *Der Yiddisher Zhurnal* (Jewish Journal) in Toronto, and *Der Kenader Yid* (Canadian jew) in Winnipeg. The *Eagle*, which began publishing in 1907, gave Canadian Jews an alternative to the New York Yiddish press and, like *The Forward,* served as an agent of subtle, gentle Canadianization and acculturation.

Writers can explore Jewish or Judaic themes in languages other than Hebrew or Yiddish or Ladino (Judeo-Spanish); they did so in earlier periods in Aramaic, Arabic, Spanish, German, Polish, and other languages. In Canada, they use English and French. A.M. Klein's and Naïm Kattan's poetry and Mordecai Richler's prose are full of Jewish references. Does this mean there has been a seamless transition from, say, Yiddish to English? No. At some point, any ethnic culture in North America is inevitably diluted as fluency in the mother tongue is lost. For now, the symbolic uses of Yiddish and Yinglish count for much, indeed more than most other immigrant languages. Hebrew is still sustained by its religious role and the tie with Israel. There is a much smaller constituency for Ladino in Canada, though scholars such as Judith Cohen at York University have been working at its preservation.

JEWISH LITERATURE AND ART

Jewish literary culture in Canada today is largely produced in English and, to a lesser degree, French. Authors such as (this is just a sampling) Leonard Cohen, Matt Cohen, Naïm Kattan, A.M. Klein, Irving Layton, Allan Levine, Eli Mandel, Seymour Mayne, Mordecai Richler, Chava Rosenfarb, Victor Teboul, Miriam Waddington, and Adele Wiseman are well-regarded Canadian writers of an older generation whose work has been influenced by Jewish history, the Jewish immigrant experience, and eternal Judaic themes. So too have been works by a younger generation such as David Bezmogis, Sheila Heti, Anne Michaels, Alison Pick, and Edeet Ravel. But their works do not speak with one voice, or one Jewish sensibility. Moreover, the degree and the nature of Jewishness in their writings and its significance remain a matter for debate.

What is Jewish about such writers? Canadian Yiddish scholar and Harvard professor Ruth Wisse has argued that we should not confuse the culture of Judaism – traditions, ideas and values – with the sociology of Jews, or what Jews happen to be doing. For her, Jewish culture must be clearly "Judaic" in its preoccupation.[17] Or at least it must be a totally enveloping entity, as was found among the pre-war Yiddish communities in Montreal, Toronto, Winnipeg, and of course

New York. According to Wisse, going to the Yiddish theatre would have been one small part of a total Jewish environment. Not so for a Canadian Jew watching Wayne and Shuster, Jerry Seinfeld, or Sarah Silverman. From her perspective, there is little today that could be construed as authentic Jewish culture in Canada. Jews writing about the daily life of Jews is not enough. Jewish art is not simply anything produced by a Jewish artist, be it a poem, a painting, or a song. The purist position argues that if it does not have authentic Judaic content, it does not qualify as Jewish culture.

My own position is less demanding. We can recognize that in North America there is no longer a holistic Judaic experience, and still find cultural significance, if not profound meaning, in the habits of everyday Jewish life. A work of Jewish art can be "about" Jews. This is a more sociological approach to the Jewish basis of Jewish art, to which I plead guilty. The difference is that between A.M. Klein's *The Second Scroll* or much of the poetry of Seymour Mayne, and the work of Mordecai Richler. The first two are in informed by Judaic tradition and lore. Publisher Malcolm Lester described Klein's work as "Jewish universalism as particularized in the Canadian experience."[18] Richler, in contrast, drew upon various Jewish experiences, and used Jewishness as a backdrop and even as a source of images or phrases. His fiction is an artistic rendering of the anthropological meaning of Jewish culture.

Jewish high culture in Canada also includes music and other art forms. Cantorial music, religious songs, or *zmirot*, classic Israeli folk music, and the newly revived klezmer music are authentic examples. Israeli popular music, of which there is plenty, is perhaps more difficult to categorize, but has an audience among Canadian Jews born in or close to Israel. Contemporary Canadian Jewish composers such as Srul Irving Glick and John Weinzweig have incorporated Jewish themes in their work. Well-crafted Judaic ritual objects such as Torah covers, seder plates, skullcaps, candlesticks, Hanukkah candelabras, or prayer shawls, also constitute clearly Jewish art forms. But Jewish painters and sculptors abound in Canada. What, if anything, about their work qualifies as Jewish art, or Canadian Jewish art? Consider a Canadian Jewish painter like Sam Borenstein, himself a product of a European Jewish background. He most often painted powerful Laurentian landscapes. But he also produced a portrait of the Montreal Jewish poet Esther Segal. And in his development as an artist, Borenstein was highly influenced by the

French-Jewish painter Chaïm Soutine. There is something going on here that is not simply Jewish, not simply Canadian, but in ways that are subtle but real, both Jewish and Canadian.[19]

FORMS OF JEWISH CULTURE

Jewish popular or folk culture can be found in Canada in many forms. One favourite is food. Jewish food is available both in strictly kosher form – under rabbinical supervision – and as "kosher style" and indeed food, kosher or not, has long been important as a marker of identity for Jews, as it has for other immigrant groups as well.[20] For most North American Jews keeping kosher is defined by a continuum, and distinctions are often made between keeping kosher in and outside of the home. In Toronto in 2005, 22 per cent of Jews surveyed claimed to be strictly kosher at home and another 28 per cent kept somewhat kosher at home.[21] In Montreal in 2010, 39 per cent of Jews surveyed said they ate kosher food at home "all the time," while 19 per cent said they ate kosher food outside the home "all the time." Over the years, kosher food has gone notably upscale in all large cities in North America. Kosher caterers have branched out into the exotic, offering mock shrimp and kosher Chinese food to discerning consumers. In 2008, the kosher food market in the United States was estimated at $12.5 billion, and had a retail value of $575 million in Canada. The North American kosher food market is estimated to have grown 15 per cent annually over the past ten years.[22]

There are an estimated 15 million "active kosher consumers" in North America. However, approximately only 15 per cent of the kosher consumers in the United States are Jewish. In Canada, the figure is 45 per cent. Among the non-Jewish consumers of kosher products are Muslims and other religious minorities, vegans and vegetarians, and non-Jews who may believe kosher products are healthier or of higher quality.[23] According to the Kashruth Council of Canada, 45,000 products carry the COR Kosher label.[24] It is not clear whether a non-Jewish consumer who accidentally purchases, say, ketchup with a Kosher label is included in the count of "active kosher consumers."

The many ways Jews keep kosher is itself a cultural phenomenon. It is too easy to poke fun at the gastronomic Judaism of "bagel and lox" Jews, who may be ignorant of the philosophy of Maimonides or the fiction of Agnon. Jewish foods in Canada are found not only in Montreal and Toronto, but in other cities as well.[25] A Jewish deli, with or without *kashrut*, has a certain distinctiveness, as does the way Jews eat, or at times overeat. Every Jewish holiday has some special food associated with it. There is matzo and horseradish on Passover, *hamantashen* (triangular-shaped pastry with prune or poppy-seed filling) on Purim, potato *latkes* (pancakes) on Hanukkah, apples and honey on the Jewish New Year, and no food on Yom Kippur. In fact, some of these foods mirror the process of embourgeoisement of the Jews. It used to be that matzo was just matzo. No longer. Now Jewish food sections in supermarkets during Passover are awash with matzo for every taste and lifestyle: egg matzo, whole-wheat matzo, onion matzo, garlic matzo, and chocolate matzo. There are even rolls, cakes, and cookies made from matzo meal. All this is a long way from "the bread of affliction" and the true meaning of Passover.

Jews love to eat, and then to complain about how they "overate," at the most recent holiday, wedding, or bat mitzvah. There is a kosher-style deli in Snowdon, a Jewish area of Montreal, called Fressers, which is Yiddish for gluttons. No festival at an Ashkenazi home, including Friday night Sabbath meals, seems complete without a fresh *challah* (egg bread), *gefilte* fish (poached deboned fish, usually carp or whitefish), chicken soup, a nice *kugel* (noodle pudding), chicken or roast beef, *knishes* (pastry stuffed with fillings like onions and potatoes or spinach), and carrot *tzimmes* (carrots cooked with prunes). Sephardic homes will have a comparable array of festival foods, such as *dafina* (a kind of *cholent,* or long simmering stew), *pastella* (like empanadas), and *mofletta* (a kind of crepe). Some Jews believe they have a special relationship with food, in much the same way that non-Jews have with alcohol. My students routinely downgrade the importance of food as a component of ethnic culture or identity. They think it is superficial. They want ethnicity, identity, and multiculturalism to be something deeper. What do they know?

Material culture – ethnic artifacts of all sorts – is another form of popular culture. Many of these artifacts are works of art; others are kitsch or Jewish bric-à-brac that is scattered throughout Jewish homes. A *mezuzah* (a decorative case containing Hebrew verses) on a doorpost, a Jewish calendar on the wall, a set of candlesticks, some Israeli or Jewish sculpture or artwork – Chagall prints are common

– or *tchotchkes* (knickknacks), some skullcaps lying around, all sig-
nify that this is a Jewish home. Many Jews wear around their neck a
Star of David or a *chai* (the Hebrew letters that spell "alive," a symbol of good luck). In my more cynical moments, I suspect there is an
unsettling correlation such that the bigger and gaudier the *chai*, the
more ignorant the Jew. Who knows ... But these symbols can also
have a material payoff. On his part-time teenage job delivering
pizzas, my son often had customers with a *mezuzah* on their doorpost. He would then flip his *chai* chain over his shirt so the Jewish
customer could see it, fishing for a bigger tip. It seemed to work.

Obviously, at one level, food and artifacts are less significant than
the ideas and values of traditional Judaic culture or the total cultural
immersion of the immigrant milieu.[26] But eating ethnic foods at holidays and other times, observing ethnic customs, and possessing ethnic artifacts are still important.[27] In a perverse way, the fact that
Jews now eat so many non-Jewish foods likely adds weight to those
occasions where Jewish foods are central. Canadian Jews are more
involved with their own popular and material culture than are other
groups. A Toronto survey asked Jews whether they consumed ethnic
food at holidays or at other times. About 90 per cent of respondents
said yes, with no decline between immigrant and third-generation
Jews.[28] We often underestimate the symbolic force of these seemingly minimal forms of Jewish identification.

THE POPULAR AND INTELLECTUAL JEWISH PRESS

Jewish culture in Canada is both reflected and shaped by a robust
media. Most prominent is the weekly newspaper, the *Canadian
Jewish News*. (Conflict-of-interest declaration: I wrote a monthly
column for the CJN for several years.) With an audited circulation
of around 40,000, the CJN is read by more than 100,000 people
each week. This includes those who access the website as well as the
hard copy. In addition, the CJN has 3,100 followers on Facebook
and 6,760 followers on Twitter.[29] There are separate Toronto and
Montreal editions which add local items to a core of national news
material. A good percentage of the Montreal edition is in French. In
this way, the CJN strives to create a national Jewish consciousness
and is a model for other ethnic community newspapers. I am amazed
to discover how wide the readership is, and that many Jews read it
from cover to cover.

Some Canadian Jewish intellectuals may criticize the CJN for being insufficiently intellectual or pluralistic or critical of Israel or the Jewish establishment. A case in point would be the fate of Dr Mira Sucharov, a regular columnist in the CJN with a progressive perspective on Israeli politics which stood out, compared to other columnists. In May of 2017, she wrote a column comparing 150 years of Canadian statehood with the fifty-year-long "occupation" by Israel of the West Bank. The column, in its content and use of the term "occupation," triggered an outburst of opposition by more pro-Israel readers. The editor, Yoni Goldstein, outlined a defence of the decision to publish based on a commitment to finding space for less conventional perspectives. But Professor Sucharov soon announced her resignation as a columnist for the CJN, thus eliminating a coherent and progressive voice from the paper.[30]

Of course, there are many other periodicals that play those important roles. The CJN thus reflects the mainstream Jewish community. On balance, the paper does hew to a kind of centre-right perspective, and is generally supportive of Israeli government positions, as shall be seen below. It covers a wide range of communal activities and reflects a diverse portrait of Judaism.[31] There are other Jewish community newspapers from coast to coast, and they too are read. In Montreal, about 76 per cent of Jews claim to read a Jewish or Israeli paper or magazine; in Toronto, 49 per cent claim to read the CJN "often."[32] About 34 per cent of American Jews claim to read a Jewish newspaper or magazine.[33] The Jewish ethnic press today in Canada is now in English or French (*La Tribune Juive* is a periodical in Quebec), and not in Yiddish. This explains in part why readership does not decline following the immigrant generation, as it does dramatically for all other ethnic groups.[34]

As successful as the Canadian Jewish press is in a communal sense, it does not, it cannot, nourish a cohesive sub-community of Jewish intellectuals with their own institutions and publications. In the United States, with a much larger Jewish population base, the "New York Jewish intellectuals," such as Irving Howe, Irving Kristol, Nathan Glazer, Norman Podhoretz, were active throughout the postwar period, talking to and arguing with each other. In recent years, American intellectuals have used Jewish journals and websites like *Commentary, Moment, Tikkun, Tablet, The Forward*, the *Jewish Review of Books*, non-Jewish periodicals like the *New York Times, New Republic*, the *Nation*, and the *New York Review of Books*, and

English versions of Israeli newspapers like *Haaretz* and the *Jerusalem Post,* to create a virtual community of American Jewish intellectuals, in print and online. The debates can turn nasty, as in any family feud, but they can also invigorate. Nothing comparable exists in Canada. There is simply an insufficient critical mass of engaged Jewish writers.[35] According to critic Robert Fulford, Canadian Jewish writers represent "separate dots of light," while in the United States they are busy "hating each other and loving each other."[36]

Despite this failure, there has been an interesting trend within the non-Jewish press. No Canadian newspaper matches the *New York Times* as a "Jewish" paper of record. Again, there are issues of critical mass. But it seems to me that over the years, mainstream national Canadian papers, including the *Globe and Mail* and later the *National Post* have been increasing news coverage and opinion pieces on Jewish issues. They in fact complement the official Jewish press. The bittersweet maxim "Jews are news" is at work. For example, just in January of 2016, the *Globe and Mail* featured a news story about the republication of *Mein Kampf* in Germany and a story about the insecurities of the Jewish community in France, as well as a debate over a mural in York University's Student Union building considered by some to be anti-Semitic.[37]

The intellectual conversation about the global future of Jewish life is rooted in the United States and Israel. All other diaspora communities are, to some extent, bystanders. In the Canadian case, it may also be that too much civility is not conducive to tough-minded polemics. Canadian Jewish intellectuals have to piggyback onto American debates, both reading them and participating in them. Canadian nationalism is not a dominant concern in the discourse of Jewish intellectuals. As mentioned earlier, in these Jewish debates there is no reflexive anti-Americanism. The ideological debates around religion and secularism, socialism or capitalism, liberalism or conservatism, Zionism and non-Zionism, in Jewish and general intellectual journals have often been generic or American. In the twenty-first century, some newer public intellectuals have emerged within the community articulating distinctive voices: for example, McGill history professor Gil Troy articulates centrist viewpoints, and Mira Sucharov of Carleton's Political Science Department, the liberal/left. Jewish studies programs nourish a significant number of academics who focus on Jewish subject matter in their teaching and research. Some of these scholars write in Canadian or general intellectual outlets on Jewish themes. The field of Canadian Jewish studies itself has emerged in recent years, and is represented by an association and a journal of the same name.

ISRAEL AND THE HOLOCAUST

Any discussion of contemporary Canadian Jewish culture must recognize the thematic roles played by Israel and the Holocaust. Many Jews likely think about these two issues far more than they think about God.

Israel is far more than just a political concern for Canadian Jews. It is a central part of day-to-day Jewish culture. About 75 per cent of Jews in Montreal and 73 per cent of Jews in Toronto had been to Israel at least once, according to surveys of 2005 and 2010. Of Montreal Jews surveyed, 87 per cent agreed that "the survival of the state of Israel was very important," and 91 per cent disagreed with the statement "If Israel ceased to exist tomorrow, it would make no significant difference to me." Thirteen per cent of Toronto Jews said that they have seriously considered moving to Israel.[38] Comparatively, the Pew survey found that only 43 per cent of American Jews in 2013 felt that caring about Israel was an "essential part of being Jewish" and only 43 per cent have travelled to Israel.[39] Approximately 23 per cent of the Canadian Jewish population can converse in Hebrew, which enhances the tie to Israel.[40] In contrast, among American Jews, only 12 per cent claim they can have a conversation in Hebrew, and only 52 per cent know the Hebrew alphabet.[41] Israel has an important place in the curriculum of Canadian Jewish schools, and many of the teachers are of Israeli origin. Most Jewish high schools sponsor summer-long tour programs in Israel for their students, and other organizations have similar summer and even year-long programs.

Many Canadian ethnic groups retain ties with an ancestral homeland, particularly within the immigrant generation. But by later generations, these links have dramatically weakened. Canadian Jews developed extensive networks of travel, philanthropy, and cultural exchanges with their "homeland," Israel. *Yom Ha'Atzmaut*, Israel's Independence Day, has become a major date on the Jewish communal and indeed religious calendar. For some Jews, Israel has become the very essence of their identity. This is reinforced because Israel, as part of the troubled Middle East, is always in the news. Jews ride the emotional rollercoaster of hope for peace and despair each time violence is renewed between Israelis and Palestinians or the Israeli government takes steps with which they disagree. The ties are also strengthened in more conventional ways, as thousands of Canadian Jews have gone on *aliyah* (emigrated to Israel) and many Israelis now live in Canada. No avenue is left unexplored to expand links with Israel. The Maccabiah Games serve to enhance the Canadian-Israeli tie through sport. Canadian philanthropy helped build the Olympic-size ice-skating rink in Metulla. Summer programs in Israel now include hockey camps for Canadian and Israeli youngsters run by Canadian hockey coaches and players. A newspaper story about Canadian Jews in Israel described ex-Montrealers Ruby and Linda Wolbromsky, and emphasized their collection of NHL hockey sticks: Jean Beliveau's, Ralph Backstrom's, and Terry Harper's, to be exact.[42] I can relate. I spent 1970–71 studying at the Hebrew University of Jerusalem. When the Stanley Cup play-offs came around, a group of us hockey-starved Montreal Canadiens fans would gather eagerly to listen to cassette tapes of play-off games.

Can anything weaken the tie to Israel? Possibly. Israel is a strong industrial or post-industrial country, developing its own cultural style. As the generation of the Holocaust in the diaspora dies off, their children and grandchildren may not share their visceral tie to Israel. The next generation of Jews will not be raised with an image of Israel as a fragile, weak state at the mercy of hostile Arab neighbours. They may sympathize more with the Palestinian cause. Meanwhile, the mainstream community supports Israel financially. Approximately 38 per cent of American Jewish charitable dona-tions go to Israel. When adjusted for inflation, American donations to Israel dropped 15 per cent from 1975–1985, rose back 15 per cent by 1995, then rose 20 per cent by 2007. Studies published by Brandeis University in 2012 and by *The Forward* in 2014 estimate that between $1.7 and $2 billion are given to Israeli causes annu-ally.[43] 12 per cent of Montreal's CJA budget in 2015–16 was allo-cated to Israel related causes, and 28 per cent of Toronto's UJA budget for 2014–15 was given to causes in Israel and overseas. These numbers are an underestimate of Canadian Jewish giving to Israel, since they do not include donations made directly to Israeli institutions. In this case, it is possible that the percentage of Canadian Jewish giving to Israel would match or exceed the American 38 per cent.[44]

The cycles of euphoria and angry despair regarding the "peace process" can have unpredictable, and contradictory, consequences. In recent years, many progressive Jews have lost heart about the prospect for a peace settlement along the lines of a two-state solution in the Middle East. At the same time, Jewish students on North American campuses report energized anti-Israel campaigns by the growing number of students supporting the BDS movement and Israel Apartheid Week. An American Jewish newspaper published a list of the forty "worst" campuses for North American Jewish students in 2016, (with perhaps suspect methodology) based largely on anti-Israel and anti-Semitic incidents and reports. The University of Toronto and McGill ranked among the five worst such universities.[45] Many Jewish supporters of Israel feel under siege, undermined by their perception of the media's misplaced evenhandedness, or at times a perception of anti-Israel bias. Jewish travel to Israel rises and falls depending on the security situation for both Jewish and non-Jewish visitors. By 2013, Canadian Jewish travel to Israel was down 2 per cent from 2012, at 72,000 visitors.[46] In general, tourism to Israel in 2014 remained similar to that in 2013 (56 per cent of tourists were Christian).[47] I recall a summer visit to Israel during the first intifada in the late 1980s. My Jerusalem hotel was nearly empty. One day, two buses pulled up to the hotel, but they were not full of North American Jewish tourists, who had stopped coming. One was a German tour, the other was Japanese. As the enthusiastic visitors spilled out of their buses, I marvelled in a bittersweet moment at the devotion of the former Axis powers ...

At present, liberal Jews critical of Israeli policies voice displeasure with the Israeli government. Should a serious attack be launched against Israel, perhaps those reservations would decrease. Certainly, tensions between the Orthodox and the non-Orthodox in Israel have eroded some liberal diaspora support. This has been expressed as feeling a growing "discomfort" in Jerusalem, or efforts by non-Orthodox Jewish women to have greater access to pray at the Western Wall where they have been surrounded by the increasingly belligerent Orthodox. For some, Israeli Judaism, formally Orthodox, was not their Judaism. A diasporic perspective argues that Jewish life in North America, for those who want to revel in it, can be just as rich as life in Israel. Israeli Judaism is a polarizing force separating a minority of Orthodox, a segment that is traditional, and a near majority who are either indifferent or hostile. In fact, the attitudes of non-Orthodox Israelis to religious Judaism can be complex and nuanced, even for those who see the Jewish New Year mainly as a time to go to the beach.[48] I recall spending a Passover in Jerusalem as a student in a Hebrew University dormitory with ten Israelis in our unit. As Passover approached, the major concern for most of my roommates was establishing a rotation for trips to the bakeries of Arab East Jerusalem to guarantee a steady supply of fresh bread.

Apart from political and cultural bonds, there are strong ties of family that bind North American Jews to Israel. There are distant cousins to visit. But over time, many scenarios are plausible. In one, the generations will die off and the cousins will become more distant. As the Sephardi population of Israel increases, family ties to the largely Ashkenazi population in North America might weaken. Israel may develop an even more indigenous Israeli culture, more removed from North American Jews. If, in this scenario, Orthodoxy and ultra-Orthodoxy in Israel continue to grow with their political power unchecked, more and more non-Orthodox Jews (and perhaps some modern Orthodox) will be disenchanted with the country.

Most Jews reflexively feel that a widening of the gulf between Israel and the diaspora would be disastrous. But this cannot be proved. Remember that the Jewish future is unpredictable. The fact is, for most of the past two millennia, the ties between diaspora Jews and Israel were weak, far weaker than they are now. This was true even for the first part of the twentieth century. If the ties were to weaken again, then non-Orthodox North American Jews might in the distant future regard Israel as Italians in North America regard Italy. Italy still means a great deal to many Italian Canadians. Israel would still be important for Jews, but it might not be central to their Jewishness. Israel could have a symbolic rather than concrete role, like the mythic Zion common throughout the pre-state centuries.

At present the ties remain fairly strong. On balance, any renewed threats to Israel's security will likely strengthen them dramatically. At the same time, there is evidence that younger, more liberal Jews may have a more nuanced commitment to Israel, related to the growth of anti-Israel sentiments on campus. In any case, visits to Israel have emerged as a key element in the strategy for Jewish continuity. In the early 1990s, Canadian philanthropist Charles Bronfman's CRB Foundation commissioned a study to understand how "the Israel experience" affected Canadian Jews.[49] It is hard to distinguish cause from effect in evaluating the link between Israel trips and Jewish identification. But adults who have been to Israel score higher on measures of Jewish involvement. The study asked them directly about experiences which had a "strong positive impact on Jewish life." The most cited response was "a trip to Israel." Similarly, for those who indicated when their commitment to Judaism crystallized, the highest response was a trip to Israel again – even higher than a birth of a child, or marriage. As a result of these findings, Bronfman helped create Birthright Israel, a program that started in 2000 to send young North American Jewish adults on free ten-day educational tours to Israel. Research suggests that this program has been very successful in terms of fostering strong connections to Israel among Jewish youth, and even in terms of stemming intermarriage rates. One recent study of the program's impact found that participants were more likely to feel very much connected to Israel compared to non-participants, and were 45 per cent more likely to be married to someone Jewish. At the same time, researchers have elucidated a critical analysis of these and other Israel trips as contributing to a narrative which obscures the oppression experienced by Palestinians in Israel and simply promotes a narrow Jewish/ Zionist nationalism.[50] It is still too early to know the very long-term impact of Birthright Israel trips, but initial results reveal an increased tie to Israel and to Jewishness. In any case, committed Jewish families include a trip to Israel, if they can, as part of the Jewish socialization of their children.

While the mainstream community remains connected to and supportive of Israel, there are emerging challenges. Progressive Canadian Jews are feeling alienated from that mainstream, and mainstream supporters feel the antagonism from critics of Israel both within and outside the Jewish community.

In recent decades, the Holocaust has also emerged as a central cultural theme of diaspora Jewish life. This has been a surprise. In the immediate aftermath of the war, North American Jews responded with silence and guilt to the horrors of the *Shoah*. Only among the sub-communities of Holocaust survivors did the memory endure. I recall going to annual Holocaust memorial events in Montreal in the late 1950s or early 1960s with my parents which were attended only by survivors themselves. Yiddish would often be spoken at these events.

The Eichmann trial, and in 1967 the Six Day War, cracked the silence. Slowly but surely, the Holocaust emerged on the Jewish community's cultural and political agenda. The NBC miniseries *Holocaust*, in 1978, brought the Shoah to a popular and non-Jewish audience in a way that previous films had not, paving the way for *Schindler's List* two decades later. No longer is the Holocaust seen as the province of Jews alone. Canadian universities offer courses in the subject which are taken by non-Jews as well. Innovative movies, dramas, or even comedies, are now produced. The hunt for Nazi war criminals emerged tentatively as a Jewish policy concern and culminated in the exposure of the Nazi past of Austria's Kurt Waldheim. (In Canada, little action has been taken. Trials in Canada and efforts at denaturalization have generally not been successful.) And the fallout from the war continues. European banks were discovered to have held on to dormant Jewish bank accounts. Crosses were erected near the gates of Auschwitz by militant Polish Catholics, to the consternation of Jews. Canadians debate whether to include a Holocaust exhibit as part of a revamped Canadian War Museum. Prosecutions in Canada were launched earlier against proponents of Holocaust denial like Ernst Zündel, Jim Keegstra, and Doug Collins (see Chapter 11 on anti-Semitism). Holocaust denier David Irving launched, and lost, a libel trial in England. Works of art stolen from Jewish owners by the Nazis were found and returned. Claims of fraud of millions of dollars were directed against the Conference on Jewish Material Claims against Germany. A public debate arose when Germany granted permission to republish an annotated version of *Mein Kampf*. And so it goes, on and on.[51]

Holocaust-related events revive old memories and animosities. A Jewish delegation accompanied Prime Minister Jean Chrétien on a visit to Auschwitz in January 1999, part of his state visit to Poland. Polish Canadians, angered by their exclusion from this part of the delegation, threatened the prime minister with political repercussions. As they reminded all who would listen, they too suffered during the war, and tens of thousands of non-Jewish Poles worked and died at Auschwitz. For Jews, it seemed like Poles were eager to muddy the waters of Jewish tragedy with their own, and also deflect attention away from consideration of possible complicity. Poles comprise the largest group of nationals among the "Righteous Gentiles" identified by the Israeli Holocaust museum, Yad VaShem, who risked their lives to save Jews during the war. But Winnipeg historian Allan Levine reminded *Globe and Mail* readers of a study by Israeli historians which concluded that "the overwhelming majority of Jews who approached Poles for help fell prey to the Nazi police or the gendarmerie, to rabid anti-Semites in Polish society and the Polish underground." Bernard Wisniewski of the Canadian Polish Congress responded to Levine's "accusatory musings" in his own op-ed article. His article is a defence of the record of Polish resistance against the Nazis replete with exculpatory quotations from Jewish scholars. Subsequent visits to Auschwitz by Prime Minister Stephen Harper and then Justin Trudeau in 2016 managed to avoid such inter-ethnic squabbling. Indeed, Prime Minister Trudeau's inscription was careful not to itemize origins of victims or perpetrators, but wrote in general terms about "humanity." In any case, Poles want nothing (like a blanket charge of collaboration) to detract from their status as victim. In this they resemble Jews.[52]

The Holocaust shapes Jewish culture and identity in many ways. The 2013 Pew Survey of American Jews found that 73 per cent of respondents agreed that "remembering the Holocaust is an essential part of what being Jewish means to them," far more than any other Jewish trait.[53] Even as the survivor generation dies off, for many of their children and other Canadian Jews it may be too soon for the terms "German," "Polish," or "Ukrainian" to evoke a neutral response. Holocaust survivors and students of the Holocaust at times engage in a grisly debate to see which European nation was the "worst" in its treatment of Jews and complicity with the Final Solution. Surprisingly, Germany is not always the first choice. My parents, both survivors, refused – perhaps illogically – to visit Poland or Ukraine after the war. The memories were too bitter. But my father visited Germany and Austria with few qualms. (For other survivors, the reverse was the case.) After my father moved to Israel, he decided to vacation one summer in the German Alps near Munich, where I visited him. The scene was Kafkaesque, and given that Kafka's sisters were liquidated by the Nazis, the term is doubly apt. His hotel was packed with aging Israelis of European extraction speaking German, many Holocaust survivors. They all seemed pleased with their holiday, and the German hotel staff was exceptionally polite.

In any case, living in Canada dulls the edge of potential confrontations and old wounds are never fully reopened. This was true for Ukrainian-Jewish relations in the wake of the Deschênes Commission on war criminals and the Demjanjuk trial in Israel. The temperature rose, but never boiled.[54]

The Holocaust fills an ideological vacuum for contemporary Jewry, apart from its specific impacts on survivors and sensitive Jews. It continually recertifies the Jewish communal claim to victimhood, which for some Jews is part of their identity. This is a valuable counterweight to the image of Jews as oppressors of Palestinians, or as wealthy supporters of the status quo. It also is a main mobilizing force for Jewish survival, and for the aggressive defence of Jewish interests. After Auschwitz, according to philosopher Emil Fackenheim, the eleventh commandment for Jews is simply to survive. "Never again" has become a rallying cry with deep resonance for modern Jews of any persuasion. It is also a warning to North American Jews to be vigilant, to act decisively for their brothers and sisters.

Indeed, over the decades, the agents of Holocaust villainy have grown and diversified. Early on, the guilty were the Nazis, or, if one preferred, the Germans. Later, guilt extended to active collaborators, including many prosecuted for war crimes. Later still, guilt extended to the Allies, who might have done more to admit Jewish refugees, or to stop the Nazi threat early on, or at least to bomb the camps and railway links so as to stop the slaughter and, after the war, to hunt down Nazi war criminals. Corporations, banks, insurance companies, museums, government agencies – German, other European, even American or British, and, who knows, maybe Canadian – are guilty. Finally, some guilt remains for North American Jewish leaders, who were not adequately militant, and even European Jews, in the persons of those who worked as *kapos* in the camp or as members of Jewish Councils. The point here is not to ascertain the accuracy or motivation behind these new stages in the evolving discourse on Holocaust guilt. Rather, the expanding universe of Holocaust guilt helps explain the staying power of the Holocaust in Jewish consciousness.[55]

The Holocaust has also invaded Canadian Jewish school curricula with a vengeance. I was a student in a Montreal Jewish day school from 1955 to 1966, and I can barely recall any discussion of or focus on the Holocaust. My children's experience in Jewish day schools has been quite different. Every year, the Holocaust played a role in books they read – in Hebrew, English, and French – and in special projects. How much is enough? The March of the Living is an annual pilgrimage in which Jewish teens are taken for a gut-wrenching tour of European death-camp sites followed by a visit to Israel. The effort is well-meaning, and two of my children went. It was a deeply moving experience. But I have no illusions. The trip may be many things, but one of them is heavy-handed shock treatment. It socializes Jewish children into a fearsome commitment to survival. Children in Jewish day schools, as well as increasing numbers of children, both Jewish and not, from other schools, are also taken on tours of Holocaust centres or museums. Holocaust survivors are routinely invited into schools to tell their stories, both to sensitize the students and undermine the Holocaust-denial movement.

This new centrality of the *Shoah* in Jewish education, and in the discourse of Jewish public life, can be a mixed blessing.[56] It risks reducing a complex and rich Jewish heritage into a vale of tears, or what historian Salo Baron called "the lachrymose" interpretation of Jewish history.[57] Jewish identities ought to be built on a positive foundation. Even Holocaust educators have twigged to the danger and begun to emphasize the rich legacy of Eastern European culture as part of their program and that of the March of the Living. Imparting the "lessons" of the Holocaust is also an ambiguous exercise. For some, the lessons are the importance of tolerance of all minorities, and a vigilant defence of human rights and freedoms. For others, the lessons may be those of an ethnocentric self-reliance and a rejection of the non-Jewish world.

Holocaust survivors have emerged as an interest group in Jewish political life. Moreover, they and their children, the "second-generation," have become the object of special curiosity and compassion by Jewish health care and social service workers. The "survivor syndrome" emerged from clinical reports and studies as a pattern of psychological disorders, including depression and psychosomatic symptoms, which allegedly did not spare their children either. Self-help groups aimed at the children of survivors proliferated in large cities, which inadvertently perpetuated the stigma. Yet my own research with Dr John Sigal calls those stereotypes into question. Looking at non-clinical (that is, more representative) samples of survivors and their children, we were struck by the resilience of survivors, despite ongoing torments, and by the high level of socio-economic achievement and psychological adjustment of the second-generation.[58]

The Jewish passion for erecting communal buildings to foster identification has been called an "edifice" complex. The Holocaust is no exception. Holocaust centres or museums have been established in Canadian cities to commemorate the tragedy. In June 2003, following a period of renovations and extension, the new permanent exhibition of the Montreal Holocaust Memorial Museum was inaugurated by Canada's prime minister and the premier of Quebec.[59] But there will be nothing on the scale of the Holocaust Museum in Washington or the Wiesenthal Museum of Tolerance in Los Angeles. The Washington Holocaust Museum reflects through its location in the US capital and proximity to the Smithsonian an integration of the Holocaust message with the core values and images of the American experience. The *Shoah* has become Americanized, but not yet Canadianized.

Indeed, in 1977 the Canadian War Museum in Ottawa announced it would include as part of an expansion plan a section devoted to commemorating the Holocaust. Some Canadian veterans' organizations opposed the idea, saying that Holocaust commemoration did not belong in a museum dedicated to the role of Canadian veterans and warfare itself. Defenders of the idea countered that the human toll of genocidal warfare was part of any modern account of war, and would also offer a perspective on Canadian involvement in the struggle against Nazism. A cynic might add that Jewish donors might also be more easily recruited to help finance the War Museum's expansion. But just as the Holocaust Museum has thrust itself, or been thrust, into the centre of American historical consciousness in Washington, so too, albeit on a lesser scale, did it begin in Canada with the debate on the War Museum. Jewish communal opinion was actually divided. Some wanted a specific Holocaust Museum. Some favoured including the Holocaust as a part of a separate museum of intolerance. The idea of a Holocaust section in the Canadian War Museum has since been abandoned, though the British War Museum in 2000 opened a permanent Holocaust exhibit. Meanwhile, Winnipeg's Canadian Museum of Human Rights, spearheaded by the Asper family, opened in 2014, and included a significant section devoted to the Holocaust. But even this was not without controversy. Many Canadian minority groups, from Ukrainian Canadians to First Nations, were concerned that their own stories of persecution and victimization deserved comparable treatment; an unstated implication was that the Holocaust ought not dominate over the concerns of other groups.[60]

Canadian artists and intellectuals have been wrestling with the Holocaust. Anne Michaels's award-winning 1996 novel, *Fugitive*

Pieces, had the Holocaust as a thematic backdrop. Earlier, the poetry
of Irving Layton and Leonard Cohen grappled with the subject.
Layton's 1968 poem "For My Sons, Max and David," a meditation
on Jewish victimhood, ends with the hard-nosed charge to his children, "Be gunners in the Israeli Air Force."[61] The Holocaust is now
an acceptable way for some largely secular intellectuals to identify
publicly as Jews, and to reconnect with a heritage which may have
been dormant for some time. Its universal message of suffering may
appeal to some of those estranged from the Jewish community and
mainstream Judaism. It is a route back without the need for synagogue attendance or ritual observance or Jewish schooling for the
kids or defending or worrying about Israel or donating to Jewish
charities or volunteering to help run Jewish agencies.

A case in point is the well-meaning 1995 volume *Beyond Imagination: Canadians Write about the Holocaust.* The essays are poignant,
insightful, and well-written. A few contributors are known scholars or
writers about the Holocaust. For at least one, the legacy of the Holocaust has been a central theme of her life. Alti Rodal, a historian of
modern Jewry and a child of survivors, has charged her children with
a demanding legacy: "You are the grandchildren of people endowed
with a powerful instinct for survival. To my mother's blessing, 'May
life be good to you,' I add: May the strength of all your grandparents
give you strength to withstand life's trials – we owe it to them. And
may the perseverance and values of their heritage be expressed through
you, within and beyond our community, so that we survive."[62]

But some contributors to the book (almost all are Jews) have a
more tenuous connection to Canadian Jewish life, and to Jewish
identity. Some are married to non-Jews. While the Holocaust troubles them, it is not a core experience which has added Jewish dimensions to their lives. Peter C. Newman writes: "I could claim neither
the exultation of actively practising the Jewish religion, nor was I a
victim of the Holocaust."[63] David Lewis Stein has started to attend
an Orthodox shul in his neighbourhood, even though he admits,
"I am not observant and my wife is not Jewish."[64] And Barbara
Kingstone writes, "I was not a very good Jew in the traditional sense.
Still am not. I don't feel threatened by some greater power if on the
high holidays I don't attend synagogue."[65] In fact, the volume is as
useful as a description of the many complex and nuanced forms of
contemporary Jewish identity among writers and intellectuals as it is
a study of the Holocaust.

JEWS AND CANADIAN CULTURE

The Jewish cultural impact on Canada has been mainly through individual artists, who have at times incorporated a Jewish sensibility. But the community has also made a collective contribution to the Canadian scene. The Segal Centre of Montreal and the Koffler Centre of the Arts in Toronto are known for their high-quality work. Both institutions are sponsored by the Jewish community but their artistic and cultural programming – in education and in performance – is available to the wider public. At times, they can be torn between filling their mandate as Jewish institutions and being part of the broader artistic and cultural community. They blur the lines between Jewish culture in Canada and Canadian Jewish culture.[66]

Just as in the American case, Canadian Jews have been prominent as authors, poets, painters, sculptors, comedians, musicians, actors, directors, producers, journalists, broadcasters, and cultural entrepreneurs. Jewish writers served as an opening wedge in the penetration of a largely anglophilic cultural establishment. They were among the first to sensitize Canadians to styles and themes different from those of the more established anglo-Canadian writers. Jews helped introduce the immigrant experience and the urban experience into the corpus of Canadian writing. The success of poet A.M. Klein, beginning in the 1930s, helped launch a Jewish Canadian tradition in both poetry and prose.

These Jewish writings – the best of them – have become accepted into the evolving Canadian literary canon. It happened later in Canada than in the United States, in part because the Jewish migration there arrived ten to twenty years before the Canadian one. As Mervin Butovsky, Concordia University English professor, noted, the American Jewish literary breakthrough began in the pre-war period, with writers like Ludwig Lewissohn, Ben Hecht, Henry Roth, and Daniel Fuchs. But "when we speak of Canadian culture at the time of large scale Jewish settlement, we are not speaking of a situation with free cultural interplay, one in which all kinds of contributions were valid. Our Canadian culture was much more akin to Anglo-Saxon culture. Our public schools were much narrower in their definition of what it meant to be a Canadian – it usually meant British style, British speech and mannerisms, and so on."[67]

For Canadian Jews, the breakthrough came in the 1950s and 1960s. Howard Roiter, professor of English at Université de Montréal, did not mince words when describing the period before the 1950s. "The problem facing the country then was that English Canadian culture was a second or third-rate imitative culture ... A culture that has been following in the footsteps of a much greater culture has an inferiority complex. It is much less open to innovation and creativity. Can you imagine Irving Layton at the Canadian Poetry Society of the 1930s? It would have been catastrophic!"[68]

Happily, there is little evidence in Canada of any resentment of this penetration by Jewish authors and a resulting "debasement" of the language. On the other hand, it is also hard to claim that Canadian publishing and literary criticism has been controlled by a cabal of Jewish writers and publishers, as was expressed about the United States by American authors such as Truman Capote or Gore Vidal. Canadian publisher Malcolm Lester recalls the interview which landed him his first job with Holt, Rhinehart and Winston in 1964. The person who hired him did so because he felt that Jews "would get the better of him." In Lester's view, the man did not think he was being anti-Semitic, but stating what he saw as a simple fact – that Jews would be better at business.[69] According to Butovsky, Adele Wiseman used to complain about the anti-Semitism of the Canadian literary establishment. But that is a minority view. Lester recalled the early role played by critic Nathan Cohen in Canadian letters, in print and on television. No one doubted that Cohen was a Jew, and indeed he had written early on for a Yiddish paper. But his style as a Canadian critic was "high mandarin, very erudite and intellectual." Robert Fulford argued that in the 1950s and 1960s, Canadian literature "did not even have a club to keep people out of, there was no door to bang at." Butovsky also recalled that literary critic Northrop Frye wrote very positively of the poetry of Irving Layton.[70] And according to critic and poet Eli Mandel, Canadian critics have welcomed themes of marginality, alienation, and a psychological or cultural doubleness.[71] Canadian Jewish writers fit right in. Certainly a preoccupation with "survival," described by Margaret Atwood as typifying English Canadian literature, also resonates well with the historic Jewish experience, though in much different circumstances. Canadian survival meant defying the weather, terrain, and, later, American power. Jewish survival referred to the dual threats of persecution and assimilation. George Woodcock said of Jewish writers, "They have revealed with a particular force and sensitivity the tensions that are characteristic of Canadian life and particularly Canadian urban life. This, it seems evident, is because the themes of which they treat with such a complex heritage of experience, the themes of isolation and division, are also the themes from which it is difficult for any writer in Canada to escape."[72]

I recognize similar patterns of cultural insecurity among Jews and Canadians. But not everyone agrees. According to Harvard critic Ruth Wisse, Atwood's pessimistic paradigm of "survival" did not resonate with Jewish sensibilities. And certainly not when lamenting the impediments of Canada's geography and climate. "Margaret Atwood's theory of Canadian literature as a mythology of survival leaves out the Jew entirely. Although she does bring in some examples from Irving Layton and Adele Wiseman, she reflects nothing of the true Jewish experience. Do you know what the term 'Canada' signified in Auschwitz? Canada was the detail that collected the possessions of incoming prisoners, it was a synonym for 'plenty.' From a Jewish point of view how can one interpret Canada as a deprived and barren country, when it is the land of all possibilities?"[73]

For some, the notion that Jewish writing deserves or has a central place in the contemporary Canadian canon reflects the status of Jews not as marginal but as a White and European group in a position of domination *vis-à-vis* non-Whites. Jews are now acceptable. And even where they seem open to racial minorities, the cultural industries that sustain the canon are accused of engaging in cultural appropriation or misrepresentation.[74] From this perspective, to say that Jews have made it into the canon is to say that Jews have shed their historic labels as victims, and are now automatically ranged with the exploiters of non-White immigrants. My own reading of the cultural scene is different. Jews and non-Whites are both making it. The gates are more open today to visible minorities and recent immigrants than was the case, say, for Jewish and other European ethnics in the 1930s. In literature, the acceptance seems unlimited. Think of successes such as Neil Bissoondath, Austin Clarke, Rohinton Mistry, Bharati Mukherjee, Michael Ondaatje, Marlene Nourbese Philip, or M.G. Vassanji, to name a few. In other areas, like music, it seems to be less. The example of rap or hip hop is a case in point.[75]

The status of Jews can seem more entrenched than that of some other groups. A very controversial 1993 Toronto production of *Showboat* exemplified that situation. The play depicted the lives of both Blacks and Whites on a gambling riverboat sailing on the Mississippi. In the eyes of some Black Torontonians, Jews were

actively involved in fostering both negative stereotypes of and contributing to the cultural appropriation of the Black experience.[76]
The author of the original 1926 play, Edna Ferber, was Jewish, as
were Jerome Kern and Oscar Hammerstein, who turned it into a
musical. So was musical impresario Garth Drabinsky, who produced
the show. The play was the opening production of the Municipal
Arts Centre of North York, where the Jewish Mel Lastman then
served as mayor. One trustee of the North York Board of Education
argued that Whites, and especially Jews, would routinely write or
produce plays casting Blacks in a negative light.[77] This was perhaps
the first Canadian episode which combined the culture wars and
Black-Jewish tensions, already old hat for Americans. For a while,
observers might have confused North York with New York.

Some liberal Jews shared reservations about the choice of *Showboat* as an opening production. The Canadian Council for Reform
Judaism supported the effort to boycott the show, as did Reform
Rabbis Gunther Plaut and Dow Marmur. The Canadian Friends of
the Hebrew University decided to cancel a fundraising evening at the
play. At the same time, Jews were upset by what they perceived as
direct or indirect anti-Semitism from the Black community, typified
by articles by Arnold Auguste, publisher of the Black community
newspaper *Share*. For Black and other non-White Torontonians, the
controversy solidified the perception of Jews not as an oppressed
minority, but as part of the city's power structure.

Such debates have continued, often related to the Israeli-Palestinian
conflict, where Jewish sensitivities, overtly or covertly, have played
a role. For example, recurring debates in Toronto and elsewhere in
Canada about the controversial play *My Name Is Rachel Corrie*,
edited and directed by Alan Rickman and Katharine Viner, have
often placed segments of the Jewish community at odds with
Canada's artistic community, as well as with Palestinian sympathizers. This play is based on the diaries of an American activist who
was killed by an Israeli bulldozer while protesting the Israeli occupation of the West Bank.[78]

Canadian Jews have been instrumental in the development of
Canadian films, theatre, and television. People like Izzy Asper of
CanWest Global, Garth Drabinsky, formerly of Livent, Harold
Greenberg of Astral, Robert Lantos of Alliance Atlantis, entertain-
ment lawyer Michael Levine, Moses Znaimer of CITY-TV, among
others, made innovative entrepreneurial contributions to popular

culture in Canada. Beginning in the 1970s, the effect is noticeable, but the total impact seems less than that found in the United States. The Jewish influence in New York and Hollywood is extensive, and often feeds into anti-Semitic stereotypes about Jewish domination of the media. Canada may not have the same critical mass of talented Jewish writers, actors, and directors; indeed, many of the best, like other talented Canadians, move south.

All this relates to English Canada. Language barriers explain the cultural gaps that persist between Jews and francophones in Quebec. With very few exceptions, like the television hostess Sonia Benezra, Jews have not played a major role in French popular culture. There are no – for the time being – francophone Jewish counterparts to the English-language poets and writers discussed above. When English Canadians watch American television shows or movies or plays, they receive a dose of culture filtered through the lens of New York or Los Angeles Jewish sensibilities. The viewers, through osmosis, become receptive to Jewish cultural styles. Think of Jerry Seinfeld, Woody Allen, Sarah Silverman, or Jon Stewart. But Jews and Jewish themes are largely absent from popular French cultural production. While the general image of the Jew has been that of the outsider, there have been sympathetic treatments of Jews, such as that in Yves Thériault's novel *Aaron*.[79] But there is nothing like the infiltration of Yiddish words into English. French dictionaries like Larousse have not in the past included Yiddish terms the way Webster and other English dictionaries have. At the same time, even here there are openings. Guy Bouthillier, head of the nationalist Société St-Jean-Baptiste de Montréal, recited a Yiddish poem at a kosher SSJB launch of three French-language books on Jewish themes in Montreal in June 2000. In general, the volume of French literary creativity by Jews in Quebec remains low but increasing. There has been a growth in the treatment of Jewish characters and themes in French artistic creativity by Québécois artists in general. A good example is the film, *Felix et Meira*, a love story about a Québécois man and a married Hasidic woman which won multiple Canadian film awards in 2016.[80]

What, if anything, is Jewish about this contribution to popular culture? Specifically, in what way do these efforts actually shape Canadian culture in a "Jewish" manner? Anti-Semites can claim that Jewish control of Hollywood is part of a Jewish conspiracy to promote Jewish interests, such as a preoccupation with the Holocaust.

(See Chapter 11 on anti-Semitism for a Canadian case in point.) In the United States, however, the conventional wisdom is that the Jewish influence, mainly through the writers and creators of movies and TV shows, has been liberalizing, in the broadest sense of the term. Sitcoms like the pioneering *All in the Family*, developed by Norman Lear, preached the tolerance and urban cosmopolitanism valued by Jewish liberals by poking fun at the conservative Archie Bunker. A similar sensibility pervaded the Canadian sitcom *The King of Kensington*, with Al Waxman portraying a good-hearted liberal Jew. Wayne and Shuster did for Canada what scores of American Jewish entertainers based in vaudeville, burlesque, and the Borscht Belt did a generation earlier for the United States. Few older Canadians can forget Wayne's portrayal of the Einsteinian Professor Weingartner, the absent-minded Jewish genius. And many older Canadian Jews will recall the Sunday-night family ritual of watching the Ed Sullivan show and *kvelling*, as Jews and Canadians, whenever Wayne and Shuster were featured. Younger generations will be familiar with Canadian Jewish comedians and actors such as Eugene Levy, Howie Mandel, Seth Rogen, and Martin Short. In the world of popular music, the Canadian Black-Jewish rapper Drake has publicly embraced his Jewish heritage, while also becoming one of the most famous music stars of his generation.

Like food, humour remains a staple of popular Jewish culture. It unites Jews, whatever their denomination or politics, and reinforces their Jewish identity with minimal obligations. In the words of (ex-Canadian) William Novak and Moshe Waldoks, editors of *The Big Book of Jewish Humor*: "It is even possible to argue that Jewish humor, which once represented a secular corner of many otherwise religious Jewish lives, has now come full circle to fulfill a kind of religious need in the lives of many non-practicing Jews."[81] The Internet helps circulate Jewish jokes with as much enthusiasm and interest as major rabbinic responsa in an earlier age. Jewish humour is seemingly distinctive. First, there is a lot of it. I own several anthologies of Jewish humour. And Jewish jokes also reinforce Jewish identity, with or without Yiddish in the punchlines. Based on the jokes my children and students recount, new generations are embracing this tradition of humour that is both self-deprecatory as well as life-affirming. Freud's 1905 quip that "A new joke is passed from one person to another like the news of the latest victory" applies to Jews.[82]

But is there a specific Jewish comedic style? I cannot identify a common thread linking Woody Allen, Sandra Bernhard, Lenny Bruce, Larry David, Jerry Lewis, Rich Little, the Marx Brothers, Jackie Mason, Don Rickles, Joan Rivers, Mort Sahl, Jerry Seinfeld, Neil Simon, Sarah Silverman, Wayne and Shuster, and Henny Youngman – except that they were and are funny. As is the case with Jewish writers, for some the Jewish content is direct, for others it is oblique. But it is there, and most Jews know it. All in all, the texture of Canadian Jewish culture is not deeper, but wider. To use assimilation as the dominant paradigm for the Jewish cultural reality is inadequate. Too much is going on.

8

The People of the Book

Jewish Education and Jewish Survival

"A man lacking instruction cannot be pious."
"Ethics of the Fathers," II: 6

In high school, I occasionally posed impertinent questions. I once asked
my Hebrew teacher the following: Suppose there was only one vacancy
in heaven and two applicants showed up at the same time. One was
Theodore Herzl, who founded modern Zionism but was thoroughly
unreligious. The other was Rabbi Akiva, the wise and devout sage
of antiquity. How would God decide who got in? My teacher pointed
toward the door and shouted, "Weinfeld, get out!"

THE SCOPE OF JEWISH EDUCATION[1]

Jewish education is a crucial element of the Jewish experience and
linked intimately to Jewish survival. Jews are called the People of the
Book, and for good reason. They were the first group to advocate
and more or less achieve universal male literacy, a requisite for being
able to read the Bible and to pray. (The Scots, under the influence of
John Knox, followed suit.) Rabbis, who are learned teachers rather
than priests, are key figures of modern Judaic life. The study of Torah
is considered the highest calling for Jews, who are commanded to
ponder the text "day and night." Indeed, the sages have written that
the requirement to study the Torah stands *keneged kulam*: as equivalent to all the rest of the commandments.

   The practical foundation upon which the study of Torah rests is a
system of Jewish education. And Jewish education today is not only
religious; it includes the study of Hebrew, Jewish history, and Jewish

literature and philosophy. Only recently have other Canadian immigrant minorities such as Muslims or Black Canadians turned their attention to educational issues specific to their group.[2] In other words, looking at Jewish education is one way to see just how different Jews are from Canadians of other ethnic and religious backgrounds.

In North America, Jewish education is available to both boys and girls, and in a variety of forms: day schools, sponsored by all denominations, including *yeshivot* for the very Orthodox; afternoon and Sunday Schools, usually sponsored by congregations but also by communities; and private tutors. In Canada over recent decades, day schools have become popular. On the other hand, more attention is also being paid to the "informal" sector of Jewish education. This includes Jewish summer camps and trips to Israel, both of which are heavily subsidized by North American Jewish communities.

A word about Jewish summer camps is in order. The impact of these camps on generations of North American Jews has been impressive, as confirmed both by anecdotes and scholarly research.[3] The camps are as diverse as North American Jewry itself. There are camps associated with specific Zionist movements, general Jewish community camps, camps associated with specific religious denominations, and privately-owned camps with Jewish owners, predominantly Jewish campers and staff, and some form of Jewish atmosphere. Some camps are basic, others very posh; in some, Jewish content is front and centre, in others, it is offered in smaller doses. But from coast to coast in Canada, Jewish identities are being forged in these camps, helped by hormones and sustained by memories.

I spent ten years, eight as a camper, at Camp Massad, a Hebrew-speaking summer camp in the Laurentian Mountains north of Montreal in the late 1950s and 1960s. Massad took Hebrew language and culture as seriously as any Jewish camp anywhere. I can still recite the Hebrew terms, coined by staffers at the camp and unknown to Israelis, for every baseball position and eventuality. (Actually, this is another affinity between Jews and Québécois, who also had to invent baseball terms in a new language!) I have no doubt that my camp experience contributed to my Jewish education and socialization as strongly as did my eleven years of Jewish day school. And I am positive most former Massadniks would agree.

No Canadian minority group has a comparably diverse and popular network of overnight summer camps. And similarly, no minority group has an educational system as extensively developed, and as multi-dimensional, as do Jews. Most of the one-morning-a-week "Saturday" schools for ethnic minorities have catered to immigrant families, and their enrolments decline dramatically after the immigrant generation. Ethno-cultural education also takes place in special heritage language or multicultural programs in public schools, sparing ethnic groups the bill.[4] Jews also benefit from these programs, and for some parents they are an acceptable alternative to Jewish schools. A good example is the Toronto District School Board, where students can earn academic credits in many language courses, including Hebrew.[5]

Even the religious aspects of Jewish education set Jews apart. Christian education does not loom large as a subject for analysts of religion in Canada. The work of Reginald Bibby, perhaps Canada's foremost sociologist studying Christianity today, has over the years devoted relatively little space to Sunday schools and mainstream Protestant and Catholic schools.[6] Bibby's national surveys show that the proportion of Canadians with school-age children who were exposed to regular religious instruction, such as Sunday school, declined from 36 per cent in 1975 to 19 per cent in 2005. The number of children who had never been exposed to religious instruction increased from 23 per cent in 1975 to over 50 per cent in 2005.[7] It is not clear what these parents thought was meant by instruction, but it was not likely to be a day school education lasting many years. In any case, these rates are far lower than for Canadian Jews. In the words of a respected Baptist minister, "Sunday School, which for two hundred years has been the major recruitment, teaching, and evangelistic arm of church life, is almost gone in Canada."[8]

Some other ethnic and/or religious schools are all-day private schools with similarities to Jewish day schools. Catholic schools are the best-known case in point, though the degree of religious instruction varies by school system and by province, and is often quite limited. Fundamentalist and Evangelical Protestant private schools take their religion very seriously. So do the Muslim schools slowly taking root, which may eventually come to approximate the Jewish day school system. Some European ethnic groups also sponsor day schools, such as the Greek Socrates school in Montreal or Ukrainian schools in Western Canada. Schools catering to First Nations students, with significant Aboriginal curricula, have also been set up. Even as Canada's atheist population has grown in recent years, so too has the number of religious private schools. For example, in

Ontario in 2006, there were 869 private schools, 410 of which were religiously defined. Roughly 80 per cent of these were associated with different Christian denominations (329 schools). The remainder included forty-seven Jewish schools, thirty-seven Islamic schools, and a Sikh school.[9] There might be more such schools in Ontario if the province extended funding to non-Catholic schools, as is done in some other provinces. Ontario has been the only Canadian province to offer full funding to Catholic schools and no direct funding to schools associated with other religious denominations. Meanwhile, provinces including Alberta, Manitoba, and Quebec provided at least partial funding to religious schools that followed the provincial curriculum, and the Atlantic Provinces provided no funding to religious schools of any denomination.[10]

The Ontario Jewish Association for Equity in Education, along with the Alliance of Christian Schools, fought the case for funding as far as the Supreme Court of Canada. In 1996 the Court ruled against them, citing the fact that Ontario Catholic Schools were constitutionally protected and the others were not, even though there was an inequity in the situation. That fight is not over. In 2005, the UN censored Ontario for religious discrimination on this matter. In the provincial election campaign of 2007, John Tory, leader of the Progressive Conservatives, included extending funding to more faith-based schools in his electoral platform. But the proposal was not well received. According to opinion polls, over 70 per cent of voters opposed the extension of funding for reasons including the belief that this would foster segregation, and that the secular state should not encourage religiosity.[11] So far, other faiths in Ontario enjoy far from equal treatment compared to the Catholics.

Providing Jewish education, from a traditional Orthodox perspective, is both a familial and a communal obligation; there is no choice in the matter. The Torah stresses the responsibility of parents to educate their children Jewishly. The Biblical commandment "*Veshinantem levanecho*" instructs Jewish fathers to teach their (male) children the basics of the Torah. But eventually parental teaching and private tutors gave way to schools. Like the creation of Jewish cemeteries and the provision of kosher slaughter for meat, the setting up of Jewish schools is now a requirement of every *kehilla*, or organized Jewish community. In the old country, the ideal marriage partner for a Jewish woman, especially if her father had money, was the brilliant rabbinical student, or *talmid chacham*. Indeed, every male child was expected to become literate in Hebrew, and poverty, in theory, was no excuse.

Jewish education is widespread among Canadian Jews. We find 65.6 per cent of Jewish children in Montreal and 37.5 per cent of Jewish children in Toronto have had some Jewish day school. The American statistic ranges between 6 and 26 per cent depending on the city.[12] Among adult Canadian Jews surveyed, 82 per cent in Montreal and 79 per cent in Toronto had received "some type of Jewish education." These figures are far higher than the national figures for Christian education. Much of this Jewish education in Canada is provided by all-day schools.[13] Formal Jewish education of Canadian Jewish children today is, on the whole, much greater than that of their Canadian-born parents or grandparents, whose education consisted mainly of tutors or Sunday schools or a few years of afternoon schools. This flies in the face of the assimilationist perspective that assumes each generation has less Judaic knowledge. These gains are most pronounced for women. The disappearance of the huge gender gaps in formal Jewish schooling is the most striking feature of postwar North American Jewish education.

The Jewish education system in Canada is extensive and intensive.[14] Canada's first Talmud Torah was started in Montreal in 1896. Toronto's first Talmud Torah was founded in 1907, and grew into the multi-branch Associated Hebrew Schools. A more Orthodox school, the Eitz Chaim, was founded in Toronto in 1915. During the First World War, Montreal's Yiddish Peretz School and the bilingual Yiddish and Hebrew Jewish People's School were founded; they have since merged. In both Toronto and Montreal, there are many educational options. Both cities boast a number of ultra-Orthodox and Hasidic schools, strictly segregated by gender, and *yeshivot* for the older male students. Other day schools span the spectrum from Modern Orthodox to Conservative to more liberal.[15] This incredible variety is a microcosm of modern Jewish life.

Montreal boasts seventeen "Jewish" daycare centres (some of these are private operations), twenty-six Jewish elementary schools, eight full-day high schools, and seven (mainly ultra-Orthodox) rabbinical schools.[16] (These numbers in Montreal and Toronto may shift from year to year.) The variety includes Sephardi/francophone as well as Ashkenazi/anglophone. In Toronto, there is also a wide array of Jewish schools. The tilt in Toronto is toward Orthodox or traditional schools, particularly at the high-school level. There is nothing yet in Toronto like the Bialik high school in Montreal, with its Yiddishist cultural orientation. However, Toronto boasts a Leo Baeck Day School (elementary) affiliated with Reform. There are twenty Jewish elementary day schools in Toronto and sixteen Jewish high school or yeshiva options, and the large majority are very traditional. Additionally, the city had forty-three Jewish after-school programs.[17] There is a wider range of Jewish high school options in Montreal. Toronto's relative strength is in Orthodox and supplementary education. Jewish day schools have sprung up throughout the country. Apart from Toronto and Montreal, one or more elementary schools are found in Ottawa, London, Hamilton, Kitchener, Winnipeg, Calgary, Edmonton, and Vancouver. Jewish high schools, whether *yeshiva*-type or general schools, are found in Ottawa, Hamilton, Winnipeg, Edmonton, and Vancouver.

Despite the general postwar increase in day schools, in more recent years, non-Orthodox Jewish high schools in Canada have been facing declining enrollments. This is due mainly to high costs, as well as the attraction of elite non-Jewish private schools. The problem has been most acute in Toronto, where tuition increased by 61 per cent between 2001 and 2011. In response, the Tanenbaum CHAT (Community Hebrew Academy of Toronto) school, where enrollment declined 37 per cent over eight years, closed its northern Toronto campus and also has decided, with two major individual donations totalling $15 million, to reduce tuition from close to $28,000 to $18,500, and to keep it under $19,000 for five years.[18] Of course the impact of these tuition decreases on enrollments remains to be seen. What is ironic is that as this retrenchment in Toronto takes place, a new $30,000,000 project is underway in Montreal to rebuild Herzliah High School despite a decline in the Montreal Jewish population.[19]

Still, day school enrollments have been higher than in the United States. In 2013, 23 per cent of Jewish adults indicated that they had at one point attended some yeshiva or Jewish day school and 59 per cent claimed that they had received some "other" type of formal Jewish education. When asked about their children's involvement, 25 per cent of American Jews said they had a child who had been enrolled in *yeshiva* or day school, and 22 per cent in some other formal Jewish education.[20] American and Canadian differences can, in part, be traced back to the constitutional difference between the two countries regarding the separation of church and state. The

Canadian tradition of public and constitutional support for religious education is a key factor making religious schooling popular and affordable. In contrast, American Jews have largely embraced the mythic image of the public school as the avenue of economic mobility and Americanization.

It is paradoxical that despite the importance of Jewish education, the vast majority of Canadian Jews are not very literate as Jews. They may be doing better than Christians or other ethnic groups, but perhaps the bar is low. To say that Jews value education is not to say that they value Jewish education to the same degree. The irony is that Jewish achievement at the level of secular education is formidable, extending into graduate and post-graduate work. But when it comes to an understanding of Jewish civilization in all its dimensions, Jews on average just scratch the surface. Jews may be the "People of the Book," but for many that book is not the Torah. Another paradox is that the function of Jewish education today is not education in the sense of imparting knowledge. Its major task is creating and nurturing the Jewish identity of students. What the home, neighbourhood, and synagogue did in the past falls now to Jewish schools. It is doubtful that Jewish schools can maximize both the creating of Jewish identity and the transmission of Jewish knowledge.

THE EFFECTS OF JEWISH EDUCATION

For some time, Jewish education has been dominated by the "vaccination" approach. Assimilation and intermarriage are the disease, and Jewish education is the vaccine. So the case for Jewish education as a sound individual and communal investment is made in terms of strengthening Jewish identity. But this instrumental model is an odd way to understand Jewish education. For most of Jewish history, Jewish identity was a given, and there was little danger that it would be lost or diluted. It was nurtured both by a hostile society and a seamless pattern linking family to synagogue to community. Jewish education did not create Jewish identity; it taught students how to be more fulfilled, more complete, and most importantly, more knowledgeable Jews. It was undertaken *li'shma*, for its own sake. Jewish education was important because knowledge was important. Studying the classic Judaic texts would make one a better human being and a better Jew. In traditional Judaic thought, the study of

Torah was something that adults (males of course) were required to do. The admonitions concerning Torah study in *Pirkei Avot*, or The Ethics of the Fathers, are directed to adults and advocate what we might today call lifelong learning. For example, Jews are instructed to set aside a fixed time for regular study, or to reflect on the optimal relation between work and study. The norm common to many non-Orthodox Jews in North America, that Jewish education and Torah study stop after a child's bar or bat mitzvah, was inconceivable for traditional Jews.

Parents and the Jewish community have faith that Jewish education will lead to stronger Jewish identification. Are they right? American research would suggest they are.[21] And a statistical analysis of ritual observance among Montreal Jews in 2010 suggested that attending a Jewish high school is the second most predictive factor of ritual observance later in life, after current denomination. Having attended a Jewish elementary school was also found to have a significant relationship with ritual adherence, but supplementary education did not. All levels of Jewish schooling were also found to have a significant impact on Jewish identity, and Jewish secondary school education was positively correlated with identification with Israel.[22] The advantages of Jewish day schools have also been reported in the general Canadian media.[23]

So we have to assume that Jewish education also has a positive impact on Judaic knowledge. Jewish students are taught facts, and Jewish skills and ideas. But we know very little of what students retain from their Jewish education. How good is their Hebrew, what do they know of Jewish history, or the Bible, or Talmud, or Jewish philosophy? Learning about something would seem to lead to knowing more about it. This is supported by the finding back in 1990 that Canadians under thirty-five – those most likely to have benefited from the increase in Jewish day school attendance – were able to converse in Hebrew better than older Jews.[24]

Research on Jewish adults does show an effect of Jewish education on subsequent Jewish identity. But the link is mysterious. Most Jews know at least one other Jew who can barely distinguish an *aleph* from a *bet* but is still highly committed. And many know the opposite, the *apikoros*, a Jew learned in Judaica who yet remains an unbeliever, disengaged from the Jewish community. But these cases do not detract from the major positive impact of education on Jewish identity, as we shall see.

There is actually a third possible effect of Jewish education which is omitted from most discussions of the topic. It can affect the type of human being one becomes. We are not certain that students with more Jewish education are more compassionate, tolerant, honest, or law-abiding, but we would like to think that those with a deeper education, with more exposure to Jewish moral teachings would also be better human beings and have more *menschlichkeit*, or decency. Within the Jewish tradition, there has always been a pre-sumed link between Judaic study and ethical behaviour – note the quotation at the beginning of this chapter. While this has generally not been a major research question, it would be worth knowing. Is there less stealing, or cheating, or gossip, or jealousy, or rudeness, or selfishness, or fighting, in Jewish day schools compared to public schools which have many Jewish students? I have no idea. A round-about approach to the question might be to compare Orthodox and non-Orthodox Jews – the former would also have more Jewish edu-cation – on measures of ethical behaviour.

The main thing scholars have studied is the net impact of Jewish education on the various attitudes and behaviours associated with living a Jewish life. Ironically, many Jews can tell horror stories about some aspect of their Jewish schooling, and many recount how Jewish school turned them off Judaism. And research suggests there is something there. In their qualitative study of "moderately affili-ated" American Jews, Steven Cohen and Arnold Eisen interviewed about sixty representative middle-of-the-road Jews and identified several "obstacles to involvement." They concluded that Jewish education was one such obstacle. "Hebrew school was consistently named, even by strongly identified Jews, as a negative feature of their childhood experience of Judaism. Jabs at Hebrew school seemed to come routinely in our interviews, almost as if they were expected and a marker of someone in the know."[25]

But this is not the last word on the matter. There are many quan-titative scientific studies of Jewish adults, usually with much larger samples. These studies generally find that Jewish education does seem to have an impact on positive outcomes. Jewish education either causes, or reinforces, Jewish identity.[26] This contradiction between the qualitative and quantitative research traditions is more apparent than real. They are both right. It is not surprising that American adults, when asked to think back to their (mainly supple-mentary) Jewish schooling, would not have fond memories. Sunday school or afternoon school took up time from socializing or other extracurricular activities. And no doubt many teachers, and the subject matter, were boring. I taught teenagers at Hebrew School from nine until noon on Sundays mornings when I was a graduate student. No matter how enthusiastic I was, I just knew they did not want to be there. They had perhaps partied late the night before and wanted to sleep in. I couldn't blame them. So those negative feelings, or recollections, are real. But the quantitative studies take a different approach. They ask not if it was fun, but if it had a positive effect years later. It may be that there is an impact of Jewish education that adults may not even realize. How many people whose parents forced them to eat vegetables and fruit instead of sweets and junk food look back fondly on the experience? Likely few. But chances are those children are healthier as adults. For many Jews, their Jewish education was like spinach. So both the qualitative anecdotes and the quantitative findings are correct. One newer problem is that Jewish parents, like all middle-class parents, have become more reluctant to force their children to do things they do not enjoy. The challenge for Jewish educators is to come up with a tasty, low-calorie, spinach ice cream …

There is no doubt there have been routes to Jewish identity outside formal Jewish education. Youth movements, Israel experiences, as well as summer camps play a role. My wife is a good example. She never had one minute of formal Jewish education. As a child, she went to synagogue on the High Holidays, perhaps. But at age thirteen, she joined Hashomer Hatzair, a socialist-Zionist youth movement, and at age seventeen, she left with her *garin*, or kibbutz group, to settle on a kibbutz in Israel. Her years with Hashomer, summers at Camp Shomria, and her three years in Israel, one on a kibbutz and two in Israeli universities, were her "Jewish education." Today, we keep a kosher home, go to synagogue, and have sent our children to Jewish day schools. But there are two other factors which can explain my wife's evolution, and which may limit its relevance for the future. First, her background. She is the daughter of Holocaust survivors and her mother tongue was Yiddish. Those facts no doubt shaped her early years in countless, if subtle, ways. Second, while she did not attend a Jewish school, her Montreal public high school, Wagar, was in a largely Jewish suburb and so was predominantly Jewish. Her peer group was totally Jewish. On major Jewish holidays, the school was empty. Her experience raises the question of the relative importance of peers compared to the formal and informal curriculum in a Jewish school. What makes Jewish education effective in reaching its goals? In terms of Jewish identity, it may well be the interaction with other Jewish kids – playing sports, doing a lab, dating – that is decisive, not the curriculum.

One reason Jewish day schools have become popular over the past few decades is they are considered good schools. They seem to prepare students well in secular subjects and for future success in university. With the exception of schools catering to ultra-Orthodox students, which do not emphasize secular studies, Jewish day schools compare well with other private or public schools. But the reason may not be the "Jewishness" of the schools. A bright and motivated peer group can promote academic achievement even more than lavish new facilities or well-paid teachers. In other words, the school climate is key. Catholic and other private schools in the United States have been more effective than public schools in teaching students from all income levels. Those schools are more disciplined, devote more class time to actual work, and assign more homework.[27] It is not because of any distinctly "Catholic" teaching. There is nothing "Catholic," or "Jewish," about doing well on a math test.

For a long time, Jewish day schools were stigmatized as being academically inferior, associated with images of ultra-Orthodox Jews uninterested in university studies. While that view has changed, there are still some parents who fear that a time-consuming Jewish education, particularly the study of a second language like Hebrew, might lead to a weaker mastery of English and other subjects. They worry that Jewish studies take time away from the more important secular subjects. In fact, the research on bilingual education offers no support for this view. A Montreal evaluation of Jewish day school students further refutes it. These students were involved in trilingual education – English, French, and Hebrew – but their academic achievements in English and secular studies were in no way impaired.[28] Many of these students also do well at the post-secondary level. Perhaps a more demanding multilingual curriculum, with both secular and religious studies, in Darwinian fashion equips Jewish students for subsequent success at university. It is also possible that students going to private schools are just brighter. Jewish day schools, like Catholic and private schools, draw a self-selected sample of students from families that value education and are able and prepared to spend more money on it. For whatever reason,

Jewish day school graduates are now found in the best Canadian and American universities. One sees knitted *yarmulkas* everywhere.

Another reason for the increase in popularity of day schools is that they are the new incubators of future Jews. More and more parents who are not themselves religious have been sending their children to Jewish day schools. Many see them as providing a better alternative to public schools, with a better peer group, less sex and drugs – which may be wishful thinking – and a way to prevent inter-marriage. Many parents want these schools to inculcate Judaism in a way they are unwilling or unable to. Other parents choose such schools because they want their children to be in school with other Jews. Their own commitment to Judaic Studies is minimal; often the children wind up socializing their parents into Judaism and Jewish life.

But these schools are not perfect. Because many schools draw upon a homogeneous middle- or upper-class clientele, there is a danger they will foster a school culture that is narrow, shallow, ethnocentric, and materialistic.[29] According to a 2013 Toronto survey, 17 per cent of respondents found that Jewish day schools "somewhat hinder integration into the secular work world," 14 per cent felt that they provide "a narrow perspective of the secular Canadian society," and 6 per cent thought that they were "deficient in substance."[30] My oldest daughter years ago came home after her first day in a Jewish kindergarten following the winter vacation. I asked her what she had learned in school that day. She answered, "Daddy, what's Barbados?" In at least two of the leading Jewish high schools in Montreal, in some past years a highlight of the school year was the annual fashion show. At some daytime school functions, there may be more nannies than parents. I have met Jewish day school graduates whose universe is confined to a narrow corridor running from Montreal or Toronto down to Boca Raton. Jewish day schools are aware of these dangers and try to counteract them with programs of exchanges and dialogues with other schools.

BARRIERS TO DAY SCHOOL EDUCATION

There are three reasons why Jewish parents might not opt for day schools for their children. One is the financial burden, which penalizes working-class and lower-middle-class parents. The costs are enormous. In Toronto in 2014, for example, fees could run to

$17,000 for a year of elementary day school, and up to $24,900 at the Tanenbaum Community Hebrew Academy (CHAT) high school. Day schools in some cities have begun to adjust tuition to reflect family income and the number of children in schools. While financial aid is often available, many parents do not like asking for it. Moreover, in some cases middle-class parents earn too much to qualify for significant aid, and are unprepared or unable to spend less in other areas. Affordability has emerged as a major challenge. In Toronto, day school tuition increased 61 per cent from 2001 to 2011. Between 2008 to 2016, enrollment at Toronto's CHAT, the community high school, declined by 37 per cent.[31]

This leads into the second reason: Jewishness is important, but not that important. A Jewish day school may be seen by some parents as providing too much Jewish education, with the risk of making their children too narrow and ill-prepared to function in a non-Jewish world. And for wealthier families, the alternative of an elite non-Jewish private school is appealing because of the perceived quality of the schools. Parents may like the uniforms, the discipline, the extra-curricular options, from drama to sports, and what seems like a tough, no-nonsense academic environment. Across Canada, there are elite private schools with growing proportions of Jewish children. Some of these schools used to have a distinct odour of anti-Semitism, and were also unaffordable. Now that Jewish parents can afford them and their children (as well as those of visible minorities) are welcome, these schools are major competition for Jewish day schools. The parents who enroll their children in them should not be considered un-Jewish, or uncommitted to the Jewish future. Not at all. Many are leaders in the community. A 2010 survey of Montreal Jews asked parents to explain why they were not sending their children to Jewish day schools. The most common reason (55 per cent) was that they wanted them to socialize in a wider milieu.[32] These parents want their children to be Jews – to be different – but not too different.

A third reason is that a Jewish day school education is too demanding for some students, as it usually results in a longer day and a dual English-Hebrew curriculum. In Montreal, a French-English-Hebrew curriculum means even greater demands. In one school system, Yiddish adds a fourth language. My youngest daughter attended a Montreal Jewish elementary school in which the day began at eight and ended at four, with just a half-hour for lunch. That is a very long day, and it started in grade one. Some students find it too much, and with homework on top, there is little time for music, ballet, sports, and just plain relaxation. An alternate option would be forms of streaming in non-Orthodox day schools, and cutting back on the hours of Judaic instruction.

THE FORM AND THE CONTENT OF JEWISH EDUCATION

There is an ongoing debate about what makes for success in education, and Jewish education is no exception. Good charismatic teachers and administrators are important. Curricular innovations also play a role, at the level of more effective pedagogy, so that graduates will actually retain more Judaic knowledge. Common sense also suggests that having fun or a meaningful and enjoyable experience is crucial, since in many cases – Sunday school and afternoon school in particular – many students may not want to be there.

In the old country, Jewish education traditionally took place in *cheders*, small schools for elementary-age male children, and in *yeshivot*, academies of higher learning aimed at male teenagers whose curriculum comprised mainly the study of Talmud. The pedagogy was not progressive, and the education was far from child-centred. Indeed, the emphasis was clearly on rote learning, on mastering the texts and the commentaries. Depending on the specific *yeshiva*, these commentaries might include traditional sources like Rashi, Maimonides, Nachmanides, Saadia Gaon, the Vilna Gaon, as well as recent ultra-Orthodox rabbis and other scholars specific to various sects. There was little interest in what the young students thought about the texts, or about any novel interpretations they might develop. In some cases, *yeshiva* students would also be exposed to minimal amounts of *musar*, a form of moral education aimed at applying Judaic principles to the real world. Originality and creativity in textual interpretation would have to wait until the end of their studies, when only the best among them would be encouraged to think independently. Some of the most ultra-Orthodox schools have recently come under legal challenge from government officials in Quebec for operating illegally or deliberately ignoring secular subjects, notably for boys.[33]

Jewish education has not been static. Many schools use modern technology such as computer programs for the study of Bible or Talmud. Judaic studies have also gone online, aimed at a variety of age groups. There has been change in content as well as in form. By the end of the nineteenth century, the influence of the *Haskalah*, or Enlightenment, extended the traditional curriculum to include elements of Jewish history and Hebrew language and literature in the Talmud Torah network of schools. In addition, a network of secular Yiddishist schools was established in Eastern Europe, and transplanted to North America. In these schools, often called "people's schools," or *folkshules*, Yiddish language and literature replaced the emphasis on Hebrew, secular ethics and social justice were stressed, and the Bible was included as literature rather than as the word of God.

Modern Jewish day schools (except for the ultra-Orthodox) seek to accomplish a dual task. They must provide their students with both a first-rate secular education and a meaningful Jewish education. The former is instrumental in getting a job and earning a living; the latter is a form of enrichment or values education. This sets many parents and Jewish educators at loggerheads. For many parents, particularly the non-Orthodox, the secular education is more important. They want top computer training, as well as sports, art, and all the main curricular subjects. But most Jewish educators are tenacious in defending the priority of the Jewish portion of the curriculum. One increasingly popular solution is to integrate the two streams where possible, in areas such as literature or history. Thus, while in general history students are learning about the French Revolution and Napoleon, in Jewish history they might be studying the impact of the Revolution and Napoleon on Jewish life in Western Europe. Another ongoing curricular debate in Jewish education concerns "*Ivrit be'Ivrit*" ("Hebrew in Hebrew"). The issue is whether all the Judaic curriculum should be taught in Hebrew, or just the Hebrew language courses. My own day school experience involved learning all Jewish studies subjects in Hebrew. In retrospect, I think I would have been better served by studying subjects like Jewish history, religion, philosophy, and perhaps literature in English, as they do in most Jewish studies courses in university.

Over the years, Jewish schools have come to emphasize the "informal" curriculum as seriously as the formal elements described above. As Jewish schools are expected to socialize children into Jewish adulthood, the informal, experiential dimensions become more important. As already suggested, simply having an all-Jewish peer group may be as important for subsequent Jewish identity as anything learned in the formal curriculum. For students in Jewish schools, plays, Holocaust memorials, sports-meets, field trips, and dances all get drafted into the cause. Many Jewish day schools facilitate Jewish dating. So do summer camps, youth groups, or Israel experiences. The object of the exercise – stated or unstated – is to channel those teenage hormones.

THE COMMUNAL POLITICS OF JEWISH EDUCATION

Although formally private, Jewish day schools in North America have become a de facto public-school system of the Jewish community. Jewish communities have taken to proclaiming in heroic fashion that no child will be denied a day school education because of inability to pay. The emergence of Jewish education, especially day schools, as perhaps the key – and most costly – element of a Canadian Jewish public agenda poses interesting problems of school independence versus communal control. Most Jewish schools zealously guard their autonomy and resist any interference in decisions made by their boards, parents, or administrators. This is a result of their histories, in which they arose as private institutions, founded by dedicated visionaries with a clear ideological focus. But as costs have risen and more schools seek assistance from the organized community, the question arises as to what influence the community can or should have on educational matters. It is useful to think of Jewish schools not as private schools but as the public-school system of the Jewish polity. If so, they must be accountable to some broad communal consensus to receive funding.

The growing concern for Jewish unity offers the best example. Imagine a school which promoted the transformation of Israel and Palestine into a single state, under eventual Palestinian control. Such a school might well fall under either extreme left-wing or certain ultra-Orthodox auspices. Or imagine a school dedicated to promoting Jewish assimilation and mixed marriage. Or a school which preached a philosophy based on the views of the Jewish Defense League's founder Meir Kahane, or those of Baruch Goldstein, who shot dozens of Arabs praying at Hebron. Or one which claimed that certain Jews, be they "black hats" or Reform, should be excluded from the Jewish community. While these are extreme examples, they raise the question of whether a core set of principles could be imposed on specific schools.[34] Could a Jewish federation insist that schools seeking its financial assistance make a commitment to inculcate the pluralistic principles of *ahavat Yisrael* or *klal Yisrael* – a love of Israel and Jewish pluralism – in some way in their curriculum? The sparks might fly. In Montreal, there are some Hasidic groups whose schools have been affiliated with BJEC, and others that are not. But in general, these ultra-Orthodox schools make little or no effort to include Israel, Zionism, and modern Jewish history in their curriculum.

Jewish day schools are not like stereotypical private schools. Many of their families are not part of a religious elite. The schools are not as well-equipped as the elite private schools. And Jewish day school parents are not all wealthy; they include the full range of economic classes. It may be useful to think about Jewish schools and their links to the Jewish community the way we analyze public schools and their link to the broader society which supports them. Educational reformers have long debated whether public schools change society or simply reflect existing arrangements. Jewish educators must wrestle with the same questions. If there is a problem of Jewish unity, can it be solved using the Jewish school system? (Anti-racist programs in public schools are an analogy. Here, the school is being used to solve the social problem of racism.) In fact, there are many programs in which Orthodox and non-Orthodox schools participate and interact socially, such as sports tournaments, song festivals, rallies, Holocaust and Israeli Independence Day events. No one knows the impact of such efforts. They likely do no harm. But they are not very meaningful encounters or structured dialogues about pluralism and tolerance. And ultra-Orthodox schools are often not involved.

The education of Jewish children has been an item on the public policy agenda in Canada for generations, particularly in Quebec. Under the British North America Act of 1867, only Catholics and Protestants were granted public education rights. In Quebec, the place of Jewish children, teachers, and parents in the Protestant and Catholic school systems was a matter of heated debate. As the Jewish population of Montreal grew, the proportion of Jewish children in the Protestant (English) school system increased. Eventually, in 1903, an act of the Quebec legislature established this access in law. Yet Jews were still not permitted to work as teachers or to be active on the Protestant School Board, even though they paid taxes. The wealthier uptown Jews argued for equality within the Protestant school system. But among some of the immigrant community, a preferred option was to create an independent Jewish School Board. This would not only enhance Jewish cultural survival, but eliminate the practice by which Jewish children were forced to participate in Christian rituals and prayer. Compromise solutions began to evolve in the 1930s, despite opposition from nationalist forces. Eventually Jewish parents and teachers were admitted into Protestant schools, and the religious character of those schools began to decline.[35] In 1970, private Jewish day schools in Quebec received recognition as Associated Schools in the public interest and were thus entitled to receive government grants for the secular portion of their school funding, as is the case with schools serving other religious and ethnic minorities. These grants continue as long as these schools continue to meet government requirements regarding the minimal hours of French instruction. Day school parents in Ontario may claim a portion of school fees as a tax deduction, which can ease the burden somewhat.

This issue highlights an important difference between Canadian and American Jews, and indeed between the two countries. American Jews, at least as represented by official organizations, have been fierce supporters of the constitutional separation of church and state. They regularly oppose any curricular or extracurricular intrusion of religious symbolism in public schools or on school grounds. No crosses, no nativity scenes, no Hanukkah lights. They usually oppose public funding of private religious schooling, seeing Jewish schools as potentially ghettoizing. American Jews and Jewish organizations are generally staunch defenders of the public-school system, since many immigrant Jewish children made their way up the occupational ladder via the public schools, and many American Jews entered the white-collar ranks as teachers and then administrators. Canada never developed an American mythology about the egalitarian nature of the public-school system, and does not have the same separation of church and state. American Jewish organizations have long supported the role of public schools in American life and have argued to eliminate or minimize the role of religion within those schools. This has included opposition to government funding for Jewish schools.[36] American Jews have always wanted desperately to become American.

The BNA Act of 1867 recognized and legitimated differences. It gave rights to speakers of English and French, and to Protestants and Catholics. This constitutional tradition has continued right through the 1982 Charter of Rights and Freedoms, with Section 27 recognizing multicultural rights. It was not unreasonable that Canadian schools should reflect, not eradicate, those cultural characteristics. Jewish communal leaders now recognize the importance of Jewish education in the fight for continuity. It was not always thus. I recall as a student attending a meeting of some wealthy Montreal Jews, around 1969 or 1970, where the aim was to sell the importance of Jewish education in general and a new program of Jewish studies for McGill University in particular. One of the philanthropists commented (I am paraphrasing), "I don't understand all this fuss about Jewish education. I never had a single day of Jewish education and that never did me any harm." Whatever their reservations, the philanthropists came through. But all the talk about the importance of Jewish education masks some painful realities. Few parents, no matter how committed to Jewish continuity, would dance for joy if their daughter – and certainly their son – told them they wanted to become a Hebrew-school teacher. Even as salaries and job security have increased, there is still a sense that Jewish teachers do not enjoy the esteem – or the income – that physicians, lawyers, and accountants do.

In the past, Israelis comprised a large percentage of the Jewish teachers in Canada. Some came on special limited-term contracts; others were immigrants. Other teachers were Holocaust survivors. Some had little training in modern pedagogic techniques, to say the least. In my eleven years of day school in the 1950s and 1960s, I can recall only two Canadian-born teachers in Judaic subjects. Let me be clear. I think my Hebrew-school teachers did a fine job. I remember most of them clearly and with affection, even after fifty years. At times, we students were rude and misbehaved, which I regret, and I spent my fair share of time getting thrown out of class. (My school was diabolically clever; when you were thrown out of class, at least in elementary school, rather than stand in the hall you had to go to the library, where there was a chance you might read a book ...) Like most of my classmates, I did not always take my Judaic studies seriously, and we tended to make more trouble for the Hebrew teachers than for those teaching secular subjects. This was generally known throughout the day school system. As the years passed, concerns were expressed that Israeli teachers, particularly those who came for just a few years, lacked the familiarity with the local scene necessary to understand their students. Who knows? In any case, the trend has been towards trying to recruit Canadian Jews, through teacher-training programs such as those which have been available at McGill and York universities.

BEYOND JEWISH SCHOOLS

Jewish education begins before elementary school and continues after high school. Jewish nurseries, playgroups, and daycare centres are now common in every Jewish community, and cater to every Jewish orientation. The segregation and socialization of Jewish children starts when they are barely toddlers. A similar explosion has taken place at the post-secondary level and beyond. Ultra-Orthodox Jewish men can continue studying, even after they get married, in adult educational institutions called *kollels*. For more secular types, the campus has become an increasingly important venue. The growth of Jewish studies courses, chairs, programs, and departments has augmented what was available from formal Jewish schools. Bible, Jewish history, Rabbinics, Jewish philosophy, Hebrew and Yiddish language and literature are the traditional core of university Jewish studies. More recently, areas dealing with the social scientific study of modern Jewish life, the Holocaust, Israel studies, or English-language Jewish literature have opened up.[37] Jewish studies courses are taught on forty Canadian campuses. The first Canadian program was launched at McGill in 1969 under the leadership of Professor Harry Bracken and Rabbi David Hartman of the Philosophy Department, and Professor Ruth Wisse of English. McGill has the only actual Department of Jewish Studies in Canada. The University of Toronto has developed a major Jewish studies program, as have Toronto's York University and Montreal's Concordia University. Many other campuses have programs, chairs, or at least courses in Judaica – quite distinct from divinity school courses in the Old Testament. (Such courses can have a Christian spin and are often taught by Christian theologians and scholars.)

University-based Jewish studies can also run into problems of bias and objectivity, albeit different from the biases of teaching Judaica in Christian seminaries. The problem is similar to that found in programs of Black or any ethnic studies, which have proliferated on North American campuses. They all run the risk of becoming hagiographic; they can become sites for communal cheerleading, for promoting group interests rather than the academy's goals of dispassionate teaching and research. Some Fredonians might want the professor of Fredonian studies to be a Fredonian, and of a certain type. If so, how critical could the Fredonian professor be about certain received wisdoms of Fredonian history, or philosophy, or communal politics, especially if the Fredonian community helped fund the program? (Do not panic. Fredonia is a fictitious country in a Marx Brothers movie.)

The first academic breaks with Jewish communal solidarity and a religious perspective took place in the nineteenth century. A scientific, non-theological Jewish studies emerged in Germany as *Wissenschaft des Judentums*, or the science of Judaism. This new field challenged the conventions of traditional Jewish learning. Texts were studied as literary or historical documents, not as the word of God. Indeed, the study of these texts became an exercise in scholarship, not in the affirmation of piety or religious commandments. Even non-Jews could pursue the scientific study of Judaism, and Orthodox rabbis frowned upon university-based Jewish studies for that reason. In the modern period, rabbis of the major denominations have all made their peace, more or less, with the academic approach to Jewish studies. Yeshiva University and the Jewish Theological Seminary, both in New York, the Hebrew Union College in Cincinnati, and the Reconstructionist College in Philadelphia are examples of how the major denominations have integrated the Western scholarly perspective into the education of young Jews and rabbis. Only the ultra-Orthodox continue to resist. It is becoming increasingly common to find rabbis with one or more graduate degree in Jewish studies to go along with their ordination. A first Canadian institution to ordain traditional rabbis, the Canadian Yeshiva and Rabbinical School, was launched in Toronto in 2011.[38] The focus was to train rabbis who would interpret *halacha* in a more liberal manner. The Rabbinical College of Canada ordains Orthodox rabbis in the Hassidic (Lubavitch) tradition. By and large, Canadian synagogues rely on Americans or on Canadians who go south for their training.

For Jewish studies, issues of objectivity and detachment remain crucial, though the fault line is both religious and communal. After all, classical Jewish learning, as in the model of the *yeshiva*, made no pretence of detachment or objectivity. Critical thinking was not encouraged. These issues appear differently in rabbinical seminaries compared to Jewish studies programs in secular universities. In

Modern Orthodox, Conservative, Reform, or Reconstructionist
seminaries, there are likely limits to the degree of critical inquiry that
Judaic scholars can pursue. (These limits will differ for each denomination.) These limits cannot, in theory, apply to the mainstream
academy, where most Jewish studies teaching takes place. Here one
can imagine the full gamut of "heretical" academics, including anti-
circumcision zealots and fiercely anti-Zionist professors. Ideally,
their academic work would consist of analysis over advocacy. Still,
professors who implicitly or explicitly criticize Judaism or mainstream Jewish communal organizations and philanthropists might
face a challenge. In some cases, they might be welcome as debunkers
of conventional wisdoms and tweakers of authority. In others, they
might become pariahs, like flat-earthers in a department of astron-
omy. Some professors of Jewish studies may not like to see themselves as role models for their students, and distance themselves
from the local Jewish community lest their "integrity" be compromised. Do Jewish studies professors have to be observant, or marry
Jews, or support Israel, or value Jewish continuity, or even be Jewish?
(My theoretical answer is "no" to all these questions. But in practical
terms, problems could arise.) Most Jewish studies professors flee
from identity politics, though others embrace it. These tensions
between academic Jewish studies and mainstream Jewish communities remain unresolved.

There are thousands of students in American and Canadian universities, mostly Jewish, who take university-level courses in Jewish
studies.[39] We know little about the impact of these courses on their
Jewish identity. On university campuses today, quite apart from formal classes, there are other options for Jewish education. Hillel and
other student groups often provide educational and cultural programs. In addition, voluntary Jewish social segregation on campuses
also plays an educational as well as social function.

I began teaching a course on the sociology of North American
Jewry at McGill in 1977: the first of its kind in Canada. I use the
Jewish example as a case study for issues in ethnic and religious
sociology in "multicultural" Canada. I estimate that at first about
one-tenth of my students were non-Jews (many dating Jews). Since
then, I would guess that the proportion of non-Jews has risen steadily
to at least 50 per cent. I would also guess that the average grades of
the non-Jews have been similar to those of the Jewish students. Why?
Perhaps some of the Jews figured that since they already had some

formal Jewish schooling, they would somehow coast through. Perhaps non-Jews have to be deeply interested to take such a course.
Among my best students ever were two non-Jews, an exchange student from Munich and a Canadian of Pakistani origin. But every
year I get several fairly assimilated Jewish students for whom my
course serves as a kind of first time and last chance exposure to some
kind of Jewish experience and knowledge, having missed out in their
earlier years. I have no idea how my course has affected them. For
some I suspect that it did more than impart information.

Jewish schools and universities are not the only arenas of Jewish
education. Other agencies have embraced Jewish family education
and adult education. Family education refers to experiential or
learning activities that involve the entire family. Such programs are
often based in synagogues, centred on holiday celebrations, and
involve families learning together. Adult education has long been a
feature of Jewish life. Among the Orthodox and ultra-Orthodox, it
is part of a long tradition in which Jews try to find time for a *shiur*,
or Talmud lesson, at a local *yeshiva* or a *beis medrash*, a house of
learning. Ultra-Orthodox Jewish males pursue advanced Talmudic
studies at *kollels* either on a full-time or a part-time basis, even after
they are married. All synagogues offer lectures, courses, or study
groups on various topics, and a variety of alternative adult institutions do so as well. Toronto boasts a *kollel* for liberal Jewish learning, affiliated with the Reform Movement; the Research Centre
of Kabbalah, which sponsors courses on the Zohar, reincarnation,
meditation, astrology, along with general principles of Kabbalah;
and the Women's Institute of Advanced Torah Study, which offers
classes from an Orthodox point of view.

Along with the academic field of Jewish studies, there has been a
proliferation of Jewish think-tanks, foundations, and research organizations that enhance the reach of Jewish scholarship not only for
academics but also for community leaders and the public. These
research institutions may be general, or focus on specific areas such
as anti-Semitism, American Jewish demography, Jewish education,
etc. As just one example, the Berman Jewish DataBank and the
Berman Jewish Policy Archives are valuable online sources of both
data and analyses abut North Jewish life; they include significant
collections relating to Canada as well.

One of the more original innovations in adult Jewish education is
the *Daf Yomi*, or daily page. It takes seven and a half years to read

the entire Talmud, at one page a day. All over the world, groups of Jewish men (and likely women) have undertaken to do just that, studying the very same page on a specific day. In the recent past, most of them would meet in groups at some point during the day. In recent years *Daf Yomi* has exploded on the internet, which means that many Orthodox participants have more flexible and impersonal options, though some face-to-face groups continue. A Jew who is travelling never has to miss a day. An original organizer in Montreal explained the attraction. It is not only simple piety that makes the *Daf Yomi* popular. He emphasized that many members in their youth had studied at *yeshiva*, only to leave it as they grew up. For some older or retired Jews, it is a way to recapture their youth.[40] Today there is a virtual explosion of websites and online materials aimed at transmitting Judaic knowledge to children. Some of these are incorporated within Jewish schools and some are developed for home use. We are not yet certain of the full impact of this technology on Jewish schooling and on the level of Judaic knowledge.[41]

These activities should surprise no one. Traditionally, Jewish learning was the obligation and duty of adults. It is mainly among the Orthodox that this admonition has been heeded. In *The Vanishing American Jew*, Alan Dershowitz concludes that an energized new commitment to a liberal, accessible Jewish education for adults holds the key to Jewish survival. He writes: "There must be classes, discussion groups, study groups, lectures, videotapes, computer programs, books, book clubs, newsletters, and other mechanisms of Jewish learning."[42] The problem with the Dershowitz solution is that all these options already exist, in synagogues and Jewish community centres, and those who partake are already among the committed, whatever their denomination.

Jewish education illustrates again how Jews are like all other groups, except very different. Most ethnic and religious groups in Canada make some efforts at socializing their children into the community and its culture. Muslim groups in Canada are developing an extensive network of schools, or *madrassahs*, and may yet approximate Jewish day school numbers. But among other groups, none come close to the quality and range of the Jewish day schools and the adult educational system. The irony is that as Jewish education increases its profile, its success is measured less by educational criteria and more by the ability to socialize Jewish children. And all things considered, that record is impressive. Yet this impressive record, notably by day schools, is at present facing serious challenges of rising tuition fees, competition from elite public schools, declining enrollments especially for the non-Orthodox schools, and resulting processes of school amalgamations and closures.

9

Jews, Judaism, and the Public Square

The Political Behaviour of Canadian Jews

"The law of the country is binding."
Talmud (Nedarim 28a)

"American Jews in the 1930s and 1940s, it is said, believed in three worlds, or, in Yiddish, *drei velt: die velt*, this world, *yenne velt*, the world to come, and – *Roosevelt*."

Anonymous

The selection of Senator Joe Lieberman as Al Gore's running mate in the 2000 US presidential election brought Jewishness to the centre of the North American political debate as never before. Lieberman was an openly observant Jew. Most Jews were elated; some were apprehensive. Subsequent analysis indicated that Lieberman's selection on the Democratic ticket did not cost the Democrats any support.[1] In 2016, the campaign of the thoroughly secular Bernie Sanders for the Democratic Party nomination reintroduced the issue of Jewishness into the American political arena, at least for American Jews if not for the wider public. So too for the roles of Ivanka Trump and Jared Kushner in the Donald Trump administration. This chapter delves into both the issues of Jews in politics and Jews and politics – the use of the political system to defend Jewish interests. While the focus is Canadian, the dilemmas are generic. We explore sensitive topics like the Jewish vote, the role of Jewish elected officials, and the informal exercise of political power and influence, through lobbying and public relations, on various public-policy issues. Herein lies yet another paradox. The more Jews participate in the mainstream of Canadian politics, the better able they are to defend their own specific interests.

Sometimes, these interests seem to clash with Canada's national interest, or with the interests of other groups.

JEWS AND THE LEFT

Jews in North America are liberal, or, to be more technical, found mainly on the centre-left half of the political spectrum. Given their relative affluence, Jews might have been expected to have abandoned liberal politics, yet they continue to support politicians and policies dedicated to reform, to equality, and to social justice for the less fortunate. It is fascinating to trace the influence of this progressive commitment on Jewish politics. More difficult is trying to account for this leftward tendency. Is there something about Jewish culture that propels people to the left, or is it simply fear of anti-Semitism or some other strategic calculations based on the Jewish position in Canadian society?

This political orientation dates from the Old Left rooted in Europe to the New Left and countercultural movements of the 1960s – from Leon Trotsky to Abbie Hoffman. American evidence consistently reveals that American Jews hold more liberal positions than non-Jews on all manner of policy issues and are also more likely to label themselves liberals. They are far more likely to think well of the American Civil Liberties Union and poorly of the National Rifle Association than are non-Jews. More important, they are the White group most loyal to the Democratic Party – well before Joe Lieberman – even after controlling for education and income.[2]

There have been fewer studies in Canada documenting the link between Jews and progressive politics. Electoral history offers some evidence. Communists J.B. Salsberg and Fred Rose were both elected in 1943 in largely Jewish ridings, the former to the Ontario Legislature and the latter to the federal Parliament from Montreal.[3] Rose, in fact, was arrested in 1945, convicted of espionage, and sentenced to six years. Released in 1951, he lived out his days in Poland. Jews were active throughout the 1930s and 1940s, along with Ukrainians and Finns, in the Communist Party as organizers and workers.[4] The Jewish labour movement in the 1930s and 1940s supported various left-wing political candidates. David and Stephen Lewis, Dave Barrett, Cy Gonick, and Gerald Caplan were prominent leaders in the New Democratic Party. In general, Jewish votes in Canada have gone to the centre/left mainstream parties. The one relevant study shows that Jews have been more likely than other Canadians to vote for the CCF/NDP or the Liberals, even taking into account factors like trade-union status, education, and economic status.[5]

There is little research analyzing recent voting preferences of Canadian Jews. Contrary to popular opinion, Jews did not shift en masse to the Conservatives during the Mulroney years.[6] One 1987 study of a non-random sample of rabbis, Jewish academics, and communal leaders aged twenty-five to forty from Montreal and Toronto found 41 per cent called themselves Liberal, 21 per cent Conservative, and 15 per cent NDP.[7] Mulroney had a deep understanding of the Jewish condition. Raised as an Irish Catholic in Quebec, he understood minority status. His wife, Mila, was the daughter of Serbs who survived the horrors of the Second World War in the former Yugoslavia. His government launched the Deschênes Commission of Inquiry of War Criminals, which aimed in part to resolve the issue of Nazi war criminals who had entered Canada illegally or secretly after the war. Throughout his tenure as prime minister and after, he displayed strong support for Israel. This was crystalized in a much-noticed major address he gave in 2003 entitled "Israel Is the New Jew."[8] With the arrival of Stephen Harper's Conservatives on the electoral scene, the Jewish vote began to drift away from the Liberals.

The Canadian Jewish community has always been more traditional, and pro-Israel, than that of the United States. Between the 1972 re-election of Nixon and the 1988 election of Bush senior, the Jewish vote for the Republican Party fluctuated around 35 per cent, dropping to 11 per cent in Bush's second term. Since then, the numbers have been steadily increasing and there is some evidence that the Jewish electorate moved closer to the Republican party during the Obama years. In 1996, 16 per cent of Jews voted Republican, rising to 30 per cent in 2012. Obama received an estimated 78 per cent of the Jewish vote in 2008 and 69 per cent in 2012.[9] Surveys of American Jews have found support of or identification with Republicans has moved from 9 per cent in 2000 to 19 per cent in 2015. The presidential election of 2016 found that about 71 per cent of Jewish voters supported Clinton and 24 per cent supported Trump. It should be noted that Jewish support for the Republicans has tended to come more from the Orthodox sectors of the community. Perhaps more telling, among the thirty Jewish members of congress following the 2016 elections, only two were Republican. While the majority of the organized Jewish community has been lukewarm to Trump, this has been due to both fears of latent anti-Semitism among some of his followers and a distaste for illiberal public policy positions. And this discomfort with Trump has percolated into Canada, where there is concern from some organizations and communal leaders about his presidency, notably in areas like immigration. Still, some strong supporters of Israel feel that a Trump administration might be more supportive of Israel than the previous Obama administration.[10]

In Canada, the twenty-first century began with the Liberal party in office, first under Jean Chrétien, then under Paul Martin. With the election of the Conservative government of Stephen Harper in 2006, the Liberal party continued to change leaders, first with Stéphane Dion in 2006 and then with Michael Ignatieff in 2008. The arrival of Stephen Harper on the political scene, first as leader of the Conservative party and then as prime minister, raised the bar in terms of government support for Israel. Harper's support for Israel, and that of his Conservative caucus, was rooted in a combination of support for a democratic but beleaguered ally, opposition to terrorism, and a foundation of Judeo-Christian affinity. After the Harper election, a sustained conversation arose about Canada's new pro-Israel foreign policy, and possible shifts to the right of Canadian Jewish voters.[11]

For a long time into the twenty-first century, Irwin Cotler played an important role in retaining Canadian Jewish loyalty to the Liberals. Cotler, a former McGill law professor and president of the Canadian Jewish congress, has been an iconic figure. An MP and then cabinet minister, he is also a revered defender of Israel and Jewish interest, a legal scholar, and a human rights advocate. Cotler left his McGill position to enter politics, winning a seat in the Liberal riding of Mount Royal. He was appointed justice minister in the Paul Martin Cabinet of 2003. For many Canadian Jews, Cotler's presence in the upper reaches of the Liberal party was reassuring, even though throughout his career there were cases where Cotler's commitment to Israel's defence put him at odds with his party.[12]

Slowly but steadily a crack began to appear in the tight bond between Jews and the Liberal Party. During the Israel-Hezbollah war in 2006, many Jews were upset when Liberal leader Michael Ignatieff suggested, during an appearance on the very popular Radio Canada TV show *Tout le monde en parle*, that the Israeli bombardment of the Lebanese Hezbollah's stronghold of Qana could be considered a war crime.[13] Contrarily, soon-to-be prime minister Harper endorsed Israel's actions as "measured." Subsequently, several high-profile Liberal Jewish supporters, including film producer Robert Lantos, entrepreneurs Gerald Schwartz and Heather Reisman, and even Cotler's wife Ariela, distanced themselves from the Liberal party.[14] It might be noted that in 2008, Ignatieff, then deputy Liberal leader, apologized for his remark in a speech at Toronto's Holy Blossom synagogue, calling it "the most painful experience of my short political career ... it was an error."[15]

In the election of 2008, Liberal party support in the four key Jewish ridings of Thornhill, York Centre, and Eglinton-Lawrence in Toronto, and Mount Royal in Montreal began to decline.[16] The Conservative Party won in Thornhill in 2008 for the first time since the creation of the riding in 1997. The Liberals also lost York Centre in the 2011 election, a seat they had held since 1962, as well as Eglinton-Lawrence, which they had held since 1979. The party did win back these two seats in the 2015 election. Mount Royal has been a Liberal stronghold from 1940 until this writing in 2017. However, according to Irwin Cotler, his 2011 victory in the riding, which is approximately 25 per cent Jewish, was despite, not because of, the Jewish vote, an estimated two-thirds of which voted Conservative.[17] This can be taken as a clear sign that Canadian Jews, notably those who prioritized the welfare and security of Israel, are moving to the right. One often cited Ipsos Reid exit poll – the only such poll – found that in 2011, 52 per cent of Jewish voters supported the Conservatives. This was far higher than any American Jewish support for Republicans.[18]

The Canadian election campaign of 2015 saw a very heated debate within the Jewish community that resonated in the general press as well.[19] Jewish voters were being targeted aggressively, by the Conservative and Liberal parties in particular. According to press reports, many Jewish voters linked support for Israel with a stand against what they perceived as growing anti-Semitism. As of this writing, scientific exit polls have yet to be released for the 2015 election, but an informal *Canadian Jewish News* poll prior to the election found that Jewish support for the Conservative Party was at 44 per cent, 4 per cent above that for the Liberals.[20]

Despite this recent movement to the right, in Canada, and to a much lesser extent in the United States, the basic affiliation of

Canadian Jews has been more left for the past century. Why do Jews have this attachment to the left?[21] One explanation is cultural. Accordingly, the historical experience of Jews as underdogs sets the foundation in some subliminal fashion. For example, Jews are reminded every Passover that they were slaves in Egypt. In addition, embedded within religious Judaism are certain tenets linked to progressive politics: the emphasis on seeking justice in this world; the prophetic yearning for peace; the preference for decent behaviour over simple sacrifices; the exhortation to act righteously; the Talmudic respect for the use of reason and the rule of law as a basis for settling disputes.[22] The idea of Jewish rationalism, as typified by the Talmud, can even be extended (all this is subconscious) to greater support for planning by governments; for example, Franklin Roosevelt's New Deal. In other words, something about being a Jew, about understanding the Jewish experience and Judaic teachings, allegedly leads to a sympathy with the underdog. In the film *The Front*, Woody Allen's character recalls a scene from his youth in which his mother complained that their maid was stealing from them. His father, more understanding, made less of a fuss, claiming, "From who else should she steal if not from us?"

But there are also social structural forces that may also have pushed Jews to the left. One argument is that Jews are liberal because their socio-demographic profile fits liberals generally. Because they are highly educated and live in large cosmopolitan cities, they tend naturally to liberal positions. Another argument claims Jews are on the left because their enemies, especially anti-Semites, have historically been on the right. It was from the liberal left that opposition to the anti-Semitism of the right was most pronounced. The left has supported civil rights for Jews since the French Revolution. Jews also tend to support progressive positions for defensive reasons. Discrimination against other groups often leads to discrimination against Jews. Racism, nativism, and anti-Semitism are expressed by the same right-wing extremist groups, as seen graphically in the summer of 2017 in the demonstrations by neo-Nazis and Klan supporters in Charlottesville, Virginia. This explains why Jews and Jewish organizations have been strong supporters of equal rights for all minorities in Canada and staunch defenders of multiculturalism.

Jews have also supported policies which reduce income differentials. This means support for the basic principles underlying the welfare state: progressive taxation, a significant package of welfare benefits, and, of course, Medicare. Why? The cultural argument sees these as an extension of Judaic values. Jews are commanded in the Torah to help the less fortunate, the poor, the orphan, the widow, and the stranger, for they too were strangers in the land of Egypt. A social structural argument might say too much inequality will lead to social instability, which has often been harmful to Jews. And when inequalities are coupled with ethnic grievances, Jews are at risk. So when Jews support elements of the welfare state, including progressive taxation or new welfare programs, they are supporting higher taxes on themselves to pay for benefits which would flow largely to non-Jews, but avoid social instability. A kind of insurance policy.

Despite the prominent roles of individual Jews in the Progressive Conservative Party and the NDP, the major consequence of these views has been postwar support for the Liberal Party. As one analyst has concluded, referring to the 1970s and early '80s, "Jews are much more likely than Protestants to vote Liberal; Jews are much more likely than Catholics to vote Liberal in Quebec, but not in English Canada, and Jews in general are overwhelmingly Liberal, particularly in Quebec."[23] The historic Jewish support for the Liberal Party begins with the fact that the highest periods of mass Jewish migration took place under Liberal governments, first under Wilfrid Laurier, and later under Louis St Laurent and Lester Pearson. (The restrictive policies of Mackenzie King's Liberals were either unknown, forgotten, or forgiven.) In the postwar period, Jews – and many other immigrants – were moving from a European experience marked by extremism of the left and right: communism and fascism and their attendant brutalities. It is likely they wanted no part of that in Canada. Seeking the relative safety of the ideological centre, immigrants, including Jews, found their home in the Liberal Party. They felt – incorrectly – that possible dangers of European-style extremism were associated with the CCF/NDP and Conservative parties. This was certainly my parents' view; it was inconceivable for them to vote for any party other than the Liberals. By the time they realized that the European analogies did not hold, Canadian Jews had grown comfortable with the Liberals' centrist welfare-state policies. But as we have seen, the twenty-first century ushered in a break with the historic tie of Jews to the Liberal party. The election of Prime Minister Justin Trudeau in 2015 may signal a return to the party. However, as of this writing, some segments of the Jewish public remain wary of the strength of the commitment of the Trudeau government to Israel's security, at least when compared to the stronger pronouncements of the Harper government. That there were only six Jewish MPs elected in 2015 and no Jewish member in Justin Trudeau's cabinet could exacerbate this apprehension. It is possible, therefore, that the Jewish vote in Canada will remain in play.

JEWISH POLITICS

Many non-Jews feel that Jews wield enormous political influence, far greater than their numbers in the electorate would warrant. Some feel that Jewish lobbies in particular are too powerful (see Chapter 11 on anti-Semitism). Jewish communal leaders and elected officials try to avoid the charge of dual loyalty when they defend Jewish interests. When I was a child, I loved to ask my father the following question; If there was a war between Canada and Israel, which country would we support?

Jews have always played significant roles in Canadian political and civic life. Even when there were only handfuls of Jews in Canada, they were contesting and winning legislative office from Quebec to the West Coast. The saga of the Hart family is well known. In 1807, Ezekiel Hart won election to the Assembly in Lower Canada for Trois-Rivières, collecting fifty-nine of 116 votes cast in a field of three candidates. He was denied his seat because he would not take the oath "as a Christian." He was elected again in 1809, and again was denied a seat simply because he was a Jew. He did not run a third time.

The good news is that the non-Jewish electors of his riding were prepared to vote at least twice for a Jew. (This pattern continues. Jewish politicians like Liberal Herb Gray from Windsor, Ontario, and NDP Premier Dave Barrett from British Columbia enjoyed success in ridings with very few Jews.) The bad news is that the controversy about the oath brought forth hoary canards of immorality and dual loyalty against Hart, and against Jews in general. An anonymous writer to *Le Canadien* asked, "By what right can a Jew who is only worried about himself and his sect expect to look after the interests of the whole nation?"[24] The fear of dual loyalty eventually became dormant, not visibly affecting the political or governmental careers of Canadian Jews.

Dormant, but not dead. Canadian Jews have never had to wrestle with the stark dilemma of a Jonathan Pollard affair, in which an

American Jew working at the Pentagon was convicted of spying for Israel in 1985 and sentenced to life imprisonment. (He was in fact released in 2015.) American Jews who felt the sentence was excessive – and from a comparative perspective it was – were deeply conflicted. But short of such drama, there have been cases in which Canadian Jews were caught in similar dilemmas. They have all dealt with Canadian policy towards Israel and the Middle East. Canada has in general been a solid supporter of Israel, but the position of the Canadian government on specific issues of Middle East policy has routinely differed from that of Israel and the major Jewish organizations. The early reluctance of the Canadian government in the 1970s to enforce action to oppose the Arab economic boycott of Israel and of Canadians doing business with Israel directly and indirectly is a case in point.[25]

The promise by Joe Clark's short-lived Conservative government to move the Israeli embassy from Tel Aviv to Jerusalem in 1979 was a major challenge. The idea raised opposition from many in pro-Arab circles, and also led to conjecture that somehow Clark's policy shift was a response to concerted pressure by Canadian Jews and their organizations, which was not the case. In 1988, as minister of external affairs, Clark was involved in a second episode. He criticized Israeli human-rights violations during the intifada at a gathering of the Canada-Israel Committee, and was greeted by a hostile reaction from his Jewish Canadian audience. That event led some commentators to raise the issue of dual loyalty and a powerful Jewish lobby. Ottawa's *Citizen* published an editorial on 12 March 1988 entitled, "The Nerve of Him: Clark Speaks the Truth." An editorial in the *Toronto Star* the same day bluntly stated that, "It was also a necessary reminder to members of the Jewish community of Canada that they are citizens of Canada, not Israel." The response in a letter to the *Star* of 15 March from Charles Zaionz and Rose Wolfe of the Ontario Region of the Canadian Jewish Congress was unusually tough: "The *Star* by questioning the loyalty of Jewish Canadians to Canada, has crossed the line from unrelenting criticism of Israeli government policy into anti-Semitism."[26]

The issue was revived again in the 1990s in the case of Norman Spector. When Spector was appointed ambassador to Israel in 1992 by Brian Mulroney's government, the idea of a Jewish ambassador to Israel seemed troubling to some Canadians. Spector was the first Jewish diplomat, let alone ambassador, posted to Israel.[27] Some objected because he had not been a career diplomat, so his appointment to a sensitive post had the appearance of patronage. But Spector's Jewishness was also a factor. Following his appointment, an Arab group condemned the appointment of, in Spector's words, "a Zionist, who was close to the Bronfmans." Spector recalls that at his committee hearing examining the appointment, "Christine Stewart looked at my CV and asked whether in light of the fact that I spoke Hebrew, I would undertake to learn Arabic. I expected she or someone would note that I was the first ambassador sent to Israel who could speak the language of the country and was shocked at the tone of her question. I committed on the spot to learn Arabic, which I did, thus becoming the first ambassador to speak either of the country's official languages."[28]

Veteran foreign affairs analyst and insider Peyton Lyon addressed these issues in an unpublished letter to the *Globe and Mail,* a copy of which he sent to me. His letter was a response to a 23 June 1998 article I wrote dealing with Hugh Segal's race for the Progressive Conservative leadership, Jewishness, and the issue of dual loyalty.[29] My article also referred positively to Spector's tenure. Lyon disagreed with my assessment of Spector. In an accompanying letter, he claimed that his views reflected "a large majority view among our professional foreign service officers." Referring to these officers, he claimed that they believed that Canadian interests and policies differed widely from those of Israel. And they resented "the lobbying that has distorted what they believe best for Canada, the States, and even Israel."

According to Lyon, the first person suggested by Ottawa as ambassador to the new state of Israel was David Croll. He claims the Israelis discouraged the appointment. "They feared that a Jewish-Canadian ambassador would be excessively concerned to demonstrate his loyalty to doubting Canadian countrymen." Regarding Spector's appointment, Lyon claims that there "never had been a Canadian policy to flatter any ethnic group by sending one of their number to the land of their heritage." In his view, it was not surprising that Jews, with only 1 per cent of the population, had not yet produced an ambassador to Israel. With regard to Spector's record, Lyon disagrees with my assessment that "by all accounts Spector's tenure was a model of fairness and defence of the Canadian interest" and claims it "evoked laughter and scorn at the weekly meeting of ex-ambassadors that I usually attend." I stand by my assessment, and can indeed recall instances when prominent members of the Canadian Jewish community objected in confidence to some of Spector's actions, feeling they tilted towards the Palestinian or Arab side. In Lyon's view, Spector's achievement "was to perpetuate doubts about Canadians who seem more responsive to the interests of their ancestral homelands than to those of Canada."[30] In other words, dual loyalty.

Another major conflict of interest for Canadian Jews took place in the fall of 1997. It concerned the use of false Canadian passports by Mossad agents in a botched assassination attempt in Jordan. The Canadian government angrily recalled David Berger, another Jewish ambassador to Israel. Norman Spector argued publicly that the use of Canadian passports by Israeli security was not news to CSIS, though it may have been to Foreign Affairs Minister Lloyd Axworthy, and that co-operation between Israeli and Canadian intelligence "goes well beyond information sharing to include some operations worthy of a James Bond thriller." As the story unfolded, a number of Jewish Canadians reported being approached by Israeli officials seeking to "borrow" their passports. At any rate, Israel issued a formal apology to Canada about the affair, and undertook measures to see it would not be repeated.[31]

How should a Canadian Jew respond to a seemingly serious conflict between Canadian government policy and the welfare of Israel? The Pollard case in the United States involved the sale to Israel of information concerning the military assets of several hostile Arab countries, which Pollard felt was crucial to Israel's strategic needs. Pollard felt that sharing the information would not harm the United States (he was wrong, since it risked compromising the network of American electronic espionage as well as blowing the cover of American agents) and that the United States should have shared it with Israel in any case. I can understand that logic, even though it defends a clearly treasonous act. Consider the following hypothetical case.

Imagine the year is 1940 or early 1941. An American of British origin working for American intelligence discovers some crucial information about plans for German air strikes into Britain. The United States is officially neutral at the time, so the information is not to be given to the British. How would we judge, legally and morally, the intelligence officer if he or she decides to violate American law, endanger American intelligence operations, and, *à la* Pollard, pass on this vital information to the British?

Jews have not been the only ones charged with dual loyalty or special pleading. The travails of the Japanese in North America during the Second World War are well known. But Catholics were also not immune. People now forget how novel – and narrow – John Kennedy's election victory was in 1960. There has still been only one Catholic president. And even in the early 1990s, New York governor Mario Cuomo, a committed Catholic, was treated with suspicion by pro-choice activists. In Canada, anti-Catholicism has been linked to anti-French prejudice, but given the proliferation of Catholic prime ministers, that issue is moot. Or is it? In recent decades in Ontario, there have been fewer Catholic than Jewish leaders of Ontario political parties or mayors of Toronto. Recently, it is Muslims and Arabs in Canada who are most likely to have their loyalties questioned. Canada's participation in the Gulf War against Iraq was tough for many Canadian Arabs and Muslims. While they were exposed to prejudice and false allegations of terrorism, many were deeply conflicted by Canada's role in that war. These issues are less acute in Canada than in the United States. Canada's weight in international affairs, and certainly in the Middle East, is far less, so the stakes are not as high. But it is premature to say that Canadian Jews whose public actions defend Jewish interests will always escape the dual loyalty accusation. They will not.

The field of diaspora studies has recognized, albeit minimally, the tensions that can arise between homeland and diasporic communities. These ties can enhance or weaken the interests of both the diasporic community and the homeland.[32] The history of Zionism offers an illuminating case study in how homelands and diasporas can try to negotiate boundaries to avoid conflicts of interest and dual loyalty allegations in Western liberal democracies. American and British Jewish community leaders were worried that support for Zionism might lead to charges of dual loyalty. Indeed, after Israeli independence in 1948, an exchange of letters between Israeli prime minister David Ben Gurion and president of the American Jewish Committee Jacob Blaustein sought to establish an agreement that Israel would not interfere in the affairs of the American Jewish community, and vice versa.[33] (Needless to say this agreement did not last long.) In Canada, moreover, tensions between a homeland and a diasporic community are not confined to the Jewish case.[34]

Indeed, my own research suggests that among Canadian Jews, one can find an undercurrent of unease regarding the potential for dual loyalties. Some years ago, I interviewed in confidence seventeen prominent Canadian Jewish figures. I asked them to indicate for whom they would root in a hypothetical Olympic match-up in soccer between Canada and Israel. This was an opening question in a longer interview. I thought this would be a fun and engaging way to begin the interviews. I was wrong. My respondents all demonstrated a great deal of discomfort in answering the question. Many were reluctant to choose, or felt the need to give long and tortured explanations for their choice.[35]

Defending Israel, and ensuring Canadian government support for Israel, will be a continuing political challenge. Canadians for Justice and Peace in the Middle East is a pro-Palestinian and anti-Israel advocacy group which seeks to bring sophisticated information and lobbying efforts to their cause. An Ekos survey they sponsored in early 2017 reveals possible slippage in Canadian popular support for Israel. About two-thirds of Canadians felt that government sanctions against Israel would be "reasonable," 78 per cent felt Palestinian calls for boycotts were "reasonable," and 46 per cent had a negative perception of the Israeli government compared to 28 per cent with a positive. The negative attitudes were also more pronounced among younger and more educated respondents, and supporters of the NDP, the Bloc Quebecois, and the Liberals; only supporters of the Conservative party were more supportive. The wording and question placement of this poll may have been such as to bias responses in an anti-Israel direction. Questions on the general idea of sanctions were posed first, and then Israel-specific questions. But regardless, large gaps in the survey response data are likely cause for concern among Canadian Jewish leaders.[36]

THE EVOLUTION OF JEWISH POLITICAL INVOLVEMENT

Jews have moved steadily into the mainstream of Canadian political life and power. Before the mass migration around 1900, their politics reflected the positions of communal leaders as merchants and professionals. By no means were all Jews well-off, and many worked as peddlers or craftsmen.[37] But few worked as unskilled labourers, and fewer still were indigent. Nevertheless, their position as a religious minority tended to make Jewish elected representatives predisposed to tolerance and sensitive to discrimination generally.

In the second half of the nineteenth century, the Eastern European Jews brought with them a tradition of left-wing politics. Among them were socialists, anarchists, and other leftists of various persuasions, as well as supporters of liberal and centrist parties. In the United States, the tie with the left is better known. German Jews in the United States supported Lincoln and the Republicans, the liberal and anti-slavery party. But by the 1930s, American Jews had begun their unbroken attachment to the Democratic Party and liberal politics. Jewish liberal support surpasses that of any White ethnic or religious group in the United States and despite their economic mobility, Jews have remained relatively loyal. According to a well-known American saying, "Jews earn like Episcopalians and vote like Puerto Ricans." In any event, Jews soon held high executive office. Judah Benjamin was the secretary of state in the Confederacy. In 1906, Theodore Roosevelt appointed Oscar Straus as secretary of commerce and labour, the first Jew in the American cabinet. "I want to show Russia and some other countries what we think of the Jews in this country," Roosevelt said to Straus when explaining his choice.[38]

In Canada, by the beginning of the First World War, several Jews had been elected as aldermen from Quebec to British Columbia. S. Hart Green was elected to sit in the Manitoba Legislature and Peter Bercovitch was elected to the National Assembly in Quebec. By the 1930s, there were three Jewish MPs: Sam Jacobs from Montreal, A.A. Heaps from Winnipeg, and Sam Factor from Toronto. David Croll won election to the Ontario Legislature in 1934, and as minister of labour and welfare was Canada's first Jewish cabinet minister. Later on, after entering federal politics and being denied a federal cabinet position, he became Canada's first Jewish senator. In the postwar period, an increasing number of Jews have held elective office, in all parties, even though they have been clustered in the centre-left part of the political spectrum.

Herb Gray became Canada's first Jewish federal cabinet minister in 1969 – six decades after Straus was appointed in the United States – in the Liberal government of Prime Minister Pierre Trudeau. The NDP has had strong representation of Jews among its leaders. Dave Barrett of British Columbia served as the first Jewish provincial premier in 1972. David Lewis was the leader of the national NDP. His son Stephen was NDP leader in Ontario and later ambassador to the United Nations. Larry Grossman was leader of the Ontario Progressive Conservatives. Three mayors of Toronto – Nathan Phillips, Phil Givens, and Mel Lastman – have been Jews. For federal Conservatives, Gerry Weiner served as cabinet minister in areas of immigration and multiculturalism in the government of Brian

Mulroney. Hugh Segal, a red Tory and later senator, has long been an insider among mainstream Conservatives, and contested the party leadership in 1998. Had Segal been successful, he would have been the first Jewish leader of one of Canada's two governing parties. In the news reports and commentary about that leadership race, the fact that he was Jewish was not mentioned. The silence was rather deafening, and contrasts with the extensive public discussion of Senator Joe Lieberman's Orthodox Jewishness in the American media. Segal's first ballot showing of less than 20 per cent was disappointing, and I would not rule out either deliberate or unconscious anti-Semitism among some right-wing Conservatives as one possible factor. Conservatives wanting to "unite the right" may have assumed that Segal would be a tougher sell to some Reformers. The Reform Party and its successor, the Alliance, did not have the same degree of extreme populism or militant Christianity reflected by people like Pat Buchanan or Pat Robertson. But its image remained problematic for many Jews.

Journalist David Frum has been a prominent neo-conservative intellectual influence in Canadian (and American) politics, and Ezra Levant, from Calgary, was a special assistant to Reform leader Preston Manning and assumed a more populist profile. In the battle for the Alliance leadership between Preston Manning and Stockwell Day, rumours about possible anti-Semitism in Day's background swirled around the candidate.[39] Whereas Manning's relations with Jews in Alberta were positive, Day was an unknown quantity. Over time, Day showed himself to be a friend of the Jewish community and a staunch supporter of Israel. The current Conservative Party, which arose from a merger with the Reform party, has continued down that path.

Apart from their role in party politics, Canadian Jews have also served as senior public servants. There have been five Jewish members of the Canadian Supreme Court: Rosalie Abella, Morris Fish, Bora Laskin, Michael Moldaver, and Marshall Rothstein, compared to eight in the United States. Given that the American Jewish population is twenty times that of Canada, the Canadian number is impressive.

Jews have moved rapidly through the ranks of the federal public service, as well as attaining influence as political advisors. For example, Bernard and Sylvia Ostry held senior cultural and economic positions respectively. Louis Rasminsky was governor of the Bank of

Canada from 1961 to 1972. Many other Jews have been prominent as provincial civil servants. Three principal secretaries to Prime Minister Mulroney were Jews: Stanley Hartt, Norman Spector, and Hugh Segal, and so were several of the closest advisors to Prime Minister Jean Chrétien: Eddie Goldenberg, Chaviva Hosek, and David Zussman. Another Jewish public servant, Mel Cappe, was named in late 1998 as the new clerk of the Privy Council. Alex Himelfarb then served as clerk from 2002 to 2006. The Harper government, despite its growing support among Canadian Jews, had fewer prominent Jewish officials. All this is a far cry from the 1930s, when unsympathetic public servants such as F.C. Blair could play a major role in preventing the immigration of German Jewish refugees. Their increasing role as elected politicians and public servants reflects the increasing sophistication and self-confidence of the Canadian Jewish community. In the words of Irving Abella, former president of the Canadian Jewish Congress, "We have clout that we never had before."[40]

What is unclear is whether the Jewishness of these politicians and public servants played any role in shaping their political thinking or their careers. My guess is that in most cases it has. In interviews with me, Hugh Segal claimed his origin as the son of a working-class Jewish immigrant in Montreal helped to develop his outlook as a Red Tory. Former cabinet minister Gerry Weiner cited his Jewish background as helping him identify with all minority groups and take a hard line against discrimination. Liberal cabinet minister Irwin Cotler's commitment to human rights and social justice has been in part nourished by his understanding of the Jewish experience.

JEWISH POLITICAL INFLUENCE

Jews try to use politics to defend their (liberal) values and Jewish interests. This is what any ethnic polity does.[41] Voting in Canada correlates with higher levels of socioeconomic status, for minorities and majorities alike. The mobilization of ethnic votes, whether in elections or even nomination meetings, is now an important new element in Canadian politics.[42] But political influence is channeled in many other ways. Jews in Canada are influential in political parties and causes, and they are prominent as donors and fundraisers (though less than in the United States), but they rarely act as part of any coordinated campaign led by formal communal organizations.

Other avenues of political influence are the informal networks linking Jewish politicians and Jewish communal leaders. A prime example is Irwin Cotler, who became an MP from Quebec in 1999 after having served as president of the Canadian Jewish Congress.

Jewish political clout is greater in the United States than in Canada. It is ironic that the separation of church and state there has made it more important for Jews to mobilize to defend their interests than it is for Jews in Canada, where religions have legal status and ethnic diversity is enshrined in the constitution. Moreover, the American political system, with its distinction between the legislative and executive branch, gives American Jews more points of leverage to influence policy. There is little in Canada – so far – to warrant a book such as the ominously titled *Jewish Power*, written by American journalist J.J. Goldberg, or *The Israel Lobby*, written by John Mearsheimer and Stephen Walt, which argues that the "pro-Israel" lobby in the US distorts American foreign policy.[43] These volumes chronicle the links between Jews, the organized Jewish community, Christian groups, the Israeli government, and the American political system, and at times read like political whodunits. American Jews are major contributors to political campaigns. In 2014, one study claimed that over a third of the top fifty political donors were Jewish, and another that the top ten were all Jewish.[44] Different studies will find different numbers depending on the year and type of political donation. These donations have gone mainly to Democratic candidates. But the overall finding is clear: wealthy Jews are major contributors to American political life.

Compared to American Jews, Canadian Jews are more likely to be foreign-born and thus less acculturated into politics. They are also a smaller proportion of the population. Moreover, the international stakes are just not as great in Canada on any issue on the Jewish political agenda, from the Middle East to repayment of Nazi-era financial claims. So Jewish political mobilization and participation in Canada is both less important and less effective. As of the end of 2016, there were ten American Jewish senators, and nineteen Jewish members of the House of Representatives, but only six Jewish members of Parliament in Canada.[45] In other words, American Jews represented 10 per cent of American Senators and 5 per cent of the House, compared to 1.75 per cent of Canadian MPs in 2016. The Jewish vote in the United States has historically been key in certain northeastern districts, as well as some in Florida and California.

This, plus the fact that Jews are more likely to vote and donate to both parties gives American Jews seemingly greater influence than numbers alone warrant.

There are no recent studies of the electoral consequences of the Canadian Jewish vote. But there are ridings in Montreal and Toronto which are heavily Jewish and which have traditionally elected Jewish representatives or those sympathetic to the political concerns of the community. None of this is a secret. Jews and other minority groups are acting more and more like interest groups. Canadian Jews are certainly concerned with Canadian policy in the Middle East, and many, through CIJA, promote Israel's interests in a non-partisan way.[46] Traditionally, policy-makers dealing with international relations have not welcomed input from any ethnic group on a homeland issue, as the correspondence from Peyton Lyon suggests.[47] Ethnic groups can be seen as promoting a special interest which may clash with so-called national interests. Ottawa mandarins might like to think that the national interest is best determined through their expertise, and in a rational, detached manner. Involving interested parties would, in this view, distort the process. But, of course, a democratic perspective on the question differs dramatically. It suggests that elites and experts should heed the voice of citizens, particularly those who are most concerned with an issue. From this perspective, minorities mobilizing to defend their interest politically are not a distortion of the democratic process. They *are* the democratic process.

LA SURVIVANCE: JEWS IN QUEBEC

The Jewish community in Quebec is a multifaceted community with a rich past and diverse present.[48] However, the Jews of Quebec are the one Jewish group in North America whose future has been clouded by political instability. Indeed, since the rise of the Parti Québécois to power in 1976, and even before, Quebec Jewry has been in "continual caucus." In Quebec, it is an open secret that Jews, the organized Jewish community, and community leaders opposed Quebec independence, and thereby the Parti Québécois, from the very start of the 1970s round of constitutional debates.[49] Jews cast almost all their votes for the Liberal Party of Quebec.

The threat of Quebec sovereignty and the reality of French nationalism has had a draining effect on Montreal Jewish life. The demographics do not look good, as many of the younger generation have moved to points west or to the United States. The High Holidays and Passover are particularly poignant times. The streets of Montreal's Jewish neighbourhoods are filled with Ontario licence plates as children visit parents and grandparents. Yet at the same time, Montreal still retains an amazingly rich Jewish communal and cultural life. I refer here to more than high per capita donations to the Federation annual appeals. The Montreal community, with all its challenges, also invested millions in an expanded new community campus for the Federation as well as renovations to the Jewish Community Centre at the turn of the century. Today, the Toronto Jewish community is roughly double the size of that in Montreal. On a per capita basis, both communities have a comparable level of cultural vitality and communal organizations. This high quality of Jewish life in Montreal remains all the more remarkable given the uncertainty that dates back to the 1960s.

The leaders of Quebec's Jewish community, notably Federation CJA, have faced difficult choices when defending Jewish interests. Members of the Montreal Jewish communal leadership have often differed with what some have called "deep Côte St-Luc," the heavily Jewish and middle-class suburb in Montreal.[50] The latter favour a more aggressive, populist opposition to sovereignty and, in particular, to further restrictions in matters of language or minority rights. They have considered the Jewish establishment too timid. In the 1980s and 1990s, some Jews supported the Equality Party, some the militant radio personality Howard Galganov. Others played leading roles in the "softer" Alliance Québec. In contrast to the hard-liners, there are other Jewish scholars and public intellectuals who continue to promote dialogue with French Quebec, including its nationalist elements. The scholarly work of Pierre Anctil, Ira Robinson, and Gérard Bouchard has contributed to the spirit of rapprochement.[51] In recent years, Jews and other allophones have begun to play a more central role in English-speaking Quebec, crowding the old dominant Anglo-Saxon and Celtic elites. Many of the major anglophone cultural institutions, like McGill and Concordia universities and the *Gazette* newspaper, have had Jewish leadership.

In Chapter 11 we explore the issue of anti-Semitism in Quebec. There is no doubt that Quebec nationalists were wary about the charges of anti-Semitism that were levelled, with his inimitable wit, by Mordecai Richler. They recoiled at the writings of Esther Delisle, who exposed the anti-Semitic and fascist leanings of Lionel Groulx,

Le Devoir, and the Quebec intelligentsia from the 1930s to the 1960s.[52] But despite the tensions, the political climate in Quebec has not been fully hostile to Jews. In the 1960s, among politically aware Jewish university students, it was common to find sympathy to the French struggle for *la survivance*. Parallels were drawn, and to some extent are still drawn, between the struggle for Hebrew in Israel and for French in Quebec. Most Jews, even as they remain strong federalists, understand the desire of a minority to resist assimilation. Even Parti Québécois governments kept open contacts with the Jewish community.

Over the decades, the situation of Quebec Jews has varied, often depending on whether a Liberal or Parti Québécois government is holding provincial power. But in broad strokes, Quebec Jews remain marginal to the political life of the province, despite some heroic exceptions such as the late Doctor Victor Goldbloom.[53] As mentioned earlier, three Jews in the postwar years were elected mayor of Toronto. This has yet to happen once in Montreal. In postwar Ontario, Jews have headed three provincial parties, Stuart Smith of the Liberals, Stephen Lewis of the NDP, and Larry Grossman of the Conservatives. No Jew has ever led a major Quebec political party. Moreover, the debate about "reasonable accommodation" and the subsequent proposed Charter of Values of the Parti Québécois government (2012–14), shook the Jewish community. The Charter of Values sought to restrict dramatically any religious apparel warn by any public servant in Quebec. This could have meant no *yarmulkas* for any doctors or high school teachers (of course this could have also eliminated the right to wear *hijab*s, turbans, and large crosses). Indeed, some elements of the Jewish community, notably the Jewish General Hospital, spoke of civil disobedience in the event that the charter passed. The Parti Québécois electoral defeat put that specific proposal to rest, at least temporarily.[54] But as of this writing, similar proposals are being debated by all major Quebec political parties.

Neither Jews nor Quebec politicians have any illusions about the convictions of Jews on constitutional issues. In a 1996 study, about 45 per cent of Montreal Jews preferred the federalist status quo, about 38 per cent a revised federalism with more provincial power, with the rest sprinkled among other options including sovereignty-association, and complete independence.[55] It is thus not difficult to estimate how Jews vote in provincial elections and how they voted in the 1995 referendum and subsequent elections. But even within this monolith there are internal divisions. The Sephardi community, notably some leaders of the then Communauté Sépharade du Québec, were less strident in their federalism. Sephardim were much less likely, at under 32 per cent, to prefer the constitutional status quo. Almost 6 per cent, three times the general communal proportion, were inclined to support either sovereignty-association or independence for Quebec. It is very unlikely, therefore, though certainly possible, that an estimated 10 per cent of Sephardi Jews voted PQ in the 1998 provincial election, as claimed in a French-language CBC TV report.[56] The point here is still that the overwhelming majority of francophone/Sephardi Jews oppose the PQ and sovereignty. It is widely known that Parti Québécois officials have hoped to attract francophone Jews to their camp, as they have tried with other French-speaking immigrant groups. For example, Évelyne Abitbol was an unsuccessful Sephardic Jewish Candidate for the PQ in the provincial elections of 2014. So far, the success of this version of "divide and conquer" has been minimal.

THE JEWISH DOMESTIC POLITICAL AGENDA

What do Canadian Jews want out of Canadian politics? The domestic political agenda of Canadian Jews can be surmised from its concerns through support for specific policies. First is support for a united Canada. It is not clear how, if at all, the election of Justin Trudeau as prime minister will impact this debate. Support for Quebec independence rises and falls; as of this writing the levels are low. While Jewish communities nationally share this federalist commitment, there has not yet emerged a concerted and effective strategy for mobilizing Jews and other citizens, and lobbying federal and provincial governments, on the federalist cause. Many Jews in Ontario and the West are ex-Montrealers and share a visceral sympathy with family and friends in Montreal. Many desire Canadian unity, while appreciating the efforts in Quebec to preserve a French identity. But at the same time, there are doubtless Canadian Jews who share the "let them go" attitude regarding Quebec. What remains unclear is what steps, if any, Jews outside Quebec would take to help Quebec Jews in the event of a rapid deterioration of the social climate there, perhaps after a "Yes" vote in yet another referendum. It would certainly put communal solidarity to the test.

A second plank in the Jewish political agenda has been support for immigration in general and Jewish immigration in particular. Traditionally, it is hard to find many Jews who would rally around a political party or movement which was, or was perceived to be, anti-immigrant. Canadian Jews seem genetically programmed to welcome immigrants, and especially refugees. The memories of the Holocaust, and of Canadian borders closed to desperate European Jews, are too fresh. Many Jews are, moreover, either immigrants or children of immigrants. This does not mean Jewish organizations advocate an open-door policy, but the Jewish community has been supportive of generous policies towards *bona fide* refugees and immigrants. This has been shown in post-2015 efforts of liberal Jewish congregations and organizations to sponsor Syrian refugees to Canada. At the same time, one wonders whether fears of terrorism and concern about a rising Muslim population in Canada, which is now three times that of the Jewish population, might in the future undercut these traditional Jewish attitudes. Indeed, it is possible that such fears also play a role in recent Jewish support for the Conservative Party, which has been tougher on Syrian refugee intake.[57]

The defence of Israel's right to live in peace and security is a third item. This does not mean that Canadian Jewish organizations, to say nothing of all Jews, inevitably support every policy of the Israel government. They do not. But the bedrock principles are pretty near inviolate. Should Israel be in unambiguous danger, almost all identifying Canadian Jews will likely defend her vigorously. Jewish organizations close ranks when the Canadian government levels serious criticism at Israel. But over the years, and within the "family," more Canadian Jews have accepted the legitimacy of dissent from specific Israeli policies, even if this may seem to endorse Canadian government policy. As far back as 1987, a Canada-wide survey of Jewish communal leaders, professors, and rabbis aged between twenty-five and forty found 56 per cent felt they had the right to criticize Israeli policies and actions publicly.[58]

In the United States, a vigorous debate has recently emerged among scholars about whether American Jews have been distancing themselves from Israel. This "distancing debate" focuses largely on younger generations and the degree to which assimilation on the one hand, and disenchantment with Israeli policies on the other, fuel it.[59] If significant distancing is taking place, which some scholars debate, the major factor is likely ongoing assimilation.[60] But other factors also play a role. One may be opposition to Israeli policies regarding the Palestinian issue. Another may be the control by the ultra-Orthodox rabbinate of religious issues in Israel. Thus, in mid-2017, diaspora-Israel relations were roiled by decisions to limit the status of non-Orthodox Jews by prohibiting gender-equal prayer space near the Western Wall in Jerusalem, and by restricting the rights of conversion under non-Orthodox auspices.[61] More recently, Jewish communal and intellectual elites in Canada and the United States have been more willing to dissent from Israeli policies than the Jewish rank and file. In Canada, such debates are emerging.[62] For example, Carleton University political scientist Mira Sucharov has been prominent in trying to craft a progressive and at times critical defence of Israel's right to exist.[63] She has done this through blogs and as a columnist for the *Canadian Jewish News* (though as described earlier, she has resigned from the paper) and in a way, has carved out space similar to that of Peter Beinart in the United States.[64] Indeed, the two appeared together in a 2016 panel discussion at the University of Toronto on the two-state solution or other options for Israel/Palestine.[65]

On the whole, Canadian Jews have been less likely to criticize Israeli policy in public than have American Jews, where petitions, counter-petitions, and op-eds in the Jewish and general press have been common.[66] Such open letters and petitions cover topics like Zionism and Israel, the occupation, and BDS initiatives on campuses. Like many Jews, I wrestle with the limits or obligations of my visceral solidarity with Israel, given my generally progressive, anti-occupation, anti-Likud posture. Sometimes I make a point of defending Israel or shading any criticism as best I can in certain social settings – like sitting around a friendly table at the McGill Faculty Club – where Middle East politics comes up frequently. This will depend on the tenor of the particular conversation and the roster of participants. At other times, I will voice serious criticism of Israeli policy. I play a tactical version of Marshall Sklare's "ambassadorial role," but this time defending Israel rather than diaspora Jews.

Where dissent has been expressed in Canada, it has often been in pages of the *Canadian Jewish News*; that is, within the tribe. Moreover, ads that have appeared have tended to be evenhanded in tone and criticism, combining a critique of Israeli policy with one of Palestinian or Arab actions. Indeed, a minority (20 to 30 per cent) of Montreal Jews surveyed in 2010 expressed disagreement with

Israel's handling of Middle East issues.[67] Canadian Jewish organizations, such as Canadian Friends of Peace Now, j space, and the more critical Independent Jewish Voices Canada, will also issue statements and articles criticizing Israeli policies to a greater or lesser extent.

Another item on the Jewish policy agenda is opposition to racism, xenophobia, and anti-Semitism, and a general support for human rights and the principles of multiculturalism. In Canada, as elsewhere in the West, this encompasses two sorts of problems. The first is the response to overt anti-Semitism. But when it surfaces, as in the actions of neo-Nazi groups, acts of vandalism, public expressions of contempt, or hate messages on the Internet, the Jewish position is generally clear. Canadian Jewish organizations support laws against hate literature and hate speech, laws promoting employment equity, and anti-discrimination legislation.

The second involves many gray areas of public policy. There are many cases where "reasonable accommodation" to Jewish religious concerns or sensibilities – in jobs, schools, or elsewhere – must be determined. The discourse of anti-Semitism is no longer really applicable to many of these kinds of issues, even though they harm Jewish interests and offend Jewish sensibilities. For example, Le Sanctuaire, a posh high-rise condo in Montreal, sought a permanent court injunction from the Quebec Superior Court against those residents who might build a *sukkah*, a makeshift hut covered with branches used by Jews during the holiday of Sukkoth, on their balconies. The issue of religious freedom was at stake, at least on the part of the religious condo owners. To adjudicate the case, the court heard conflicting expert testimony from two rabbis. Eventually, the court sided with Le Sanctuaire, citing the testimony of their expert witness, Rabbi Barry Levy. In his view, residents could use *sukkahs* at local synagogues. It was not religiously crucial for Jewish residents to have *sukkahs* on their own balconies.[68] But eventually this case, known as the Amsallem case, went all the way to the Supreme Court. The ruling there then favoured the condo resident rather than Le Sanctuaire. The Court argued that what was decisive was not one or another rabbinic interpretation of the religious issue. Rather, what mattered was that the defendant had a sincere belief that he had to have his own *sukkah* in order to fulfill the religious commandment.[69] It remains to be seen whether this precedent will be extended to other cases where individual understandings of faith obligations will trump expert religious authority.

We can imagine other examples. Schools, other government services, and businesses must accommodate the religious requirements of Jewish workers or employees. How far, say, should the Canadian Armed Forces go to accommodate religious requirements of an Orthodox Jewish recruit? Where do you draw the line between legitimate debate over aspects of the Holocaust and Holocaust denial and hate speech? What of possible challenges to kosher ritual slaughter on the grounds that it is perceived by some animal rights advocates as inhumane? Suppose activists decide, as an extension of the opposition to female genital operations, that male circumcision is a form of criminal assault. Indeed, this is precisely the point that has been made by Professor Margaret Somerville, of the McGill University Centre for Medicine, Ethics, and Law. Dr Somerville has argued that in almost all cases, male circumcision is therapeutically unnecessary and therefore criminal assault.[70] She recognizes that circumcisions done for religious reasons might deserve a different approach. Rather than prosecute Jews, it may be possible to engage in dialogue with rabbis to lead them to modify their views, in the light of new medical evidence. Presumably laws would be drafted, and then Jews could be persuaded through dialogue to abandon the practice. Though this is all well-meaning, it would bring us to a new form of medieval disputation in which Jews had to defend their faith against non-Jews. In fact, in several European countries, there has been intense political debate about restricting both male circumcision and kosher slaughter.[71]

I have reviewed many relevant studies and am not persuaded of the harm caused by *milah*, or circumcision. In fact, quite the opposite. Male circumcision is a desirable intervention to prevent sexually transmitted diseases, including HIV/AIDS.[72] Moreover, there is no epidemiological evidence that Jewish boys or men have historically suffered higher rates of disease or death or any adverse long-term outcomes associated with the procedure. The major problem for opponents seems to be pain and possible harmful after-effects for the infant. Painkilling ointments can alleviate the discomfort. There should be no religious objection to such a modification. As for post-circumcision traumas, there is no evidence that Jewish boys become undernourished, or develop a weaker bond with their mothers. In any case, it would be a political nightmare for Jews if this budding movement grew to the point where legislation criminalizing circumcision were anticipated. Some Jews do indeed refuse to circumcise their children, and they have that legal right. Indeed, some Jews may even support the intactivist movement in Canada.[73] However, prohibiting all Jews from doing so would be quite something else. The level of civil disobedience this inspired would be staggering.[74]

Opposition to anti-Semitism blends in with support for multiculturalism, which legitimates the Jewish concern with cultural survival. The ideology of multiculturalism also blends with Jewish liberalism since they both reach out to underdogs and victims. Jews, like other minorities, see in the public rhetoric around multiculturalism symbolic recognition of their valued place in Canada. Indeed, as I have been arguing throughout this book, Jews are a multicultural group *par excellence*. Jews do what they can to preserve multiculturalism, in fact and as a symbol.

A final item on the Canadian Jewish agenda is support for the welfare state. This has also been seen in American surveys of Jewish opinion on domestic policy questions.[75] Jews, more than most, seem to see value in an activist government, as seen in the United States by the Democratic tilt. Of course, part of this support reflects the Jewish belief that it is right to help the unfortunate. Case closed. But there may be another reason, perhaps subconscious, for their support of the public sector. Jews are overrepresented in the health, scientific, research, social service, and educational professions, all of which rely in one way or another on government spending. Thus there may be self-interest, intentional or unintentional, in Jewish support for a strong public sector. While state services may flow to the poor or general population, who are less likely to be Jews, the salaries of the deliverers of service are more likely to flow to Jews, as middle-class professionals. Jewish organizations, in general, steer clear of positions on economic policy. But one exception to this has been the opposition of Jewish welfare organizations both in Canada – at the federal and provincial levels – and the United States to budget cuts in the areas of health and social services.[76] Those cuts have downloaded many of the welfare burdens to private agencies in general and Jewish agencies in particular.

COALITION POLITICS AND PARTISAN POSITIONS

There is strength in numbers, especially for minorities. Jewish politicians, public servants, advisors, voters, and, of course, donors can do only so much.[77] Wherever possible, Canadian Jewish organizations have also used a coalition approach. Jews have deliberately played a key role within the human rights and anti-racist community in Canada, as they have historically in the United States. Jews have joined with other minority ethnic, racial, or religious organizations, human-rights groups, and labour unions on matters of common interest.[78]

In the United States, these coalitions have historically been linked to the Democratic Party. In Canada, the coalitions have tended to be more non-partisan and ad hoc. One exception was the coalition among the organized Jewish, Italian, and Greek communities in Quebec to support the Charlottetown accord, extending into the 1995 referendum debate in Quebec. The collaboration continued despite differences in the social, political, and cultural characteristics of the three communities.[79] The three groups were largely federalist, and hoped that constitutional reform would defuse the separatist threat. The accord represented an effort to amend the constitution with the consent of Quebec. The Canadian Jewish Congress entered the Tripartite Coalition with the National Congress of Italian Canadians and the Hellenic Canadian Congress, and together the group played a visible role. In the autumn of 1991, they toured several Canadian cities. They presented a brief to the Beaudoin-Dobbie Special Committee in February 1992, and while there were some reservations, they agreed in August 1992 to support the accord. So did B'nai Brith, and so did Pioneer Women-Na'amat Canada, which suspended its membership in the National Action Committee on the Status of Women when the latter came out against the accord. There is no way of knowing to what extent these political representations by the Jewish community (and other ethnic groups) affected sentiment either among Canadian Jews or in the country as a whole. There was strong support for the accord in those areas of Montreal and Toronto with large Jewish concentrations. In Quebec, 57 per cent of the population voted "no," but in the largely Jewish provincial riding of D'Arcy-McGee, the "yes" vote came in at 92 per cent. In Toronto, the "yes" vote in areas with large Jewish concentrations – Willowdale, St Paul's, Don Valley East, Eglinton-Lawrence – came in around 60 per cent.

On the other hand, Jews in the West were less committed to Charlottetown than were Eastern Jews, who saw the issue as much as a Jewish issue as one dealing with constitutional change. Calgary's *Jewish Free Press* published the results of a non-scientific hotline poll in its 30 October 1992, issue. Of those who responded, 87.5 per cent reported they had voted "no." (That may have overstated Jewish opposition.) Clearly, regional sentiments played a role in how Jews viewed the accord, and perhaps even the importance of national unity. In the West, the Jewish grassroots may have felt less obliged to support the directives of the national Jewish elite organizations, catching the very populist spirit that sunk both the Meech Lake and Charlottetown accords. The tripartite coalition predictably raised the ire of Quebec sovereigntists. In an interview with the *Canadian Jewish News* on 24 June 1993, Parti Québécois Premier Jacques Parizeau described the role of Jewish leaders as "extremely dangerous." This view foreshadowed his harsher comment that "money and the ethnic vote" had cost the Parti Québécois the 1995 referendum.[80]

The future of Canadian ethno-racial coalition politics is dicey. The multicultural community includes a range of groups that can be divided into two rough categories. One comprises older, European groups, largely Canadian-born, who are doing well economically. Their concerns are cultural retention and status politics. The second comprises groups that are more recent, mainly non-White, immigrant, and low-income. Their concern is mainly the fight against racism and discrimination. Canadian Jews have shared the concerns of both groups and have managed to ally themselves with both, a tough balancing act. But these two groups really have different priorities. If the multicultural coalition comes apart due to racial polarization, the Jewish community will find itself in a delicate situation. Jewish self-perception as a vulnerable group will clash with the fact of Jewish success in Canada, particularly in the eyes of other groups.[81]

Black-Jewish relations in Canada are still good, at least compared to the United States, where the historic liberal alliance involving Blacks, Jews, and labour has been fractured over issues like affirmative action. More recently, the embrace by Black Lives Matter of support for BDS and critique of Israel as an apartheid state has added a new division.[82] Perhaps Black-Jewish relations are better in Montreal than in Toronto. In Toronto, Jews are more easily identified with the White majority. They are true insiders, whereas Black Torontonians are not. On the other hand, both Black and Jewish Montrealers are identified more as non-francophone (Haitians excepted) and federalist groups. They are both outside the conception of "*un vrai Québécois.*" The bonds may be tighter. No research studies address this issue.

How long can this Canadian inter-group honeymoon last? The political demography for Canadian Jews may be changing in a more challenging direction as the proportion of visible minority immigrants increases. This is not because of anti-Semitism on the part of visible-minority immigrants. In advocating its interests, the Jewish community has been able to draw upon common experiences with other European immigrant groups for whom the Holocaust and support for Israel are part of a shared historical discourse. Rituals like Remembrance Day on 11 November and symbols like the swastika or the death camps still resonate for the European groups and sustain the image of the Jew as a victim. Many visible-minority Canadians do not share the same historical frame of reference, or to the same degree. This is certainly true for the increasing numbers of Arab and/or Muslim immigrants. These groups bring their own historical legacies of slavery and colonialism, of economic exploitation, of warfare, and even genocide. For some of them, Jews and Israel are allied with the wealthy, with Western powers, and with colonial exploiters.

Canadian Jews have so far been able to retain their moral standing as a victim community in alliance with visible minority groups when dealing with issues of racism. This is due to an extreme racist right that targets both Jews and non-Whites. And employment equity in Canada has yet to engender the conflict and tensions it has between Jewish and Black Americans. There is also no parallel in Canada to the influence of Louis Farrakhan and the Black Muslims within the Black community. But in both Canada and the United States, the growth of Muslim and/or Arab origin groups through immigration will pose specific challenges for Jews seeking to defend Israel's interests. If the Canadian scene is a generation behind the United States, then Canadians can soon expect to experience the same types of identity politics, cultural wars, and inter-group and foreign policy confrontations.[83] A harbinger of such tensions years earlier was the flap over the Toronto production of *Showboat* in the fall of 1993, described in Chapter 7.[84]

But if Jews, or the Jewish lobby, may be perceived as powerful, the truth is more nuanced. The Jewish lobby is far from omnipotent. As is the case with most pressure groups, it is hard to win on every issue. The Canadian Jewish community tried to mobilize action against Nazi war criminals in Canada; it took close to forty years for any progress to be made. A crystallizing event in the campaign was the Deschênes Commission of Inquiry on War Criminals, established in 1985, in which the Canadian Jewish Congress and the League for Human Rights of B'nai Brith found themselves opposed at Commission hearings by two Ukrainian groups. So much for ethnic coalitions. The ultimate recommendations by the Commission, and actions taken since by the War Crimes Unit in the Department of Justice, have generally fallen short of the hopes of the Jewish community.[85] Similar allegations were made about personnel at the Immigration and Refugee Board.[86] As described earlier, for some years, members of the Immigration and Refugee Board would routinely, and to great embarrassment for Canadian Jews, grant refugee status to "Jewish" refugee claimants from Israel. There have been other policy failures. The decision of Joe Clark's government in 1979 to move the Canadian embassy in Israel to Jerusalem from Tel Aviv proved a fiasco. Efforts of Jews in Ontario to obtain equitable government financial support for Jewish day schools via court rulings or new legislation have been unsuccessful. In 2007, organizations in the Canadian Jewish community lobbied unsuccessfully to extend key sections of the anti-terrorism legislation which had been passed by parliament after 9/11. More generally, efforts by the Canadian Jewish community to influence Canadian voting at the UN in a pro-Israel direction during pre-Harper Liberal governments had at best mixed results.[87]

On the other hand, even if the track record is not perfect, Jews have a strong sense of their own political strength and the linkage between the Jewish community and the government. The setbacks described above are not really major. True, a 2005 Toronto survey found that 55 per cent of Jews who had heard of the Toronto Jewish Congress did not know what it did.[88] But generally Jewish organizations are, or seem to be, more effective than those of other minority groups. Jews have tended to be more aware of the existence of their communal organizations than other ethnic groups in Toronto.[89] Jews perceive a higher degree of political efficacy on the part of their communal leaders, in terms of influencing politicians, even if they are fuzzy on the organizational details.

This relative confidence in the political acumen of Jewish communal leadership will be tested in the near future. The issue of conflicts of interest – dual loyalty – for Jewish public servants or politicians will resurface periodically. Canadian Jews may witness the fraying of their coalition strategies with visible minority groups. Defending Israel will become an increasing challenge and may move the community to the right. Yet it is not clear if the Canadian Jewish community will retain its more recent affinity with Conservative Party and conservative politics.

10

A Holy Nation

Canadian Judaism between Tradition and Modernity

"Hear, O Israel: The Lord our God, the Lord is One."
Deuteronomy 6:4

A joke making the rounds on the Internet claims that most Jewish holidays can be described in nine words: "They tried to kill us. They failed. Let's eat."

UNDERSTANDING JUDAISM: GOD AND SPIRITUALITY

To understand Canadian Jews, even secular Jews, we must understand Judaism.[1] The Jewish religion affects all spheres of Jewish life, directly or indirectly. In its current diversity, Judaism incarnates the paradox of the Jewish experience – the blending of the traditional and the modern. The roots of Judaism run deep. But contemporary Judaism is a mix of constancy and change, well adapted to uncertain times. For Jews as a whole, the tensions created by these opposites – even when they result in conflict – are ultimately beneficial. All religions are still struggling to find their place in Western societies that are formally secular and rational. Judaism is doing rather well.

For many Christian believers, Jews are those cantankerous people who refused to accept the divinity of Jesus. But Judaism and Christianity have much in common, beginning with the fact that Jesus was a Jew. Both revere the Old Testament, both are basically monotheistic and more or less believe in the same God, both subscribe to common codes of human conduct and values. These commonalities are often labelled as "Judeo-Christian" for convenience, though that term bothers some traditional Jews and, for all I know, some fundamentalist Christians. (More recently the term "Abrahamic faith" has emerged to describe the three monotheistic faiths, Judaism, Christianity, and Islam. And indeed, there are religious and cultural affinities between Islam and Judaism.) In any case, Canadian Jews and Christians by and large draw upon a European heritage, despite the origins of both religions in the hills of Judea. This is true also for Sephardi Jews from North Africa or the Middle East, where French, British, and Spanish influences loomed large. Judaism and Christianity have evolved in tandem with – though not without conflict – the basic tenets of liberal democracy.

But there are differences. The conventional wisdom, which I think is right, is that Judaism is more concerned with actions, while Christianity is more concerned with faith. The Jewish religion is built largely on 613 *mitzvot*, or commandments, often onerous, which is why, in scripture, Judaism is compared to a yoke. At an interfaith dialogue I attended some years ago, the late American Jewish intellectual Milton Himmelfarb turned to one of the panelists and asked in all sincerity: "Tell me, what do Presbyterians *do?*" He brought down the house.

At the risk of oversimplifying, salvation in Christianity is largely a result of belief in Jesus Christ. A very strict embrace of any Jesus-centred Christianity would yield, *reductio ad absurdum*, the following: Hitler on his deathbed, should he sincerely give himself to Christ, would be saved. Good works are highly desirable but not mandatory for access to the Christian afterlife. However, for traditional Judaism, believing in God is not enough. Salvation also requires performing many rituals and good deeds.[2]

As a result, social scientific studies of Judaism in the postwar period are primarily behavioural. I confess that I too, as a sociologist, have shared this bias. Spiritual experience is valuable, but it must be accompanied by action. Most of the studies of Jewish religiosity therefore focus on easily measurable behaviours: denominational affiliation, synagogue membership and attendance, and observance of domestic religious rituals. The assumption is that people who carry out more of these behaviours more frequently are more "religious." However, counting these kinds of behaviours does not measure their intensity, or their spiritual meaning to individuals. There are limits to this approach, recognized by the Judaic tradition itself.

A Hasidic tale describes a barely literate young Jew at Yom Kippur services. Instead of reciting the prayers, which he cannot do, but wanting to participate, he emits a loud whistle. God is so moved by the boy's sincere whistle that He answers the prayers of the entire congregation.

Conventional social research on Judaic observance will miss the importance of that whistle. As a result, relatively little is known about what faith really means to most Canadian and American Jews.[3] Most religious Jews do not get mushy about finding God or salvation. Most do not ponder the nature of heaven or hell, of angels or Satan. But they do feel a strong identification with the Jewish people, and an appreciation of Jewish culture, religious rituals, and religious texts. To what extent are God and spirituality part of the lives of Canadian Jews? Is prayer a meaningful part of Jewish religious life, or is prayer mainly ritual and rote? The answer will vary by denomination.

Anyone who has seen committed Orthodox and ultra-Orthodox Jews praying in synagogue will have witnessed clear expressions of spiritual devotion, or *kavanah*. Such Jews will periodically immerse themselves into a trancelike condition, eyes closed, rocking back and forth in religious rapture. Public displays of such religious fervour are expected and encouraged, but perhaps not everyone attains unambiguous transcendence. Some may not get past the performative aspect of ritual, or what sociologists call "the presentation of self."[4] This is not to suppose that for Orthodox Jews every minute spent in synagogue is deeply private and spiritual. On the contrary. In Orthodox congregations, a loud buzz of conversation often drowns out the cantor. Many people feel knowledgeable enough about what is going on to pay little attention to the service. Some may feel that they know more than the rabbi himself, and maybe they do. In Conservative and Reform congregations, the services tend to be more decorous and deferential. Congregants are less confident in their knowledge, so they follow the service more closely.

For those who are not formally Orthodox, there can still be spiritual moments, and unscripted paths to religious experience. My wife is an interesting example. As a child, she almost never went to synagogue. As we raised a family, we joined a Reconstructionist congregation and began to go more often, for all the major holidays. But then, after losing both her parents within the space of a year, she found that saying *kaddish* every Shabbat brought her tremendous comfort and peace. She continued going throughout the year-long mourning period for each parent. My case is different. I recall a Friday night, not in Jerusalem, but in the tiny synagogue in New Delhi, in the mid-1980s. As a visitor, I was given the honour of leading the service. At that time, the official Jewish population of New Delhi was listed as only nine families, yet they held Shabbat services and even published a quarterly newsletter. I asked the community leader whom they counted when trying to make a *minyan*, given the small population. I will never forget his response, a model for Jewish inclusiveness: "We can't be choosy." Singing the Friday night prayer *Lecha Dodi* in such a forsaken, remnant Jewish community filled me with a sense of awe and mystery.

In about 2010, I started to attend weekly Sabbath services in my synagogue. I do not care for prayer, so I would time my arrival for the later reading of the Torah portion, then a sermon, and some congregational singing near the end. (I enjoy congregational singing. Other Jews prefer the operatic voices of cantors, or the near-professional quality of some synagogue choirs.) I enjoy a good sermon. My synagogue encourages questions and comments from the congregation after the sermon. I like the democratic angle of that custom, though the odd time you have to suffer through some long-winded inanity. I should note that I sit in a regular spot, alone, in my own little private space. In some ways, this may be a kind of meditation, or indeed, of spirituality. After the service I enjoy the socializing of the *kiddush* (light meal) with a group of regulars. I know Jews for whom the *kiddush* is the major incentive for attending services. One Jewish academic routinely rates the food on a ten-point scale. For some Jews, like Christians, the congregation is like an extended family. As French sociologist Émile Durkheim (himself a son of a rabbi) understood, religion is a social more than a spiritual activity; and this is true even for Orthodox Jews.[5] All this emphasis on communal bonding may be an overly Durkheimian approach to religion, but it works for me and for many others, Jew and Gentile alike.

American evidence confirms that Jews downplay the general importance of religion and God. Surveys of Americans find that Jews are the least likely Americans to answer that their religion is "very important." The 2013 Pew survey found that only 26 per cent of Jews, versus 56 per cent of the general American population, agreed or agreed strongly that religion is very important to them.

For declared Christians, this number was 69 per cent. The Pew survey also found that only 34 per cent of American Jews were absolutely certain they believed in God or a universal spirit, compared to 69 per cent of the US general public and 78 per cent of Christians. Among American Jews, 15 per cent argue that being Jewish is mainly a matter of religion, and another 23 per cent that it is a mixture of both religion and ancestry or culture. Moreover, 29 per cent felt that a person can be Jewish if he/she does not believe in God, and 34 per cent felt one could be Jewish and also believe that Jesus was the Messiah.[6] These findings should surprise no one. There is a venerable tradition of Jewish folklore about Jewish atheists.

Still, it would be wrong to assume that God and spirituality are totally removed from the lives of average Canadian Jews. In moments of crisis, God reappears; there are no atheists in a foxhole. And certainly, Jews who have had a traditional Jewish education may have a dormant religious sensibility which can reawaken as needed. Prayer is a spiritual exercise that can have profound effects. Years ago, a friend of mine who had just become a quadriplegic was fighting off an infection in hospital. His grieving father – an educated, sophisticated, albeit traditional, European Jew – was at his side. I remember vividly how the father passed his days wrapped in his *tallis* (prayer shawl) and *tefillin* (phylacteries), pacing the corridors and reading *tehillim* (psalms). The infection passed, and his son survived. Another story: When my wife was expecting our third child, she decided to include a midwife in the birthing experience. I felt a bit marginalized, with a deep need to do something. So I sat in the hospital room and read my favourite Judaic text, the *Pirkei Avot*, or Ethics of the Fathers. Here, too, the prayers must have worked, as our daughter was born healthy and whole. When I find myself with an ethical or moral problem I often turn to Judaic ethical teachings, summoning snippets of texts to help light the way. (This seems similar to the Christian posture of "What would Jesus do?") I would not call myself very religious, though I suppose this qualifies as religious behaviour.

When our children asked us if there really was a God, we were actually stuck for an answer. We finally came up with the following: "While we are not sure if there is a God or not, it is better to act as if there is." In classic Judaism, spirituality is something obtained through obeying the commandments and living ethically in the real world – working, raising a family, dealing fairly with friends and community, and, of course, studying Torah. No one is encouraged to live on a mountaintop and meditate. Traditional Judaism does not venerate monks and mystics. Being a good Jew does not require separation from the material world.

In recent decades there are clear signs of a new focus on spirituality within Judaism.[7] In some circles there is an interest in Hasidic tales. New Age influences are reflected in a concern with kabbalah and Jewish mysticism. Buddhism attracts some Jews who seek to meld it with Judaic teachings. The attractions of meditation and mindfulness are becoming more pronounced. Indeed, my Reconstructionist congregation in Montreal features a weekly meditation *minyan*. Clearly these approaches can appeal to some Jews who find the older religious models dry and formulaic.

THE EVOLUTION OF JUDAISM

Judaism has never been static. Priestly Judaism, which included sacrificial ritual at Solomon's temple in Jerusalem, was dominant during the pre-exilic period. Following the exile and the destruction of the temple in 70 AD, rabbinic Judaism emerged as the dominant form. Even here, doctrinal disputes around the interpretation of text arose between the more liberal school of Hillel and the more conservative school of Shammai. A rabbi's role is that of teacher and scholar, rather than priest or holy man. He is called upon to issue authoritative interpretations of the Torah and to solve disputes of a legal or quasi-legal nature. Rabbis, like scholars and judges, could and did disagree with each other. The Torah, and the corpus of Jewish law which evolved from it, deals with both the relationship between humans and God and the relations of humans to each other.

After the destruction of the temple, rabbinic academies proliferated, and a body of commentary known as Oral Law developed. Eventually, these commentaries were recorded and codified, first into the Mishnah, written in Hebrew in approximately 200 AD. Then a commentary on the Mishnah written in Aramaic, known as the Gemara, was compiled and codified around 500 AD. The Mishnah and Gemara together constitute the Talmud. The Talmud is a huge, multi-volume work which might best be compared to a contemporary collection of Supreme Court decisions with accompanying explanatory notes, amicus briefs, and expert testimony. Eventually, a consensus emerged, distilled from the Talmud and other commentary, as to the proper form of ritual and observance. These laws and guidelines are described as *halacha*, or "the way," and some were codified in the Middle Ages in a text called the *Shulchan Aruch*, or the "Set Table."

Until the twentieth century, most religious Jews could be classified as Orthodox; even if they occasionally deviated from strict observance, there was no question as to the normative standard, the *halacha*. Yet religious Judaism, then and now, never had a single hierarchical structure like that of the Catholic Church. Jews have never had a Pope. Various rabbis claim authority by dint of their intellectual reputation, charisma, and organizational power, and numbers of followers. Today, pluralism is rampant both within religious movements and among them. Reform Judaism emerged in Germany in the nineteenth century and espoused a liberal, rational, and universalist philosophy. The original objective was to eliminate the nationalistic as well as supernatural elements within Judaism, so there was little use of Hebrew, no Zionism, no concept of a chosen people, and no miracles. Conservative Judaism was developed later in the United States at the end of the nineteenth and in the early twentieth century, by scholars associated with the Jewish Theological Seminary in New York. Conservative Judaism sought to synthesize elements of Reform and Orthodoxy, to become an authentic American version of Judaism. It created a more traditional form of religious expression which took *halacha* as a guide, but which countenanced deviations where considered appropriate, like driving to Sabbath services.[8] In recent decades, the progressive Reconstructionist and Jewish Renewal movements, among others, have emerged as even more modern and egalitarian Jewish religious options.

Canadian Jewish denominations are usually affiliated with American umbrella organizations. In the United States, Reform Judaism was the first branch to institutionalize, but German Jewish Reform made a negligible impression in Canada and has never caught up. The anti-Zionism of the early Reform movement did not sit well with the Eastern European Jewish community in Canada. Reform temples in Canada are affiliated with the Union of American Hebrew Congregations. Conservative congregations are affiliated with the United Synagogue of America. Orthodox congregations include much greater diversity and a looser organizational framework. They range from small, informal synagogues, or *shtibels*, to Modern Orthodox congregations in large new facilities. Many

Orthodox synagogues are affiliated with the American Union of Orthodox Congregations, but by no means all.

THE CONTEMPORARY SCENE

In Canada today, the boundaries between Judaism and Christianity, and between religious and secular Judaism, have become more permeable. As described earlier, there are thousands of Jews who are no longer "religious," and their numbers are growing. In the twenty-first century, some Canadians who are Jewish by ethnic origin do not claim the Jewish religion and some Canadians who are Jewish by religion do not claim Jewish ancestry (e.g. converts). In 2011, 309,650 Canadians claimed single or multiple Jewish ethnic ancestries, 329,500 Canadians claimed Jewish religion, and there was an estimated total of 385,345 Jews.[9] The fact that the Canadian census allows only one response to the question, "What is your religion?" means that the religious variable is less and less helpful in understanding the profile of Canadian Jewry.[10] More and more Canadians are being raised in families where there are joint Jewish and non-Jewish religious traditions.

But some self-declared Jewish atheists or agnostics, as well as some of those who rarely attend synagogue, will still engage in some religious practices and observances. For example, in Montreal in 2010, 87 per cent of Jews said they attended a Passover seder, and 76 per cent said they fast on Yom Kippur "all the time."[11] But there are now more Jews with mixed Christian and Jewish ancestry, through conversion and/or mixed marriage. One can imagine that many blended Jewish families in Canada in December celebrate a form of "Chrismukah." At bar and bat mitzvah celebrations which involve a convert, Jewish parents have to be careful when delivering a charge to their child. "You are now following in the footsteps of your ancestors – or at least some of your ancestors."

Efforts to convert Canadian Jews to Christianity have been ongoing. For example, a full-page ad in the *Globe and Mail* before Christmas 1998 asked this jarring question in the boldest print: "Is it reasonable to be Jewish and believe in Jesus?" The ad featured fifteen smiling adults and one baby, who claim, "Maybe the most reasonable thing – the most Jewish thing – we have ever done is to believe in the Messiah." Note that this ad does not promote the glories of Christianity. Rather, it singles out a specific minority group, and implies that Jews who reject Jesus are irrational. While I am sure such ads upset many Jews, there is no way to prevent newspapers from accepting them. It violates no law. Of course, newspapers are not obliged to accept such ads, which is quite a different story ...

Consider the following. Is there a point at which such ads, were they to proliferate in newspapers, on television and radio, on buses and subways, on lawns and balconies, would begin to encroach upon the constitutional guarantee of freedom of religion? There is no doubt the Canadian Charter of Rights and Freedoms prohibits forced conversions and discrimination on the basis of religion. But is that all? Imagine a barrage of such ads and posters assaulting Jews as they went about their daily life. In any event, as of 2016, according to Ben Volman, a senior representative of the Union of Messianic Jewish Congregations in Toronto, there were about a dozen Messianic-Jewish congregations in Canada, numbering about 1,200 formal adherents, though it is claimed there are many others who display interest. The core belief of this movement is the Jewish origin and character of Jesus, who remains the Jewish son of God. A typical congregation would comprise original Christians and original Jews in roughly a 50–50 ratio. Many members would themselves belong to mixed-marriage families. Some of the congregations might tilt more to Judaic observance, others more to Christian. A good many of these adherents would describe themselves as Jewish, in one sense or another, and would celebrate Jewish holidays.[12] But there should be no doubt that most Jewish community leaders, lay or religious, and most academic researchers, would – rightly or wrongly – not include these individuals within any count of the Jewish population in Canada.

Of course Jews can fight back against conversion efforts. Historically, Jews have never been very active proselytizers, at least not since the days of the Roman Empire. Perhaps this is because the playing field has never been level and Jews, like other minorities, would never want to risk a backlash by an angry majority. (Imagine if Muslims in North America or Europe were to embark on an aggressive public campaign to recruit and convert Christians. It would certainly fan the flames of racism.) The closest thing to in-your-face conversion efforts have been those of the Lubavitcher Hasidim, aimed at wayward fellow Jews. Yet I know Jews who find the Lubavitchers' efforts almost as annoying as those of the Jews for Jesus.

Some Jews have suggested that the time is right for some gentle persuasion directed at willing or curious Christians. A synagogue in Los Angeles began the process, and soon after a Conservative synagogue in Montreal gingerly followed suit, with an ad not in the mainstream press but in the *Canadian Jewish News*. Addressed to Jews, the ad asks: "Are you dating someone who is not Jewish? Do you know a non-Jew who is interested in Judaism? Conversion to Judaism is an option." The ad then offers information about conversion classes. A discussion with the rabbi responsible revealed that the motivation behind the ad was not really to convert gentiles. The motives were more parochial. One was that Orthodox conversions were apparently becoming more lengthy and onerous. The other was a desire to present the Conservative option as an alternative to the more "suspect" Reform conversions.[13] So the motive was more market share than a mission to the Gentiles. Had the Conservative movement been really serious about converting Gentiles, they might have taken out the ad in the mainstream press.

So boundaries will be ever more porous, and labels that are fixed become less accurate. Because of mixed marriage, there are more and more Jews creating hybrid religious Jewish identities, à la Chrismukah ... Unitarian church services and congregations include many people who are Jewish (and some may also attend Jewish religious services as well). But the synagogue is the centre of contemporary Judaism. The Hebrew term for synagogue is *beit knesset*, which means house of assembly. So it should not anger purists that synagogues have become *de facto* mini Jewish community centres. Apart from the holding of services, synagogues run study groups, sponsor lectures, and organize bridge clubs, youth groups, bazaars, drama productions, and sports events. They hold activities celebrating the various holidays, and they organize trips to Israel, casino nights and other fundraisers, and so on.

There is a spectrum of religiosity among Jews. In the second decade of the twenty-first century, for those Canadian Jews who identify religiously, about 24 per cent in Montreal and 14 per cent in Toronto are Orthodox (10 per cent in the United States), 15 per cent in Montreal and 37 per cent in Toronto are Conservative (18 per cent in the United States), 5 per cent in Montreal and 19 per cent in Toronto are Reform (35 per cent in the United States). The remainder belong to other denominations including Reconstructionism (3.8 per cent in Montreal and 1.7 per cent in Toronto), Humanism

(1.1 per cent in Montreal and 1.9 per cent in Toronto), and New Age (0.7 per cent in Montreal and 0.5 per cent in Toronto). Approximately 16 per cent of Jews in both cities preferred the title "just Jewish," and 8 per cent in Montreal and 9 per cent in Toronto considered themselves secular Jews. One-quarter of the population in Montreal and Toronto were unaffiliated, compared with 30 per cent in the United States.[14] This confirms the relative strength of Reform in the United States and Orthodoxy in Canada. It is worth noting that in Montreal, there is a large Sephardic population for which the denominational categories of Conservative and Reform are not very pronounced. Sephardi synagogues are Orthodox in practice, but Sephardi respondents may not choose the designation. A 2010 survey of Montreal Sephardim found that over one third simply identified themselves as "traditional" Jews.[15] Canadian Jews who are lapsed Orthodox or even Conservatives also might choose the term "traditional" more than Americans do.

Jews in general are not avid synagogue-goers, even if they belong to one. In 2010, 60 per cent of Montreal Jews were paying members of a synagogue. The membership figure was 50 per cent in Toronto and 46 per cent in the United States. The pattern of memberships followed roughly the pattern of denominational identification. According to the Montreal survey, 18 per cent of respondents attended synagogue on Shabbat all the time, whereas 42 per cent of respondents never attended on Shabbat. In terms of attendance on High Holidays, 66 per cent said they attended all the time, 9 per cent said usually, just over 12 per cent said sometimes, and just under 12 per cent said never.[16] A 2005 Toronto survey found a bit more attendance. 51 per cent of respondents attended religious services only on High Holidays, or on High Holidays and a few other times, 17 per cent attended only on special occasions, and 8 per cent attended very rarely or never. In terms of more regular attendance, 4.5 per cent of respondents attended at least once a month, 5.8 per cent several times a month, 8.3 per cent about once per week, and 5.1 per cent more than once per week.[17] In every North American study of synagogue involvement, attendance is more likely for those who are Orthodox, moderate for those who are Conservative, and least for those who are Reform or other. But there is still incongruence in the denominational patterns. For example, 71 per cent of nominally Orthodox Jews in Toronto attend synagogue at least once a month, far more than the other denominations. But where are the other 29 per cent? Some of those absent may be older Orthodox women, among whom attending services is less common. In addition, many Jews who call themselves Orthodox and belong to Orthodox congregations may not be fully observant in their private lives. On the other hand, about 16 per cent of Toronto's Reform Jews attend regularly.[18] One of the perplexing challenges in understanding Judaism is how to compare the religiosity of, say, a self-defined "Orthodox" Jew who attends services monthly and a Reform Jew who attends weekly.

Canadian Christians generally attend services more frequently than Jews. One study reported that monthly church attendance declined from 38 per cent in 1989 to 28 per cent in 2009. There is some debate as to whether this decline is leveling off. The decline seems most pronounced for the Roman Catholic population of Quebec (from 44 per cent in 1989 to 20 per cent in 2009), but is holding steady for Canadian Protestants (an estimated 1 per cent increase between 1989 and 2009).[19] Earlier, Christian service attendance rates were in a sort of free fall. Weekly service attendance declined from 53 per cent in 1957 to 23 per cent in 1990.[20] By comparison, in the United States, a 2014 Gallup Poll found that 75 per cent of Mormons, 53 per cent of Protestants, 50 per cent Muslims, 45 per cent Catholics, and only 19 per cent of Jews attended religious services almost every week.[21]

As of this writing, it is hard to predict future patterns of church/synagogue attendance in Canada. Leaving aside survey trends, there is a sense in which Christianity, at least in its non-fundamentalist or non-evangelical variant, has been declining. In part because of the new multicultural political reality, in part because of natural processes of erosion, Christianity may be losing its self-confidence. I see this starkly during the Christmas season. Conservative commentators in Canada and the US at times refer to this as "the war on Christmas." Some Christians have become afraid to wish people "Merry Christmas" lest they catch a non-Christian or atheist and give offence. A colleague who was involved in anti-racist efforts in Canada used to bristle when Air Canada personnel, some years back, would wish him "Merry Christmas" as he disembarked. But I never felt offended when non-Jews wished me a Merry Christmas. My late father, a Holocaust survivor, greatly enjoyed Christmas carols. I still wish my Christian friends, even if no longer practising, a Merry Christmas. In any event, almost everywhere the inoffensive

"Happy Holidays" and "Season's Greetings" reign triumphant. Hanukkah, Kwanzaa, Ramadan, and Passover seem to have nearly crowded out Christmas and Easter in daycares, schools, and radio morning shows.

Perhaps I am too pessimistic about Christianity and its future. Perhaps a decline in church attendance or in adherence to formal organized churches is not the same thing as a decline in Christian spirituality or a belief in God or a reverence for Jesus Christ.[22] On the one hand, the percentage of atheist and agnostic Canadians has been rising steadily, reaching 23 per cent in 2011. But on the other hand, there is evidence of a growing spirituality among Canadians, which may be distinct from traditional religious beliefs and church attendance.[23] Anecdotal reports describe corporate spirituality seminars and people studying the Bible. And according to a research poll commissioned by the *National Post*, only half of Canadians say they are religious but two-thirds say they are spiritual. Additionally, 25 per cent of respondents who did not identify with a religion expressed a belief in God.[24] I am uncertain about what spirituality actually means. My behaviourist bias wants to see actions, even though as described above elements of spirituality have clearly intruded into my own synagogue attendance.

Many Canadian Jews belong to congregations which do not correspond to their own identification, and some belong to more than one. A few belong to synagogues both at home and in Florida. When it comes to congregational membership, Canadian Jews and Christians differ. Christian congregational membership has declined dramatically, even more than their attendance. Recent Canadian surveys find significant declines in membership among mainstream protestant denominations such as Anglican, United Church and Presbyterian. For example, membership in the Anglican Church has fallen by 53 per cent over the previous 40 years and continues to fall roughly 2 per cent each year.[25] Jews are far more likely to belong to congregations even if they rarely attend. For example, in Toronto, almost 50 per cent of Jews claim they are paying members of a synagogue.[26] So are Jews hypocrites for belonging to synagogues but not attending? Not really. Being an official member of a congregation may have more symbolic and communal meaning for Jews. Judaism, perhaps more than Christianity, can be expressed religiously in many ways other than weekly attendance at services, mainly through major annual holidays and life-cycle rituals.

DENOMINATIONAL CHALLENGES

In both Canada and the United States, each of the three major Jewish denominations has been undergoing dramatic changes, at times involving painful soul-searching. Before looking at the denominations themselves, we should note that all of them are marked by tensions between the left and the right and between elite and folk religion. The left-right split means simply that every denomination can be understood as having a liberal and conservative wing. These factions will, at times, conflict with each other while finding common ground with adjacent wings of other denominations. So the traditional wing of the Conservative movement shares some affinities with the liberal (modern) wing of Orthodoxy. At times, tensions within denominations can be as intense as those between them, in the same way that civil wars are unusually ferocious. In the case of Orthodoxy, it may be more useful to speak of a wide continuum of possible options, from Modern Orthodox to ever more pious ultra-Orthodox groups. In this type of Orthodox one-upmanship, the Orthodox compete to see who can be most scrupulous in terms of *halachic* observance. Charles Silberman described this move to hyper-stringent observance as belonging to the "*chumrah*-of-the-month club," a *chumrah* being a more demanding religious obligation.[27]

Often, the left-right distinction among the Orthodox is expressed by where one eats, trusting the observance of the dietary laws. For the most pious, the label of "kosher" on a food product does not suffice. Most Hasidic Jews, for example, would probably not eat a meal containing meat in the home of a Modern Orthodox Jew, and certainly not in my home, even though it is nominally "kosher." They are making the right decision. In my home, we keep two sets of regular dishes, and two sets of Passover dishes. But we do bring non-kosher food in and eat it on paper plates. So, like many Canadian Jews, our dishes are reasonably kosher, but our stomachs are *treif*, or unclean. Some Jews who keep kosher will eat fish or salads in a non-kosher restaurant; others will not. One of the more frequent topics of debate in strictly Orthodox circles concerns which products are revealed to be unkosher, and which kosher, and according to which groups' supervision, and why.

The second distinction is between elite and folk religion. According to social scientist Charles Liebman, every one of the denominations, and perhaps every religion, includes a doctrinal set of prescriptions mandated by the elite; that is, rabbis and religious scholars. These are combined with a populist set of practices and attitudes which emanate from the religious folk themselves.[28] These are the things people do, as opposed to what they ought to do. Elite religion flows from the top down, while folk religion flows from the bottom up. Most of the members of Orthodox, Conservative, Reform, and Reconstructionist congregations have not studied in depth the range of theological writings of their respective rabbinic authorities or gurus, from David Hartman to Abraham Joshua Heschel to Eugene Borowitz to Mordecai Kaplan. Many, perhaps most, do not know the "official" denominational position on various issues, from dietary laws to the status of women to Sabbath observance. They just evolve their own approaches, their own compromises based on daily efforts to make sense of their lives. At times, a dialectical relation between elite and folk Judaism can lead to cross-denominational creativity. For some people, Conservative Judaism represents the incarnation and institutionalization of elements of folk Orthodoxy. For the majority of Jews who are "moderately affiliated," a new form of folk religion is liberal individualism, a pick-and-choose approach to belief and sentiment which downplays the role of any religious elites or organizations. Indeed, in their study of such Jews, Steven Cohen and Arnold Eisen identified "rabbis and congregations" encountered by young adults or newlyweds as obstacles to adult Jewish involvement or participation.[29] In matters of religion, Jews, and many Christians, like to do their own thing.

How are the denominations in North America doing?[30] By all indicators, Orthodoxy is the most vibrant. It is losing the fewest adherents, and its large families are adding to the population base. Ultra-Orthodoxy, whether Hasidic or *yeshiva*-based, epitomizes this vitality; their communities, synagogues, and schools are bursting with children. The Orthodox see themselves, with some justification, as the guarantors of the Jewish future in the face of assimilation. Indeed, all indicators of assimilation, notably mixed marriage, are lower for the Orthodox. Trends in Jewish day school attendance in Montreal and Toronto, as in the United States, illustrate this Orthodox resurgence, where increasing proportions of students are attending Orthodox and ultra-Orthodox schools.[31]

It is hard to overemphasize how unexpected this Orthodox resurgence has been. No social scientist who studied North American Jewish life prior to the 1970s anticipated it. On the contrary, it was felt as axiomatic by observers, like pioneer sociologist Louis Wirth, that Orthodoxy in North America was doomed. It was too much at odds with the prevailing culture, too Old World, too opposed to modernity.[32] Of course Wirth, a professor at the University of Chicago, was an assimilated German Jew, so perhaps some of that was a personal prejudice. These views were part of the general social scientific infatuation with modernization. Accordingly, ethnic cultures and religion, and certainly religious fundamentalism, would fade as societies became more educated, urbanized, industrialized, and cosmopolitan, and as the immigrants to the new world gave way to native-born generations. This, too, was wrong. Indeed, right-wing or fundamentalist Christians, Muslims, and Jews have shown themselves adept at utilizing elements of modernity, like YouTube and other websites and apps, to help propagate their conservative message. The Lubavitch Hasidim were among the first to pioneer the use of worldwide live TV when they began broadcasting the *farbrengen*, a festive communal meal, and commentaries of the late *Rebbe*. In addition, a form of "Modern Orthodoxy" developed in the postwar period which sought to integrate faith with active participation in the secular world. One study of Orthodox life in Toronto's suburbia has found a remarkable degree of adaptability. The expansion of Orthodox day schools as well as the development of a sophisticated "religious consumerism" allow these Jews to enjoy their lives with a degree of material sophistication.[33]

In the twenty-first century, Orthodoxy has been moving to the right. Triumphalism has caused strains between the newly militant Orthodox and the Modern Orthodox on issues such as ties with non-Orthodox Jews. Some Modern Orthodox are embarrassed by the exclusiveness of the militant Orthodox just as some supporters of the Lubavitch Hasidim are embarrassed by the efforts of certain Lubavitchers to argue that the late *Rebbe* remains alive in some Elvis-like way, a kind of messiah, and is "continuing his work," as one follower told me.[34] The left wing of Orthodoxy, or the Modern Orthodox, have some elements in common with the right-wing Conservatives, though less so recently. And the right wing of Orthodoxy embraces increasing degrees of piety and religiosity, typified by the tendency among the youngest generation to become more devout than their parents. An example of the strength of Orthodoxy are the *baalei teshuva* – adherents of a kind of born-again movement – who move from limited or moderate levels of Judaism to very pious Orthodoxy and ultra-Orthodoxy.[35] Specific *yeshivas* in Israel cater to these new seekers, though some in the Orthodox community remain skeptical about their commitment. A program of deliberate outreach – some might say intra-Jewish proselytizing – has been developed by the Aish HaTorah organization, which has developed a massive database of emails and a variety of online programming, reaching tens of thousands of participants in North America.[36] One can argue that cult-like elements have seeped into the new Orthodox fervour.

Reform Judaism in Canada has never been as stridently doctrinaire as American Reform. It has been more ethnic, more open to Israel, more open to particularism, all without losing the traditional Reform concern with social justice, universalism, and integration into host societies. In a sense, Reform in Canada anticipated the evolution of American Reform in the postwar period, which now embraces Hebrew, and Israel, and other elements of tradition. At the same time, Reform has, paradoxically, had to embrace increasingly marginal Jews and innovations to accommodate mixed-marriage families.[37] It is common for Orthodox and Conservative Jews to condemn Reform for its seeming association with assimilation. And, indeed, most studies find that Reform Jews are most "assimilated" and most likely to be in a mixed marriage. But it would be foolish to assume that Reform in any sense "causes" assimilation. None of the studies can solve the problem of self-selection. Jews who are already more prone to assimilation or more predisposed to greater contact with the non-Jewish world are also more likely to choose or to have been raised in Reform (and like-minded) families. Reform Jews are simply articulating a liberal version of Jewish identification that works for them.

A far more sympathetic interpretation of Reform Judaism would be to see it as occupying the front lines in the desperate struggle *against* assimilation. Reform congregations are the most likely to include non-Jews as members or associate members so Reform congregations wrestle regularly with setting boundaries between Jewish and non-Jewish members. Reform is most involved with outreach to those on the margins, seeking, often against great odds, to bring them back to the fold. Their congregations wrestle with issues like how or whether non-Jewish spouses of temple members can participate in the services or congregational life. To most of the Orthodox this is lunacy, as well as heresy. But from a different perspective, this is rescue. A pro-continuity case can be made for both a hard and soft line on such questions. Of course, for Reform rabbis, conversion remains preferable, but Reform has no choice but to try to navigate the uncharted waters of mixed marriage, in which Jews with non-Jewish spouses and children try to find a workable approach that will not alienate the family from Judaism.

All denominations have conversion classes. These cater to some individuals but mainly serve couples where there is a prospect of marriage. They get the job done, though the Orthodox will not recognize non-Orthodox conversions. More provocative are outreach programs aimed at married couples where the non-Jewish partner is not planning to convert but the couple wishes to retain some familial tie to Jewish life – typically expressed as, "We will raise the children with both religions, and when they are older they can choose." Reform or Reconstructionist synagogues in Montreal and Toronto routinely sponsor programs for intermarried families.[38]

The fact is that all liberal congregations are doing the community's dirty work without receiving much thanks. They are providing a last-ditch option for linkage with the Jewish community for those dangerously close to the way out. In doing so, they are also inadvertently perpetuating the Orthodox stereotype of Reform as being very weak on authentic Judaic content.

A Jew goes to an Orthodox rabbi and asks, "Rabbi, can you give me a *bracha* (blessing) on my new Jaguar?" The rabbi answers, "What's a Jaguar?" The Jew then asks the same question of a Reform rabbi, who answers, "What's a *bracha*?"

Conservative Judaism has had a checkered history, and is currently the denomination which faces the most challenges. The denomination had been seen as the ideal model for North American Judaism. The strength of Conservatism is in its origins in North America. It was an indigenous response of New York's Jewish Theological Seminary, designed as an alternative for children of East European immigrants straying from Orthodox Judaism. It was homegrown, pragmatic in the best American sense, and tailored to the dilemmas of North American life. It strove for compromise with *halacha* and created institutions like the Jewish community centre. At one point, it was predicted that it would outstrip all rivals, drawing left-wing Orthodox and right-wing Reform into the fold, producing a consensual North American Judaism.

But Conservative Judaism has been beset with its own left-right conflicts. Historically, the tensions between the elite rabbis and the folk have been severe.[39] Canadian Conservative Judaism is generally more traditional than American Conservatism. In the United States, it has been a battleground on the status of women, though moving steadily to an egalitarian position. Still, rather than offering a happy medium, Conservatism may appear inadequate compared to either the absolute gender egalitarianism of Reform and Reconstructionism and their relative acceptance of LGBTQ members and intermarriage, or the self-confident traditionalism of Orthodoxy. Indeed, because of the hostile Orthodox stance on Reform and Conservative conversions, Conservatism has often found itself in an uneasy alliance against Orthodox exclusivism. Conservative Judaism has never lost its affinity with the turbulent Jewish student movements of the 1960s, which spawned countercultural movements like the *Havurot* and other innovations. *Havurot* are small intimate congregations of Jews seeking a more experimental and informal community of faith. An example of Conservative innovation is the *Rabbi's Manual* published by the Conservative Rabbinical Assembly. It includes new blessings for sending children away to college or to camp and, like the new Conservative prayer book *Sim Shalom*, does away with masculine names for God such as "Lord" or "King." In the words of sociologist Samuel Heilman, "It's *The Jewish Catalog*, thirty years later."[40]

In the twenty-first century, Conservative Judaism has seen its problems grow. As traditional Jews have moved towards Orthodoxy and liberal Jews have moved towards Reform, Conservative Judaism is experiencing a loss of numbers and institutional vibrancy in both Canada and the United States. Data from the 2013 Pew survey outlined the numerical weakness in Conservative Judaism. What is unclear is whether this decline will continue, or whether the Conservative Jewish movement can stage a comeback.[41]

DILEMMAS OF CANADIAN JUDAISM

Judaism in Canada is a branch-plant operation. Reform, Conservative, and Reconstructionist Judaism in Canada are all dependent on their American counterparts for infrastructural support and, more importantly, for the major rabbinic seminaries. These rabbis in Canada must be trained in the United States. As mentioned earlier, there are some Orthodox rabbinic seminaries in Canada, but the larger institutions such as Yeshiva University are south of the border.[42] Historically, the majority of pulpit rabbis in Canada have been American. Only recently has there been an increase in Canadians who receive ordination in the United States and then return to Canada. The situation is less pronounced in Jewish communal service, though leadership positions in many federations have been filled by American-born professionals. All this is reminiscent of the 1960s plaint about the preponderance of American professors in Canadian universities. Canadian universities solved the dependency problem either by hiring Canadians trained in the United States or beginning to recognize the value of Canadian PhDs. But unlike the resulting expansion of Canadian universities and a shift in hiring, a large number of Rabbinical seminaries have not emerged in Canada. Canadian Jews still do not have the necessary critical mass, and so the American institutions – Orthodox, Conservative, Reform, and Reconstructionist – continue to serve the Canadian market.

Is this a problem? Perhaps. American rabbis are initially unfamiliar with the Canadian scene. Some in Montreal have never learned French well or become very familiar with the history of French-English relations. Among leading "Canadian" Judaic thinkers have been Dr Emil Fackenheim, Rabbi Gunther Plaut, and Rabbi Dow Marmur of Toronto, and Rabbi David Hartman of Montreal. All of these philosophers and rabbis were immigrants to Canada, born and raised in Europe or New York. With its ties to the United States and to Israel, Canada has not yet been able to generate or sustain original creative movements of Jewish theology and philosophy.

Even Canadian Jewish contributions to religious custom, or *minhag*, have been few. Among the best known are the unique customs which used to occur in Montreal and Toronto – and I presume other communities – during the Passover seders, which used to conflict with the Stanley Cup playoffs. Jews are passionate hockey fans, like all Canadians. Many seders were routinely punctuated by kids and some adults excusing themselves, finding a TV, and then updating everyone on the score. A close game in the third period, or worse, in overtime, would be a real test of commitment and further incentive to finish the seder quickly. For me, a loss by the Canadiens would take the joy out of the celebration. The whole thing is parodied in "A Montrealer Seder," a fictional ethnographic study in *The Big Book of Jewish Humor* which is read as a regular feature of my seders. Let me commend it to everyone:

Another unique Montrealer custom concerns the afikomen. The father sends the youngest child to search for it, and upon finding it, the child runs back to the table and whispers in his father's ear. The father then jumps to his feet, raises his hands skyward, and shouts "Agol, Agol!" The rest of the males then rise with their arms raised and respond, "Ahllo Habs, Ahwei-Ahwei."[43]

FAITH AND PEOPLEHOOD

The Jewish religion, Jewish people, and the land of Israel are intimately linked, making it easy to be religious without much theology. Passover is a holiday celebrating the national liberation of the Jewish people, contrasting the value of freedom with the horror of slavery. Even the Sabbath, arguably the paradigmatic religious event in the Jewish calendar, has a national/ethnic subtext. The requirements of Sabbath observance, like the prohibitions of kashrut, do more than separate the sacred from the profane. They separate Jews from non-Jews. As essayist Ahad Ha'am once put it, "It is not that the Jews keep the Sabbath, it is that the Sabbath keeps the Jews."[44] In sociological terms, all of Judaism is a thoroughly ethnic religion. (There are some similarities with German Mennonites and with the various Orthodox churches. Most Greek Orthodox are also Greek.) Converts not only embrace the Jewish faith but, as we are taught in the story of Ruth in the Bible, join the Jewish people. The Reform movement tried to create a purer form of intellectualized religion, based on universal principles and ideals, and failed. Ritual and peoplehood have crept back in.

Judaic observance relates to ethnicity and community in a number of ways. First, while some Jewish holidays emphasize normative ethical issues such as the need for repentance on Yom Kippur, many others commemorate specific national-historical events such as the exodus from Egypt (Passover), wandering through the desert (Sukkoth), and receipt of the Torah (Shavuot). The Passover seder includes the saying, "Next year in Jerusalem," which Jews today may assume has a territorial or Zionist rather than spiritual meaning. Holidays which emerged later, like Hanukkah and Purim, celebrate historic confrontations with external oppressors in ancient Israel or in the diaspora.

Two new holidays have emerged in recent years, capturing a communal dimension of the Jewish experience. These are Yom Ha'Shoah, which commemorates the Holocaust, and Israel's Yom Ha'Atzma'ut, or Independence Day. Both of these have no historical/theological significance as related to the Torah and the Bible, yet are included in any Judaic website listing holidays. Modern philosophers wrestle with their meaning, and try to ascribe a post hoc religious significance to them around the motif of redemption. They are routinely commemorated in one form or another in synagogues of all branches of Judaism. Prayers for Israel are part of the Sabbath service. Some congregations give a certificate for trees planted in Israel as a bar or bat mitzvah present. So Judaism is tied to the Jewish people, and both are tied to Israel.

Second, in all branches of Judaism, though less in Reform and Reconstructionism, Hebrew dominates as the language of prayer and reading of the Torah. There is no movement afoot to parallel the Catholics' rejection of Latin. Even Reform Judaism has increased the use of Hebrew in the service and now requires Hebrew language study as an element of Reform education. Hebrew is the language of the Jewish people, and links all Jews together in time and space. The Biblical Hebrew used in prayer also serves to separate the sacred and the profane, which is, after all, one of the central purposes of organized religion.

Third, prayer is a social activity, requiring a quorum of ten. Jews cannot recite the prayer for the dead, the *kaddish*, without a quorum. Jews must pray with other Jews, not as isolated mystics. In short, the Jewish religion embraces both universal and particular elements functional for Jewish survival. Conversion to Judaism is thus more difficult than acceptance of Christianity. It can entail casting one's lot with the Jewish people, linking one's fate with the horrors of the Holocaust – and with anti-Semitism today – as well as possibly developing a deep empathy with Israel and her travails. It also involves adopting a repertoire of religious rituals, Hebrew prayers and songs, customs, and foods that play a role in specific holidays.

THE NUTS AND BOLTS OF RELIGIOUS OBSERVANCE

Some years ago, for reasons that are unclear – it may have had something to do with the death of my father – I decided to build a *sukkah*, the temporary hut for the holiday of Sukkoth, and did so every year

while my children were young. I enjoyed the physical work of erecting it, the exotic nature of it, the involvement of family in putting it
up. I am proud to say it was an authentic Canadian *sukkah* – I used
wooden skis and hockey sticks for the roof, on which I laid the covering of branches. I would buy a *lulav* (a bundle of green plants) and
etrog (a citron – a lemon-like fruit). We said the blessings a few
times, but didn't make a point of eating a full meal in the sukkah.
Just having it around for seven days was enough.

For Jews, religion often means doing, and they do a lot more than,
say, Methodists. First and foremost, Canadian and American Jews
observe Jewish life-cycle rituals.[45] Even largely assimilated Jews, if
they marry other Jews, have some sort of a Jewish wedding. (And
even mixed marriages will often incorporate Jewish elements in the
service.) If they later have a boy, they will usually have a circumcision. Increasingly ceremonies for baby girls have evolved, which
range from naming ceremonies called *simchat ha'bat* to a *brit banot*,
which can include immersing the girl in water.[46] They will likely then
provide their children a bar or bat mitzvah ceremony. (The terms
"bar mitzvah" and "bat mitzvah" are perhaps the most misused
in Jewish life. In Hebrew *"bar mitzvah"* is *not* a noun referring to
a party or ritual. It is the designation of the boy who at thirteen
becomes someone who must obey the commandments. So to say "I
went to a bar mitzvah" is like saying, "I went to a thirteen-year-old
boy." The correct form would be to say "I went to a party celebrating
David's becoming a bar mitzvah," or, more loosely, "I went to a bar
mitzvah party.") And last but not least, Jews will observe some form
of *shiva* for their dead, and will themselves choose to be buried
according to Jewish ritual, and in a Jewish cemetery.

Since life-cycle rituals are infrequent, they are more likely to be
observed. But they certainly can be onerous. A bar or bat mitzvah
can monopolize a family's psychic energy for six months or more.[47]
And the cost is a real burden. Some families have taken to combining
the celebration with a family trip to Israel. The emotional impact of
coming of age at the Wailing Wall or on Masada is great, but for
parents it is also one more event to plan, and to pay for. It is really a
rite of passage for the whole family, and is probably more stressful
for the parents preparing the festivities than for the boy or girl. I
speak from experience.

Is it worth it? No one knows if having a bar or bat mitzvah celebration contributes significantly to a child's future Jewish commitment.

The celebration, however, honours not just the adolescent but the family, and by extension the community. Like a Jewish wedding, these occasions are public statements about commitment to Jewish continuity. I might cry at *simchas* because of the public display of solidarity with a Jewish community still burdened with memories of the Holocaust. A Jewish wedding, with the promise of children, is a slap in the face of anti-Semites. These events are a celebration of Jewish life by the family and friends, who are representatives of the entire community.

For this reason, the presence of grandparents at these celebrations – or their saddening absence – is a big deal. They symbolize the generational chain of Jewish continuity. At the celebrations for our children, my wife and I included a slide show with photos of recently deceased grandparents as well as other European relatives who died before or during the Holocaust, an idea we copied from some friends. As children of Holocaust survivors, we felt a special obligation to Jewish memory. It is also a ritual during such festivities to thank all the out-of-town relatives and friends who have travelled a great distance to attend. The farther flung the guest list, the better. These are tribal sentiments. They blur the line between the personal, the familial, and the communal, which can be a strength of religious ritual generally and Judaism in particular. The deliberate melding of these three domains should not obscure the coming-of-age value of the bar and bat mitzvah. For some youngsters, the event, especially the preparation of the Torah portion and the increasingly common *d'var torah*, or sermon-like speech, may be traumatic or exhilarating, or both.

Perhaps the most onerous life-cycle ritual is the saying of *kaddish*, the prayer for the dead. It requires those Jews who accept the traditional burden to attend morning, afternoon, and evening services (the latter two are generally combined) every day for eleven months, in order to find a minyan. Reform and Reconstructionist Jews generally say it only on Sabbath during the year of mourning. But Jews saying a daily *kaddish* will go to elaborate lengths to find a *minyan* during the day, and still attend synagogue if they happen to be travelling. When my mother died in the early 1970s, I was a single graduate student at Harvard. The small Cambridge synagogue heroically tried to offer twice-daily services, even though the Jewish population base consisted of a few "townies" and a collection of university students who lived in the area. I became a morning regular, and my

commitment was strong because I felt I just could not let the synagogue down. I worried that getting up at half past six would cramp
my limited social life. But it was not too bad.

Observing a period of *shiva*, a week of intense mourning after the
burial, is another powerful ritual observed to some degree by most
Jews. I have seen Christian friends show up for work a couple of
days after the death of a loved one, looking haggard, lost, and for-
lorn. Jews who sit *shiva* stay home for the week or designated time
period and are visited by friends of the deceased, both close and
distant, who console them. In many cases, daily services take place in
the home, transforming it into a sort of synagogue, and light food is
served after the morning services. Often, family friends will supply
food for the week. At times, the crowd of visitors becomes a social
gathering, where old acquaintances see each other – though it may
not reach the level of festivity found at Christian wakes. The blurring
of the personal, the familial, and the communal is again obvious.

Apart from life-cycle events, Jews also observe key yearly holidays. As sociologist Marshall Sklare noted about American Jews,
Canadian Jews also tend to observe holidays which are infrequent,
which can be invested with universal or modern themes, which
do not demand social isolation, which have a counterpart in the
Christian calendar, and which are child-centred.[48] This could explain
why more Jews in both Canada and the United States light Hanukkah
candles than fast on Yom Kippur, though the latter is arguably the
most important holiday. Hanukkah comes once a year, while lasting
eight days. It parallels Christmas in timing and in the practice of gift-
giving. It celebrates the struggle for freedom by Jews against colonial
invaders, a universal message. And it is profoundly child-centred,
given the gift-giving, the lighting of candles, and the spinning of the
dreidel. These traits also explain the popularity of Passover. The
feast celebrates the universal holiday of freedom, parallels Easter,
and the seder is often child-centred. The absence of these themes
may also explain why complete Sabbath observance, such as not
using electricity, is rare except among the strictly Orthodox.

The most faithfully observed rituals are Passover seders (92 per
cent in Toronto and 94 per cent in Montreal), lighting Hanukkah
candles (84 per cent in Toronto and 88 per cent in Montreal), and
fasting on Yom Kippur (71 per cent in Toronto and 76 per cent in
Montreal). These are all higher in Canada than in the United States.
In 2012, 70 per cent of Americans Jews attended a Passover seder

and 53 per cent fasted on Yom Kippur. Sabbath observance is marked by a range of rituals and practices – 47 per cent of Jews in Toronto and 48 per cent of Jews in Montreal light Sabbath candles compared to only 23 per cent in the United States. Similarly, 36 per cent of Jews in Toronto and 41 per cent of Jews in Montreal say they keep kosher all the time, whereas only 22 per cent of American Jews claim to do so.⁴⁹ But as already described, keeping kosher involves a mish-mash of competing definitions and practices, from "kosher style" to the ultra "glatt kosher." This populist variation confirms the centrality of Jewish folk religion as well as the old Jewish proverb "Every Jew makes his own Sabbath." Every Jew makes his or her own *kashrut*. Kosher restaurants incur onerous costs. They pay more for kosher meat, they must pay for the services of a recognized *mashgiach*, or food inspector, and they close on the Sabbath and Jewish holidays. Jewish delis feature the less expensive "kosher style" option.

Food intersects culturally with Judaism in other ways. Jews have become infatuated with Chinese food in North America. There are kosher Chinese foods and restaurants, and no kosher caterer is without a strong Chinese menu, including "mock shrimp."

A Jew and a Chinese man are arguing. The Chinese man says his people have been around for four thousand years. The Jew says his people have been around for five thousand years. Asks the Chinese man, "Well, what did you people eat for the first thousand years?"

RELIGIOUS VARIATION

Levels of religious observance in Canada vary by region and by social characteristics. They are higher in Montreal and Toronto, and lower in Western communities. Interestingly, there is no evidence of decline in religious observance among younger Jews. Likely due to the higher fertility rates of religious Jews, there are more younger Jews who are observant, have a more Jewish social network, and live in Jewish neighbourhoods.⁵⁰ Levels of observance are, of course, highest among Orthodox Jews, followed by Conservative and Reform. A fully observant Jew must, in theory, recite prayers three times a day, and many Orthodox men do so. Most Conservative synagogues also feature daily services. By contrast, daily prayers are not required for Reform or Reconstructionist Jews or more liberal movements.

Religious expression is no longer easily described by the conventional denominations. As mentioned, New Age synagogues affiliated with the Jewish Renewal Movement try to create a level of spirituality that is absent from the mainstream. New forms of "secular" Jewish associations have developed in Toronto and Montreal, seeking to celebrate holidays without the overlay of belief, perhaps the best proof of the non-theological nature of Jewish religiosity. *Havurot*, or small independent congregations, stressing informality, innovation, and community, have sprung up. So have egalitarian Orthodox *minyans*, congregations which follow Orthodox traditions but have complete gender equality, like the The First Narayever in Toronto. Both respond to perceived needs that were not met by established denominations.

Orthodoxy is less entrenched in the West Coast. Indeed the boundaries of the major denominations no longer hold in a frontier society where traditions are weak. A 1999 ad for an assistant rabbi by a self-described liberal congregation in Vancouver described the 525-family congregation as "completely egalitarian, yet also has two days of Rosh Hashana. Conversions are *ke'dat halacha*, and Jewish identity is established through matrilineal descent or conversion."[51] This unnamed congregation clearly does not conform to the accepted doctrines of the major denominations. New Age Judaism is alive and well. Vancouver's Or Shalom Spiritual Community embraces the environmental movement with "religious" zeal. In their previous rabbi's view, "Eating food grown or produced in a way that is destructive to the earth is not kosher. We are not allowed to participate in things that destroy the earth." That means no foam plates or plastic cutlery, and a preference for locally grown foods. The Pacific region of the Canadian Jewish Congress debated a position paper on the environment, with the involvement of their rabbi.[52]

Jews in Vancouver have had to be resourceful. One informal *havura* of five or six couples, with children, would get together once a month for Friday-night potluck Shabbat dinners, and would also meet around holidays. They would attend each other's life-cycle celebrations. The group was drawn from different synagogues, and included converts to Judaism. Few of the members had Jewish roots in Vancouver, so what they created was a surrogate extended family, with a warm, *heimish* (home-style) atmosphere. For all this experimentation, it is paradoxical that the glue that held this surrogate family together has been Shabbat and the accompanying ritual, which imposes an inevitable commitment.

There is a relation between these experiments and the established denominations. Many of the innovators are themselves products of mainstream denominations. Mordecai Kaplan, founder of Reconstructionism, as well as the leaders of Camp Ramah and the *Havurah* movement, emerged out of Conservative Judaism. Many of the innovations – those that stand the test of time – are slowly being accepted by synagogues. Eco-Judaism has been prefigured by forms of Judaic social consciousness and the concern shared by the Jewish Renewal movement and other progressive Jews for *tikkun olam*, or the healing of the world.

A new major challenge faces Jewish religious life in Canada as well as the United States. Judaism, as I have argued, has been a largely communal religion. Even more than other faiths, religious observance is rooted in the collectivity. Yet an individualist ethic has spread throughout religious life in recent decades, particularly among the more liberal religious movements. In the words of sociologists Wade Clark Roof and William McKinney, "Of all the recent religious changes in America, few are more significant or more subtle than the enhanced religious individualism of our time. Americans generally hold a respectful attitude toward religion, but also they increasingly regard it as a matter of personal choice or preference."[53] Individuals are charting their own journey, by themselves or with like-minded groups. For "moderately affiliated" Jews, religion is becoming a cafeteria, and prescriptive texts more like a menu from which individuals can pick and choose.[54] This trend is more pronounced in the United States, but it is growing in Canada.

For most Canadian Jews, religious life takes place in the mainstream synagogues. Synagogue politics can be nasty, even if based on seeming trivialities. Congregations can break apart as a result of clashes of personality, doctrine, or combinations of the two. Rabbis are often targets, with supporters and the disgruntled in opposing camps. One such case occurred in an Orthodox synagogue. A clash between supporters and opponents of the incumbent rabbi blended into an earlier disagreement about the *mechitza*, or partition, separating men from women. The two factions were split over whether it was several inches too high or too low. I am not making this up. Much later, the rabbi left the congregation.

A Jew is marooned on a desert island for twenty years and finally rescued. He shows his rescuers what he has built. "These are the two synagogues." They ask why one Jew needs two synagogues. He explains; "Simple, this is the synagogue that I pray in, and this other one, ha, I would never set foot in it!"

There may be more tensions between and within the ultra-Orthodox and Modern Orthodox than within any of the other movements. But the major fault line is between the Orthodox and the non-Orthodox.

RELIGIOUS PLURALISM, RELIGIOUS CONFLICT

Religion has in recent years taken over from differences in ethnicity, class, and political ideology as a major basis of conflict within the Jewish community. With the rise in intermarriage, tensions have mounted over the issues of "Who is a Jew?" and "Who is a rabbi?" This is the Jewish version of religious wars found in most other faiths. None is immune: Shias versus Sunnis, Catholics versus Protestants, fundamentalist Protestants versus liberal Protestants. To an outsider, the grievances can seem picky. Reform Judaism differs explicitly with Orthodoxy and Conservatism by accepting patrilineal descent as equal to matrilineal descent as a basis for being a Jew, and recognizing women and LGBTQ rabbis. Moreover, Orthodox rabbis do not accept as "legitimate" marriages and conversions carried out under Reform, and often Conservative, auspices. (No Reform or Conservative rabbi would challenge the status of an Orthodox convert – at least not yet.)

Because of intermarriage, non-Orthodox conversion, and the large numbers of mixed marriages and "Jews by choice," there are now in Canada tens of thousands of Jews who are not recognized by the Orthodox. This position derives support from Israel, where issues of marriage and family status are administered by the official rabbinate, which is resolutely Orthodox. (Christians and Muslims in Israel are also governed by their respective religious bodies.) Reform and Conservative rabbis, while often devoted to Israel, are second-class clerics. Given that 80 per cent of the population of Canada – and Israel – is non-Orthodox, the possibilities for friction are large. One rabbi argued to me that the rising intermarriage rates were decisive in increasing the tensions. Another pointed out that some of the tensions have always been there but have been exacerbated by polarization in Israeli politics. Most Orthodox rabbis have tended to be pro-Likud, while more of the others have tended towards Labour. The assassination of Israeli prime minister Yitzhak Rabin in 1995 was a flashpoint in several Canadian Jewish communities. For example, Montreal Reconstructionist Rabbi Ron Aigen was quoted in the *Gazette* as claiming that the Orthodox rabbinate in Israel had "blood on their hands." Many in the Orthodox community were outraged, but Orthodox and militant Zionist Rabbi Reuben Poupko defended Aigen and did not isolate him.[55]

The kind of invective common in New York (or Jerusalem) is not as prevalent in Canada. As Toronto Rabbi Moshe Shulman explained, the non-Orthodox in Canada are more traditional than in the United States, so there is more crossover and less tension.[56] Tensions are lower, but still present. A liberal rabbi recounted how in the early 1980s, two Orthodox rabbis, including one with whom he had been very friendly, refused to join him to sit on a conversion Beth Din. He was also dismayed to find that Orthodox *mohels* refused to circumcise the children of some of his converts.

How to assess the seriousness of these divisions? For the vast majority of Jews, the doctrinal differences that define these conflicts do not intrude on their daily lives. Most Jews voluntarily and happily self-segregate. They are not forced to interact with those with whom they disagree. They go to synagogue, educate and raise their children, and socialize with Jews with whom they get along. Moreover, in the view of Toronto Reform Rabbi John Moscowitz, friendships exist between the Orthodox and the non-Orthodox. Conservative Rabbi Baruch Frydman-Kohl noted that while some Jews live separately in terms of public religiosity, that is not the whole story. At the personal level, people discover commonalities when meeting in business or at social gatherings. He sensed that many in Toronto's Modern Orthodox community are open to more public relationships with the non-Orthodox.[57] A case in point is my own course on the sociology of Jews in North America at McGill University. For the past several years, I have invited a Reform rabbi and an Orthodox rabbi to speak together to the students about the challenges and strengths facing their respective denominations. It has been truly remarkable to see the warmth and mutual respect they display towards one another.

Nevertheless, it is always unpleasant when Reform or Orthodox Jewish leaders are quoted in the *Canadian Jewish News* making nasty remarks about each other. But these displays of intolerance may have little impact on the larger community. Orthodox Jews, for the most part, marry other Orthodox Jews. This is even truer for the ultra-Orthodox. And what if an Orthodox and non-Orthodox Jew fall in love? The issue resolves itself one way or another. If the family of the Orthodox Jew is not satisfied, then perhaps, to keep the peace, the other partner will embrace Orthodoxy. If not, maybe the Orthodox family will grudgingly accommodate themselves to the marriage, which may produce a blended religious lifestyle sometimes called Conservadox. Or the lovers will decide not to marry. Or they may marry and break, at least temporarily, with one or both sets of parents. Sad, but not the end of the world. Disagreements with parents happen often, for all sorts of reasons, to all sorts of couples. I see very little evidence that problems of cross-boundary marriages have reached crisis proportions for North American Jews.

For several years, annual Simchat Torah celebrations in Montreal included several synagogues: Orthodox, Conservative, Reconstructionist, and Sephardic. This involved dancing with the Torahs on the street in front of the Orthodox synagogue. But that was Montreal. To risk an unfair generalization, it seems tensions among the denominations have been greater in Toronto. One Toronto scholar said that a multidenominational Simchat Torah rally could not take place in that city: "The Orthodox would not play ball, the Reform would find it unseemly to dance in the street, the Conservatives would worry that the insurance on the Torahs would not permit them being in the street. And whoever was planning the event would forget to invite the Reconstructionists." According to one rabbi, Toronto's dynamics are like those of Baltimore and Cleveland, while Montreal's are like those of Boston and more liberal parts of New York Orthodoxy. In Montreal, the Orthodox rabbis may be more focused on community and communal solidarity, while in Toronto it has fallen to Conservative and Reform rabbis to play larger communal roles.

Another rabbi claims that in Toronto, Orthodox congregations are more homogeneous, with more members who are personally' very observant. Certainly, I have found it common to hear non-Orthodox Jews in Toronto lament the increasing power of the "black hats" with a venom not found in Montreal. In Montreal, Orthodox congregations tend to be more eclectic; many are at best institutionally Orthodox. People join because their parents were members rather than for any deep personal conviction. The Montreal Orthodox rabbinate has no choice but to act accordingly, and thus more tolerantly.

None of the denominations is homogeneous, and the same applies to their rabbis. In Montreal in 2016, there was a Jewish marriage officiated by both an Orthodox and a Reform rabbi. One Orthodox rabbi describes a nuanced approach to his faith. He endorses an "uncompromising" commitment to *halacha*. Yet he laments the frequent description of Orthodoxy as "right-wing." His view of Orthodoxy entails no ghetto walls, no closure from the outside world. He concedes that when a Jew attends a Reform or Conservative service, it is a "positive Jewish experience." But it is hard to imagine ultra-Orthodox rabbis and even many Orthodox rabbis, whether in North America or in Israel, agreeing with him. There are also internal divisions within liberal ranks, such as Reform and Reconstructionism. Some rabbis will perform mixed marriages, others will not. Some will refuse to officiate at a bar mitzvah ceremony, regardless of which parent is Jewish, if told by a mixed married couple that their child "is being raised in both religions." Some liberal rabbis in Canada do not mind.

A major area of controversy has been the status of women and, to a lesser extent, the LGBTQ community. The Reform and Reconstructionist denominations have achieved complete gender equality. In addition, most of these also accept ordination of lesbian rabbis, and may perform same-sex marriages or alternative ceremonies. And in many Conservative congregations, seating is mixed, women are counted in the minyan, and serve as rabbis, cantors, and synagogue presidents. The text of prayers has also been amended to avoid sexist language and to omit certain phrases or prayers which might offend women. An example is the deletion of an offending morning benediction in which men bless God for not creating them women. Another is the inclusion of Sarah, Rebecca, Rachel, and Leah, along with Abraham, Isaac, and Jacob, in the major prayer, the *shmoneh esrei*.

Some Orthodox Jewish women are engaged in struggles, too, though the parameters are far different. Orthodox inequalities are pronounced. We have already discussed the problem of granting a *get*, or divorce decree. There seems to be only a minority Orthodox constituency for exploring the ordination of women, or for mixed seating, or indeed for full gender equality. A few Orthodox women and prayer groups have experimented with all-women services in which they fulfil the various functions, including chanting the Torah portion, permissible if no men are around. The tensions within Orthodoxy will increase as more women pursue higher-level Jewish studies, including Talmud. On the one hand, parts of Orthodoxy are moving to the right; on the other hand, more liberal elements of Orthodoxy are seeking to create spaces for learned women who are given a form of ordination as a "*Rabba*" or "*Maharat,*" which can allow them to assume some quasi-rabbinical functions. There, the debate is not yet settled. In this area, the Canadian Jewish response is usually influenced by developments in American rabbinical seminaries, but with a time lag.[58]

The Canadian religious community has begun to confront and adapt to issues of homosexuality. The LGBTQ organization Kulanu in Toronto listed twenty-two "LGBTQ-friendly" congregations in the city: five Conservative, three Orthodox, seven Reform, one Reconstructionist, and the remaining unaffiliated. Of the eleven that said they perform same-sex weddings, none were Orthodox or Conservative. Rabbis in Vancouver and Edmonton have also indicated that they would perform same-sex weddings. Rabbi Alan Bright of Montreal's Conservative Shaare Zedek Congregation claimed that Montreal Conservative Rabbis were not yet comfortable marrying gay couples.[59]

The first gay synagogue was organized in Los Angeles in 1972; since then, the jewishLGBTnetwork.com lists approximately 100 "LGBT friendly" synagogues in the United States. The rise of "gay-friendly" synagogues has called into question the attraction of mainly gay synagogues.[60] Individual gay and lesbian Jews belong to all types of congregations but it is only among Reform or Reconstructionist Jews that the status of LGBTQ Jews, couples, or rabbis is fully equal. The legitimacy of ordaining LGBTQ rabbis was established by the Reform's Central Conference of Reform Rabbis in 1990. The prominent Reform Temple Emanuel in Montreal hired a lesbian rabbi, Lisa Grushcow, in 2012.

As these examples indicate, nowhere are Jewish pluralism and conflict more evident than in the religious arena. But the impact of these tensions on daily life is minimal. Moreover, they are clear signs of adaptation, vitality, inclusiveness, and creativity.

11

Sticks, Stones, and Social Relations

The Evolving Forms of Anti-Semitism

"Come, let us deal wisely with them; lest they multiply, and it come to
pass, that, when there befalleth us any war, they also join themselves
unto our enemies, and fight against us, and get them up out of the land."

Exodus 1:10

"An anti-Semite is someone who hates Jews more than is really necessary."

Isaiah Berlin

Until the 1960s, one could argue that anti-Semitism was the dominant fact of North American Jewish life. For the next three to four
decades, assimilation gained ground as the main focus of scholarly
and communal concern. But in the twenty-first century, it is fair to
say that anti-Semitism, often linked to anti-Israel expressions and
Zionism, and encouraged by some of the discourse that surfaced
with Trump's election, has re-emerged both on the communal agenda
and in the private concerns of Canadian Jews.

In my McGill University course on the sociology of North
American Jewry, taught since 1977, I have often asked my Jewish
students (about half the class) how many of them have been victimized by anti-Semitism. Most say they have. I then ask for details.
Most often they report reading anti-Semitic graffiti in the bathrooms
or hearing upsetting JAP jokes. One student told of a grade-school
teacher who had made an explicitly anti-Semitic remark. When I
asked what happened, the student replied that she told her parents,
who then told the school administration, who then reprimanded the
teacher. End of story. Almost none of the students had been beaten
up, and none had been given a lower grade in school, been denied a

job or paid lower wages, been denied accommodation or service, or
had their property vandalized or defaced. But most of them felt sincerely that they had been victimized. Jewish students, like all other
minority students, also claim to be affected by micro-aggressions:
indirect, subtle, or unintentional prejudice or discrimination (often
verbal) against members of a marginalized group. More recently,
I have met with Jewish students at McGill who have felt highly
stressed and victimized – as Jews – by Israel Apartheid and BDS
(boycott, divestment, and sanctions) campaigns on campus. And
research has found this feeling is now common among Jewish
students elsewhere.[1]

I personally have never experienced any episode in which I was
directly victimized as a Jewish person. I was never assaulted by
anti-Semites on the street. As a teenager, I took a summer job in a
hardware store in the French East End of Montreal. I was the only
Jewish or English-speaking worker in the place. After a few days, I
noticed another employee was yelling in my direction across the
store, "Hey, rabbi, rabbi!" This was the first time I had encountered racial taunting. I wondered how to respond; the fellow was
older and bigger than I was. Luckily, a few days later, I realized he
had been calling out to his friend at the other end of the store. The
friend's name was Robert, which in French slang or *joual* came
close to "rabbi" ...

Almost every adult non-Jew I have encountered professionally
and socially has been, in my view, either neutral – often curious –
or philo-Semitic. Obviously, I do not socialize with anti-Semites.
University faculties today are not crawling with overt bigots, despite
the fears of some activists in the antiracist movement. And perhaps
my view of what constitutes anti-Semitism is distorted because of
my exposure, through my family and my academic studies, to the
Holocaust. Most older Canadian Jews will tell a far different story,
sometimes about street fights, more often about the Jewish equivalent of the rude Anglo saleslady in Eaton's department store in
Montreal sixty years ago telling francophones to "speak white."

Understanding anti-Semitism in Canada means understanding the
paradoxical relationship between two divergent trends. On the one
hand, compared with earlier periods of Canadian history (and certainly by comparison with most Western societies), anti-Semitism in
Canada today is not a major problem. By conventional measures
it is in decline. On the other hand, the anti-Semitism which does

remain, and the new forms which have emerged, are all the more disturbing and difficult to overcome.

If this book had been written in the 1950s, this chapter would be as large as several others combined. Jews in Canada, and indeed in the United States, were part of a still profoundly marginal and insecure community. Intermarriage and assimilation were not recognized as major threats, since non-Jews were not eager to marry Jews. The key issue facing Jews in their private and public lives was discrimination, in its many forms. Quotas, formal and informal, still operated in universities and corporate boardrooms. An effective legal structure dealing with human rights, non-discrimination, and expressions of hate did not exist. Negative and demeaning stereotypes about Jews were widespread in all segments of the Canadian public. Jews faced discrimination in employment, in accommodation, and in housing. Jewish children in public schools were usually expected to take part in all manner of Christian rituals and prayer. There were no human rights acts or human rights commissions, no hate literature laws, no constitutional protections. Jewish Holocaust survivors still had to overcome resistance to enter Canada after the war.[2] Jews still lived in a profoundly Jewish solitude, for reasons of choice and reasons of exclusion. Many Jews were uncomfortable with non-Jews, and vice versa.

Throughout most of the twentieth century, the fledgling social scientific study of Jews in North America focused on anti-Semitism and inter-group relations. This paralleled the preoccupation of postwar scholars working in the more general area of prejudice and racism. It was anti-Semitism that made Jews interesting. The landmark study *The Authoritarian Personality*, published in 1950, looked at the causes of anti-Semitism and fascism. Other general American studies of prejudice in the 1950s dealt equally with anti-Black racism and anti-Semitism within a broader framework.[3] In addition, several studies focusing directly on anti-Semitism were published in the 1960s and 1970s.[4] The first major research projects on American Jewish life in general included studies of social relations, exclusion, and by extension subtle forms of anti-Semitism. There was no concern with Jewish identity or culture. This dates back to the pioneering sociological study of Chicago Jews by Louis Wirth, *The Ghetto*, first published in 1926. Later research in the 1950s and 1960s focused on Jewish life in the new postwar suburbs, or in the "gilded ghetto," far from immigrant neighbourhoods. These

American studies did not focus on glaring or violent anti-Semitism, but on day-to-day interactions between Jews and their non-Jewish neighbours.[5]

In Canada, the pioneering study of Forest Hill in Toronto, *Crestwood Heights* by John Seeley and associates, included sections describing Jewish interactions with the majority non-Jewish populations. Canadian Jews in the 1950s played down their Jewish identity, still insecure in their new-found middle-class suburban status.[6] But despite the general improvement in social conditions for Jews in recent decades, anti-Semitism remains a defining feature of the Canadian Jewish consciousness. The most successful book ever written on a Canadian Jewish topic was *None Is Too Many*, exploring Canada's closed-door policy toward Jewish refugees before and during the Second World War.[7]

In many ways, perceptions of anti-Semitism today are determined by memories and the received wisdom of the past. Things were indeed much worse for Canadian Jews two or three generations ago, and earlier. But how bad were they? The Canadian experience, both past and present, has been relatively benign for Jews. There have been no forced conversions, no expulsions, no pogroms, no crematoria, no Nuremberg Laws, not even a Dreyfus affair and related organized anti-Semitism. No political party or movement of any consequence has had Jewish issues as a central plank. There was no historic legacy of a "Jewish problem" crying out for a political solution, final or otherwise, in North America. The anti-Semitism of Social Credit in Alberta, like that of American populism, remained on the fringe geographically and politically. In Quebec and Ontario, both elite and populist anti-Semitism were the norm, in attitudes if not behaviours. But Jews were never the absolute pariahs they were in Europe, and occasionally in Arab/Muslim countries. French-English polarization and the victimization of First Nations and non-White minorities assured Jews a margin of acceptability and buffered the hatred. It is not even clear that any individual Canadian Jews have been murdered by anti-Semites, as happened in the United States in notorious cases like the 1915 lynching of Leo Frank.[8]

After the 1950s, the American appetite for both public and private expressions of anti-Semitism shrank even further, though they may now be taking new forms, as we shall see.[9] There has been a similar slow but steady improvement in Canada. Not only is discrimination in the public sphere now against the law, but the prevalence of stereotypes and prejudice has declined as well. Declined, but certainly not disappeared. It is important to recognize the distance travelled by Canadian Jews. But it is also important to recognize that anti-Semitism persists among certain fringe elements of the far right, notably those involved in Holocaust denial. In addition, it remains present in the holding and asserting of negative stereotypes, and residual discomfort in social interactions. And as we observed in Chapter 9 on politics, it may be manifested as insensitivity to Jewish interests, which leads to policies that can be harmful to Jews, notably regarding Israel.

There are different ways of defining and measuring anti-Semitism. It is important to get a sense of the spectrum of meanings. Some anti-Semitism has been explicitly mandated in, or permitted by, legislation, or so interpreted by courts. The Canadian Constitution, which includes the British North America Act, itself contains a form of legal discrimination against Jews in the area of educational rights. Protestants and Catholics enjoy educational rights unavailable to Jews and other religious minorities. For a long time, anti-Semitism was not even illegal in Canada. It was not uncommon in the 1930s and 1940s for resorts, employers, and landlords to discriminate openly against Jews. Universities and hospitals were more subtle, but as effective. A CJC study in 1934 uncovered such extensive anti-Semitism, most of it relatively legal, that the report was never released lest it prove demoralizing to Canadian Jews and help legitimate anti-Semitic expressions.[10]

The force of law and jurisprudence in Canada today protects Jews and other minorities from such open discrimination. The role of government has shifted away from oppression of Jews and other minorities such as the 1930s immigration restrictions or the Chinese head tax. The shift took place in stages. From the postwar period to the 1960s, governments adopted a neutral posture, not actively discriminating but also not rigorously proscribing discrimination. By the 1960s, we saw a move toward a new role for the government as protector of minorities. This is typified by the adoption of the non-discriminatory immigration points system, and the enactment of human rights legislation at provincial and federal levels.[11] Nevertheless, as we have already seen, there remain clear cases where law, or the interpretation of law, can harm Jewish interests. These often deal with "reasonable accommodation." How far should public institutions go to accommodate Jewish concerns such as exams on Jewish holidays or the right to build a synagogue in an area not zoned for it?

Everyday anti-Semitism consists of acts by individual Canadians or institutions which may or may not be illegal but which do harm Jews. Some of these acts are clearly motivated by anti-Jewish feeling, like an employer choosing not to hire a Jew. Others may be unintentional and simply have harmful consequences, like scheduling examinations on Passover. (Note that the inadvertent scheduling of exams on Passover, for example, could be described as systemic anti-Semitism; a subsequent court challenge that failed might be considered by some to be legal or state-sponsored anti-Semitism.)

Overt expressions of anti-Semitism can come in many forms from acts of serious personal violence, which are rare, to the defacement of property, which is more common. Another type is overt discrimination in employment or in any other public domain. This, too, is rare, or at least ineffectual, given that Canadian Jews are doing well economically. This form of discrimination can be discovered by documenting socio-economic inequalities in official income statistics, as well as in field studies of discrimination, or by looking at cases reported to human rights commissions. Such cases include harassment as well as explicit acts such as not hiring or firing, denial of promotions, or paying unequal salaries. Verbal insults or internet postings such as Holocaust denial are another form of anti-Semitism. And anti-Semitism is often a real or perceived subtext in recent heated campus debates about Israel or Zionism.[12] Of course, casual private comments or expressions might be found offensive by Jews, as a form of micro-aggression, even when they are not intended to be hurtful.

Another type of anti-Semitism is attitudinal. This is often hidden, and in some cases can blend in with the micro-aggressions mentioned above. Most anti-Semites do not act out their prejudices or even express them in public (although they may express them to selected friends and neighbours), because it is politically incorrect or because they risk some sort of sanction. We know from surveys that some Canadians hold negative attitudes about Jews. Some of these attitudes are clearly vicious, while others are stereotypes ranging from benign to misinformed. This prejudice does not translate into real discrimination except in rare cases. The effects of these attitudes are sometimes seen in what social scientists call "social distance," which measures the propensity of groups to interact socially with each other. But social distance is not necessarily what it seems. Often it may be Jews themselves who choose to keep their distance, reflecting a fear of anti-Semitism or simple preferences.

And there is more. Studies of racism in Canada or elsewhere almost never focus on the attitudes of minorities toward majorities. Some Jews hold negative stereotypes about non-Jews, and they are just as demeaning. The same is true for other visible minority groups, who may hold negative views about Whites or Europeans that border on racism. The belief that only the powerful can be racist is prevalent among sociologists, as majority groups generally wield greater power to harm minority groups than the reverse. Though minority groups usually lack the power to implement their racist views, intergroup relations have increasingly become a two-way street. To deny that minorities, including Jews, can hold prejudicial views, is to deprive them of their cultural agency. And to fail to analyze these views is to miss an interesting dynamic. It is not clear how many Jews believe, for example, that every non-Jew is a potential anti-Semite. Or that non-Jews drink too much, or have different cultural styles. But some do. As a result, they may be happy to socialize mainly with other Jews. In addition, some Jews in North America benefit from "white privilege" compared to racialized, non-White minorities.[13]

Anti-Semitism can permeate both high culture and popular culture. Historically, this began as anti-Judaism, and would include the theological conviction that Jews were Christ-killers, and that Judaism posed a threat to Christianity. Today it may be more subtle, like the use of terms such as "Christian" morality rather than "Judeo-Christian." Beyond that, it includes demeaning images of Jews in literature or intellectual discourse or daily language, or the absence of Jews or Jewish themes in Canadian cultural production. The images of Shylock, or of rapacious Jewish businessmen, or the use of "Jew" as a verb, are well-known examples. This type of cultural anti-Semitism was far more prevalent in the past in both English and French Canada. If it exists today, it must contend with the unexpected spread of a general tolerance and even with philo-Semitism, in which others find Jews and Jewish culture exotic and interesting. Examples are the increasing fascination with the Holocaust on the part of many sympathetic non-Jews and the widespread admiration of the late Leonard Cohen. In a way, curiosity and admiration are eating into fear and dislike.

THE HISTORICAL BACKGROUND

Anti-Semitism in Canada dates back to before Confederation. It was found among both the French and English communities, and was largely religious in character. The conflict over the election in 1807 of Ezekiel Hart to the legislative assembly of Lower Canada included elements of anti-Semitism, though scholars debate whether it was his Jewishness or his affinity with the English which was decisive. Indeed, a theological anti-Semitism existed throughout the pre-Confederation era, even in the near absence of Jews.[14] In French Canada, a steady stream of anti-Semitic thought was present, some home-grown and some imported from France. The Dreyfus case galvanized French and Catholic anti-Semitism in Canada around the turn of the century. Many publications and personalities supported anti-Dreyfusard sentiments. Some newspapers published the anti-Semitic tracts of Edouard Drumont. A persistent drumbeat of anti-Semitism in Quebec to 1914, which would eventually grow louder, reflected not only theological prejudice but acts of street vandalism as well.[15]

In English Canada, the prevailing anti-Semitism can be gleaned from the credit-rating reports of R.G. Dun and Company in the mid-1800s, which are replete with derogatory comments and stereotypes about Jews and Jewish businessmen.[16] Theological anti-Semitism was expressed in evangelical and missionary activity aimed at converting Jews in Canada, and supporting such efforts elsewhere.[17] English Canada also developed a brand of "intellectual" anti-Semitism, typified by the writings of Goldwin Smith in the late nineteenth century. Smith, a scholar and writer with wide-ranging interests, was a classic liberal on issues such as separation of church and state. Yet beginning in the 1870s, his writings contain many anti-Semitic thoughts and references. He criticized Judaism as a tribal religion, condemned an alleged Jewish materialism, and raised the canard of Jewish dual loyalty. Smith, who influenced Vincent Massey and Mackenzie King among others, helped set the stage for twentieth-century anti-Semitic prejudice while giving such views a gloss of respectability.[18] Anglo anti-Semitism of this type helped feed into discrimination at Canadian universities. Jewish enrollment at McGill declined between 1925 and 1935 from 25 to 12 per cent of the student population.[19] Anti-Semitism was less prevalent in the West at the turn of the century, due in part to the absence of entrenched anglo elites in an essentially polyglot and immigrant pioneering society. But even though the western Canadian press was supportive of the Dreyfusards in France, some papers would occasionally publish implicitly anti-Semitic articles and did not attack anti-Semitic ideas per se.[20]

Canadian anti-Semitism reached its peak in the 1930s. Explicitly fascist organizations existed in both English and French Canada. In English Canada, it fed on a base of Anglo-Saxon nativism and unemployment. The 1930s saw the development of swastika clubs and associations. Indeed, the swastika figured in the largest Jewish-Gentile riot in Canadian history, which broke out in 1933 in Toronto's Christie Pits after a baseball game between a largely Jewish team and an Anglo-Saxon club.[21] The formation of a Swastika Club at Balmy Beach that year had been followed by sporadic clashes between supporters and young Jews.[22] In Christie Pits, thousands of combatants were involved. The event traumatized Toronto Jews at the time, and old-timers still recall the riot, but there was no loss of life and few serious injuries.

Movements such as the Canadian Union of Fascists took root in Ontario and western Canada, inspired by Oswald Mosely's British Union of Fascists. Adrien Arcand, a Quebec fascist and anti-Semite, also extended his activities into Ontario. A national fascist convention in 1938 attracted an estimated 1,500 to 2,500 participants, but their ultimate success was limited.[23] Indeed, among English Protestants in Canada, there was consistent opposition to the various anti-Semitic policies of the Third Reich. This opposition on the part of the Protestant clergy was welcomed by Jews, though it was perhaps not as vociferous as it could have been.[24]

In Quebec, the situation was more serious. Opposition to conscription helped fuel traditional anti-Semitic sentiments, and vice versa. Moreover, in the inter-war period, French nationalism embraced three themes, all of which fed anti-Semitism: re-francization, with Jews being identified with the English; promoting French entrepreneurs through the *"achat chez nous"* movement, which involved boycotting Jewish firms; and anti-immigration sentiments.[25] The conservative Catholic Church in Quebec opposed liberal and radical tendencies identified with Jews at home and abroad.[26] Father Lionel Groulx expressed sympathies with certain anti-Semitic currents as well as fascist governments, though there is debate among scholars as to the degree and influence of his anti-Semitism. Even more pronounced was the steady anti-Semitism in articles, letters, and columns published in the influential newspaper *Le Devoir*.[27] In comparison to the English press, or to the Protestant churches, the silence from mainstream Quebec circles about the defence of European Jews or anti-Semitism generally was marked.[28] In 1934, Dr Samuel Rabinovitch, a top graduate from the Université de Montréal's medical school, was awarded an internship at Montreal's Notre Dame Hospital. In protest, all of his fellow non-Jewish interns walked out, soon joined by interns in other Catholic hospitals. Eventually, the doctor resigned his appointment. More telling, the interns' strike enjoyed support from all sectors of Quebec society, including *Le Devoir*.[29]

Adrien Arcand formed his National Social Christian Party on a Nazi model in 1934. His brand of anti-Semitism influenced popular French-language newspapers like *Le Patriote* and *Le Goglu*. Moreover, the conservative and nationalist Quebec government of Maurice Duplessis offered an environment in which more extreme forms of anti-Semitism could thrive. For example, the unopposed passage of the Padlock Law in 1937 enabled the government to close any establishment used to propagate communism, but ignored fascist and anti-Semitic organizations.[30] To be sure, Arcand's movement numbered only in the hundreds, not thousands. It petered out during the course of the war, though elements of anti-Semitism animated the Bloc Populaire and the anti-conscription movements. But the bald fact that over 80 per cent of Quebec voters, and more among francophones, rejected the possibility of conscription in the referendum in the spring of 1942 is revealing. And distressing. Quebec intellectuals have yet to have an honest confrontation with that vote, and indeed with that period. Esther Delisle's second book (published in 1998) dealing with the anti-Semitism and Nazi sympathizers in the postwar period was, like her first, greeted with a blend of silence and contempt.[31] The contrast with the eager *mea culpas* and enthusiastic reception in English Canada of Irving Abella and Harold Troper's *None Is Too Many* is stark.

While organized anti-Semitism was weaker in western Canada, there was some among immigrant German communities, most notably Mennonites.[32] Anti-Semitism in the West also drew some strength from Social Credit and Prairie populism, which attacked the influence of "Eastern bankers," presumably some Jewish, whose high interest rates penalized farmers. Social Credit premier William Aberhart of

Alberta did not openly espouse anti-Semitic views, unlike the British founder of Social Credit, Major Douglas. But Norman Jacques, Social Credit MP from 1935 to 1949, would routinely rail in the Commons against "the international financial conspiracy." Ernest Manning, father of Reform Party founder Preston, fought the Douglasite anti-Semitic tendencies in the party in the 1940s.[33]

After the war, political anti-Semitism was largely discredited, but there remained a strong residue of popular anti-Semitic sentiment. A national survey at the end of the war found that most Canadians ranked Jews as among the least desirable immigrants to the country.[34] But slowly, over the decades, as educational levels rose and as the notion of human rights took root, anti-Semitism became less acceptable as both private attitude and public expression.

THE CONTENT OF EXTREME ANTI-SEMITISM

By the end of the twentieth century, there were a number of extreme right-wing groups in Canada who espoused elements of fundamentalist Christianity, anti-Semitism, xenophobia, Islamophobia, anti-communism, and racism. Among the better known were the Western Guard, the Ku Klux Klan, the Heritage Front, and various skinhead movements.[35] Most of the organizations were small and unimportant. But some were not. Anti-Semitism is purveyed regularly by extremist fringe groups through magazines and books, which are read devotedly by followers. When police seize arms caches from these groups, they often find White supremacist literature nearby. And, of course, anti-Semitic tropes, notably the Jews or Zionists as conspirators against the West, are found on many racist websites. Islamist and jihadi websites will also argue that Zionism and/or Israel are regularly conspiring against Islam and Islamic states.

The content of traditional explicit anti-Semitism in the West can be reduced to four types.[36] First is religious anti-Semitism that feeds on the hoary "Christ-killer" theme. The Jewish refusal to accept Christ stands as a permanent challenge to Christianity. Some evangelical Christians continue to call routinely for the conversion of the Jews, as in the *Globe and Mail* ad described earlier. The modern version of religious anti-Semitism is a far cry from the gross calumnies common in the past, like blood libels or linkage of Jews with the devil or Antichrist. Messianic Jewish groups like Jews for Jesus speak fondly of Jews, Judaism, and of Israel; they simply want Jews to accept a better, a more complete alternative. But they can pose a challenge to Judaism, and have deliberately targeted Russian Jews, whose Jewish learning and identity are weak. The Jewish community lobbied Bell Canada to exclude the institutions run by Jews for Jesus from the telephone directory's listing of synagogues. But in 2016, typing "synagogue" in the business directory of Canada411.ca still yielded a list the fourth item of which was "messianic synagogue." Some years ago, I decided to explore the movement. I wrote a letter to a Canadian representative, claiming I was a Jew who was having doubts about my faith. I received back some pamphlets and a personalized three-page, single-spaced letter urging me to make contact. I was impressed with their apparent sincerity, but make no mistake: attempts to get Jews to abandon their "misguided" religious beliefs can be perceived by some Jews as a form of anti-Semitism.

A second type is racist anti-Semitism, rooted in biology, not belief. According to this view, Jews are either non-human, sub-human, or at the very least biologically distinct: a different race from Aryans or other Caucasians. Racist anti-Semitism reached its nadir in Nazi films, writings, and propaganda, in which Jews were described as parasites and depicted as mice. According to this line of prejudice, the Jewish inclination toward usury or crime was a biological trait and therefore neither political emancipation nor religious conversion would solve the biological problem. Only extermination, or genocide, would suffice. The medieval myth of the Jews as devils with horns linked both themes.[37]

Then there are two types of political or economic anti-Semitism. Right-wing anti-Semitism opposes Jews because they are either liberal or socialist or communist. Jews are the ultimate modernizers and urbanites, challengers of the old order, opposed to monarchs and aristocrats and even to capitalists. The image of the Jew as a Bolshevik subversive epitomizes the fears of right-wing anti-Semites. More recently, Jews tend to be identified with liberal or progressive positions – pro-choice, pro-sex education, pro-gay rights, earning the enmity of the religious right.

Left-wing anti-Semitism naturally takes the opposite tack. It opposes Jews because they are seen as arch-capitalists, greedy exploiters of the working class devoted to moneymaking and material pursuits. The image of Rothschild, of Jewish bankers and financiers, captures its essence. This strain goes back again to the Middle Ages, when the image of the Jew as usurer or moneylender gained currency. Marx himself used satire and invective to establish the link between Jews and capitalism.

This strain of prejudice had a populist variant among Ukrainian peasants in the seventeenth century and among inner-city Black Americans as well as French Canadians in the twentieth century. In all these cases, Jews were assumed to hold the levers of power, when in fact they did not. It has another variant which sees Judaism (like other religions) as socially conservative on a host of issues. And yet another attacks Zionism as reactionary nationalism, and Israel and her Jewish supporters as an extension of Western imperialism aimed at oppressing Arabs.

How can Jews be simultaneously a religious group and a racial group, communists and capitalists, freethinkers and ultra-Orthodox? How do all these contradictory representations of Jews hang together in the minds of anti-Semites? The answer is conspiracy theory. The myth of a Jewish conspiracy resolves these contradictions, since all types of Jews are thus part of one overarching conspiracy – aided by Jewish control of the media – to achieve world domination.[38] Hitler's *Mein Kampf*, in its section dealing with the Jews, contains elements of all four types of anti-Semitism, as well as a section on the international Jewish conspiracy. A sampling:

Religious anti-Semitism: "His [Jewish] spirit is inwardly as alien to true Christianity as his nature two thousand years previous was to the great founder of the new doctrine … Christ was nailed to the cross while our present day party Christians debase themselves to begging for Jewish votes."[39]

Racial anti-Semitism: "The mightiest counterpart to the Aryan is represented by the Jew." Jews are a "typical parasite" and a "noxious bacillus." "The Jew has always been a people with definite racial characteristics and never a religion."[40]

Right-wing anti-Semitism: "All at once the Jew becomes liberal and begins to rave about the necessary progress of mankind … From now on the worker has no other task but to fight for the future of the Jewish people."[41]

Left-wing anti-Semitism: "He [the Jew] begins to lend money as always at usurious interest ... Finance and commerce have become his complete monopoly."[42]

The role of the press in concealing the international Jewish conspiracy: "Freemasonry is joined by a second weapon in the service of the Jews: the press ... To what extent the whole existence of this people is based on a continuous lie is shown incomparably by the Protocols of the Elders of Zion so infinitely hated by the Jews. They are based on a forgery, the Frankfurter Zeitung moans and screams once every week; the best proof they are authentic."[43]

Such vicious expressions of hate did not die with Hitler. Anti-Semitism in Canada today downplays (but does not ignore) the religious and racial theme while emphasizing elements of the left- and right-wing positions and, of course, the linchpin, conspiracy theory, applied to all manner of world events. Anti-Semites seek some degree of plausibility, and political and economic arguments seem more likely to be supported by "facts" and half-truths than debates about religious doctrine or Jews as a race. Conspiracy theories in general have gained a certain degree of acceptance, particularly after the John F. Kennedy assassination and as historical revisionism has come into fashion. Thus, John Ross Taylor, a leader of the Western Guard, believed that in the 1970s, Canada had been embroiled in a secret civil war between Anglo Freemasons and Jewish Freemasons. The latter were supported by Pierre Trudeau, René Lévesque, France, and Russia. To take another example, veteran Canadian right-wing extremist Ron Gostick argued he was not anti-Semitic but just opposed to political Zionism. Nevertheless, he has written that the US Supreme Court's 1954 school desegregation decision was a Jewish plot, that the Anti-Defamation League promotes hate and bigotry, that Anne Frank's diary is a fraud, and that Jews and communists are behind increases in anti-Semitic incidents.[44] An essay written by one of Jim Keegstra's students (see below) brings the message home clearly: "The Jews since 1976 have financed and supported the spread of Communism because it is a step toward what they must feel is heaven. Their heaven would be a New World Order under a One World Government. This government, of course, would be led by these cutthroats themselves."[45]

HATE SPEECH, FREE SPEECH

The expression of direct or indirect anti-Semitism is often defended by claims of freedom of speech. The case of the late British Columbia columnist Doug Collins is revealing. For years, Collins's column in the *North Shore News* had infuriated Jews, among others. A column he wrote on 9 March 1994 went too far for one irate Jewish reader, who took action against Collins under the British Columbia Human Rights Act. The relevant section of the act prohibits publication of material which is "likely to expose a person or a group or class of persons to hatred or contempt because of the race, colour, ancestry, place of origin, religion, marital status, family status, physical or mental disability, sex, sexual orientation, or age" of that person or group or class.

The column in question dealt with the movie *Schindler's List*, and was entitled "Hollywood Propaganda." The column is well-written, full of sarcasm and invective, designed to push Jewish buttons while promoting a cynical distrust of Jews. It is also an unambiguous piece of Holocaust denial. Both the tone and thrust of the column are captured by Collins's use of the term "Swindler's List" to describe the movie. The column cleverly compares movies like *Schindler's List* to the work of Goebbels. It calls the figure of six million Jews who died "nonsense." It focuses on Jewish producers wanting to "cash in" on the Holocaust, reviving the image of the money-crazed Jewish capitalist. Most of all, the column develops the idea of a conspiratorial Jewish-controlled Hollywood that deliberately disseminates Holocaust-related films that defame Germans while serving the needs of Jews and Israel.

I served as an expert witness in this case for the attorney general of British Columbia, to make the point that hate speech can harm its targets and indeed society as a whole. Let me be clear. I am not one of those anti-racists who advocates extensive use of hate speech laws. I take seriously the concerns of civil libertarians and supporters of free speech. The law should be used sparingly; if everything is racism or genocide or hate speech, then nothing is. While there have been cases where certain forms of campus speech have properly come under regulation through the use of "trigger warnings" for courses or lectures, or attempts to avoid "offensive" material, "thought police" should not reign supreme. But the Collins column was a clear example of Holocaust denial and hate speech. If this column was not hate speech, in my view, nothing was.

The Collins column is best understood in its socio-cultural context. Most overt anti-Semitism in Canada has relied on the myth of an international Jewish or Zionist conspiracy dating back to the *Protocols of the Elders of Zion.* A potent new element in the arsenal is Holocaust denial. This is promulgated under the guise of free speech, or academic freedom, or the value of a relativistic approach to the search for truth.[46] In fact, one Canadian survey in 1985 found that only 50 per cent of Canadians agreed that about six million Jews were killed in the Holocaust. Moreover, about 16 per cent claimed that the Holocaust was "partly" the fault of Jews themselves.[47]

Knowledge about the Holocaust remains uneven in Canadian society. A 2005 survey of the Canadian population found that 7 per cent had never heard of the Holocaust, 13 per cent among those aged eighteen to twenty-four. Forty per cent knew that the estimated figure of murdered Jews was six million, but 16 per cent thought it was less than one million. In any case, 55 per cent said they wished to learn more about the Holocaust.[48] Holocaust ignorance resurfaced during the election campaign of 2015. Alex Johnstone, an NDP candidate from Ontario, and a long-time school trustee and public-school official, admitted that she was unfamiliar with the fact that Auschwitz was a death camp during the Second World War.[49]

Ignorance about the Holocaust differs from outright anti-Semitism, but the onslaught of revisionism that has caused some skepticism and doubt about the Holocaust is often correlated with anti-Semitic views. In 1985, Canadians who felt that Jews were "too powerful" were more likely to blame the Holocaust on its victims and to say the estimate of six million was too high.[50] This despite the fact that the staunchest of Holocaust deniers insist that they are not anti-Semitic; they are simply researchers pursuing the "truth."

Three Canadian Holocaust denial cases in the 1980s led to a great deal of media attention, and were precursors of the Collins case. Ernst Zündel was a German-born publisher of materials denying the Holocaust and preaching a Jewish international conspiracy for world domination. He was prosecuted under an obscure Criminal Code provision against the spreading of false news. After an original conviction, he was eventually acquitted by the Supreme Court, which found the original statute unconstitutional. During his trial, expert witnesses testified that the concentration camps were really resorts, which was duly reported in the media. Is there a danger in prosecuting Holocaust deniers such that the coverage of the trials might spread their message? Unlikely. Ernst Zündel himself had welcomed the free publicity his trial brought him. But Canadians who followed media coverage of the Zündel trial did not have higher levels of anti-Semitism than others, or increasing doubt about the Holocaust. My guess is that people who were clear in their views on Zündel – pro or con – were more likely to follow the issue in the media. If so, press coverage of these issues would simply reinforce pre-existing views. Moreover, journalistic reports of the contents of hate speech are very different from hate speech itself.

In fact there is no evidence that such media coverage led to an increase in anti-Semitic belief.[51] As of 2001, Zündel had left Canada for the United States. In 2003, he was deported back to Canada for overstaying a US visa, detained for two years, then deported to Germany where he faced charges for Holocaust denial dating from the 1990s. He was convicted in 2007, then released in 2010, and died in 2017.

In another case, Jim Keegstra was a social studies teacher in Eckville, Alberta. He was initially prosecuted in 1985 under the hate literature laws in the Criminal Code for "willfully promoting hatred" against the Jewish people. He taught his high-school students that the events of Western history were largely the result of an international Jewish conspiracy.[52] The case eventually wound up in the Supreme Court, which upheld the constitutionality of hate literature laws as a legitimate restriction of free speech under Section One of the Charter of Rights and Freedoms. Keegstra was convicted, and sentenced to a one-year suspended sentence, one year of probation, and 200 hours of community service.

Another case involved New Brunswick school teacher Malcolm Ross. As a mathematics teacher, Ross did not import his Holocaust revisionism into the classroom. But his students knew about those views, which he expressed in public outside of class. Ross was prevented from returning to teaching in a decision by a Human Rights Tribunal which was upheld by the Supreme Court.[53]

The tensions between the right to free speech and hate speech laws will never be resolved.[54] New cases with slightly different twists, in new jurisdictions, will doubtless arise. For example, hate messages on the unregulated Internet and on social media are a troubling new version.[55] Nonetheless, as an academic, I have a reflexive appreciation of free speech. The American First Amendment is clearly a more eloquent and more consistent defence of free speech than that contained in the Canadian Charter of Rights and Freedoms. However, there is a role for carefully crafted and judiciously applied restrictions on hate speech. There are two clashing visions of a dangerous slippery slope in the debate on free speech and hate speech. From the civil libertarian perspective, restricting hate speech leads to greater restrictions on controversial or provocative speech, and any speech that anyone might find offensive. Political correctness would reign supreme. On the other hand, one racist column might become ten or a thousand, legitimating and exacerbating latent bigotry in the population until it is too late.

In my testimony in the Collins case, it was fairly easy to demonstrate that the material in the column conformed to classic Holocaust denial and anti-Semitism and that such material can cause, and has in the past caused, harm to targeted minorities. In Canada, these are not hypothetical issues. Some anti-Asian writings in mainstream British Columbia newspapers in the first decades of the twentieth century would be classified as hate speech by current standards. They prepared the public for the wartime internment of Japanese Canadians.[56] Another grotesque example was the fixation on Jewish noses and circumcision found in *Le Devoir* in the 1930s.[57] The initial decision in the Collins case supported Collins and his newspaper. The reasoning of tribunal member Nitya Iyer seemed highly complex. On the one hand, she found that the relevant section of the British Columbia legislation, prohibiting public speech "likely to expose" minorities to hatred, was indeed constitutional. And she found the Collins column "obviously anti-Semitic," and that it reinforced "negative stereotypes" of Jews with a meaning that was "offensive and harmful." She found the tone of article to be "nasty" and "mean-spirited." She also agreed that Jews were "extremely vulnerable to persecution and discrimination." But despite all this, she found that the content and tone of the column, taken together, did not capture the "degree of calumny, detestation, and vilification" signified by "hatred and contempt." She reasoned that the relevant statute did not restrict all anti-Semitic expression, even "all offensive and injurious anti-Semitic expression," only those that she claimed signified "extreme emotions of ill-will towards their targets."[58] In effect her reasoning would protect clever, witty, sophisticated hate speech, while penalizing gross and grotesque hate speech which could be considered as extreme. "Jews are evil hateful scheming bastards" might violate the statute, but "Swindler's list" does not.

The problem with her reasoning is that the witty and sophisticated Collins column may be more effective in spreading hatred of Jews than any outright statement of prejudice would be.

Collins and the newspaper were ably defended by attorney David Sutherland. One of the tough questions he posed to me was about the differences between the free-speech environment in America and that in Canada, where federal and provincial statutes place clear limits on free speech. If such laws protect minorities vulnerable to hate speech, like Jews, then it would stand to reason that Jews in the United States, denied those protections, would be much worse off. He wondered if that, in fact, was the case. The fact – which he probably knew – is that, in general, American Jews do not feel threatened or worse off. I had to scramble to refute his reasoning, like a graduate student at an oral examination. Luckily, I knew that the comparative evidence was not conclusive. The only relevant study found no difference in levels of day-to-day anti-Semitism when it compared anti-Semitic incidents collected by B'nai Brith in the two countries from 1982 to 1992.[59] Still, the best I could do was to argue that the position of American Jews was more precarious than their level of integration might suggest. After all, Jews in the Weimar Republic were doing very well on socio-economic measures before Hitler's rise to power. But economics is not everything. The socio-political environment affects the actual, perceived, and potential well-being of Jews. I argued that American White supremacist, racist, and extremist groups, often armed and militaristic, with links to militias and right-wing organizations, are more prolific than in Canada, and more dangerous, as seen in the Oklahoma City bombing. And there was no ready analogue in Canada to Pat Buchanan and Pat Robertson then (or extreme supporters of Donald Trump more recently), as mainstream political forces who could attract elements of anti-Semitism. American Jews were and remain apprehensive about perceived anti-Jewish positions and ties to the Christian right. The Reform Party in Canada, at that time, did not come close.

Collins's victory was short-lived. A second tribunal was held in early 1999. This time, four columns were at issue, including the one from the 1997 case. And this time tribunal member Tom Patch found that while individually the columns might not rise to the level of hatred envisioned by the legislation, taken together they did cross the line. Collins and the *North Shore News* had to pay the complainant, Harry Abrams, two thousand dollars. This ruling stressed the concept of the quantity as much as the quality of the expression as determining whether some expression is hate speech. The ruling was well-meaning but it actually muddied the waters for future decisions, since there may not be a reliable formula for assessing the quality and the quantity of speech required to yield a measure of hate.

A key benefit of hate speech legislation is its symbolism. It makes minorities feel better about themselves, and more secure. It also sends a signal to Canadians that public expressions of bigotry are unacceptable. Striking down such laws runs the risk of sending out the opposite message. The same could be said about the periodic debate about doing away with multicultural policy in Canada. In my view, symbols are very important. They define who we are.

Canada's various hate speech laws in the Criminal Code and in provincial statutes recognize that absolutes are rare in the world, and that more often principles will jostle against one another. When that happens, we have a court system to sort things out. Prosecutions should be rare, to avoid the stifling effect of self-censorship on debate and ultimately freedom. The laws should not be used capriciously. They are a kind of societal insurance policy. The ideas of free speech were nurtured to protect political reform and new ideas. In fact, in almost all court cases challenging these laws as restricting speech, the defendants are racists or pornographers – a far cry from Galileo and Voltaire. So far, free speech remains vigorous in Canada and in the many European countries which have comparable, or even tougher, legislation.

EXAMPLES OF CANADIAN ANTI-SEMITISM

Canadian episodes of overt anti-Semitism are uncommon. Most cases that get publicity deal with grey areas of public policy where Jewish interests or sensibilities are at stake, like the sukkah on the condo balcony discussed earlier. That proceeding was one where both parties were private citizens. In other instances, Jews have found themselves confronting state agencies directly. The infamous "Matzogate" flap in Quebec during Passover in 1997 is a case in point. Kosher-for-Passover products, coming in limited supply from the United States, were suddenly barred from Quebec because they had English-only labels. One hopes that was the result of a too-rigid obedience to language policy rather than anti-Semitism. But it is a fair bet that new cases will come along regularly to pit Jewish rights against some other legitimate government policy.

The most acute examples of policy-based anti-Semitism concern Israel. In its most extreme form we have anti-Zionism. Understanding the link between anti-Semitism and anti-Zionism implies weighing the perceptions of self-declared victims over motivations of perpetrators, as happens with cases of racism and sexism as well. Thus, opposing the right of Jews to a state of their own, given the fact that millions of Israeli Jews already live in such a state and would defend its existence, is for most Jews unambiguous anti-Semitism. To be blunt, for many it is a call for a de facto genocide against Israeli Jews. But what of opposition to one or more Israeli policies? This is obviously more complex. After all, much of the Israeli electorate at any time, from left to right, opposes some Israeli policy, and they are not anti-Semitic. However, that is not the point. Although overt anti-Semitism has become unfashionable, anti-Zionism and opposition to Israeli security policies by non-Jews can be perceived as anti-Semitism by many Jews. For most mainstream Canadian Jews, campaigns promoting B D S and campus Israel-Apartheid Week are perceived as anti-Semitic. All these issues are currently hotly debated within the Canadian Jewish community, and within Canadian campus life. In early 2017 an American Jewish newspaper, the *Algemeiner*, published a list of the forty North American campuses most hostile to Jewish students. University of Toronto ranked number three, and McGill number four.[60] Many or most of the indicators had to do with anti-Israel activity. Needless to say, officials at Canadian universities were quick to denounce the study. It is certainly true that on the whole, life is pleasant for Jewish students on Canadian campuses. But it is equally true that a recent increase in anti-Israel activities, including B D S efforts, has made many Jewish students uncomfortable. To take McGill University as an example, beginning in the 2010s, attempts to pass B D S resolutions by the student body, a decision by the campus newspaper to censor pro-Israel articles, and a controversial tweet by a student involved in campus governance to "punch a Zionist" have added to tensions for Jewish students on campus. And of course, McGill is not unique.[61]

Policies that would weaken Israel in the face of real threats can be seen as anti-Semitic in their effect, if not always in their motivation. In Canada, the pursuit of a more "even-handed" position on the

Middle East has been perceived by many as code for tilting away from strong support for Israel. Canada's voting record on UN resolutions during Liberal governments in the pre-Harper period included routine condemnations of Israeli policy.

The Canadian government evinces no overt anti-Semitism, and universities and hospitals boast many Jewish students, professors, doctors, administrators, and deans. Still, anti-Semitic events occur regularly.[62] One prominent source of data is the annual report on anti-Semitic incidents of the League for Human Rights of B'nai Brith. The report counts incidents of both vandalism and harassment clearly motivated by anti-Semitism. Since 1982, when the report was first issued, the number of incidents documented has increased dramatically. The count remained in two digits up until 1988. The number of incidents reported for 2014 was 1,627, compared to 240 reported for 1998. Of these recent incidents, 84 per cent were counted as harassment, 15 per cent as vandalism, and 1 per cent violence. But we must be cautious; no Canadian should conclude that anti-Semitism has increased five times over the past fifteen years. Much of the increase comes from more effective collection procedures. There has also been an explosion of anti-Semitic comments online. But this activity does correspond to the increase in certain forms of Holocaust denial, anti-Israel and anti-Zionist commentary, and hate speech in Canada. The regional breakdown of reported incidents in 2014 is as follows: 259 took place in Quebec and Atlantic Canada, 961 in Ontario, 34 in the Parries and Nunavut, 37 in Alberta and the Northwest territories, 15 in British Columbia and the Yukon, and an estimated 321 online. In terms of the Canadian metropolitan centers with the largest Jewish populations, 109 incidents were reported in Toronto, 88 in Montreal, 39 Ottawa, 33 in Calgary, and 25 in Winnipeg.[63]

What sorts of incidents are these? The following descriptions from the League's 2014 annual report gives us a sense of the range. In terms of vandalism, examples include a fire set behind a synagogue in Montreal, stickers placed along the Danforth in Toronto saying "Holocaust is a Jewish invention," graffiti on a Winnipeg synagogue saying "Free Palestine," and "F*ck Israel" painted on a roadway in Calgary. In terms of harassment, examples include a man in Montreal threatening Hassidic children playing in a schoolyard and a woman in a Winnipeg doctor's office being told that "Hitler was right." Harassment is even more widespread online, where people are often held less accountable for their actions. Reported cases in 2014 include Nazi-themed toys being sold on eBay, and multiple blogs and news sites running stories titled "The Jewish Takeover of Canada." In terms of violence, luckily there are fewer examples. In Montreal, a Jewish man was ambushed and beaten unconscious, and eggs were thrown at Hassidic Jews, and in both Winnipeg and Calgary, several assaults leading to hospitalization of victims took place during pro-Israel rallies.

Data on anti-Semitism is also available through official law-enforcement records. A 2010 report on law enforcement studies in Canada and the US found that Jews were "overwhelmingly and disproportionately" the target of hate crimes when compared with other religious minorities.[64] The Annual Hate/Bias Crime Statistical Report released in 2014 by the Toronto Police Department found that Jews were the most targeted of all minority groups, with fifty-two reported incidents. The second and third most targeted groups were the LGBTQ and Black communities, with thirty-four and twenty-nine reported incidents respectively.[65]

In Canada in 2012, 30 per cent of reported hate crimes (419 incidents) were classified as religious hate crimes. Crimes targeting Jews accounted for 58 per cent of these incidents. Of all police-reported hate crimes, 17 per cent were directed against Jews, and 3 per cent against Muslims. When one considers that the Muslim population in Canada is roughly three times larger than the Jewish population, this evidence demonstrates a higher level of anti-Semitism than of Islamophobia. This may partly be due to reporting bias in that Muslim Canadians are more likely to be immigrants, and therefore might feel less comfortable reporting such attacks. A total of 242 hate crimes targeting the Jewish community were reported to police in 2012, 85 per cent of which were classified as non-violent offences. Included in the 15 per cent classified as violent, are uttering threats (46 per cent), and assault (18 per cent).[66]

As mentioned, Canadian campuses have now become the scene of specific forms of anti-Semitism relating to Israel. Many Jewish students find these efforts offensive and distressing. Events like Israel Apartheid Week, or petitions to support BDS directed against Israeli companies, companies that do business with Israel, and Israeli academics and universities, have proliferated. In many cases, they have created a hostile environment for Jewish students on campus despite the fact that supporters of these efforts claim that they are in no way anti-Semitic and only directed against Israeli policies. A 2015 survey of American and Canadian Jewish university students found high levels of perceived anti-Semitism and, notably, that Canadian universities represented higher levels of anti-Semitism than their American counterparts.[67] One such incident took place at McGill University in February 2016, where a BDS motion was first passed at a student union meeting but then rejected in an online ratification vote. Jewish students reported increasing tension on campus, exemplified by a statement found on a social media site, "Little Zionist Jewboys not happy that McGill students don't support their genocide."[68]

But is this a "great deal" of anti-Semitism? Obviously, perceptions are shaped by media reporting of individual incidents, so that the extent of bigotry is inevitably overstated. Both the League and police services claim that reported incidents represent 10 per cent of all cases. If so, in 2014 there may actually have been 16,000 episodes. Each one can hurt dozens or thousands of Jews, depending on the degree of publicity.

ANTI-SEMITIC PREJUDICE AND JEWISH-NON-JEWISH INTERACTIONS

Prejudice is not illegal. People have a right to their negative stereotypes and a right to socialize with those who are like them. Some Jews themselves may hold negative stereotypes of non-Jews and be uncomfortable in mixed social settings; others are uncomfortable with other kinds of Jews. Still, it is important to stress the long-term trend of increasing acceptance. Ironically, the rising rate of intermarriage, while of concern to many Jews, is also an indicator of social acceptance by non-Jews.

But how extensive is anti-Semitic prejudice, and where is it concentrated? One national survey in 1984 found that one in seven Canadians held negative attitudes toward Jews; the rest were either positive or neutral. More recent research has found generally low levels of attitudinal antisemitism in Canada. For example, a 2008 Leger Marketing poll found 13 per cent of Canadians had an "unfavourable opinion" of Jews. This breaks down to 7 per cent in English Canada and 27 per cent in French Canada. In comparison, 7 per cent of Americans and 9 per cent of British respondents had unfavorable opinions of Jews. For comparative purposes, 36 per cent of Canadians had an unfavorable opinion of Muslims (33 per cent in

English Canada and 49 per cent in French Canada).[69] A 2009 Angus Reid Poll commissioned by *MacLean's* found that 72 per cent of Canadians had a positive view of Christianity, 53 per cent of Judaism, and 28 per cent of Islam. Respondents in Ontario were the most favorable towards Judaism, at 59 per cent, and those from Quebec were the least, at 36 per cent.[70] A 2014 survey of International anti-Semitism by the Anti-Defamation League used an eleven-item index to measure anti-Semitism. Respondents who answered probably true to six of the following eleven items were labelled anti-Semitic:

1 – Jews are more loyal to Israel than to [this country/the countries they live in].
2 – Jews have too much power in international financial markets.
3 – Jews have too much control over global affairs.
4 – Jews think they are better than other people.
5 – Jews have too much control over the global media.
6 – Jews are responsible for most of the world's wars.
7 – Jews have too much power in the business world.
8 – Jews don't care what happens to anyone but their own kind.
9 – People hate Jews because of the way Jews behave.
10 – Jews have too much control over the United States government.
11 – Jews still talk too much about what happened to them in the Holocaust.

The survey found a 14 per cent anti-Semitic index score for Canada. This compares with 9 per cent for the US, 8 per cent for the UK, 5 per cent for the Netherlands, 27 per cent for Germany, and 37 per cent for France.[71]

Another study found that religiosity is no longer a source of anti-Semitism; those who believed that a "Christian commitment was needed for salvation" were not more apt to be anti-Jewish.[72] Contact with Jews also plays a role. Canadians who had met at least one Jew were less likely to be prejudiced. A 2009 survey found that 76 per cent of Canadians with Jewish friends were favorably disposed towards Judaism, while only 34 per cent of people with no Jewish friends had a favorable opinion of Judaism.[73] In this study it is not clear what is cause and what is effect.

Distrusting Jews in positions of political power is another common indicator of anti-Semitism. In the 1980s, the percentage of Canadians who claimed they would not vote for a Jew hovered in the single digits (American surveys had similar findings).[74] According to the 2014 Anti-Defamation League survey, 23 per cent of Canadians believe Jews have too much power in the business world and in international financial markets, and 18 per cent believe Jews hold too much control over the global media.[75] A 2009 study by the ADL found that 16 per cent of Americans believe "Jews have lots of irritating faults," and 12 per cent feel that "Jews are not as honest as other business people."[76] Although the corresponding statistics were not gathered in Canada, Canadians score higher than Americans on all measures of anti-Semitism available for both countries, so it is likely no different for anti-Semitic stereotypes.

As always, it is hard to interpret such survey questions when they focus on attitudes rather than behaviours. The Bibby surveys also shed light on the social acceptability of intermarriage. From 1975 to 1995, there was a clear increase in the approval of interfaith marriages. For marriages between Protestants and Jews, the increase in approval went from 80 to 90 per cent, and for Catholics and Jews, from 78 to 89 per cent. So about one-tenth of Canadians still disapprove. By comparison, the approval rate for marriages between Whites and Blacks was only 81 per cent (but up from 57 per cent in 1975).[77] A 2009 survey found that Judaism ranks only behind Christianity as an acceptable religion for the children of Canadians who would intermarry; 56 per cent claimed it was acceptable for their child to marry a Jew.[78] As we have seen in chapter 5, the actual rates of Jewish intermarriage have increased as well.

Manuel Prutschi of the Toronto Jewish Congress feared that simple survey data may underestimate the nature and extent of anti-Semitism. The renewed intifada in 2000 unleashed a wave of anti-Jewish incidents, many emanating from Arab and/or Muslim communities. Moreover, the more recent violent flare-ups with Gaza and South Lebanon also intensified anti-Semitism in Canada and abroad. A September 2006 Léger survey for the Association for Canadian Studies found a higher proportion of the population in Quebec (38 per cent), compared to the total Canadian average of 31 per cent, attributed the conflict in Lebanon to "Israel's actions in the Middle East."[79]

Survey researchers have learned the trick of asking respondents how "others" view minority groups. This can avoid the problem of people understating their own negative opinions. An early 1970s study of the perceived social standing of various groups found that English Canadians ranked Jews behind the French and other Western and Central European groups, but just ahead of Southern and Eastern Europeans, and non-Whites.[80] These assessments of "social standing" have been matched by later studies which have looked at the degree of comfort which Canadians feel around Jews and other groups. Though somewhat dated, a 1991 national survey offers interesting insights. It found that 64 per cent of Canadians felt "very comfortable" around Jews. That figure was higher than for a list of visible minorities, which ranged from 43 per cent for Sikhs to 61 per cent for Black West Indians. But that 64 per cent was below other European-origin groups, and even the Chinese, who scored 69 per cent. (It is always hard to figure out what these numbers mean. Only 83 per cent of Canadians felt very comfortable around British-origin Canadians.) British-origin Canadians were by far the most comfortable with Jews. Italian, French, Ukrainian, and German Canadians, all with similar rankings, followed them. Jews, for their part, felt reasonably comfortable around British, French, and Italian Canadians, and least comfortable with Germans, no doubt a residue of the Second World War.[81] Is the fact that 36 per cent of other Canadians did not feel very comfortable with Jews cause for alarm? Likely not. There is a difference between not feeling "very comfortable" around Jews, and feeling unease or active dislike. The Bibby national survey for 1995 found only 6 per cent claiming to be "uneasy" around Jews. This was lower than for comparable visible minority groups, with East Indians and Pakistanis leading at 15 per cent.[82]

So far we have focused mainly on majority attitudes towards Jews. But remember, there are likely many Jews who are "not very comfortable" around non-Jews.

An Orthodox Jew goes to university and for the first time tries to sustain a conversation with a non-Jew. At a loss for subject matter and feeling increasingly uncomfortable, the Jew finally asks, "So tell me, does Christmas come early or late this year?"

Jews tend to establish their friendships with other Jews. This is probably a result of their comfort levels, not any exclusion on the part of non-Jews. Moreover, younger Canadian Jews are as likely as seniors to have a mainly Jewish circle of friends. In a 2005 survey of Jews in Toronto, where Jews comprised perhaps 4 per cent of the population, 45 per cent of respondents said that all or almost all of their close friends were Jewish, 34 per cent said most were Jewish, 15 per cent said some were Jewish, 4 per cent said few were Jewish, and 2 per cent said none were Jewish. So roughly 80 per cent said that most of their friends were Jewish. Additionally, 70 per cent of respondents with children said that all or most of their children's friends were Jewish.[83]

We can push this far beyond issues of friendship and social comfort levels. To what extent would non-Jews take serious risks to defend or protect Jews? Failed lessons of the Holocaust, of non-Jewish bystanders who did not help Jews, hang heavy in the shadows. How many Canadians in British Columbia opened up their homes and hid Japanese neighbours who sought to avoid relocation? There are no known cases. But Jews should not be self-righteous. How many of them would have been prepared to do so? I don't know how far I would have gone. Our commitments to "others" are best understood when put to the most extreme tests, when there is real inconvenience, even danger, to our well-being.

The good news is that contact with Jews is associated with lower levels of anti-Semitism. The bad news is that many Canadians, particularly those who do not live in major cities, have minimal contact with Jews. In one survey, only 17 per cent of Canadians said they "often" had contact with Jews; 34 per cent of English-speaking Canadians and fully 68 per cent of francophone Canadians reported no contact at all with Jews.[84] These levels were comparable to those for Asian and Black Canadians. In 2009, 45 per cent of Canadians reported having Jewish friends, from a high of 61 per cent in Ontario to a low of 20 per cent in Quebec.[85] Given the finding that knowing at least one Jew reduces prejudice, it is possible that much of the greater anti-Semitism among francophones in Quebec may reflect a lack of contact.

Anti-Semitism in Quebec, past and present, has a distinctive edge to it. There has never been a collective reckoning in Quebec, as took place in English Canada with the publication of None Is Too Many, with the depth and breadth of anti-Semitism of the 1930s and 1940s.[86] Of course in Quebec today, anti-Semitism is more than the residue of staunch Catholicism. The larger issue is that Jews in

Quebec are federalists, and are perceived as such by Quebec nationalists and *independentists*. In a 2007 poll, 41 per cent of French speakers in the province agreed with the statement, "Jews want to impose their customs and traditions on others," while 31 per cent agreed that "Jews want to participate fully in society."[87] Jacques Parizeau's attack against "money and the ethnic vote" after the 1995 referendum jarred many Jews. While Parti Québécois leaders have generally opposed anti-Semitism, Jews fear French nationalism like they fear all ethnic nationalistic movements. On the other hand, higher levels of attitudinal anti-Semitism in Quebec today have *not* been associated with any increases in overt anti-Semitic acts by individuals or by the government. Indeed, Quebec has long supported government aid to Jewish schools whereas Ontario has not. Nevertheless, a series of high profile episodes of anti-Semitism in Quebec have jarred many Quebec Jews. For example, in 1990, Pierre Péladeau, a prominent Québec businessman and father of former Parti Québécois leader Pierre Karl Péladeau, told a Québec newsmagazine that he has great respect for Jews but "they take up too much space."[88] More recently, in 2014, the well-known Québec radio host Gilles Proulx stated on air that Jews manipulated world governments and took economic control of the countries in which they lived, and Louise Mailloux, a PQ candidate, publicly expressed her belief that kosher food is a scam, and that its proceeds may be funding religious wars.[89]

Regardless of the evidence, North American Jews themselves perceive a significant amount of anti-Semitism. According to the 2013 Pew survey, 43 per cent of American Jews, compared with 24 per cent of the American public, felt that "there is a lot of discrimination against Jews."[90] In terms of Canadian numbers, a 2005 survey of Jews in Toronto found that 13 per cent of respondents believed "there is a great deal of anti-Semitism in Toronto," 65 per cent believed "there is some," 20 per cent believed "there is little," and 0.5 per cent believed there is no anti-Semitism; the remainder were unsure. The same survey found that 45 per cent of respondents had personally experienced anti-Semitism at least once, and 11 per cent had experienced anti-Semitism within the last two years.[91] A 2013 survey found that 61 per cent of Jews in Toronto felt that anti-Semitism had increased in the past decade, whereas 6 per cent thought it had decreased.[92] Perhaps the conclusion is that Toronto Jews feel that anti-Semitism is relatively low, but increasing. Jews in Montreal feel that fighting local anti-Semitism should be the third most pressing community priority after helping the Jewish poor/elderly and families in crisis, and Jews in Toronto feel that it is the second most pressing after helping the Jewish elderly.[93]

So, many Canadian Jews, like Jews anywhere in North America or Europe, like many racialized minorities, may believe themselves to be potential victims. The idea of "systemic" discrimination does not require specific episodes of victimization. There is an ideology of omnipresent anti-Semitism which is quite clearly, and understandably, part of modern Jewish identity. It explains the potency of the Holocaust for Jews far removed from the death camps in Europe, and why Jews who are affluent, indeed well integrated, will still feel insecure. Of course, Jews know from their history that danger can always lurk. During the debate on the dangers of Iran acquiring nuclear weapons, many Jewish communal leaders evoked the metaphor of 1938 to describe their current fears.[94] Surveys may not pick up resentments which are no longer expressed even confidentially to pollsters. But the basic facts remain. Things have been, and could be, a lot worse ... yet the Jewish community remains on guard.

EPILOGUE

A Canadian Jewish Model?

Jewish life in Canada is a success story compared to other Jewish diaspora cases and to other minority groups in Canada. Like most social scientists, I am programmed to think about societies in a critical fashion. In fact, there are many tensions, conflicts, and dilemmas facing Canadian Jewry. This book has outlined them in unsparing detail. But Canadian Jews, through their diversity, seem to possess the resources to meet these challenges and make sense of the multiple paradoxes of the Canadian Jewish experience. The pieces of the mosaic fit together well. An equilibrium balances the forces of tradition and change, and of separation and inclusion.

The twin goals of Canadian multiculturalism are to allow minorities to integrate into and participate in Canadian life while retaining, to a meaningful extent, their particular culture and identity. The Canadian Charter of Rights and Freedoms, Section 15, emphasizes equal opportunity for participation in Canada life. Section 27 emphasizes the acceptability, and indeed the desirability, under multiculturalism of strengthening minority identities. Generally, these goals require a tradeoff of some sort. It is hard to maximize both. But compared to other diaspora Jewish communities, or to other Canadian minorities, or to Canadian Jewry generations ago, Canadian Jews today are doing well on both counts.

Indeed, Jewish life in North America benefits from the reduction of serious differences between key cultural and social features of Jewish life and the surrounding community. Sociologists Richard Alba and Sylvia Barack Fishman have described this American Jewish condition and its usefulness for integration. Alba has focused on the "blurring" of boundaries which has occurred, which is different from assimilation in the classic formulation.[1] Fishman has described a "coalescence "of Jewish and American values and norms, which differs from a conventional model of compartmentalization of Jewish and non-Jewish identities.[2] Both apply to the Canadian Jewish case as well.

The Jewish community in Canada is on its way to becoming the second most-important diaspora Jewish community. The quality of Jewish life in Canada is relatively high. Canadian Jews rank with Americans in terms of freedom and affluence but they enjoy a deeper Jewish cultural and communal life. This ability to participate fully in Canadian life while retaining a rich heritage is the mysterious essence of the Jewish experience. In this sense, the Jewish community can be seen as a poster child for Canadian multiculturalism. The environment for Jews in Canada may have been more nurturing, and less abrasive, than that in the United States or Europe.

But Canadian Jewish life is not static and may yet approximate the American model. The advantages of a more recent and relatively larger Jewish immigration will likely fade. The much-vaunted Canadian rhetoric and policies of multiculturalism will likely not stem the tide of assimilation, or at least transformation. The north-south links between the two Jewish communities are formidable, and cross-border marriages will likely increase. As the Old World influence recedes, a new variant of Jewish civilization will emerge in Canada, likely along American lines.

Note that I do not equate this future convergence with any likely disappearance of Judaism in Canada, or indeed, in the United States. Jewish life will survive. Even high levels of mixed marriages will be mitigated by new forms of creative identification and voluntary affiliation, and demographic replenishment – more babies – from the thriving Orthodox and ultra-Orthodox communities. And this survival will persist even without the frenetic efforts of "continuity" committees aimed at cultural engineering. The innovation found at present in Jewish life flows both from the bottom up, reflecting real creativity and concern, and from the top down, as in the Birthright/ Taglit program of subsidized trips for young Jews to Israel.

Jews are an extremely diverse group and that diversity can be seen as a strength. Pluralism is becoming more and more pronounced, and at times leads to friction. But this fractious pluralism has paradoxically always been, and remains, a source of strength, innovation, and vitality. And as I have argued, the daily tensions are minimized

through the voluntary segregation that accompanies Jewish pluralism. Jews live near, marry, socialize, pray, and join organizations
with Jews who are like them. Moreover, from these frictions can
emerge creative solutions. Conflict and debate are signs of life. Jews
care about their future.

I cannot predict if the fault line between the Orthodox and non-
Orthodox, in Israel and in the diaspora, will become an unbridge-
able chasm. I likewise cannot predict if these "Who is a Jew?"
tensions will lead to an irreparable gulf between non-Orthodox
diaspora Jews, even the generally pro-Israel Canadian community,
and Israel. But even if such splits emerge, Jewish life will continue.

Jewish communal unity is, in the main, a myth. Moreover, the
dominant metaphors for Jewish experience since the Bible have been
loss and schism: expulsion from the Garden of Eden, the genocide of
the Flood, the destruction of Sodom and Gomorrah, the break
between Ishmael and Isaac, the attraction of the Golden Calf, the
mysterious disappearance of the ten lost tribes, the split of the post-
Solomonic Kingdom of Israel, the destruction of the two temples,
the expulsions, civil war among the Jews themselves in the early
Israelite kingdoms. Antagonisms within and between Jewish groups
were the norm, even in the idealized Eastern European "world of our
fathers" and in the early decades of the last century in North America.
Jewish life in the diaspora has survived for centuries without unity
and, indeed, without close ties to Israel and if need be, it will again.
Not only Judaism has survived sharp internal divisions. So have
Christianity and Islam.

But these apocalyptic scenarios are far off for Canadian Jewry. In
terms of the Canadian environment, it is still impossible to predict
the denouement of the Quebec independence movement, and therefore the long-term future of Quebec Jews. It is also not clear how
the political preferences of Canadian Jews will evolve in the Justin
Trudeau era and beyond. But at present, life remains good for
Canadian Jews, faced with a range of rich cultural and communal
options, from the traditional to the trendy. Anti-Semitism is not
gone, and the growth of new forms of anti-Semitism linked in reality
or perception to anti-Zionist and anti-Israel perspectives is a new
and major challenge. But traditional anti-Semitism remains increasingly irrelevant to the daily lives and opportunities of Canadian
Jews. Jews are less an object of disdain, and more an object of admiration or at least curiosity, as rising intermarriage rates confirm.

But I do reach one conclusion which bothers me. As a sociologist, I have long espoused a comparative approach to the study of all minority groups, including Jews. I have done that in this volume and I routinely encourage my students to do comparative research papers, arguing that an excellent way to understand group X is by comparison with group Y. One of my mentors, Professor Seymour Martin Lipset, argued that such comparative study would inevitably confirm the old adage attributed to the German poet Heinrich Heine that "the Jews are like everyone else, except more so." By this is meant that Jewish social patterns such as low fertility, universal post-secondary education, urbanization, and liberalism are simply precursors of general societal trends.

I now have serious doubts. The comparative approach may have a built-in bias towards assuming basic commonalities – differences in degree but not in kind. I have come to question the utility of routine comparisons between Jews and other groups, and am still pondering that. As I have argued, Jews are like everyone else, but different. Not better, but different. There are too many paradoxes which confound normal theories about and expectations of other minority groups. More and more, Canadian Jews strike me as being in the main distinct, rather than as easily comparable to other groups. While Jews are a multicultural group par excellence, I am not convinced that Jews can or should be a poster group for multicultural policy in Canada. The successful Jewish model may not be replicable by other groups because a unique set of circumstances work in the Jewish favour. This uniqueness is a combination, as we have seen, of particular social contexts and of a unique cultural heritage, and may owe little or nothing to government policies.

The official rhetoric of multiculturalism nourishes a tolerant environment for Jews. But the roots of Jewish success long predate official multiculturalism. This is not a criticism of government policy; I have no doubt that multiculturalism as policy and rhetoric taps into a core Canadian value, and its message is important for Canada as a whole and for minorities in particular. But it is not clear if the policy is easily exportable. One day, years ago, a Japanese social scientist came to my office. He was part of a delegation of seven Japanese scholars spending the summer in Canada to study multiculturalism. Each scholar was assigned one ethnic group; my visitor was studying Jews. Why the mission? Japan, though roughly 99 per cent ethnic Japanese, was worried about increasing diversity from other Asian countries. In order to be prepared, what better model to study than Canada, which enjoyed and still enjoys a worldwide reputation of inter-group harmony and tolerance? These scholars assumed that studying the experience of Jews or Italians or other minorities in Canada might help Japan cope with social strains caused by increases in its Filipino or Thai community. Well, perhaps it was useful, but I have doubts. I am not sure what lessons the fate of Canadian Jews had for, say, Filipinos in Japan.[3]

It is also not clear if all or most Canadian minority groups will be able to emulate the success of Canadian Jews. All are unique but, with apologies to Lipset and George Orwell, Jews may be more unique than others. They have several strengths which help them realize multicultural objectives. These strengths derive ultimately from Jewish culture and history, from the social characteristics of Jews, and from the interaction between the two.

First, as analyzed throughout this volume, Jews are both a religious and ethno-cultural group. This gives them an unusually large repertoire of cultural traits: languages, literature, a homeland, festivals, beliefs, art, music, rituals, customs, and foods. To these one can add chosen elements of religious observance. Moreover, Jewish religious requirements – whether for kosher food or the need to care for less fortunate Jews – reinforce the need for developing a Jewish polity. This large repertoire relates to the diversity within the community. No minority group is better equipped for survival.

Second, Jews have a two-thousand-year experience as a diaspora community, with the vast majority of the group outside the homeland. This is not the case for most other immigrant minority groups. Being a minority is second nature to Jews, as are forms of voluntary self-governance. Jews were practising "multiculturalism" long before the concept became fashionable. No group – not Italians, not Ukrainians, not Chinese – has such a dense network of self-governing organizations.

Third, Canadian Jews are overwhelmingly White and can therefore pass easily into the mainstream, unlike visible minorities. They are not trapped at the bottom of a racist stratification system based on skin colour. That status falls to First Nations, to Blacks, to Asian groups. There is no tradition of a festering "Jewish Question" in Canada. Jews in North America have never been the most oppressed group, the eternal other, as was the case in Europe. They could belong. My own experience has been that Canadian Jews do not dwell on or recognize the advantages of white privilege but the advantages are there nonetheless.

Fourth, the peculiarities of Jewish history, as well as some cultural legacies, have led to high socio-economic achievements in what is now a relatively open, non-discriminatory society. This success surpasses most other groups. This Jewish affluence, and Jewish philanthropy – rooted in both cultural traditions and social circumstances – provide the foundation for the proliferation of communal organizations and thereby for Jewish survival. The will to survive is not enough. Jews also have the means.

And lastly, more than specific multicultural policies, the non-separation of church and state in Canada has enabled Jewish schools to benefit from government support in some provinces. As a result, Jewish schools have thrived in Canada. No other minority group has such a comprehensive and diverse school system. Muslims may soon approximate this model. But at present, this system gives Jews survival advantages that other minority groups cannot match.

If we put all this together, it is not clear how much other Canadian groups can learn from the Jewish experience. The Canadian ideology of multiculturalism legitimates and reinforces traits which have long been part of the Jewish experience. The diversity of Jewish life provides many options to negotiate tensions between tradition and modernity. A series of coincidences have created the situation where Jewish communities in Canada can make the best of their immediate options. New forms of real or perceived anti-Semitism may pose increasing challenges. But for the present and near future, Canadian Jewry, with its paradoxes and challenges, survives and thrives.

APPENDICES

Counts of the Canadian Jewish Population

The tables below are taken from Morton Weinfeld and Randal F. Schnoor, "The Demography of Canadian Jewry, the Census of 2011: Challenges and Results," in *American Jewish Yearbook 2014*, ed. Arnold Dashefsky and Ira Sheskin (Springer, 2015), 285–300. Reprinted with permission.

Table 1
Jews and Jewish characteristics in Canada, 1991–2011

	1991	1996	2001	2006	2011
JEWS (ethnic ancestry)	369,600	351,705	348,605	315,120	309,650
JEWS (religion)	318,185	N/A	329,995	N/A	329,500
TOTAL JEWS (JSD)	356,315	N/A	370,505	N/A	385,345
ISRAEL place of birth	*Not available	15,510	13,550	21,320	25,145
ISRAEL ethnic ancestry	*Not available	*Not available	6,060 (SR 1,395) (MR 4,660)	10,755 (SR 2,520) (MR 8,235)	15,010 (SR 2,695) (MR 12,320)
HEBREW Mother tongue (Single response)	11,525	13,125	12,430	17, 630	18, 105
HEBREW Able to converse	52,450	60,740	63,670	67,390	70,695
YIDDISH Mother tongue (Single response)	21,400	21,415	19,295	16,295	14,930
YIDDISH Able to converse	53,420	46,635	37,010	27,605	23,750

Table 1 above presents the results of the 2011 NHS and earlier census for variables relating to the size of the Jewish population, 1991–2011. The count of Jews by religion is 329,500, up slightly from 318,185 in 1991, an *increase* of 3.6 per cent. The count of Jews by ethnic origin is at 309,650, *down* significantly and steadily from 369,600 in 1991, a *decrease* of 16.2 per cent. The *Jewish standard definition* count of Jews, which combines those who claim Jewish religion with those who claim Jewish ethnicity and no religion, is at 385,345, up from 356,315 in 1991, an increase in twenty years of 8.2 per cent. This means that there were in 2011 about 55,000 Canadians who claimed Jewish ethnic origin, but no religion. Accordingly, Jews comprised 1.17 per cent of the Canadian population in 2011.

Table 2
Jewish populations based on standard and revised definitions,
2011 National Household Survey

	Jewish standard definition	Revised Jewish definition
Halifax CMA	2,080	2,120
Montréal CMA	89,665	90,780
Toronto CMA	186,010	188,715
Ottawa CMA	13,850	14,010
Hamilton CMA	5,055	5,110
Kitchener CMA	1,970	2,015
London CMA	2,610	2,675
Windsor CMA	1,475	1,520
Winnipeg CMA	13,260	13,690
Calgary CMA	8,210	8,340
Edmonton CMA	5,440	5,550
Vancouver CMA	25,740	26,255
Victoria CMA	2,630	2,740
Total Canada	385,345	391,665

Charles Shahar, Research and Evaluation specialist for the Jewish Community Foundation of Montreal, and consultant to the Jewish Federations of Canada – UIA, has computed a preliminary revised estimate of the Canadian Jewish population, using a *Revised Jewish Definition*, and we present some results using this definition.[1] It is possible that this definition will become the one used for future Jewish communal planning purposes. The 2011 *Revised Jewish Definition* incorporates more than just the Jewish religion and Jewish ethnicity variables from the National Household Survey. Specifically, it enlarges the definition of Jewish to include individuals with (a) no religious affiliation and Israeli by ethnicity, (b) no religious affiliation and having knowledge of Hebrew or Yiddish as a "non-official" language, (c) no religious affiliation and born in Israel and (d) no religious affiliation and living in Israel in 2006. Shahar confirms that there were virtually no individuals (such as Arab Israelis) who were wrongly identified as Jews according to the *Revised Jewish Definition*.

In Table 2 we see counts of the Canadian Jewish population in 2011, using the standard and revised Jewish definitions, for Canada and for several key cities. This procedure added an additional 6,320 Jews to the total Canadian count, for a total of 391,665. This is at best a modest increase of roughly 1.6 per cent compared to the previous definition.

Table 3
Jewish population distribution, provinces and territories,
2011 National Household Survey, revised Jewish definition

Province / territory	Jewish population	% of Canadian Jewish population
Nova Scotia	2,910	0.8
New Brunswick	860	0.2
Newfoundland/Labrador	220	0.1
Prince Edward Island	185	0.0
(Total Atlantic Canada)	(4,175)	(1.1)
Quebec	93,625	23.9
Ontario	226,610	57.9
Manitoba	14,345	3.7
Saskatchewan	1,905	0.5
Alberta	15,795	4.0
British Columbia	35,005	8.9
Yukon	145	0.0
Northwest Territories	40	0.0
Nunavut	20	0.0
Total Canada	391,665	100.0

Table 3 presents the 2011 totals using the Revised Definitions, for the Canadian provinces and Territories. Ontario continues to emerge as the dominant province, just as Toronto has emerged as the dominant metropolis.

Table 4
Jewish population of Canada: historical summary

	Jewish population	# change from previous census	% change from previous census
2011	391,665	+17,605	+4.7
2001	374,060	+14,950	+4.2
1991	359,110	+45,245	+14.4
1981	313,865	+27,315	+9.5
1971	286,550	+32,182	+12.7
1961	254,368	+49,532	+24.2
1951	204,836	+36,251	+21.5
1941	168,585	+12,819	+8.2
1931	155,766	+30,321	+24.2
1921	125,445	+50,685	+67.8
1911	74,760	+58,267	+353.3
1901	16,493	–	–

Table 4 presents a historical evolution of the Canadian Jewish population. Note the data for 1991, 2001, and 2011 are computed using the revised Jewish definition, 1971 and 1981 using the Jewish standard definition, and earlier estimates were derived from ethnic or religious counts.

APPENDIX TWO

Sources of Evidence

My arguments in this revised book rest mainly on three major sources of evidence. The first is the scholarly research and writing that deals with various aspects of Jewish life in Canada and the United States. Where few or no Canadian studies exist, I rely on American research where it applies. The core is the scholarly literature as found in monographs and academic articles. I include here also the use of newspapers and popular magazines, both Jewish and non-Jewish, and websites of various organizations. The latter are particularly useful for recent events and trends for which scholarly analyses are not yet available. I have not tried to integrate every academic thesis or article ever written on a Canadian Jewish topic or to provide an exhaustive review of media portrayals of Jews or Jewish issues. But I try to include reports of recent events as well as research studies.

The second source is a set of interviews conducted mainly but not only in 1999–2000 with a cross-section of Jews, and my own ongoing observations of Jewish settings across Canada. These interviews and observations are designed to tap into the sentiments of Canadian Jews from the ground up. In general, I have avoided speaking only to the many celebrities and *machers*, or bigshots, in the Canadian Jewish scene – the Canadian Jewish "rich and famous" – and the official heads of the major Jewish organizations. Though some names are named, there is little gossip and few personality profiles. That would be another, albeit interesting, book. I used contacts, friends of friends, names I was given by others, and tried to reflect the diversity which is so much a facet of Canadian Jewish life. At times I have kept the identity of the informants confidential.

The third source is statistical, surveys of Canadian and American Jews and national census data. Census data are reported from 1991 to 2011 to illustrate trends as well as current characteristics. The main American source is the *A Portrait of Jewish Americans: Findings from a Pew Research Center Survey of U.S. Jews*, published in 2013, though occasional references are made to previous national surveys such as the national Jewish population studies of 1990 and 2000.[1] The main Canadian surveys, and the ones which are most recent, are Charles Shahar's *2011 National Household Survey: The Jewish Population of Canada,* which includes nine sections (Basic Demographics; Jewish Populations in Geographic Areas; Jewish Seniors; The Jewish Poor; The Jewish Family; Intermarriage; Immigration and Language; Core FSU Jews; and the Sephardic Community), and the Montreal counterpart, *2011 National Household Survey: The Jewish Community of Montreal*.[2] Also often referenced are Shahar's 2005 survey of the Toronto Jewish community and 2010 survey of the Montreal Jewish community.[3] To illustrate trends, I also refer to other surveys, including previous surveys of the Jewish communities of Montreal in 1996;[4] one taken of Jewish households in Toronto in 1990;[5] one taken of the entire Canadian Jewish community in 1990;[6] and a survey of seven ethnic groups in Toronto directed by sociologist Raymond Breton and his colleagues, which included 168 Jews out of a total of 2,338 respondents, taken in 1979.[7]

How reliable are these surveys? Finding a truly random and representative sample of Jews is a daunting task, given that Jews are a small minority of the population. It is easier in Canada than in the United States since the Canadian census, which collects data on Jews, offers a basis for verifying the accuracy of any survey. There are different ways to draw a Jewish sample. While all the surveys I have used have limitations, they meet accepted standards when used appropriately.

Finally, I will on occasion use personal and familial anecdotes to make a point. Why not? My family illustrates some of the themes of Canadian Jewish life, from postwar migration to religious evolution. I will also not shrink from using jokes, some of the classic genre. To try to explain Jewish life without recourse to the vast storehouse of Jewish humour makes little sense to me, like coffee without cake. Jokes do not come from nowhere. They are a vital folkloric counterpoint to the stodgy tools of social science. They are a distillation of a wide-ranging social experience and a source of essential truths. Besides, since when does a Jew need an excuse to tell a joke?

Bibliographic Essay

The following is a selection of books and sources, by no means exhaustive, that have been written on aspects of contemporary Canadian Jewish life.

A brief yet informative overview of the Canadian Jewish experience, with an engaging collection of photographs, is Irving Abella's *A Coat of Many Colours* (Toronto: Lester and Orpen Dennys, 1990). The pioneering history of Canadian Jewry was written by the journalist B.G. Sack in Yiddish in 1948, translated into English as *History of the Jews in Canada* (Montreal: Harvest House, 1965). Gerald Tulchinsky's two-volume study of Canadian Jewry is the definitive history. Volume 1, *Taking Root: The Origins of the Canadian Jewish Community* (Toronto: Lester Publishing, 1992), ends at about 1920 while volume 2, *Branching Out: The Transformation of the Canadian Jewish Community* (Toronto: Stoddart, 1998), continues into the 1990s. Louis Rosenberg's *Canada's Jews: A Social and Economic Study of the Jews of Canada* (Montreal: Canadian Jewish Congress, 1939), republished by McGill-Queen's Press in 1993, is a detailed socio-demographic study of Canadian Jewish life in the 1920s and 1930s, relying on census data and other statistics. Ira Robinson's edited volume *Canada's Jews: In Time, Space, and Spirit* (Boston: Academic Press, 2013) is a collection of essays capturing a wide range of past and present issues in the field of Canadian Jewish studies. It extends an earlier anthology in the field, *The Canadian Jewish Studies Reader* (Calgary: Red Deer Press, 2004), edited by Richard Menkis and Norman Ravvin. Morton Weinfeld, William Shaffir, and Irwin Cotler, *The Canadian Jewish Mosaic* (Toronto: John Wiley and Sons, 1981) was an early collection of original articles on the topic, while Robert Brym, William Shaffir, and Morton Weinfed, eds., *The Jews in Canada* (Don Mills, ON: Oxford University Press, 2010) is an anthology of published social scientific articles.

There are a number of regional works, many on Quebec. Michael Brown's *Jew or Juif? Jews, French Canadians and Anglo-Canadians, 1759–1914* (Philadelphia: Jewish Publication Society, 1987) is a historical account of the Jewish experience in Quebec. A French-language overview of Quebec Jewry can be found in *Juifs et réalités juifs au Québec*, edited by Pierre Anctil (Quebec: Institut québécois de recherche sur la culture, 1984). Joe King's *From the Ghetto to the Main: The Story of the Jews in Montreal* (Montreal: Montreal Jewish Publication Society, 2000) and Mackay L. Smith's *Jews of Montreal and Their Judaisms: A Voyage of Discovery* (Montreal: Aaron Communications, 1998) are readable overviews of Jewish life in Montreal. Two collections of essays on Montreal Jewish culture and society edited by Pierre Anctil, Mervin Butovsky, and Ira Robinson, published by Véhicule Press, are *An Everyday Miracle: Yiddish Culture in Montreal*, 1990, and *Renewing Our Days: Montreal Jews in the Twentieth Century*, 1995. A recent collection of essays on Quebec Jewry is Pierre Anctil and Ira Robinson, eds., *Les communautés juives de Montréal: Histoire et enjeux contemporains* (Sillery, QC: Septentrion, 2010). Pierre Anctil's *Histoire des Juifs du Québec* (Montreal: Éditions du Boréal, 1917) reviews four centuries of Jewish life in Quebec. Stephen Speisman's *The Jews of Toronto: A History to 1937* (Toronto: McClelland and Stewart, 1979) is an account of the development of the communal and organizational structure of Toronto Jewry. So too is Jack Lipinsky's *Imposing Their Will: An Organizational History of Jewish Toronto, 1933–1948* (Montreal and Kingston; McGill-Queen's University Press, 2011). Arthur Chiel's *The Jews in Manitoba* (Toronto: University of Toronto Press, 1961), Cyril Leonoff's *Pioneers, Pedlars, and Prayer Shawls* (Victoria: Sono Nis Press, 1978), and Sheva Medjuck's *Jews of Atlantic Canada* (St. John's: Breakwater Press, 1986) describe the history of the Jews in Manitoba, British Columbia, and Atlantic Canada, respectively. A collection of articles dealing with the links between Canadian and American Jewry from a borderlands perspective is Barry L. Stiefel and Herman Tesler-Mabe, eds., *Neither in Dark Speeches nor in Similitudes: Reflections and Refractions between Canadian and American Jews* (Waterloo: Wilfrid Laurier University Press, 2016).

Several studies focus on specific issues. Joseph Kage's *With Faith and Thanksgiving* (Montreal: Eagle Publishing, 1962) is a pioneering review of Jewish immigration to Canada, and the role of JIAS in particular. Lita Rose Betcherman's *The Swastika and the Maple Leaf* (Toronto: Fitzhenry and Whiteside, 1975) is a detailed review of the development of fascist antiSemitism during the 1930s. A broader review of anti-Semitism in Canada from a variety of perspectives and covering the early colonial period to the present can be found in *Anti-Semitism in Canada: History and Interpretation*, ed. Alan Davies (Waterloo: Wilfrid Laurier University Press, 1992). Ira Robinson's *A History of Anti-Semitism in Canada* (Waterloo: Wilfrid Laurier University Press, 2015) surveys Canadian anti-Semitism past and present. Another collection of essays is that edited by Derek Penslar, Michael Marrus, and Janice Gross Stein, *Contemporary Antisemitism: Canada and the World* (Toronto, University of Toronto Press, 2005). Esther Delisle's two historical volumes on Quebec anti-Semitism, *The Traitor and the Jew* (Montreal: R. Davies Publishing, 1992) and *Myths, Memory, and Lies: Quebec's Intelligentsia and the Fascist Temptation, 1939–1960* (Westmount: R. Davies Multimedia, 1998), have stirred opposition in Quebec. Franklin Bialystok's *Delayed Impact: The Holocaust and the Canadian Jewish Community* (Montreal: McGill-Queen's University Press, 2000) reviews the effect of Holocaust survivors on Canadian Jewish life.

A number of studies have focused on specific cases of anti-Semitism, public policy, and intergroup relations. Irving Abella and Harold Troper, *None Is Too Many* (Toronto: Lester and Orpen Dennys, 1982), is a study of Canada's restrictive immigration policy toward Jews before, during, and after the Second World War. Harold Troper and Morton Weinfeld, *Old Wounds: Jews, Ukrainians, and the Hunt for Nazi War Criminals in Canada* (Toronto: Viking, 1988), is a study of the relationship among Jews, Ukrainians, and the Canadian government in the face of the Deschênes Commission of Inquiry on War Criminals in Canada. Howard Margolian's *Unauthorized Entry: The Truth about Nazi War Criminals in Canada, 1945–56* (Toronto: University of Toronto Press, 1999) explores the interaction of the Canadian government and Jewish community concerning the issue at the time. Cyril Levitt and William Shaffir, *The Riot at Christie Pits* (Toronto: Lester and Orpen Dennys, 1987), is a study of a major riot between Jews and Gentiles in Toronto in the early 1930s. Richard Menkis and Harold Troper's *More Than*

Just Games: Canada and the 1936 Olympics (Toronto: University of Toronto Press, 2015) describes the Canadian response to the attempted boycott of the Berlin Olympics of 1936.

Etan Diamond's *And I Dwell in Their Midst: Orthodox Jews in Suburbia* (Chapel Hill: University of North Carolina Press, 2000) is a study of Orthodox Jewish life in Toronto. *The Jews in Canada*, ed. Robert Brym, William Shaffir, and Morton Weinfeld (Toronto: Oxford University Press, 1993), is a collection of social scientific articles dealing with various aspects of contemporary Jewish life. An earlier collection of such research is *The Canadian Jewish Mosaic*, ed. Morton Weinfeld, William Shaffir, and Irwin Cotler (Rexdale: John Wiley of Canada, 1981). An early study of changes in Canadian Jewish identity is that of Evelyn Kallen, *Spanning the Generations* (Toronto: Longmans, 1973). A collection of essays as well as biographical information on individual Canadian Jews is *Canadian Jewry Today: Who's Who in Canadian Jewry*, ed. Edmond Y. Lipsitz (Toronto: J.E.S.L. Education Products, 1989, and the third edition in 2000). Daniel Elazar and Harold Waller's *Maintaining Consensus: The Canadian Jewish Polity in the Post-War World* (Lanham, Maryland: University Press of America, 1990) is an analysis of the internal political organization of the Jewish community in Canada. An interesting collection of essays on sociopolitical aspects of Canadian Jewish life is *Multiculturalism, Jews, and Identities in Canada*, ed. Howard Adelman and John H. Simpson (Jerusalem: The Magnes Press, Hebrew University of Jerusalem, 1996). Harold Troper's *The Defining Decade: Identity, Politics, and the Canadian Jewish Community in the 1960s* (Toronto: University of Toronto Press, 2010) focuses on the 1960s as marking the transition of Canadian Jewry into a more modern era. A study of the constitutional documents of the Canadian Jewish community is Daniel Elazar, Michael Brown, and Ira Robinson, eds., *Not Written in Stone: Jews, Constitutions, and Constitutionalism in Canada* (Ottawa: University of Ottawa Press, 2003).

Archival material on Canadian Jewry can be found in the Canadian Jewish Congress National Archives in Montreal, in the Ontario Region cjc Archives in Toronto, and in various collections at the National Archives of Canada in Ottawa. Much of the cjc archival material has been published by David Rome in a series called Canadian Jewish Archives. Other archival sources include the Jewish Public Library in Montreal and the Jewish Historical Societies of

British Columbia and of Western Canada. Bibliographies include
David Rome, Judith Nefsky, and Paule Obermeir, *Les Juifs du
Québec: Bibliographie retrospective annotée* (Montreal: Institut
québécois de recherche sur la culture, 1981); Susan Vadnay, *A
Selected Bibliography of Research on Canadian Jewry, 1900–1980*
(Ottawa: Mimeo, 1991); and Stuart Schoenfeld and Dwight
Daigneault, *Contemporary Jewish Life in Canada; A Bibliography*
(Toronto: Centre for Jewish Studies, York University, May 1992).

Several social scientific journals have featured articles dealing with
Canadian Jewish life. These include *Canadian Jewish Studies, Canadian Ethnic Studies, Canadian Journal of Sociology, Contemporary
Jewry, Canadian Review of Sociology and Anthropology*, and the
Jewish Journal of Sociology.

Notes

INTRODUCTION

1 Charles Silberman, *A Certain People* (New York: Summit Books, 1985).
2 Calvin Goldscheider, *Jewish Continuity and Change* (Bloomington: Indiana University Press, 1986).
3 Alan M. Dershowitz, *The Vanishing American Jew* (New York: Little, Brown and Company, 1997); Elliott Abrams, *Faith or Fear: How Jews Can Survive in a Christian America* (New York: The Free Press, 1997); Jack Wertheimer, *A People Divided: Judaism in Contemporary America* (New York: Basic Books, 1993); Samuel G. Freedman, *Jew vs Jew: The Struggle for the Soul of American Jewry* (New York: Simon and Schuster, 2000); Luis Lugo, Alan Cooperman, Gregory A. Smith, Conrad Hackett, Cary Funk, Neha Sahgal, Phillip Connor, Jessica Hamar Martinez, et al., *A Portrait of Jewish Americans: Findings from a Pew Research Center Survey of U.S. Jews* (Washington, DC: Pew Research Center's Religion and Public Life Project, 2013).
4 Simon Rawidowicz, "Israel, The Ever-Dying People," in *Israel: The Ever-Dying People, and Other Essays* (Cranbury, NJ: Associated University Presses, 1986), 53–4.
5 See David Vital, *The Future of the Jews* (Cambridge, MA: Harvard University Press, 1990); Bernard Wasserstein, *Vanishing Diaspora: The Jews in Europe since 1945* (Cambridge, MA: Harvard University Press, 1996); Michael Lipka, "The Continuing Decline of Europe's Jewish Population," *Fact Tank: News in the Numbers* (Pew Research Center), 9 February 2015.
6 Sergio DellaPergola, "World Jewish Population, 2014," *The American Jewish Year Book, 2014*, ed. Arnold Dashefsky and Ira M. Sheskin, vol. 114 (Springer, 2015), 301–93.

7 Milton Gordon, *Assimilation in American Life: The Role of Race, Religion, and National Origins* (New York: Oxford University Press, 1964), 147. Kallen developed the idea of cultural pluralism in articles written in *The New Republic*, and apparently was the first to use the term in 1924.

8 Paul Yuzyk, *Ukrainian Canadians: Their Place and Role in Canadian Life* (Toronto: Ukrainian Canadian Business and Professional Federation, 1967), 74.

9 Louis Rosenberg, *Canada's Jews: A Social and Economic Study of Jews in Canada in the 1930s*, ed. Morton Weinfeld (Montreal: McGill-Queen's University Press, 1993; originally published in Montreal by The Canadian Jewish Congress, 1939). Rosenberg was an interesting character. He was a lifelong Zionist and socialist. While working for the Jewish Colonization Association in western Canada, he was active in the CCF. And while doing his research on Canadian Jewish life he published, under the pseudonym of Watt Hugh McCollum, the popular anti-capitalist tract *Who Owns Canada? An Examination of the Facts Concerning the Concentration of the Ownership and Control of the Means of Production, Distribution and Exchange in Canada* (Regina: CCF Research Bureau, 1935).

10 Ernest van den Haag, *The Jewish Mystique* (New York: Stein and Day, 1969).

11 Raphael Patai, *The Jewish Mind* (New York: Charles Scribner's Sons, 1977), 8.

12 Desmond Morton and Morton Weinfeld, introduction to *Who Speaks for Canada? Words That Shape a Country*, ed. Desmond Morton and Morton Weinfeld (Toronto: McClelland and Stewart, 1998, xvi–xx).

13 United Nations Development Programme, *Human Development Report 2015*, http://report.hdr.undp.org; The Canadian Press, "Canada Picked among Best Places to Live," CBC, 28 May 2013.

14 Lugo et al., *A Portrait of Jewish Americans*; Statistics Canada, "Religion (108), Immigrant Status and Period of Immigration (11), Age Groups (10) and Sex (3) for the Population in Private Households of Canada, Provinces, Territories, Census Metropolitan Areas and Census Agglomerations, 2011 National Household Survey." NHS Data Tables, Catalogue number 99-010-X2011032.

15 Historian Jonathan Sarna emphasizes the influx of North African Jews to Montreal and their unique influence on strengthening tradition. Gunther Plaut, Biblical scholar and rabbi emeritus of Holy Blossom in Toronto, focuses on the greater proportion of Holocaust survivors in Canada. He recalls that at Canadian Jewish Congress meetings during the 1960s,

"speakers could talk Yiddish in a debate and no translation was deemed necessary. In those days, too, half my Temple Board could speak or understand it." Sociologist Robert Brym also does not feel that the differences stem from innate social and political features of Canada and the United States States. "I feel that too much is often made of Canadian multicultural policies as a force perpetuating ethnic culture, including Jewish culture; we're no more of an ethnic mosaic, and no less an ethnic melting pot, than the U.S.A." Sociologist William Shaffir recognizes the role of immigration, but "is not entirely convinced that the two communities will, over time, display common features." Political scientist Daniel Elazar and sociologist Stuart Schoenfeld stress that Canada does not share the rigorous American separation of church and state, which works to strengthen Jewish communal life and education. These views were sent to me in personal communications. Sociologists Jeffrey Reitz and Raymond Breton have questioned whether this celebrated melting pot versus mosaic distinction really makes a difference in the lives of minorities in Canada and the United States in *The Illusion of Difference: Realities of Ethnicity in Canada and the United States* (Toronto: C.D. Howe Institute, 1994).

16 For an exception, see Harold Troper and Morton Weinfeld, *Old Wounds: Jews, Ukrainians, and the Hunt for Nazi War Criminals in Canada* (Markham, ON: Viking, 1988).

17 Seymour Martin Lipset, "The Study of Jewish Communities in a Comparative Context," *The Jewish Journal of Sociology* 5, no. 2 (1963): 157–66.

18 Max Weber, *The Protestant Ethic and the Spirit of Capitalism*, trans. Talcott Parsons (New York: Charles Scribner and Sons, 1958). Weber argued that certain tenets of Protestantism were more conducive than Catholicism for the kinds of innovative and risk-taking behaviours needed for capitalist entrepreneurs.

CHAPTER ONE

1 Irving Abella, *A Coat of Many Colours: Two Centuries of Jewish Life in Canada* (Toronto: Lester and Orpen Dennys, 1990); Gerald J.J. Tulchinsky, *Taking Root: The Origins of the Canadian Jewish Community* (Toronto: Lester Publishing Co., 1990); Gerald J.J. Tulchinsky, *Branching Out: The Transformation of the Canadian Jewish Community* (Toronto: Stoddart, 1998).

2 Raphael Patai, *Tents of Jacob: The Diaspora, Yesterday and Today* (Englewood Cliffs, NJ: Prentice Hall, 1971). This volume is a good source for the internal group differences described below.

3 Louis Rosenberg, *Canada's Jews: A Social and Economic Study of the Jews of Canada* (Montreal: Canadian Jewish Congress, 1939, republished by McGill-Queen's Press in 1993).

4 Some of these differences were captured in the letters to the editor of *The Forward*, the Yiddish daily in New York. See Isaac Metzker, ed., *A Bintel Brief: Sixty Years of Letters from the Lower East Side to the Daily Forward* (New York: Doubleday, 1971).

5 Jean-Claude Lasry, "A Francophone Diaspora in Quebec," in *The Canadian Jewish Mosaic*, ed. Morton Weinfeld, William Shaffir, and Irwin Cotler (Toronto: John Wiley and Sons, 1981), 221–40; Jean-Claude Lasry, "Sephardim and Ashkenazim in Montreal," *Contemporary Jewry* 6, no. 2 (1983): 26–33; William F.S. Miles, "Between Ashkenaz and Québécois: Fifty Years of Francophone Sephardim in Montréal," *Diaspora, a Journal of Transnational Studies* 16, no. 1/2 (Spring/Fall 2007): 29–66.

6 Nicholas Wade, "Africans Exhibit Jewish Ancestry," *The Gazette*, 9 May 1999; Edith Bruder, *The Black Jews of Africa: History, Religion, Identity* (New York: Oxford University Press, 2008).

7 An example is the cephalic index, the ratio of the distance from the top of one ear to the other divided by the distance from the forehead to the back of the head.

8 Patai, *Tents of Jacob*; Raphael Patai, *The Myth of the Jewish Race*, rev. ed. (Detroit: Wayne State University Press, 1989).

9 Richard M. Goodman, *Genetic Disorders among the Jewish People* (Baltimore: Johns Hopkins University Press, 1979), 29.

10 For a review of these and other cases, see Hillel Halkin, "Wandering Jews – and Their Genes," *Commentary*, 1 September 2000, 54–61.

11 Melvin B. Heyman, "Lactose Intolerance in Infants, Children, and Adolescents," *Pediatrics* 118, no. 3 (2006): 1279–86; Jessica Mozersky, *Risky Genes: Genetics, Breast Cancer, and Jewish Identity* (London: Routledge Taylor and Francis Group, 2013); Jewish Genetic Disease Consortium, "Jewish Genetic Diseases," http://www.jewishgeneticdiseases.org/jewish-genetic-diseases/.

12 Ivan Oransky, "Studies of Mental Illness Train Spotlight on Genes," *The Forward*, 20 August 1999; Ido Efrati, "Scientists Discover Gene That Predisposes Ashkenazi Jews to Schizophrenia," *Haaretz*, 26 November 2013.

13 Rosenberg, *Canada's Jews*, see chapter 9. In fact, the Jewish death rate was 5.5 per 1,000 compared to 10.3, and the Jewish infant mortality rate was 39.8 per 1,000 compared to 82.4.

14 Odin Anderson, "Infant Mortality and Social and Cultural Factors: Historical Trends and Current Problems," in *Patients, Physicians and*

Illness Sourcebook in Behavioral Science and Medicine, ed. Egbert Gartly Jaco (Glencoe, IL: The Free Press, 1958), 21–2.

15 David Mechanic, "Religion, Religiosity, and Illness Behavior: The Special Case of the Jews," *Human Organization* 22, no. 3 (1963): 206.

16 Sheryl Gay Stolberg, "Concern among Jews Is Heightened as Scientists Deepen Gene Studies," *New York Times*, 22 April 1998, A24.

17 Ernest van den Haag, *The Jewish Mystique* (New York: Stein and Day, 1969), see chapter 1; Arno G. Motulsky, "Possible Selection Effects of Urbanization on Ashkenazi Jews," in *Genetic Diseases among Ashkenazi Jews*, ed. Richard M. Goodman and Arno G. Motulsky (New York: Raven Press, 1979), 301–14.

18 Thorstein Veblen, "The Intellectual Pre-eminence of Jews in Modern Europe," *Political Science Quarterly* 34 (1919): 3–42.

19 JINFO.org, "Jewish Nobel Prize Winners," last modified 2016, http://www.jinfo.org/Nobel_Prizes.html.

20 Raphael Patai, *The Jewish Mind* (Detroit: Wayne State University Press, 1977), 317–18, 339–41.

21 Lee D. Cranberg and Martin L. Albert, "The Chess Mind," in *The Exceptional Brain: Neuropsychology of Talent and Special Abilities*, ed. Loraine K. Obler and Deborah Fein (New York: Guilford Press, 1988); William D. Rubinstein, "Jews in Grandmaster Chess," *Jewish Journal of Sociology* 46 (2004): 35–43.

22 Bertha Brody, *A Psychological Study of Immigrant Children at Ellis Island* (Baltimore: Williams and Wilkins, 1926); Thomas Sowell, "Race and IQ Reconsidered," in *Essays and Data on American Ethnic Groups*, ed. Thomas Sowell and Lynn Collins (Washington, DC: The Urban Institute, 1978); Thomas Sowell, *Race and Culture: A World View* (New York: Basic Books, 1994), see chapter 6.

23 Margaret E. Backman, "Patterns of Mental Abilities: Ethnic, Socioeconomic, and Sex Differences," *American Educational Research Journal* 9 (1972): 1–12. The advantage in the math and verbal tests ranged from one-half to a full standard deviation.

24 Christopher Jencks, "What Color Is IQ? Intelligence and Race," in *The Fallacy of IQ*, ed. Carl Senna (New York: The Third Press, 1973), 39.

25 For a review of all these studies, see Miles D. Storfer, *Intelligence and Giftedness: The Contributions of Heredity and Early Environment* (San Francisco: Jossey-Bass Publishers, 1990), 316–17.

26 Kevin Marjoribanks, "Ethnic and Environmental Influences on Mental Abilities," *American Journal of Sociology* 78 (1972): 323–37. The Jewish advantages in the verbal and numerical tests were almost one and a half

standard deviations. For related controversies, see Richard E. Nisbett, "Heredity, Environment, and Race Differences in IQ: A Commentary on Rushton and Jensen," *Psychology, Public Policy, and the Law* 11, no. 2 (2005): 302–10.

27 For a review, see Storfer, *Intelligence and Giftedness*, 324–9; Paul Burstein, "Jewish Educational and Economic Success in the United States: A Search for Explanations," *Sociological Perspectives* 50, no. 2 (2007): 209–28; Gregory Cochran, Jason Hardy, and Henry Harpending, "Natural History of Ashkenazi Intelligence," *Journal of Biosocial Science* 38, no. 5 (2006): 659–93.

28 Arthur Koestler, *The Thirteenth Tribe: The Khazar Empire and Its Heritage* (New York: Random House, 1976).

29 Ibid.; Shlomo Sand, *The Invention of the Jewish People*, trans. Yael Lotan (London: Verso, 2009); Tudor Parfitt, *The Lost Tribes of Israel: The History of a Myth* (London: Weinfeld and Nicholson, 2002). An entire issue of the journal *Human Biology* was devoted to this controversial question (vol. 86.6, 2013).

30 See Joshua Trachtenberg, *The Devil and the Jews: The Medieval Conception of the Jews and Its Relation to Modern Antisemitism*, 2nd ed. (Philadelphia: Jewish Publication Society, 1983).

31 See Rich Cohen, *Tough Jews* (New York: Simon and Schuster, 1998). There has been scholarly discussion of the tension between the Jewish body and the Jewish mind. See for example Sander Gilman, *The Jew's Body* (New York: Routledge, 1991), and Sander Gilman, *Smart Jews: The Construction of the Image of Jewish Intelligence* (Lincoln: University of Nebraska Press, 1996).

32 Robert Slater, *Great Jews in Sports* (New York: Jonathan David Publishers, 1983).

33 Peter Levine, *Ellis Island to Ebbets Field: Sport and the American Jewish Experience* (New York: Oxford University Press, 1992).

34 Stanley R. Barrett, *Is God a Racist? The Right Wing in Canada* (Toronto: University of Toronto Press, 1987); Paul Lungen, "Jews Most Targeted Group in Hate Crimes: Toronto Police," *Canadian Jewish News*, 21 March 2016.

35 Benedict Anderson, *Imagined Communities: Reflections on the Origin and Spread of Nationalism* (London: Verso, 1991).

36 Charles Shahar, *Jewish Life in Montreal: A Survey of the Attitudes, Beliefs and Behaviours of Montreal's Jewish Community* (Montreal: Federation CJA, 2010); Charles Shahar and Tina Rosenbaum, *Jewish Life in Greater Toronto: A Survey of the Attitudes and Behaviours of Greater Toronto's Jewish Community* (Toronto: UJA Federation, 2005).

37 Jewish Federation of Greater Vancouver, "Birthright Israel – Canada Israel Experience," last modified 2016, http://www.jewishvancouver.com/israel-and-overseas/israel-and-overseas-experiences/taglit-birthright-israel; "Is Birthright Working?" *Hamilton Jewish News*, 5 April 2015, https://hamiltonjewishnews.com/israel/is-birthright-working; The Azrieli Foundation, "Azrieli Foundation Pledges $5 Million to Birthright Israel Foundation of Canada," 3 February 2015. http://www.azrielifoundation.org/2015/02/azrieli-foundation-pledges-5-million-to-birthright-israel-foundation-of-canada/.

38 See Jennifer Keishin Armstrong, *Seinfeldia: How a Show about Nothing Changed Everything* (New York: Simon and Schuster, 2016).

39 Marcel Danesi, "Ethnic Language and Acculturation: The Case of Italo-Canadians," *Canadian Ethnic Studies* 17, no. 1 (1985): 88–103.

40 Raymond Breton, "Institutional Completeness of Ethnic Communities and the Personal Relations of Immigrants," *American Journal of Sociology* 70 (1955): 93–205.

41 Jean Paul Sartre, *Anti-Semite and Jew* (New York: Schocken, 1948).

CHAPTER TWO

1 In this section I rely heavily on the ideas in my chapter, "Between Quality and Quantity: Demographic Trends and Jewish Continuity," in *Creating the Jewish Future*, ed. Michael Brown and Bernard Lightman (Walnut Creek, CA: Altamira Press [Sage], 1998), 216–33.

2 Letter to the editor, *The Jerusalem Report*, 31 October 1996.

3 Samuel Liberman and Morton Weinfeld, "Demographic Trends and Jewish Survival," *Midstream* 24 (November 1978): 9–19.

4 David Singer, "Living with Intermarriage," in *American Jews: A Reader*, ed. Marshall Sklare (New York: Behrman House, 1983), 395–412.

5 Steven M. Cohen, "Cohen Defends His Views," *Moment* 20 (April 1995), 68–9; Luis Lugo, Alan Cooperman, Gregory A. Smith, Conrad Hackett, Cary Funk, Neha Sahgal, Phillip Connor, Jessica Hamar Martinez et al., *A Portrait of Jewish Americans: Findings from a Pew Research Center Survey of U.S. Jews* (Washington, DC: Pew Research Center's Religion and Public Life Project, 2013).

6 Milton Himmelfarb and Victor Baras, *Zero Population Growth – For Whom? Differential Fertility and Minority Group Survival* (Westport, CT: Greenwood Press, 1978).

7 John A. Hostetler and Gertrude Enders Huntington, *The Hutterites in North America* (New York: Holt, Rhinehart and Winston, 1980); Rod Janzen and Max Stanton, *The Hutterites in North America* (Baltimore,

MD: Johns Hopkins University Press, 2010); Yossi Katz and John Lehr, *Inside the Ark: Hutterites in Canada and the United States* (Regina, SK: Canadian Plains Research Center Press, University of Regina, 2012).

8 Rosenberg, *Canada's Jews*, see chapter 9. For a general discussion of the links between smaller family size and achievement, see Judith Blake, *Family Size and Achievement* (Berkeley: University of Californian Press, 1989).

9 There are exceptions to every rule. High intermarriage rates in Weimar Germany did not prevent Hitler's rise to power. And in the former Yugoslavia, high rates did not prevent wholesale atrocities by Serbs, Croats, Kosovar Albanians, and Bosnians against each other. On the other hand, there is a strong current of anthropological reasoning dating back to Levi-Strauss which endorses an alliance theory of exogamy.

10 Readers will discern a strand of sociobiological reasoning in this argument.

11 Lila Sarick, "Diaspora Reacts to Kotel and Conversion Decisions," *Canadian Jewish News*, 6 July 2017, 20.

12 Lewis A. Coser, *The Functions of Social Conflict* (Glencoe, IL: The Free Press, 1956).

13 See Table 1 in Appendix 1. For a detailed discussion of the 2011 count of Canadian Jews and the impacts of the ethnic origin and religion questions, see Morton Weinfeld and Randal F. Schnoor, "The Demography of Canadian Jewry, the Census of 2011: Challenges and Results," in *The American Jewish Yearbook, 2014*, ed. Arnold Dashefsky and Ira Sheskin (Springer, 2015), 285–300.

14 Joanna Stark Glassman, "The Relationship between Jewish Ethnic and Religious Identity" (MA thesis, Department of Counselling Psychology, University of British Columbia, 1992), quoted in *Focus for the Future*, report no. 5 (Vancouver: Jewish Federation of Greater Vancouver, November 1993).

15 To be sure, the Canadian gain of 14.2 per cent is deceptive. Most of the increase comes from the category of secular/ethnic Jews. If we look at just those who claim to be Jewish by religion, the increase is from 296,000 to 318,070, an increase of only 7.5 per cent. This is the category likely to contain fewer secular or assimilated Jews. Still, this is an increase.

16 Lugo et al., *A Portrait of Jewish Americans*. Data from the Pew 2014 American Religious Landscape Study, which measured only religious identification, found more optimistic numbers. The Jewish religious proportion was 1.9% of the American population, up from 1.7% in 2007. Alan Cooperman and Becka A. Alper, "The Jewish Place in America's Religious Landscape" (paper presented at the Association of the Sociology of Religion, Montreal, 14 August 2017).

17 Lila Sarick, "Changes in Census Question Led to Dramatic Undercounting of Canadian Jews: Researchers," *Canadian Jewish News*, 31 October 2017.

CHAPTER THREE

1 Luis Lugo, Alan Cooperman, Gregory A. Smith, Conrad Hackett, Cary Funk, Neha Sahgal, Phillip Connor, Jessica Hamar Martinez et al., *A Portrait of Jewish Americans: Findings from a Pew Research Center Survey of U.S. Jews* (Washington, DC: Pew Research Center's Religion and Public Life Project, 2013); Statistics Canada, "Religion, Age Groups, Sex, Selected Demographic, Cultural, Labour Force and Educational Characteristics for the Population in Private Households of Canada, Provinces, Territories, Census Metropolitan Areas and Census Agglomerations, 2011 National Household Survey," NHS Data Tables, Catalogue number 99-010-X2011037.

2 Irving Abella, *A Coat of Many Colours: Two Centuries of Jewish Life in Canada* (Toronto: Lester and Orpen Dennys, 1990), 6–7.

3 Joseph Kage, *With Faith and Thanksgiving: The Story of Two Hundred Years of Jewish Immigration* (Montreal: Eagle Publishing, 1962).

4 Stephen Birmingham, *The Grandees: America's Sephardic Elite* (New York: Harper and Row, 1971).

5 Lloyd Gartner, "Immigration in the Formation of American Jewry, 1840–1925," in *The Jew in American Society*, ed. Marshall Sklare (New York: Behrman House, 1974), 31–50.

6 Kage, *With Faith and Thanksgiving*, 263.

7 Gerald J.J. Tulchinsky, *Taking Root: The Origins of the Canadian Jewish Community* (Toronto: Lester Publishing Co., 1990), 57–8.

8 Stephen Birmingham, *Our Crowd: The Great Jewish Families of New York* (New York: Harper and Row, 1967).

9 Kage, *With Faith and Thanksgiving*, 27. In 1851, Jews were found in nine towns, and by 1871, in twenty-nine towns.

10 Haim H. Ben-Sasson, *A History of the Jewish People* (Cambridge, MA: Harvard University Press, 1976), 757.

11 Louis Rosenberg, *Canada's Jews: A Social and Economic Study of Jews in Canada in the 1930s*, ed. Morton Weinfeld (Montreal: McGill-Queen's University Press, 1993), 135–6.

12 Kage, *With Faith and Thanksgiving*, 24.

13 Gartner, "Immigration in the Formation of American Jewry."

14 Abella, *A Coat of Many Colours*, 87, 112; Stephen Speisman, *The Jews of Toronto: A History to 1937* (Toronto: McClelland and Stewart, 1979), 57.

15 Kage, *With Faith and Thanksgiving*, 30–1.

16 See Erna Paris, *Jews: An Account of Their Experience in Canada* (Toronto: Macmillan, 1980), and Abella, *A Coat of Many Colours*.

17 Thomas Kessner, *The Golden Door: Italian and Jewish Immigrant Mobility in New York City, 1880–1915* (New York: Oxford University Press, 1977); Rosenberg, *Canada's Jews*, 162.

18 Irving Abella and Harold Troper, *None Is Too Many: Canada and the Jews of Europe, 1933–1948* (Toronto: Lester and Orpen Dennys, 1982).

19 Kage, *With Faith and Thanksgiving*, 129.

20 Myra Giberovitch, "The Contribution of Holocaust Survivors to Montreal Jewish Community Life," *Canadian Ethnic Studies* 26, no. 1 (1994): 74–85. Franklin Bialystok, *Delayed Impact: The Holocaust and the Canadian Jewish Community* (Montreal: McGill-Queen's University Press, 2000).

21 William B. Helmreich, *Against All Odds: Holocaust Survivors and the Successful Lives They Made in America* (New York: Simon and Schuster, 1992), 264.

22 The American population estimate is from Sidney Goldstein, "American Jewry: A Demographic Profile," in Sklare, *The Jew in American Society*, 101. The Canadian figure is from Kage, *With Faith and Thanksgiving*, 261.

23 Rabbi Gunther Plaut, personal communication, 31 December 1997.

24 Jean-Claude Lasry, "Sephardim and Ashkenazim in Montreal," in *The Jews in Canada*, ed. Robert J. Brym, William Shaffir, and Morton Weinfeld (Toronto: Oxford University Press, 1993), 395–401; Jean-Claude Lasry, personal communication, 18 August 1998.

25 Charles Shahar and Randal Schnoor, *A Survey of Jewish Life in Montreal, Part II* (Montreal: Federation of Jewish Community Services of Montreal, 1997); Charles Shahar, *2011 National Household Survey: The Jewish Community of Montreal* (Jewish Federations of Canada UIA, 2015); Statistics Canada, NHS Data Tables, Catalogue number 99-010-X2011037.

26 Jean-Claude Lasry, "A Francophone Diaspora in Quebec," in *The Canadian Jewish Mosaic*, ed. Morton Weinfeld, William Shaffir, and Irwin Cotler (Toronto: John Wiley and Sons, 1981); Lasry, "Sephardim and Ashkenazim in Montreal"; Morton Weinfeld, "The Jews of Quebec: An Overview," in Brym, Shaffir, and Weinfeld, *The Jews in Canada*, 171–92.

27 Charles Shahar, *Sépharade 2000: Challenges and Perspectives for the Sephardic Community of Montreal* (Montreal: Federation CJA, 2000), 52.

28 William F.S. Miles, "Between Ashkenaz and Québécois: Fifty Years of Francophone Sephardim in Montréal," *Diaspora: A Journal of Transnational Studies* 16, no. 1/2 (Spring/Fall 2007): 29–66.

29 Yaacov Glickman, "Russian Jews in Canada: Threat to Identity or Promise of Renewal?" in *Multiculturalism, Jews, and Identities in Canada*, ed. Howard Adelman and John H. Simpson (Jerusalem: Magnes Press, 1996), 192–218; Rina Cohen, "The New Immigrants: A Contemporary Profile," in *From Immigration to Integration: The Canadian Jewish Experience*, ed. Ruth Klein and Frank Diamant, Millennium ed. (Toronto: Institute for International Affairs of B'nai-Brith Canada and Malcom Lester, 2001), 213–27; Larissa Remennick, "Russian Jews in the Global City of Toronto: A Pilot Study of Identity and Social Integration," *Espace populations sociétés* 1 (2006): 61–81. http://eps.revues.org/1235. The Russian migration has raised the spectre of a new Jewish association with organized crime with international dimensions, in Canada as well as the United States, Israel, Russia, and elsewhere in Europe. It fits models of crime associated with earlier waves of Jewish immigrants.

30 Roberta L. Markus and Donald V. Schwartz, "Soviet Jewish Émigrés in Toronto: Ethnic Self-identity and Issues of Integration," in Brym, Shaffir, and Weinfeld, *The Jews in Canada*, 402.

31 Charles Shahar, *2011 National Household Survey: The Jewish Population of Canada* (Jewish Federations of Canada – UIA, 2014), Part 7, Immigration and Language, Table 2.

32 Lugo et al., *A Portrait of Jewish Americans*.

33 Ministry of Immigration and Absorption, *1998 Annual Report on Immigration and Absorption in Israel* (Jerusalem, 1998).

34 Jewish Virtual Library, "Immigration to Israel: Total Immigration from FSU, 1948–Present," last modified 2016, https://www.jewishvirtuallibrary.org/jsource/Immigration/FSU.html.

35 Tzila Baum, personal communication, 20 January 1998.

36 Gerald Gold and Rina Cohen, "The Myth of Return and Israeli Ethnicity in Toronto," in Adelman and Simpson, *Multiculturalism, Jews, and Identities in Canada*; Cohen, "The New Immigrants," 221.

37 Shahar, *2011 National Household Survey: The Jewish Population of Canada*, Part 7, Immigration and Language, Tables 2 and 7b.

38 Lugo et al., *A Portrait of Jewish Americans*.

39 Haim Handwerker, "How Many Israelis Live in America, Anyway?" *Haaretz*, 20 June 2014.

40 Gold and Cohen, "The Myth of Return."

41 Uriel Heilman, "Israel Tries to Lure Back Expats," *Canadian Jewish News*, 15 December 2011; Alissa Breiman and Eran Shayshon, "Expanding the

Tent to Include Half a Million Israeli Expats," *The Times of Israel*, 11 November 2012.

42 See Robert F. Barsky, "Refugees from Israel: A Threat to Canadian Jewish Identity?" in *Multiculturalism, Jews, and Identities in Canada*, 219–62; Irwin Cotler, "Refugees, Human Rights, and the Making of Israeli Foreign Policy," in *Still Moving: Recent Jewish Migration in Comparative Perspective*, ed. Daniel Elazar and Morton Weinfeld (New Brunswick, NJ: Transaction Publishers, 2000), 265–84.

43 Inna Tsinman Grebler, "Canada's Acceptance of Refugee Claimants from Israel," *Canadian Jewish News*, 12 August 2009.

44 Cotler, "Refugees, Human Rights, and the Making of Israeli Foreign Policy," 271.

45 Ron Csillag, "Canada Continues to Accept 'Refugees' from Israel," *Canadian Jewish News*, 17 August 2000, 22.

46 Shahar, *2011 National Household Survey: The Jewish Population of Canada*, Part 7, Immigration and Language, Table 6.

47 For a discussion of nested integration, the integration of Jews, and the role of JIAS and other agencies, see Morton Weinfeld, "The Integration of Jewish Immigrants in Montreal: Models and Dilemmas of Ethnic Match," in Elazar and Weinfeld, *Still Moving*, 285–98.

48 Anna Rubalsky, personal communication, 28 January 1998.

49 Daphne Gottlieb Taras and Gerry Beitel, *Preliminary Analysis, Jewish Community Council Survey January 30, 1997* (Calgary: Jewish Community Council, 1997).

50 Shahar, *2011 National Household Survey: The Jewish Population of Canada*.

51 Anne Kilpatrick, "The Jewish Immigrant Aid Services: An Ethnic Lobby in the Canadian Political System" (MA thesis, Department of Sociology, McGill University, 1993).

52 BC Almanac, "Refugee Crisis: Vancouver Jewish Temple Raises $40K to Sponsor Syrian Family," CBC News, 18 November 2015; Amanda Jelowicki, "Westmount Synagogue Sponsors Syrian Refugee Family," *Global News*, 18 September 2015; Arno Rosenfeld, "Canadian Jews Leery of Ottawa's Stance on Refugees," *Times of Israel*, 17 July 2013.

53 Bob Luck of JIAS, Montreal, personal communication, 24 August 1998; Uriel Heilman, "Seeking Newcomers Overseas, Winnipeg Jews Don't Get What They Expected," *Jewish Telegraph Agency*, 25 March 2014.

54 Statistics Canada, NHS Data Tables, Catalogue number 99-010-X2011032.

55 Lugo et al., *A Portrait of Jewish Americans*.

56 Bialystok, *Delayed Impact*.

57 Nancy Tienhaara, *Canadian Views on Immigration and Population: An Analysis of Post-War Gallup Polls* (Ottawa: Department of Manpower and Immigration, 1974), 59.

58 Rod McQueen, "Special Report: The Rich List," *National Post*, 22 April 2000, E2.

59 Lasry, "A Francophone Diaspora in Quebec," 232.

60 Shahar, *Sépharade 2000*. The study is based on a survey of 441 adults in Montreal, drawn from a sample of Sephardi-sounding names in the Montreal telephone directory, the Combined Jewish Appeal list, and the *Voix Sépharade* mailing list. So the sample is not random, and might tend to undercount Sephardi women married to non-Sephardi and non-Jewish men.

61 Sheldon Gordon, "Quebec Sephardim Make Breakthroughs," *The Forward*, 2 April 2004.

62 Rosenberg, *Canada's Jews*, 289. When adjusted for urban-rural difference (Jews were heavily urbanized and crime rates are always higher in cities), the Jewish rate fell to 226.

63 Metzker, *A Bintel Brief*; Gerald J.J. Tulchinsky, *Branching Out: The Transformation of the Canadian Jewish Community* (Toronto: Stoddart, 1998), chapter 7; Cyril H. Levitt and William Shaffir, *The Riot at Christie Pits* (Toronto: Lester and Orpen Dennys, 1987).

64 Eugene Orenstein, "Yiddish Culture in Canada: Yesterday and Today," in *The Canadian Jewish Mosaic*, 293–314.

65 Jean R. Burnet and Howard Palmer, *Coming Canadians: An Introduction to a History of Canada's Peoples* (Toronto: McClelland and Stewart, 1988).

66 Rosenberg, *Canada's Jews*, 19, 23.

67 AntiDefamation League, *Anti-Semitism and Prejudice in America, 1998 Survey*, http://archive.adl.org/antisemitism_survey/survey_main.html#. V2GmQYRllAY; AntiDefamation League, *Global 100: An Index of Anti-Semitism, 2015 Update*, http://global100.adl.org/public/ADL-Global-100-Executive-Summary2015.pdf

68 Rosenberg, *Canada's Jews*, 31–6.

69 Speisman, *The Jews of Toronto*, 82–93; Rosenberg, *Canada's Jews*, 31–6.

70 Rosenberg, *Canada's Jews*, see chapter 23; Abella, *A Coat of Many Colours*, 91; Arthur A. Chiel, *The Jews in Manitoba: A Social History* (Toronto: University of Toronto Press, 1961).

71 Abraham Arnold, "The Mystique of Western Jewry," in Weinfeld, Shaffir, and Cotler, *The Canadian Jewish Mosaic*, 260.

72 For more information on the past and present of Jewish communities outside Montreal and Toronto, see Ira Robinson, "Atlantic Canada," 149–51;

Ellen Scheinberg, "Jewish Life in Ontario Outside of the Metropolis," 215–40; Ira Robinson, "Winnipeg," 241–4; Debbie Shocter, "Saskatchewan, Alberta, and the North," 245–62; Cyril Leonoff and Cynthia Ramsay, "Vancouver," 263–75, all in *Canada's Jews: In Time, Space and Spirit*, ed. Ira Robinson (Boston: Academic Studies Press, 2013).

73 Mitch Potter, "Canada May Be Better Haven than Israel for French Jews, Says Rabbi," *The Star*, 14 January 2015.

74 Shahar, *2011 National Household Survey: The Jewish Population of Canada*, Part 2, Jewish Populations in Geographic Areas.

75 Sydney Goldstein and Alice Goldstein, *Jews on the Move: Implications for Jewish Identity* (Albany: State University of New York Press, 1996), 291. In 1991, Jews comprised about 14 per cent of the population of the city of New York, and 11 per cent of the suburbs, both down slightly from earlier years as the American Jewish population spreads south and west.

76 Shahar, *2011 National Household Survey: The Jewish Population of Canada*, Part 2, Jewish Populations in Geographic Areas.

77 Gershon Hundert, personal communication, 21 August 1998.

78 Interview with Franklin Bialystok, 30 March 2001.

79 As examples see Morley Torgov, *A Good Place to Come From* (Toronto: Lester and Orpen, 1974) and Fredelle Bruser Maynard, *Raisins and Almonds* (Toronto: General Publishing, 1972).

80 Sheldon Maerov, personal communication, 12 December 1997.

81 Philip Moscovitch "Russian Jews Find a New Home in Halifax," *Jewish Federations of Canada*, 8 July 2014.

82 Sheva Medjuck, "Jewish Survival in Small Communities," in Brym, Shaffir, and Weinfeld, *The Jews in Canada*, 363.

83 Michele Byers and Evangelia Tastsoglou, "Negotiating Ethno-cultural Identity: The Experience of Greek and Jewish Youth in Halifax," *Canadian Ethnic Studies* 40, no. 2 (2008): 5–33.

CHAPTER FOUR

1 John A. Porter, *The Vertical Mosaic: An Analysis of Social Class and Power in Toronto* (Toronto: University of Toronto Press, 1965), 287.

2 Wallace Clement, *The Canadian Corporate Elite: An Analysis of Economic Power* (Toronto: McClelland and Stewart, 1975), 237–8.

3 Peter C. Newman, *The Canadian Establishment*, vol. 1 (Toronto: McClelland and Stewart, 1975).

4 Irving Abella, *A Coat of Many Colours: Two Centuries of Jewish Life in Canada* (Toronto: Lester and Orpen Dennys, 1990), 12, 38.

5 See Gerald J.J. Tulchinsky, *Taking Root: The Origins of the Canadian Jewish Community* (Toronto: Lester Publishing Co., 1990), 133–4.
6 Abella, *A Coat of Many Colours*, 135–43; Tulchinsky, *Taking Root*, 214–23.
7 Stephen Speisman, *The Jews of Toronto: A History to 1937* (Toronto: McClelland and Stewart, 1979), 195–7.
8 Abella, *A Coat of Many Colours*, 194–5.
9 Morton Weinfeld, "The Ethnic SubEconomy: Explication and Analysis of the Jews of Montreal," in *The Jews in Canada*, 218–37.
10 Abella, *A Coat of Many Colours*, 143, 109.
11 Thomas Kessner, *The Golden Door: Italian and Jewish Immigrant Mobility in New York City, 1880–1915* (New York: Oxford University Press, 1977); Louis Rosenberg, *Canada's Jews: A Social and Economic Study of Jews in Canada in the 1930s*, ed. Morton Weinfeld (Montreal: McGill-Queen's University Press, 1993), see chapters 16 and 17.
12 Ibid., 162. The actual percentages reveal the dramatic differences. 18 per cent of Jews were merchants compared to 3 per cent for all Canadians; 30 per cent were clerks compared to 13 per cent, while only 6 per cent were unskilled workers compared to 33 per cent.
13 Ibid., 169, 176.
14 Ibid., 191, 214.
15 Watt Hugh McCollum, *Who Owns Canada? An Examination of the Facts Concerning the Concentration of the Ownership and Control of the Means of Production, Distribution and Exchange in Canada* (Regina: CCF Research Bureau, 1935).
16 See Clement, *The Canadian Corporate Elite*; Newman, *The Canadian Establishment*; Porter, *The Vertical Mosaic*.
17 Ibid.
18 Weinfeld, "The Ethnic Sub-Economy."
19 About 28 per cent of the third generation said most of their clients were Jewish, 61 per cent said they were either self-employed of worked for Jewish firms, and 28 per cent said most of their business associates were Jews.
20 Jeffrey Reitz, "Ethnic Concentrations in Labour Markets and Their Implications for Ethnic Inequality," in *Ethnic Identity and Equality: Varieties of Experience in a Canadian City*, ed. Raymond Breton, Wsevolod W. Isajiw, Warren E. Kalbach, and Jeffrey G. Reitz (Toronto: University of Toronto Press, 1990), 92–165. The survey included 168 Jewish respondents: 64 first-generation immigrants, 64 second-generation, and 40 third-generation. Reitz found that among third-generation Jews, 33 per

cent were employed in occupations of Jewish concentration, 43 per cent were self-employed, 26 per cent worked in a Jewish-run business, and 54 per cent had "more than a few" Jewish customers or clients. The Jewish proportion of the Toronto population was between 3 and 4 per cent.

21 Reza Nakhaie, Xiaohua Lin, and Jian Guan, "Special Capital and the Myth of Minority Self-Employment: Evidence from Canada," *Journal of Ethnic and Migration Studies* 35, no. 4 (2009): 625–44; Statistics Canada, NHS Data Tables, Catalogue number 99-010-X2011037.

22 The directory was a project of The Jewish Business Network, directed by Rabbi Ronnie Fine of Lubavitch, and founded in 1992. It had as its main activity a series of monthly luncheons, each of which could draw up to 200 people.

23 To date, there have been five Canadian Supreme Court Justices: Rosalie Abella, Morris Fish, Bora Laskin, Michael Moldaver, and Marshall Rothstein.

24 Statistics Canada, NHS Data Tables, Catalogue number 99-010-X2011037.

25 Samantha Grossman, "And the World's Most Educated Country Is ..." *Time*, 27 September 2012.

26 Charles Kadushin, *The American Intellectual Elite* (Boston: Little, Brown, 1974).

27 Seymour Martin Lipset and Everett Carl Ladd, Jr, "The Changing Social Origins of American Academics," in *Qualitative and Quantitative Social Research, Papers in Honor of Paul F. Lazarsfeld*, ed. Robert K. Merton, James S. Coleman, and Peter H. Rossi (New York: The Free Press, 1979), 326.

28 Luna Goriss, "Jewish Nobel Prize Winners," *About.com*, http://judaism. about.com/od/culture/a/nobel.htm.

29 Daniel Golden, "In Effort to Lift Their Rankings, Colleges Recruit Jewish Students." *The Wall Street Journal*, 29 April 2002.

30 Porter, *The Vertical Mosaic*, 501.

31 Richard L. Ogmundson and James A. McLaughlin, "Changes in an Intellectual Elite 1960–1990: The Royal Society Revisited," *Canadian Review of Sociology and Anthropology* 31, no. 1 (1994): 1–13.

32 Ibid., 7.

33 Statistics Canada, NHS Data Tables, Catalogue number 99-010-X2011037.

34 Ibid. In 2011, the Canadian unemployment rate was 7.8 per cent, and for Jews it was 6.6 per cent.

35 Morton Weinfeld, Randal F. Schnoor, and David S. Koffman, "Overview of Canadian Jewry," in *American Jewish Yearbook 2012*, vol. 109–12, ed. Arnold Dashefsky and Ira Sheskin (Springer, 2012), 55–90.

36 Jacob Berkman, "At Least 139 of the Forbes 400 Are Jewish," *Jewish Telegraphic Agency* 5, October 2009.

37 AFL-CIO, "100 Highest Paid CEOs," last modified 2014, http://www. aflcio.org/Corporate-Watch/Paywatch-2014/100-Highest-Paid-CEOs.

38 The sources for the information which follows are published lists of wealthy Canadians, taken from books which update the analyses of John Porter, Wallace Clement, and Peter C. Newman, and from magazine and newspaper articles. By examining first and second names, consulting with informants, and checking with basic references like *Canadian Who's Who*, I count those who appear to be Jewish. Some errors creep in; people who are Jewish may have been omitted, and some who are not may be mistakenly so identified and counted. My apologies to those mislabelled, but these few cases will not detract from the general patterns and do not affect the orders of magnitude.

39 Peter C. Newman, *The Acquisitors: The Canadian Establishment*, vol. 2 (Toronto: McClelland and Stewart, 1983); Diane Francis, *Controlling Interest: Who Owns Canada?* (Toronto: Macmillan, 1986). The ten families are: Bronfman (Charles and Edgar), Ivanier, Steinberg, Posluns, Bronfman (Edward and Peter), Reichmann, Mann, Wolfe, Singer, and Belzberg.

40 *Financial Post Magazine*, January 1996, 14.

41 *National Post*, 22 April 2000, section E.

42 *Canadian Business* 72, no. 14 (7 August 2000), 60–107. This list includes both public and privately held corporations, as well as real estate and other assets.

43 "Canada's Richest People 2015," *Canadian Business*, 15 January 2015.

44 Jean-Benoit Nadeau, "Les grandes fortunes du Québec," *L'actualité*, 11 January 2011.

45 Hugh Mackenzie, "Canada's CEO Elite 100: The 0.01%," *The Canadian Centre for Policy Alternatives*, January 2012.

46 Peter C. Newman, *Titans: How the New Canadian Establishment Seized Power* (Toronto: Viking, 1998).

47 Ibid., 121–2.

48 Ibid., 583.

49 Boundless, University of Toronto, "Donor Listing," 2015, http://boundless. utoronto.ca/our-supporters/donor-listing/; University of Toronto, "National Report" Division of Development and University Relations, 1998.

50 Rosemary Sexton, *The Glitter Girls* (Toronto: Macmillan, 1993), 58.

51 James Torczyner, "The Persistence of Invisible Poverty among Jews in Canada," in *The Jews in Canada*, 379–94.

52 Shahar, *2011 National Household Survey: The Jewish Population of Canada*, Part 4, The Jewish Poor.

53 Statistics Canada, "Selected Demographic, Cultural, Educational, Labour Force and Income Characteristics (730), First Official Language Spoken (4), Age Groups (8D) and Sex (3) for the Population of Canada, Provinces, Territories, Census Metropolitan Areas and Census Agglomerations, 2011 National Household Survey." NHS Data Tables, Catalogue number 99-010-X2011043.

54 Shahar, *2011 National Household Survey: The Jewish Population of Canada*, Part 7, Immigration and Language, Table 16.

55 Ibid.

56 Statistics Canada, NHS Data Tables, Catalogue number 99-010-X2011043.

57 Charles Shahar, Morton Weinfeld, and Randal Schnoor, *Survey of the Hassidic and Ultra-Orthodox Communities in Outremont and Surrounding Areas* (Outremont: Coalition of Outremont Hassidic Organizations, 1997).

58 Randal F. Schnoor, "Tradition and Innovation in an Ultra-Orthodox Community: The Hasidim of Outremont," *Canadian Jewish Studies* 10 (2002): 53–73.

59 Jeffrey Reitz, "Ethnic Concentrations in Labour Markets."

60 Jason Z. Lian and David R. Mathews, "Does the Vertical Mosaic Still Exist? Ethnicity and Income in Canada, 1991," *Canadian Review of Sociology and Anthropology* 35, no. 4 (1998): 461–82.

61 Peter S. Li, *Ethnic Inequality in a Class Society* (Toronto: Wall and Thompson Press, 1988), 116.

62 Monica Boyd, "Gender, Visible Minority and Immigrant Earnings Inequality: Reassessing an Employment Equity Premise," in *Deconstructing a Nation*, ed. Vic Satzewich (Halifax: Fernwood Publishing, 1992), 305.

63 James Geschwender and Neil Guppy, "Ethnicity, Educational Attainment, and Earned Income," *Canadian Ethnic Studies* 27, no. 1 (1995): 67–84.

64 Peter S. Li, "The Market Value and Social Value of Race," in *Racism and Social Inequality in Canada*, ed. Vic Satzewich (Toronto, ON: Thomson Educational Publishing Inc., 1998), 115–30.

65 Krishna Pendakur and Ravi Pendakur, "Color by Numbers: Minority Earnings in Canada 1995–2005," *Journal of International Migration and Integration* 12 (2011): 305–29.

66 Maryam Dilmaghani, "Religiosity, Human Capital Return and Earnings in Canada," *International Journal of Social Economics* 39, no. 1–2 (2011): 55–80.

67 Li, *Ethnic Inequality in a Class Society*, 102. Jews averaged an extra $1,300 for each year of schooling compared to the average Canadian figure of $800.

68 Nathan Hurvitz, "Sources of Motivation and Achievement of American Jews," *Jewish Social Studies*, October 1961, 217–23.

69 Weber, *The Protestant Ethic and the Spirit of Capitalism*; Werner Sombart, *The Jews and Modern Capitalism* (London: Collier, 1962).

70 Andrew Greeley and Peter Rossi, *The Education of Catholic Americans* (Chicago: Aldine Publishing Company, 1966); Andrew M. Greeley, *Ethnicity in the United States: A Preliminary Reconnaissance* (New York: John Wiley, 1974).

71 James Coleman, Thomas Hoffer, and Sally Kilgore, *High School Achievement: Public, Catholic, and Private Schools Compared* (New York: Basic Books, 1982).

72 Stephen L. Morgan and Jennifer J. Todd, "Intergenerational Closure and Academic Achievement in High School: A New Evaluation of Coleman's Conjecture," *Sociology of Education* 82, no. 3 (2009): 267–85; Maureen Hallinan and Warren N. Kubitschek, "A Comparison of Academic Achievement and Adherence to the Common School Ideal in Public and Catholic Schools," *Sociology of Education* 85, no. 1 (2012): 1–22.

73 Statistics Canada, "Ethnic Origin (101), Age Groups (10), Sex (3) and Selected Demographic, Cultural, Labour Force, Educational and Income Characteristics (327) for the Population in Private Households of Canada, Provinces, Territories, Census Metropolitan Areas and Census Agglomerations, 2011 National Household Survey," NHS Data Tables, Catalogue number 99-010-X2011036.

74 See Shahar, Weinfeld, and Schnoor, "Survey of the Hassidic and Ultra-Orthodox Communities."

75 Miriam Slater, "My Son the Doctor: Aspects of Mobility among American Jews," *American Sociological Review* 34 (1969): 359–73.

76 Nathan Glazer, "American Jews and the Attainment of Middle-Class Rank," in *The Jews: Social Patterns of an American Group*, 138–46; Barry R. Chiswick and Jidong Huang, "The Earnings of American Jewish Men: Human Capital, Denomination, and Religiosity," *Journal for the Scientific Study of Religion* 47, no. 4 (2008): 694.

77 Naomi Fejgin, "Factors Contributing to the Academic Excellence of American Jewish and Asian Students," *Sociology of Education* 68, no. 1 (1995): 18; Yongmin Sun, "Cognitive Advantages of East Asian American Children: When Do Such Advantages Emerge and What Explains Them?" *Sociological Perspectives* 54, no. 3 (2011): 377–402.

78 Pat Johnson, "Cost of Being Jewish," *The Jewish Independent*, 21 September 2001; Paul Lungen, "Day School Fees Vary across Canada," *Canadian Jewish News*, 2 September 2014; Yael Miller, "The Cost of Keeping Kosher," *Haaretz*, 10 October 2011; Sarah Boesveld, "As Bar and Bat Mitzvahs Become More 'Over the Top,' Parents Say the Jewish Tradition Is Still Meaningful," *The National Post*, 18 October 2013.
79 Sexton, *The Glitter Girls*, 150–1.
80 Newman, *Titans*, 333.
81 Boesveld, "As Bar and Bat Mitzvahs Become More 'Over the Top.'"

CHAPTER FIVE

1　See Sylvia B. Fishman, "The Changing American Jewish Family Faces the 1990s," in *Jews in America: A Contemporary Reader*, ed. Roberta Rosenberg Farber and Chaim I. Waxman (Hanover, NH, and London: Brandeis University Press and University Press of New England, 1999), 51–88. For a Canadian perspective see Norma Joseph, "Jewish Women in Canada: An Evolving Role," in *From Immigration to Integration: The Canadian Jewish Experience*, ed. Ruth Klein and Frank Diamant, Millennium ed. (Toronto: Institute for International Affairs of B'nai-Brith Canada and Malcom Lester, 2001), 182–95. For recent studies of changes in Jewish family structure, see Sylvia B. Fishman, *Transformations in the Composition of American Jewish Households* (American Jewish Committee, 2010), and "Refiguring the American Jewish Family," *Journal of Jewish Communal Service* 89, no. 1 (2014): 7–19.
2　Paula Hyman, "Introduction: Perspectives on the Evolving Jewish Family," in *The Jewish Family, Myths and Reality*, ed. Steven M. Cohen and Paula Hyman (New York: Holmes and Meier, 1986), 2–3; Henri Grégoire, *Essai sur la régénération physique, morale, et politique des juifs* (Devilly, France: Metz, 1789), 36.
3　ChaeRan Freeze, "The Litigious Gerusha: Jewish Women and Divorce in Imperial Russia," *Nationalities Papers* 25, no. 1 (1997): 89–101.
4　Isaac Metzker, ed., *A Bintel Brief: Sixty Years of Letters from the Lower East Side to the Daily Forward* (New York: Doubleday, 1971).
5　See Gladys Rothbell, "The Jewish Mother: Social Construction of a Popular Image," in Cohen and Hyman, *The Jewish Family, Myths and Reality*, 118–30.
6　Yael Israel-Cohen, "Jewish Modern Orthodox Women, Active Resistance and Synagogue Ritual," *Contemporary Jewry* 32, no. 1 (2012): 3–25; Jewish Orthodox Feminist Alliance, https://www.jofa.org.

7 Batya Ungar-Sargon, "Orthodox Yeshiva Set to Ordain Three Women. Just Don't Call Them 'Rabbi,'" *Tablet Magazine*, 10 June 2013; Barbara Silverstein, "Have Female Rabbis Hit the Proverbial Stained Glass Ceiling?" *The Star*, 6 September 2013; Michael Kaminer, "First Woman in Her Job, Toronto Rabbi Yael Splansky Has Big Plans," *The Forward*, 30 June 2014; Janice Arnold, "Female Jewish Clergy Discuss Professional Challenges," *Canadian Jewish News*, 19 October 2012.

8 Norma Joseph, "Personal Reflections on Jewish Feminism," in *The Canadian Jewish Mosaic*, ed. Morton Weinfeld, William Shaffir, and Irwin Cotler (Toronto: John Wiley and Sons, 1981), 205–21.

9 Norma Joseph, personal communication, 28 January 1998.

10 Sheva Medjuck, "If I Cannot Dance to It, It Is Not My Revolution: Jewish Feminism in Canada Today," in *The Jews in Canada*, ed. Robert J. Brym, William Shaffir, and Morton Weinfeld (Toronto: Oxford University Press, 1993), 338.

11 Silverstein, "Have Female Rabbis Hit the Proverbial Stained Glass Ceiling?"; Kaminer, "First Woman in Her Job."

12 For a discussion of feminism and Judaism, including new rituals, see Sylvia B. Fishman, "Negotiating Egalitarianism and Judaism: American Jewish Feminisms and Their Implication for Jewish Life," in Farber and Waxman, *Jews in America*, 163–90; Elyse Goldstein, ed., *New Jewish Feminism: Probing the Past, Forging the Future* (Woodstock, VT: Jewish Lights Publishing, 2008).

13 Norma Joseph, personal communication, 28 January 1998.

14 Statistics Canada, NHS Data Tables, Catalogue number 99-010-X2011037.

15 Luis Lugo, Alan Cooperman, Gregory A. Smith, Conrad Hackett, Cary Funk, Neha Sahgal, Phillip Connor, Jessica Hamar Martinez et al., *A Portrait of Jewish Americans: Findings from a Pew Research Center Survey of U.S. Jews* (Washington, DC: Pew Research Center's Religion and Public Life Project, 2013).

16 Moshe Hartman and Harriet Hartman, *Gender Equality and American Jews* (Albany: State University of New York Press, 1996), 33.

17 Statistics Canada, NHS Data Tables, Catalogue number 99-010-X2011037.

18 Statistics Canada, NHS Data Tables, Catalogue number 99-010-X2011036.

19 Medjuck, "If I Cannot Dance to It."

20 Barry Chiswick, "Working and Family Life: The Experiences of Jewish Women in America," in *Papers in Jewish Demography*, ed. Sergio DellaPergola and Judith Even, 283. Jerusalem: Hebrew University of Jerusalem, 1997.

21 Byron G. Spencer, "Labor Supply and Investment in Child Quality: A Study of Jewish and Non-Jewish Women: A Comment." *Review of Economics and Statistics* 74, no. 4 (1992): 721–5.

22 Paul Ritterband, "Jewish Women in the Labor Force." New York: Center for Jewish Studies, Graduate Center, City University of New York, 1990.

23 Chiswick, "Working and Family Life," 285–6.

24 Medjuck, "If I Cannot Dance to It."

25 Fishman, "Refiguring the American Jewish Family," 9–12. See also H. Hartman and M. Hartman, *Gender and American Jews: Patterns in Work, Education and Family in Contemporary Life* (Waltham: Brandeis University Press, 2009).

26 Ruth K. Westheimer and Jonathan Mark, *Heavenly Sex: Sexuality in the Jewish Tradition* (New York: New York University Press, 1995). Also see Shmuley Boteach, *Kosher Sex: A Recipe for Passion and Intimacy* (New York: Doubleday, 1999).

27 See Alan Fisher, "The Jewish Electorate: California, 1980–86," in *Jews and the New American Scene,* ed. Seymour Martin Lipset and Earl Raab (Cambridge: Harvard University Press, 1995), 131–50; Herbert McClosky and Alida Brill, *Dimensions of Tolerance: What Americans Believe about Civil Liberties* (New York: Russell Sage, 1983), 404–6; Steven M. Cohen, "Religion and the Public Square: Attitudes of American Jews in Comparative Perspective, Part Two," in *Jerusalem Letter* (Jerusalem: Jerusalem Center for Public Affairs), 1 August 2000.

28 Mark D. Regnerus and Jeremy E. Uecker, "Religious Influences on Sensitive Self-Reported Behaviors: The Product of Social Desirability, Deceit, or Embarrassment?" *Sociology of Religion* 68, no. 2 (2007): 145–63.

29 Mark D. Regnerus, *Forbidden Fruit: Sex and Religion in the Lives of American Teenagers* (New York: Oxford University Press, 2007).

30 Edward Laumann, John H. Gagnon, Robert T. Michael, and Stuart Michaels, *The Social Organization of Sexuality* (Chicago: University of Chicago Press, 1994), Table 5.1C.

31 William E. Mann, ed., *The Underside of Toronto* (Toronto: McClelland and Stewart, 1970), 160–1.

32 Joseph J. Levy and Eleanor Maticka-Tyndale, *Sexualité, contraception, et SIDA chez les jeunes adultes* (Montreal: Méridien, 1992).

33 Fishman, *Refiguring the American Jewish Family*, 8; Shahar, *2011 National Household Survey: The Jewish Population of Canada*, Part 5, The Jewish Family, iii.

34 Special communication from Warren Clark, Statistics Canada, 20 September 1998.

35 Louis Rosenberg, *Canada's Jews*, 298.

36 Adam H. Koblenz, "Jewish Women under Siege: The Fight for Survival on the Front Lines of Love and the Law," *University of Maryland Law*

Journal of Race, Religion, Gender and Class 9, no. 2 (Fall 2009): 259–302; Lydia M. Belzer, "Toward True Shalom Bayit: Acknowledging Domestic Abuse in the Jewish Community and What to Do about It?" *Cardozo Journal of Law and Gender*, 2005:2, 241–82; Jewish Coalition Against Domestic Abuse, http://jcada.org.

37 Act to End Violence against Women, "Programs and Educational Resources," last modified 2011. http://www.acttoendvaw.org/programs-and-educational-resources.php.

38 Esther East and Elke Stein, "Project S.A.R.A.H.: A Domestic Violence Program Eroding Denial in the Orthodox Jewish Community in New Jersey," *Journal of Jewish Communal Service* 83 (2008): 223–8; Shoshana Ringel and Rena Bina, "Understanding Causes of and Responses to Intimate Partner Violence in a Jewish Orthodox Community: Survivors' and Leaders' Perspectives," *Research on Social Work Practice* 17, no. 2 (2007): 277–86; Shalom Task Force, "Working with Couples and Families in the Orthodox Jewish Community," 2014, http://www.shalomtaskforce. org/articles/working_with_couples_and_families_in_the_orthodox_jewish_ community1.

39 Irv Binik (psychologist and sex therapist), personal communication, 11 September 1998.

40 Hurvitz, "Sources of Motivation and Achievement of American Jews"; Fred Strodtbeck, "Family Interaction, Values, and Achievement," in *The Jews: Social Patterns of an American Group*, ed. Marshall Sklare (Glencoe, IL: The Free Press, 1958), 147–68.

41 Zena Smith Blau, "The Strategy of the Jewish Mother," in *The Jew in American Society*, ed. Marshall Sklare (New York: Behrman House, 1974), 165–88.

42 Ronald Freeman, Pascal Whelpton, and Arthur Campbell, *Family Planning, Sterility, and Population Growth* (New York: McGraw-Hill, 1959), 110.

43 Bernard Farber, Charles Mindel, and Bernard Lazerwitz, "The Jewish American Family," in *Ethnic Families in America*, ed. Charles Mindel and Robert Habenstein (Amsterdam: Elsevier North Holland, 1976), 359.

44 Lugo et al., *A Portrait of Jewish Americans*.

45 Shahar, *2011 National Household Survey: The Jewish Population of Canada*, Fertility Rates of Canada's Jewish Population, Table 1, 2.

46 Leo Davids, "Marital Status and Fertility among Sub-groups of Canadian Jews," in Brym, Shaffir, and Weinfeld, *The Jews in Canada*, 320. Davids used those who spoke Yiddish at home as a proxy for Hasidim. He looked at the number of children aged from birth to four years old per

1,000 women aged fifteen to forty-four. The figure for all Canadian Jews was 279, while that for Yiddish-speakers was 1,122. Lugo et al., *A Portrait of Jewish Americans*. According to the Pew Report, the Orthodox fertility rate is 4.1 compared to 1.9 for other Jews.

47 Medjuck, "If I Cannot Dance to It," 336–7.
48 Ibid, 337.
49 Yael C.B. Machtinger, "Socio-legal Gendered Remedies of Get Refusal: Top Down, Bottom Up," in *Women's Rights and Religious Law: Domestic and International Perspectives*, ed. Fareda Banda and Lisa Fishbayn Jofee (New York: Routledge, 2016), 223–54; Yael C.B. Machtinger, "To Shame or Not to Shame," *Canadian Jewish News*, 4 August 2016.
50 Shahar, *2011 National Household Survey: The Jewish Population of Canada*, Part 5, The Jewish Family, Table 3A.
51 Rosenberg, *Canada's Jews*, 93.
52 Shahar, *2011 National Household Survey: The Jewish Population of Canada*, Part 5, The Jewish Family. The percentage of divorced or separated Jews was 4.4 per cent in Montreal, 5 per cent in Toronto, and 6.1 per cent in Vancouver. The percentage in common-law relationships was 2.2 per cent in Montreal, 2 per cent in Toronto, and 5.4 per cent in Vancouver. The percentage of Jews living in single-parent families was 7.4 per cent in Montreal, 6.6 per cent in Toronto, and 9.5 per cent in Vancouver.
53 Erin Dym, "New Single Parent Support Group Takes Off," *Canadian Jewish News*, 6 June 2014.
54 Rebecca Adams, "Jewish Matchmaking Is Alive and Well, with Some Post-Shtetls Updates," *The Huffington Post*, 19 June 2014.
55 Cara Stern, "Matchmaking Site Hopes to Pair Young Jews," *Canadian Jewish News*, 5 March 2013.
56 Adams, "Jewish Matchmaking."
57 Sheri Shefa, "Cover Story: Will Hookup Apps Replace Matchmakers?" *Canadian Jewish News*, 10 February 2015.
58 JDate.com, "The Leading Jewish Singles Network! Explore the Possibilities," Spark Networks, A Leading Provider of Iconic, Niche-Focused Brands. Retrieved 6 December 2012, from http://www.spark.net/portfolio/jdate-com/.
59 Shiryn Ghermezian, "*Daily Beast* Writer Describes Her Week on 'Jewish Tinder': More Attractive Guys than Usual Dating Site," *The Algemeiner*, 5 January 2015, https://www.algemeiner.com/2015/01/05/daily-beast-writer-describes-her-week-on-jswipe-more-attractive-guys-than-usual-dating-site/.
60 Mirian Pullman Friedman, "New Jewish Matchmaking: A Quantitative Analysis of JDate Users," *Journal of Jewish Communal Service* 84, no. 3/4 (Summer/Fall 2009): 345–52.

61 Lisa Scherzer, "Looking for Mr. Goodstein: When Gentile Singles Seek Jewish Mates," *Interfaith Family.com*, December 2002. http://www.interfaithfamily.com/relationships/interdating/Looking_for_Mr_Goodstein_When_Gentile_Singles_Seek_Jewish_Mates.shtml.

62 Sarah E. Richards, "You Don't Have to Be Jewish to Love JDate," *New York Times*, 5 December 2004.

63 Lisa M. Brown, Penny S. McNatt, and Gordon D. Cooper, "Ingroup Romantic Preferences among Jewish and Non-Jewish White Undergraduates," *International Journal of Intercultural Relations* 27, no. 3 (May 2003): 335–54.

64 I thank Dr Randal Schnoor for much of the information and insights into gay Jewish life in Toronto.

65 Fishman, "Refiguring the American Jewish Family," 13–14. Jonathan Krasner, "Same-Sex Couple Families and the American Jewish Community," in *Love, Marriage, and Jewish Families: Paradoxes of a Social Revolution*, ed. Sylvia Barack Fishman (Waltham, MA: Brandeis University Press, 2015).

66 Reginald Bibby, *Beyond the Gods and Back: Religion's Demise and Rise and Why It Matters* (Lethbridge, AB: Project Canada Books, 2011), 87.

67 Dena S. Davis, "Religion, Genetics, and Sexual Orientation: The Jewish Tradition," *Kennedy Institute of Ethics Journal* 18.2 (2008): 125–48; Randal F. Schnoor, "Being Gay and Jewish: Negotiating Intersecting Identities," *Sociology of Religion* 67 (2006): 43–60.

68 Harvey Cohen, personal communication, 27 October 1997.

69 Riva Gold, "Ga'ava Provides Social Network, Support for GLBT," *Canadian Jewish News*, 11 June 2008.

70 Jewish in Montreal, "Support Group for Jewish Families with Gay Children." http://www.jewishinmontreal.com/Support-Group-for-Jewish-Families-with-Gay-Children.html.

71 Jodie Shupac, "How LGBTQ Inclusive Are Toronto Shuls?" *Jewish Independent*, 27 June 2014; Out and Proud Program, "LGBTQ-Positive Faith Groups and Places of Worship," *Children's Aid Society of Toronto*, 2012, http://www.torontocas.ca/app/Uploads/diversity/outandproudworship.pdf.

72 Michael Lemberger, "Gay Synagogues' Uncertain Future," *Tabletmag.com*, 11 March 2013.

73 Jodie Shupac, "LGBTQ Inclusion: How Welcoming Are Conservative Shuls?," *Canadian Jewish News*, 23 June 2014.

74 Naomi Grossman, "The Gay Orthodox Underground," *Moment* 28, no. 2 (April 2000): 54. While there are individual gays and lesbians in Canadian

Orthodox synagogues, there is not, as yet, a well-developed underground movement of Orthodox gays as in the United States.

75 Randal F. Schnoor and Morton Weinfeld, "Seeking a Mate: Inter-Group Partnerships among Gay Jewish Men," *Canadian Ethnic Studies* 37, no. 1 (January 2005): 21–39.

76 Ibid.

77 Carlos A. Godoy L., "Jewish Groups Are on the Front Lines of LGBTQ Issues," *Canadian Jewish News*, 19 July 2016.

78 "Tel Aviv Declared World's Best Gay Travel Destination," *Haaretz*, 11 January 2012; Diaa Hadid, "In Israeli City of Haifa, a Liberal Arab Culture Blossoms," *New York Times*, 3 January 2016; Lulu Garcia-Navarro, "Israel Presents Itself as Haven for Gay Community," *NPR*, 4 June 2012.

79 Michael Kaminer, "'Pinkwashing' Washed Out at Toronto Gay Pride," *The Forward*, 30 June 2014; Mira Sucharov, "Israel's 'Pinkwashing' Is Not Whitewashing," *The Huffington Post*, 19 June 2012; Ben Cohen, "Pinkwashing? Try 'Progwashing,'" *Canadian Jewish News*, 27 March 2012.

80 Shahar, *2011 National Household Survey: The Jewish Population of Canada*, Part 3, Jewish Seniors, Table 3.

81 Lugo et al., *A Portrait of Jewish Americans*; Sergio DellaPergola, "World Jewish Population, 2012," in *American Jewish Yearbook 2012*, vol. 109–12 (Springer, 2012), 213–83.

82 Ira Sheskin, *Comparisons of Jewish Communities: A Compendium of Tables and Bar Charts* (Berman Jewish Data Bank, 2015).

83 Shahar, *2011 National Household Survey: The Jewish Population of Canada*, Part 3, Jewish Seniors, Table 2; Rohan Kembhavi, "Canadian Seniors: A Demographic Profile," *Elections Canada*, November 2012.

84 Carolyn Rosenthal, "Aging in the Family Context: Are Jewish Families Different?" in Brym, Shaffir, and Weinfeld, *The Jews in Canada*, 344–57.

85 Shahar, *2011 National Household Survey: The Jewish Community of Montreal*; Shahar, *2011 National Household Survey: The Jewish Population of Canada*, Part 3, Jewish Seniors, Table 5. 64 per cent of Montreal Jewish seniors live with their spouses; 29 per cent live alone; 2 per cent live with nonrelatives; 6 per cent live with children.

86 Charles Shahar, *Jewish Life in Montreal: A Survey of the Attitudes, Beliefs and Behaviours of Montreal's Jewish Community* (Montreal: Federation CJA, 2010).

87 Charles Shahar, *Jewish Retirement Residence Survey* (Ottawa: April 2015), https://fedweb-assets.s3.amazonews.com/fed-10/2/Community Survey Jewish Retirement Residence Survey, April 2015.pdf.

88 Susan Cogan and Hazel Orpen, *Housing Needs of the Jewish Community of Greater Vancouver* (Vancouver: Tikva Housing Society, 2015), http://tikvahousing.org/wp/wp-content/uploads/2014/04/Tikva-Survey-Final-Report-March-23-2015.pdf.

89 John Sigal and Morton Weinfeld, *Trauma and Rebirth: Intergenerational Effects of the Holocaust* (New York: Praeger, 1989), 95.

90 Rosenthal, "Aging in the Family Context," 351.

91 Shahar, *2011 National Household Survey: The Jewish Population of Canada*, Part 6, Intermarriage, Tables 6A, 6B, 6C; Angus Reid Institute, "Religious Trends: Led by Quebec, Number of Canadians Holding Favourable Views of Various Religions Increases," Public Interest Research, 4 April 2017, http://angusreid.org/religious-trends-2017/.

92 We exclude the *halachic* point that the children of intermarried Jewish women are Jewish. A recent American study by Bruce Phillips reported below found – the "good" news – that 12 per cent of the children of mixed-married Jews went on to marry Jews, a kind of return inmarriage. The "bad" news is that 88 per cent did not.

93 Jay Brodbar-Nemzer, Steven M. Cohen, Allan Reitzes, Charles Shahar, and Gary A. Tobin, "An Overview of the Canadian Jewish Community," in Brym, Shaffir, and Weinfeld, *The Jews in Canada*, 60–1. Intermarriage among Toronto Jews is more prevalent among fourth-generation Canadian Jews than among first or second; 43 per cent to under 10 per cent.

94 Ibid.; Charles Shahar and Randal Schnoor, *A Survey of Jewish Life in Montreal, Part II* (Montreal: Federation of Jewish Community Services of Montreal, 1997).

95 Bruce A. Phillips, *Re-examining Intermarriage: Trends, Textures, Strategies* (New York: The American Jewish Committee and the Susan and David Wilstein Institute of Jewish Policy Studies, n.d.). For this study, in 1993 Phillips contacted 1,123 respondents of the 1990 NJPS who were currently or previously married and under fifty years old, and interviewed 580. In 1995, he also interviewed 256 non-Jewish spouses.

96 Peter Y. Medding, Gary A. Tobin, Sylvia Barack Fishman, and Mordechai Rimor, "Jewish Identity in Conversionary and Mixed Marriages," in Farber and Waxman, *Jews in America: A Contemporary Reader*, 226–60.

97 One third said "Christian only," and one-quarter said "no religion" and "both" respectively. Phillips, *Re-examining Intermarriage*.

98 Shahar, *2011 National Household Survey: The Jewish Population of Canada*, Part 6, Intermarriage, Table 16.

99 Lugo et al., *A Portrait of Jewish Americans*.

100 Shahar and Rosenbaum, *Jewish Life in Greater Toronto*, 62.

101 Shahar, *Jewish Life in Montreal.*

102 Micah Sachs and Edmund Case, *What We Learned from the Fourth Annual December Holidays Survey* (Interfaith Family, 2007), http://www.interfaithfamily.com/files/pdf/WhatWeLearnedfromthe2007December HolidaysSurvey.pdf.

103 Alan M. Dershowitz, *The Vanishing American Jew* (New York: Little, Brown and Company, 1997).

104 Francine Klagsbrun, "Survey Says Intermarriage Is O K," *Moment* 28, no. 2 (April 2001): 32; Lugo et al., *A Portrait of Jewish Americans.*

105 Shahar and Schnoor, *Summary of Jewish Life in Montreal*, Part II, 34.

106 Charles Shahar and Tina Rosenbaum, *Jewish Life in Greater Toronto: A Survey of the Attitudes and Behaviours of Greater Toronto's Jewish Community* (Toronto: U J A Federation, 2005); Lila Sarick, "Shift in How We Talk about Intermarriage," *Canadian Jewish News*, 20 July 2016, 8–9.

107 Reginald Bibby, *The Bibby Report: Social Trends, Canadian Style* (Toronto: Stoddart, 1995), 54.

108 "Canada Is Leading the Pack in Mixed Unions," *Maclean's*, 29 July 2014.

109 See Sylvia B. Fishman and Steven M. Cohen, "Family, Engagement, and Jewish Continuity among American Jews," *The Jewish People Policy Institute*, June 2017.

110 See Theodore Sasson, Janet Krasner Aronson, Fern Chertok, Charles Kadushin, and Leonard Saxe, "Millennial Children of Intermarriage: Religious Upbringing, Identification, and Behavior among Children of Jewish and non-Jewish Parents," *Contemporary Jewry* 37 (2017): 99–123.

CHAPTER SIX

1 Irving Abella, *A Coat of Many Colours: Two Centuries of Jewish Life in Canada* (Toronto: Lester and Orpen Dennys, 1990); Gerald J.J. Tulchinsky, *Taking Root: The Origins of the Canadian Jewish Community* (Toronto: Lester Publishing Co., 1990); Gerald J.J. Tulchinsky, *Branching Out: The Transformation of the Canadian Jewish Community* (Toronto: Stoddart, 1998); Stephen Speisman, *The Jews of Toronto: A History to 1937* (Toronto: McClelland and Stewart, 1979). The argument that the Jewish community remained essentially fragmented is mine, not theirs.

2 Tulchinsky, *Taking Root*, see chapter 13.

3 Lewis A. Coser, *The Functions of Social Conflict* (Glencoe, I L: The Free Press, 1956).

4 Selma Stern, *The Court Jew: A Contribution to the History of Absolutism in Central Europe* (Philadelphia: Jewish Publication Society, 1950).

5 Mark Zborowski and Elizabeth Herzog, *Life Is with People* (New York: Schocken, 1962).

6 John Kralt, *Atlas of Residential Concentration for the Census Metropolitan Area of Montreal and Atlas of Residential Concentration for the Census Metropolitan Area of Toronto* (Ottawa: Multiculturalism Canada, 1986); Warren E. Kalbach, "Ethnic Residential Segregation in an Urban Setting," in *Ethnic Identity and Equality: Varieties of Experience in a Canadian City*, ed. Raymond Breton, Wsevolod W. Isajiw, Warren E. Kalbach, and Jeffrey G. Reitz (Toronto: University of Toronto Press, 1990), 92–134; Philippe Apparicio, Xavier Leloup, and Philippe Rivet, "La diversité montréalaise à l'épreuve de la ségrégation: Pluralisme et insertion résidentielle des immigrants," *Journal of International Migration and Integration* 8, no. 1 (2007): 63–87; Mohammad Qadeer and Sandeep Agrawal, "Ethnic Enclaves in the Toronto Area and Social Integration: The City as Common Ground." http://www.metropolis.net/pdfs/Evolution of Ethnic Enclaves-Oct27.pdf; Mohammad Qadeer, Sandeep K. Agrawal, and Alexander Lovell, "Evolution of Ethnic Enclaves in the Toronto Metropolitan Area, 2001–2006," *Journal of International Migration and Integration* 11, no. 3 (2010): 315–39. Two observations from the recent research stand out. Firstly, only a minority of each ethnic group in the CMA live in enclaves. Secondly, Jews had the highest proportion (49 per cent) of their population living in an enclave.

7 T.R. Balakrishnan and Feng Hou, "Residential Patterns in Cities," in *Immigrant Canada: Demographic, Economic, and Social Challenges*, ed. Shiva Halli and Leo Driedger (Toronto: University of Toronto Press, 1999); Daniel Hiebert, *A New Residential Order? The Social Geography of Visible Minority and Religious Groups in Montreal, Toronto, and Vancouver in 2031* (Government of Canada, July 2012), http://www.cic.gc.ca/english/resources/research/residential.asp.

There are several ways social scientists measure this concentration. One is simply to compute the proportion of a group living in the fewest numbers of census tracts for a given city. For example, how many census tracts might it take to tally up 90 per cent of the Jews in a given city? If Jews were randomly distributed throughout a city, it would require about 90 per cent of the tracts. As we have seen, in 2006, for Jews in Toronto this required only 30 per cent of the census tracts. Jews are therefore far more concentrated than other minority groups. Another technical measure is an "index of dissimilarity." This is a measure that ranges from zero to one, with zero meaning no concentration and one meaning complete segregation. The index measures the proportion of a group that would have to be reshuffled in a city to approximate the distribution of the key comparison group,

British-origin or French in Montreal. A score of zero denotes a distribution exactly the same as that of the majority group, suggesting very little residential concentration. Studies of Jewish concentration using earlier data as measured by these indices was greater in every Canadian city (except Victoria) and compared to every major Canadian ethnic or racial group.

8 Kalbach, "Ethnic Residential Segregation in an Urban Setting."

9 Judith R. Kramer and Seymour Leventman, *Children of the Gilded Ghetto* (New Haven, CT: Yale University Press, 1961); John Seeley, Alexander Sim, and Elizabeth W. Loosley, *Crestwood Heights* (Toronto: University of Toronto Press, 1956).

10 Amitai Etzioni, "The Ghetto – A Re-evaluation," *Social Forces*, March 1959: 255–62.

11 Jay Brodbar-Nemzer, Steven M. Cohen, Gary A. Tobin, Allan Reitzes, and Charles Shahar, "An Overview of the Canadian Jewish Community," in *The Jews in Canada*, ed. Robert J. Brym, William Shaffir, and Morton Weinfeld (Toronto: Oxford University Press, 1993), 39–72.

12 Charles Shahar and Randal Schnoor, *A Survey of Jewish Life in Montreal* (Montreal: Federation of Jewish Community Services of Montreal, 1997), 38–9. A survey of Montreal Jews in 1991 found about 48 per cent claimed that "all or most" of their neighbours were Jews and another 39 per cent that "some" were Jews. Even more revealing, in a 1996 Montreal survey, 44 per cent said it was "very important" and 38 per cent that it was "somewhat important" that they live in a neighbourhood with a sizeable Jewish population.

13 Wsevolod W. Isajiw, "Ethnic Identity Retention," in Breton et al., *Ethnic Identity and Equality*, 57; Charles Shahar and Tina Rosenbaum, *Jewish Life in Greater Toronto: A Survey of the Attitudes and Behaviours of Greater Toronto's Jewish Community* (Toronto: UJA Federation, 2005).

14 Daphne Gottlieb Taras and Gerry Beitel, *Preliminary Analysis, Jewish Community Council Survey January 30, 1997* (Calgary: Jewish Community Council, 1997). The study surveyed 680 Jews in 1996. The Montreal, Toronto, and Calgary surveys used different sampling techniques: Jewish community lists, Jewish-sounding names, or a more random procedure. They all came up with similar results.

15 Marshall Sklare and Joseph Greenblum, *Jewish Identity on the Suburban Frontier: A Study of Group Survival in an Open Society* (New York: Basic Books, 1967), 287–8.

16 Charles R. Snyder, "Culture and Jewish Sobriety: The Ingroup-Outgroup Factor," in *The Jews: Social Patterns of an American Group*, ed. Marshall Sklare (Glencoe, IL: The Free Press, 1958), 560–94; Raphael Patai, *The*

Jewish Mind (New York: Charles Scribner's Sons, 1977), 433–46; personal communication with Montreal bartender Michael Goldman, 28 October 1997. This was also confirmed in an interview with a hotel banquet-hall manager. Another way to estimate Jewish drinking patterns is to compare the total alcohol consumption per capita per year of Israel with other countries. World Health Organization data for 2010, from their Global Status Report on Alcohol, is revealing. Israel ranked 142, with 2.8 litres. Belarus ranked first, at 17.5. Even recognizing that maybe 18 per cent of the Israeli population is Muslim, the difference is dramatic. There is little debate that Jews drink to excess less often than non-Jews, though some claim they are drinking more than they used to.

17 Raymond Breton, "Institutional Completeness of Ethnic Communities and the Personal Relations of Immigrants," *American Journal of Sociology* 70 (1955): 93–205.

18 Daniel Elazar, *Community and Polity: The Organizational Dynamics of American Jewry* (Philadelphia: Jewish Publication Society, 1976). With political scientist Harold Waller, Elazar has also written a major study of the Canadian Jewish polity: *Maintaining Consensus: The Canadian Jewish Polity in the Postwar World* (Lanham and Jerusalem: University Press of America and the Jerusalem Center for Public Affairs, 1990).

19 Abella, *A Coat of Many Colours*, 154–64, 189–90.

20 Andy Levy-Ajzenkopf, "Is CIJA Better or Worse than What Came Before?," *Canadian Jewish News*, 27 March 2013.

21 Andy Levy-Ajzenkopf, "Legitimacy Questions Continue to Plague CIJA," *Canadian Jewish News*, 23 December 2011.

22 Zach Paikin and James Gutman, "It's Time to Bring Back Canadian Jewish Congress," *Canadian Jewish News*, 20 November 2015; David Noble, "The New Israel Lobby in Action," *Canadian Dimension*, 1 November 2005.

23 Harold Troper and Morton Weinfeld, *Old Wounds: Jews, Ukrainians, and the Hunt for Nazi War Criminals in Canada* (Markham, ON: Viking, 1988).

24 David Taras and Morton Weinfeld, "Continuity and Criticism: North American Jews and Israel," in *The Jews in Canada*, ed. Robert J. Brym, William Shaffir, and Morton Weinfeld (Toronto: Oxford University Press, 1993), 293–310.

25 Elazar and Waller, *Maintaining Consensus*.

26 Morton Weinfeld and William Eaton, *A Survey of the Jewish Community of Montreal* (Montreal: Jewish Community Research Institute, 1979); Charles Shahar, *Jewish Life in Montreal: A Survey of the Attitudes, Beliefs and Behaviours of Montreal's Jewish Community* (Montreal: Federation CJA, 2010); Shahar and Rosenbaum, *Jewish Life in Greater Toronto*.

27 Michael Grange and Andrew Willis, "Teeing Up for Snob Appeal," *Globe and Mail*, 6 September 2003.

28 Morton Weinfeld, "Canadian Jews, Dual/Divided Loyalties, and the Tebbit Cricket Test," *Canadian Ethnic Studies* 43, no. 3 (2011): 59–80.

29 Carl E. James, *Perspectives on Racism and the Human Services Sector* (Toronto: University of Toronto Press, 1996).

30 Harold Troper and Morton Weinfeld, "Diversity in Canada," in *Ethnicity, Politics, and Public Policy: Case Studies in Canadian Diversity*, ed. Harold Troper and Morton Weinfeld (Toronto: University of Toronto Press, 1999), 3–25; Morton Weinfeld, "The Challenge of Ethnic Match: Minority Origin Professionals in Health and Social Services," in Troper and Weinfeld, *Ethnicity, Politics, and Public Policy*, 117–41.

31 See Alissa Levine, "Female Genital Operations: Canadian Realities, Concerns, and Policy Recommendations," in Troper and Weinfeld, *Ethnicity, Politics, and Public Policy*, 26–53; Stephanie Levitz, "Government Poll's Results Suggest Wide Support for Tory Niqab Position," *The Huffington Post*, 24 September 2015.

32 See note 1 in this chapter.

33 These issues are explored in *Ethnicity, Politics, and Public Policy in Canada*.

34 Josh Nathan-Kazis, "26 Billion Bucks: The Jewish Charity Industry Uncovered," *The Forward*, 24 March 2014.

35 Lauren Markoe, "Study: Most Jewish Charitable Giving Goes to Jewish Groups." *The Washington Post*, 16 January 2014.

36 Arnold Dashefsky and Bernard Melvin Lazerwitz, *Charitable Choices: Philanthropic Decisions of Donors in the American Jewish Community* (Lanham, MD: Lexington Books, 2009).

37 Bobby Kleinman, personal communication, 6 October 1997.

38 Gary A. Tobin and Aryeh Weinberg, *A Study of Jewish Foundations* (Institute for Jewish and Community Research, San Francisco, 2007).

39 Brodbar-Nemzer et al., "An Overview of the Canadian Jewish Community"; Shahar, *Jewish Life in Montreal*; Shahar and Rosenbaum, *Jewish Life in Greater Toronto*; Luis Lugo, Alan Cooperman, Gregory A. Smith, Conrad Hackett, Cary Funk, Neha Sahgal, Phillip Connor, Jessica Hamar Martinez et al., *A Portrait of Jewish Americans: Findings from a Pew Research Center of U.S. Jews* (Washington, DC: Pew Research Center's Religion and Public Life, 2013). Though the dollar amounts referred to here are given in their countries' respective currencies, they are an accurate reflection of the different rates of gift-giving, as the average American income is higher than the Canadian.

40 Norbert Fruehauf, "The Bottom Line: Major Gifts to Federation Campaigns," in *Contemporary Jewish Philanthropy in America*, ed. Barry A. Kosmin (New York: Rowman and Littlefield, 1991), 173–85.

41 Federation CJA Impact Report, 2015, http://www.federationcja.org/media/mediaContent/PAA_15102_Impact_book_digital.pdf; UJA Federation of Greater Toronto, "UJA Annual Campaign" Report to the Community, Annual Report for 2015, United Way, Toronto and York Region, http://www.ujafederation.report/campaign/annual-campaign.

42 Bobby Kleinman, personal communication, 5 July 2000.

43 UJA Federation of greater Toronto, http://jewishtoronto.com/ujais/jewish-foundation; The Jewish Community Foundation of Montreal, http://www.jcfmontreal.org/en/foundation+at+40/; The Jewish Foundation of Manitoba: Financial Statements, 2014, http://www.jewishfoundation.org/documents/2014JFMFinancialStatements-FINAL.pdf.

44 *Directory of Foundations and Grants* (Toronto: Canadian Centre for Philanthropy, 1997).

45 Greenberg, "I'll Give It My Way"; Kosmin, "Dimensions of Contemporary American Jewish Philanthropy." Another study of data from the *American Foundation Directory* for 1987, ten years earlier than the Canadian data cited above, provides details of 5,148 private American foundations with either assets greater than one million dollars or giving greater than US$100,000. There were 355 foundations which specified Jewish giving, or 7 per cent of the total – much less than the Canadian 29 per cent cited above – though still above the 2 per cent of Jews in the population. Religious causes were popular. There were 437 that specified Protestant giving and 155 for Catholic giving. There were seventy-five entries targeting Israel compared to only four for Italy and three for Poland.

46 Martin Turcotte, "Charitable Giving by Canadians," in *Canadian Social Trends*, Statistics Canada, 16 April 2012; Ida E. Berger, "The Influence of Religion on Philanthropy in Canada," *Voluntas* 17 (2006): 115–32.

47 Reginald Bibby, *Unknown Gods: The Ongoing Story of Religion in Canada* (Toronto: Stoddart, 1993), 107.

48 Elazar and Waller, *Maintaining Consensus*.

49 Brodbar-Nemzer et al., "An Overview of the Canadian Jewish Community," 46; Shahar, *Jewish Life in Montreal*; Shahar and Rosenbaum, *Jewish Life in Greater Toronto*.

50 Shahar, *Jewish Life in Montreal*.

51 Shahar and Rosenbaum, *Jewish Life in Greater Toronto*.

52 Lugo et al., *A Portrait of Jewish Americans*.

53 Raymond Breton, "The Ethnic Group as a Political Resource in Relation to Problems of Incorporation: Perceptions and Attitudes," in Breton et al., *Ethnic Identity and Equality*, 196–255.

54 Franklin Bialystok, "NeoNazis in Toronto: The Allan Gardens Riot," *Canadian Jewish Studies*, special issue, "New Perspectives on Canada, the Holocaust, and Survivors," vols. 4 and 5 (1996–97): 1–38.

55 Weinfeld and Eaton, *A Survey of the Jewish Community of Montreal*; Shahar, *A Survey of Jewish Life in Montreal*, 26; Breton et al., *Ethnic Identity and Equality*. In Montreal, as far back as 1979, only 16 per cent claimed that the "leadership of the Jewish community" represented the interests of "a few Jews." Most felt that leaders were in touch with the majority. In 1996, only 4 per cent claimed they were dissatisfied with the level of services provided by the Jewish federation. The situation was very similar in Toronto. By and large Jewish Torontonians, compared to other groups, are most likely to feel ordinary community members have much to say about how things are run, that their leaders are concerned with community problems and interests, and that leaders seek to get community approval. In addition, Jews are the most likely group to feel their leaders are taken seriously by politicians, and have enough connections to do their job.

56 Harold Waller, "The Canadian Jewish Polity: Power and Leadership in the Jewish Community," in *The Jews in Canada*, 254–69.

57 Jean R. Burnet and Howard Palmer, *Coming Canadians: An Introduction to a History of Canada's Peoples* (Toronto: McClelland and Stewart, 1988).

58 Breton, "The Ethnic Group as a Political Resource."

59 See Steven Cohen and Arnold Eisen, *The Jew Within: Self, Community, and Commitment among the Variety of Moderately Affiliated* (Boston: The Susan and David Wilstein Institute, 1998).

60 Dr Frank Guttman, personal communication, 4 February 1998.

CHAPTER SEVEN

1 Enoch Padolsky, "Canadian Ethnic Minority Literature in English," in *Ethnicity and Culture in Canada: The Research Landscape*, edited by John Berry and Jean Laponce (Toronto: University of Toronto Press, 1994), 361–86.

2 Ladino (Judeo-Spanish), Arabic, and Judeo-Arabic have been spoken by Sephardi immigrants to Canada. For some Sephardi Jews, these languages

continue to fulfil many of the symbolic and ritualistic functions that Yiddish does for Ashkenazi Jews. But they are no longer used for daily communication, and did not establish themselves in an institutional sense as did Yiddish.

3 Leo Davids, "Hebrew and Yiddish in Canada: A Linguistic Transition Completed," *Canadian Jewish Studies* 18/19 (2011): 39–76.

4 Joe Friesen, "Yiddish Finding a Way to Survive in Canada," *Globe and Mail*, 7 December 2012; Josh Dehaas, "Yiddish Lives on Canadian Campuses," *Macleans*, 22 December 2011.

5 Davids, "Hebrew and Yiddish in Canada"; See Table 1 in the Appendix.

6 Naghmeh Babaee, "Heritage Language Learning in Canadian Public Schools: Language Rights Challenges" (PhD diss., Department of Education, University of Manitoba, 2012).

7 Davids, "Hebrew and Yiddish in Canada."-

8 Charles Shahar, Morton Weinfeld, and Randal Schnoor, *Survey of the Hassidic and Ultra-Orthodox Communities in Outremont and Surrounding Areas* (Outremont: Coalition of Outremont Hassidic Organizations, 1997).

9 Shahar, "Sépharade 2000," 12.

10 Jeffrey Shandler, *Adventures in Yiddishland: Postvernacular Language and Culture* (Berkely, CA: University of California Press, 2005).

11 Marcel Danesi, "Ethnic Language and Acculturation: The Case of Italo-Canadians," *Canadian Ethnic Studies* 17, no. 1 (1985): 88–103.

12 See Irving Howe, *World of Our Fathers* (New York: Simon and Schuster, 1976), 588.

13 Rebecca Margolis, "Culture in Motion: Yiddish in Canadian Jewish Life," *Journal of Religion and Popular Culture* 21 (2009): 1–51; Pierre Anctil, "'Nit ahin un nit aher': Yiddish Scholarship in Canada," *Canadian Jewish Studies* 21 (2013). For a more popular exposition, see the work of Canadian Michael Wex, *Born to Kvetch: Yiddish Language and Culture in All Its Moods* (New York: St Martin's Press, 2005).

14 Elizabeth Bromstein, "Queer Klezmer," *Now Toronto*, 2 September 2004; Kathleen Peratis, "And the Award Goes to … Queer Yiddishkeit," *The Forward*, 23 February 2007; Dana Astmann, "Freylekhe Felker: Queer Subculture in the Klezmer Revival," in *Discourses in Music* 4, no. 3 (University of Toronto, 2003), http://library.music.utoronto.ca/discourses-in-music/v4n3a2.html.

15 Bromstein, "Queer Klezmer."

16 See Ira Robinson, Pierre Anctil, and Mervin Butovsky, *eds., An Everyday Miracle: Yiddish Culture in Montreal* (Montreal: Véhicule

Press, 1990); and Orenstein, "Yiddish Culture in Canada: Yesterday and Today."

17 See Ruth Wisse, Mervin Butovsky, Howard Roiter, and Morton Weinfeld, "Jewish Culture and Canadian Culture," in *The Canadian Jewish Mosaic*, ed. Morton Weinfeld, William Shaffir, and Irwin Cotler (Toronto: John Wiley and Sons, 1981), 315–42. For a general review of Canadian Jewish writing, see Alex Hart, "Jews in English Literature," in *Canada's Jews: In Time, Space, and Spirit*, ed. Ira Robinson (Boston: Academic Studies Press, 2013), 361–411.

18 Malcolm Lester, personal communication, 10 September 1998.

19 For a review of the work of Sam Borenstein, see William Kuhns and Leo Rosshandler, *Sam Borenstein* (Toronto: McClelland and Stewart, 1978). For a general review of the contributions of various Canadian Jewish artists, see Loren Lerner and Suzanne Rackover, "Jews and Canadian Art," in Robinson, *Canada's Jews*, 422–41.

20 Luis Lugo, Alan Cooperman, Gregory A. Smith, Conrad Hackett, Cary Funk, Neha Sahgal, Phillip Connor, Jessica Hamar Martinez et al., *A Portrait of Jewish Americans: Findings from a Pew Research Center Survey of U.S. Jews* (Washington, DC: Pew Research Center's Religion and Public Life Project, 2013).

21 Charles Shahar and Tina Rosenbaum, *Jewish Life in Greater Toronto: A Survey of the Attitudes and Behaviours of Greater Toronto's Jewish Community* (Toronto: UJA Federation, 2005).

22 Agriculture and Agri-Food Canada, *The Specialty Food Market in North America* (Government of Canada Report, 2012).

23 Leona Reynolds-Zayak, *Consumer Trends in the Canadian Kosher Market* (Alberta Agriculture: Food and Rural Development, March 2004).

24 Agriculture and Agri-Food Canada, *The Specialty Food Market in North America*.

25 Bonny Reichert, "Latest Wave of Jewish Cuisine Is Unapologetically Ethnic," *Globe and Mail*, 24 February 2015.

26 Mervin Butovsky, in Wisse et al., "Jewish Culture and Canadian Culture," 319.

27 For an analysis of North American Jewish food habits, see Jonathan Deutsch and Rachel D. Saks, *Jewish American Food Culture* (Westport, CT: Bison Books, 2009).

28 Wsevolod W. Isajiw, "Ethnic Identity Retention," in *Ethnic Identity and Equality: Varieties of Experience in a Canadian City*, ed. Raymond Breton, Wsevolod W. Isajiw, Warren E. Kalbach, and Jeffrey G. Reitz (Toronto: University of Toronto Press, 1990), 68–9.

29 The *Canadian Jewish News*, www.cjnews.com/media-kit; www.cjnews.com/about-us.
30 Yoni Goldstein, "From Yoni's Desk: A Response to a Controversial Column," *Canadian Jewish News*, 5 May 2017; Mira Sucharov, "Why I'm Resigning My *CJN* Column," *Canadian Jewish News*, 2 June 2017.
31 See Pierre Anctil, "Aspects de la thématique juive dans le *CJN*, édition de Montréal, 1977–1982," *Canadian Ethnic Studies* 16, no. 1 (1984): 29–57.
32 Charles Shahar, *Jewish Life in Montreal: A Survey of the Attitudes, Beliefs and Behaviours of Montreal's Jewish Community* (Montreal: Federation CJA, 2010); Shahar and Rosenbaum, *Jewish Life in Greater Toronto*.
33 Yoel Cohen, *God, Jews and the Media* (London: Routledge, 2012), 272.
34 Isajiw, "Ethnic Identity Retention," 84.
35 From the late 1970s through the 1980s, there was an attempt to transform the periodical *Viewpoints* into a Canadian Jewish intellectual journal, led heroically by William Abrams and his wife Jeannette in Montreal. (I was involved in the effort.) For a time, it was included as a supplement to the *CJN*, which solved its distribution problem. It never really established a significant, independent constituency.
36 Robert Fulford, personal communication, 28 April 1998.
37 Jens Hack, "Demand for Reprint of Hitler's 'Mein Kampf' Overwhelms German Publisher," *Haaretz*, 8 January 2016; Angela Charlton, "Jews in France Ask: Is Wearing the Skullcap a Risk or a Religious Right?," *Globe and Mail*, 14 January 2016; Konrad Yakabuski, "The York Mural Controversy: When Art and Politics Collide," *Globe and Mail*, 27 January 2016.
38 Shahar, *Jewish Life in Montreal*; Shahar and Rosenbaum, *Jewish Life in Greater Toronto*.
39 Lugo et al., *A Portrait of Jewish Americans*.
40 Of course, there may variation in understanding what a "conversation" can entail. See Table 1 in the Appendix.
41 Lugo et al., *A Portrait of Jewish Americans*.
42 Leora Frucht, "Israel's Canadian Content," *The Gazette*, 26 April 1998.
43 Eric Fleisch and Theodore Sasson, *The New Philanthropy: American Jewish Giving to Israeli Organizations* (Maurice and Marilyn Cohen Center for Modern Jewish Studies, Brandeis University, April 2012), http://www.brandeis.edu/cmjs/pdfs/TheNewPhilanthropy.pdf.
44 Josh Nathan-Kazis, "26 Billion Bucks: The Jewish Charity Industry Uncovered," *The Forward*, 24 March 2014; Fleisch and Sasson, *The New Philanthropy*; Benjy Cannon, "American Jews, Money, and the Israel-Palestine Conflict," *Open Democracy*, 9 April 2014; "2015–16 Allocations

Snapshot," *Federation CJA*, federationcja.org; "Annual Report 2014–2015," *UJA Federation of Greater Toronto*.

45 "The 40 Worst Colleges for Jewish Students, 2016: The Algemeiner's 1st Annual List of the US and Canada's Worst Campuses for Jewish Students," *The Algemeiner*, https://www.algemeiner.com/the-40-worst-colleges-for-jewish-students-2016/.

46 "Annual Tourism Report, All Time Record for Israel," *Independent Media Review Analysis*, 9 January 2014.

47 "3.3 Million Visitors to Israel in 2014," *Israel Ministry of Foreign Affairs*, 5 January 2015, http://mfa.gov.il/MFA/PressRoom/2015/Pages/3-3-million-visitors-to-Israel-in-2014.aspx.

48 Pew Research Center, *Israel's Religiously Divided Society*, 8 March 2016, http://www.pewforum.org/2016/03/08/israels-religiously-divided-society/.

49 "The Israel Experience: Summaries of Research Papers Prepared for the CRB Foundation" (Montreal, CRB Foundation, March 1992).

50 Leonard Saxe, Michelle Shain, Graham Wright, Shahar Hecht, Shira Fishman, and Theodore Sasson, *The Impact of Taglit-Birthright Israel: 2012 Update*, Cohen Center Publications (Waltham, MA: Brandeis University, 2012).

51 Alison Flood, "New Edition of *Mein Kampf* Set to Land on German Bestseller Lists," *The Guardian*, 13 January 2016; Sam Sokol, "Holocaust Claims Conference Fraud Likely 'Much Higher' than $57 Million," *Jerusalem Post*, 8 July 2015; Lila Sarick, "Cover Story: Returning Nazi-Looted Art in Canada," *Canadian Jewish News*, 19 July 2015; Steve Busfield, "Irving Loses Holocaust Libel Case," *The Guardian*, 11 April 2000; Deborah Lipstadt, *Denying the Holocaust: The Growing Assault on Truth and Memory* (New York: Plume, 1994).

52 Jeff Sallot, "Polish Canadians Vent Anger at PM," *Globe and Mail*, 23 January 1999, A5; Allan Levine, "The Prime Minister, Auschwitz, and the Battle for Memory," *Globe and Mail*, 26 January 1999, A17; Bernard Wisniewski, "What the Polish Christian Stake Is in Auschwitz," *Globe and Mail*, 8 February 1999, A13. The recent controversy over the alleged role of Poles in the massacre of the Jews of the town of Jedwabne in 1941 is a new flashpoint. See Jan T. Gross, "Annals of War," *The New Yorker*, 12 March 2001, 64–71; Murray Brewster, "Justin Trudeau Pays Emotional Visit to Auschwitz," *CBC News*, 10 July 2016.

53 Lugo et al., *A Portrait of Jewish Americans*.

54 Harold Troper and Morton Weinfeld, *Old Wounds: Jews, Ukrainians, and the Hunt for Nazi War Criminals in Canada* (Markham, ON: Viking, 1988).

55 David Cesarani and Paul A. Levine, eds., *Bystanders to the Holocaust: A Re-Evaluation* (London: Frank Cass Publishers, 2002).

56 For a provocative review of the topic, see Peter Novick, *The Holocaust in American Life* (Boston: Houghton Mifflin, 1999).

57 David Engel, "Crisis and Lachrymosity: On Salo Baron, Neobaronianism, and the Study of Modern European Jewish History," *Jewish History* 20, no. 3 (2006): 243–64.

58 John Sigal and Morton Weinfeld, *Trauma and Rebirth: Intergenerational Consequences of the Holocaust* (New York: Praeger, 1989). Dr Sigal was a psychologist and psychoanalyst associated with the Institute of Community and Family Psychiatry of the Sir Mortimer B. Davis Jewish General Hospital in Montreal.

59 The Canadian Jewish Heritage Network, "Montreal Holocaust Memorial Centre," last modified 2014, http://www.cjhn.ca/en/permalink/cjhn45523.

60 Ira Basen, "Memory Becomes a Minefield at Canada's Museum for Human Rights," *Globe and Mail*, 20 August 2011; Graeme Hamilton, "Canada's Human Rights Museum Was Meant as a Unifying Force, but, So Far, Has Only Inspired Criticism," *The National Post*, 27 September 2013.

61 Reprinted in *Beyond Imagination: Canadians Write about the Holocaust*, ed. Jerry S. Grafstein (Toronto: McClelland and Stewart, 1995), 78.

62 Alti Rodal, "Legacies: A Second Generation Reflects," in Grafstein, *Beyond Imagination*, 60–75.

63 Peter C. Newman, "The Guns of Biarritz," in Grafstein, *Beyond Imagination*, 1–7.

64 David Lewis Stein, "Dress British, Think Yiddish," in Grafstein, *Beyond Imagination*, 121.

65 Barbara Kingstone, "A Journey into the Holocaust," in Grafstein, *Beyond Imagination*, 127.

66 A classic case took place in the early 1970s, when Montreal's Saidye Bronfman Centre was scheduled to produce *The Man in the Glass Booth* by Robert Shaw. The play deals with the Holocaust, is loosely based on the Eichmann trial, and blurs the clear distinctions between the guilty and the victims. Organizations of Holocaust survivors were deeply offended and demanded that the Saidye Bronfman Centre cancel the play. They did, to charges that artistic freedom was compromised – it was – and this led to the departure of the Centre's artistic director.

67 Butovsky, in Wisse et al., "Jewish Culture and Canadian Culture."

68 Howard Roiter, in Wisse et al., "Jewish Culture and Canadian Culture," 320.

69 Malcolm Lester, personal communication, 10 September 1998.

70 Mervin Butovsky, personal communication, 10 October 1997; Malcolm Lester, personal communication, 10 September 1998; Robert Fulford, personal communication, 28 April 1998.

71 Eli Mandel, "The Ethnic Voice in Canadian Writing," in *Identities: The Impact of Ethnicity on Canadian Society*, ed. Wsevolod W. Isajiw (Toronto: Peter Martin, 1977), 57–68.

72 George Woodcock, *Mordecai Richler* (Toronto: McClelland and Stewart, 1971), 20–1.

73 Wisse et al., "Jewish Culture and Canadian Culture," 330. For a review of English-language Canadian Jewish literature, see Alex Hart, "Jews in English Literature," in *Canada's Jews: In Time, Space, and Spirit*, ed. Ira Robinson (Boston: Academic Studies Press, 2013), 361–411.

74 Peter S. Li, "The Multicultural World of Visible Minorities and the Art World in Canada," *Canadian Review of Sociology and Anthropology* 31, no. 4 (November 1994): 365–91.

75 For a discussion of the difficulties facing hip-hop and rap music in Canada, see Rebecca J. Haines, "Break North: Rap Music and Hip Hop Culture in Canada," in *Ethnicity, Politics, and Public Policy: Case Studies in Canadian Diversity*, ed. Harold Troper and Morton Weinfeld (Toronto: University of Toronto Press, 1999), 54–88.

76 Howard Adelman, "Blacks and Jews: Racism, AntiSemitism, and *Showboat*," in *Multiculturalism, Jews, and Identities in Canada*, ed. Howard Adelman and John Simpson (Jerusalem: Magnes Press, 1996), 128–78; Frances Henry, Carol Tator, Winston Mattis, and Tim Rees, *The Colour of Democracy* (Toronto: Harcourt Brace, 1995), 218–23.

77 Ibid., 222.

78 "Toronto Theater Won't Stage *My Name Is Rachel Corrie*," CBC News, 22 December 2006; George Perry, "Review: *My Name Is Rachel Corrie*," *Mooney on Theater*, 21 October 2012.

79 Yves Thériault, *Aaron* (Waterloo, ON: Wilfrid Laurier University Press, 2007).

80 Of course, there are likely political and strategic considerations at work here. Still, in the 1930s, the same SSJB lobbied the Canadian government to keep Jews out. For a review of recent treatments of Jewish themes in French literature in Canada, see Chantal Ringuet, "Jews in French Literature," in Robinson, *Canada's Jews*, 412–21; Brendan Kelly, "*Felix et Meira* Explores Love across the Cultural Divide," *Montreal Gazette*, 29 January 2015.

81 William Novak and Moshe Waldoks, eds., *The Big Book of Jewish Humor* (New York: Harper and Row, 1981), xviii–xix.

82 Ibid., xviii. Jewish jokes, and the attitudes surrounding this Jewish celebration of humour, can be found on the YouTube channel "Old Jews Telling Jokes." A famous *Seinfeld* episode also exemplifies this when a Gentile character, a dentist, converts to Judaism "because of the jokes."

CHAPTER EIGHT

1 This chapter, while revised and expanded, draws from my chapter "The Educational Continuum: A Community Priority," in *From Immigration to Integration: The Canadian Jewish Experience*, ed. Ruth Klein and Frank Diamant, Millennium ed. (Toronto: Institute for International Affairs of B'nai-Brith Canada and Malcom Lester, 2001), 197–213.

2 See Peter Li, *The Chinese in Canada*, 2nd ed. (Toronto: Oxford University Press, 1998). This does not mean that such books, which present overviews of Canadian minority groups, are flawed but rather that the issue of ethnic or religious education is not central to the group's agenda. There are exceptions for other groups. See Jasmin Zine, *Canadian Islamic Schools* (Toronto: University of Toronto Press, 2008); George J. Sefa Dei and Arlo Kempf, *New Perspectives on African-Centred Education in Canada* (Toronto: Canadian Scholars' Press Inc., 2013).

3 Steven M. Cohen, Ron Miller, Ira M. Sheskin, and Berna Torr, *Camp Works: The Long-Term Impact of Jewish Overnight Camp* (Foundation for Jewish Camp, Spring 2011).

4 Jim Cummins, "Heritage Language Learning and Teaching," in *Ethnicity and Culture in Canada: The Research Landscape*, ed. Harold Troper and Morton Weinfeld (Toronto: University of Toronto Press, 1999), 435–56.

5 Toronto District School Board, "Languages," last modified 2014, http://www.tdsb.on.ca/HighSchool/YourSchoolDay/Curriculum/Languages.aspx.

6 Reginald Bibby, *Beyond the Gods and Back: Religion's Demise and Rise and Why It Matters* (Lethbridge, AB: Project Canada Books, 2011); Reginald Bibby, *Unknown Gods: The Ongoing Story of Religion in Canada* (Toronto: Stoddart, 1993).

7 Bibby, *Beyond the Gods and Back*, 13.

8 Bibby, *Unknown Gods*, 99.

9 Deani A. Van Pelt, Patricia A. Allison, and Derek J. Allison, "Ontario's Private Schools: Who Chooses Them and Why?" in *Studies in Education Policy* (Vancouver: The Fraser Institute, May 2007), https://www.fraserinstitute.org/sites/default/files/OntariosPrivateSchools.pdf.

10 William Hoverd, Erin LeBrun, and Leo Van Arragon, "Religion and Education in the Provinces of Quebec and Ontario," n.d., http://

religionanddiversity.ca/media/uploads/religion_and_education_in_the_provinces_of_quebec_and_ontario_report.pdf.

11 Jeffrey Reitz, Rupa Banerjee, Mai Phan, and Jordan Thompson, "Race, Religion and the Social Integration of New Immigrant Minorities in Canada," *International Migration Review* 43, no 4 (2009): 695–726.

12 Charles Shahar, *Jewish Life in Montreal: A Survey of the Attitudes, Beliefs and Behaviours of Montreal's Jewish Community* (Montreal: Federation CJA, 2010); Charles Shahar and Tina Rosenbaum, *Jewish Life in Greater Toronto: A Survey of the Attitudes and Behaviours of Greater Toronto's Jewish Community* (Toronto: UJA Federation, 2005).

13 Shahar, *Jewish Life in Montreal.* In a survey of Montreal Jews, 42 per cent of respondents received a Jewish elementary day-school education; 27 per cent attended a Jewish high school. The drop-off in day school education after elementary school, and after bar or bat mitzvah, is common; what is surprising is that the retention rate is as high as it is. About 65 per cent of Montreal parents said their school-age children are currently attending a Jewish day school. These rates may be high because of provincial funding, as mentioned earlier, to help meet the needs of Jewish schools in Quebec. Levels in Toronto would be slightly less.

14 The system in Canada is more comprehensive than that in the United States or in Europe. Only Jewish communities in South Africa, Australia, and in some Latin American countries compare with Canada in the degree to which children are given a day-school education.

15 For a review, see Yaacov Glickman, "Jewish Education: Success or Failure," in *The Canadian Jewish Mosaic*, ed. Morton Weinfeld, William Shaffir, and Irwin Cotler (Toronto: John Wiley and Sons, 1981), 113–28.

16 "Montreal Jewish Education: Daycare and Nursery," *Montreal Jewish Directory*; "Schools," Bronfman Jewish Education Center, http://www.jewishinmontreal.com/Category/Montreal-Jewish-Education/Daycare-and-Nursery/.

17 Associated Hebrew Schools of Toronto, "About," last modified 2016, http://www.ahschools.com/about/jewish-toronto.

18 Lila Sarick, "Cover Story: Jewish High Schools Struggle with Enrolment," *Canadian Jewish News*, 25 March 2015; Lila Sarick, "Dwindling Affordability Puts Day Schools at Crossroads," *Canadian Jewish News*, 1 February 2017; Lila Sarick, "Tanenbaum CHAT Closes Northern Campus and Slashes Tuition," *Canadian Jewish News*, 7 March 2017.

19 Janice Arnold "New $30-million Herzliah High School Taking Shape," *Canadian Jewish News*, 20 July 2017.

20 Luis Lugo, Alan Cooperman, Gregory A. Smith, Conrad Hackett, Cary Funk, Neha Sahgal, Phillip Connor, Jessica Hamar Martinez et al., *A*

Portrait of Jewish Americans: Findings from a Pew Research Center of U.S. Jews (Washington, DC: Pew Research Center's Religion and Public Life Project, 2013).

21 Gabriel Horenczyk and Hagit Hacohen Wolf, "Jewish Identity and Jewish Education: The Jewish Identity Space and Its Contribution to Research and Practice," in *International Handbook of Jewish Education*, ed. Helena Miller, Lisa D. Grant, and Alex Pomson (Netherlands: Springer, 2011), 183–201.

22 Shahar, *Jewish Life in Montreal.*

23 Paul Attfield, "Jewish Schools Give Kids Identity, Academics and Connectedness," *Globe and Mail*, 25 September 2014.

24 Jay Brodbar-Nemzer, *A First Look* (Toronto: Toronto Jewish Congress, 1991), 54.

25 Steven Cohen and Arnold Eisen, *The Jew Within: Self, Community, and Commitment among the Variety of Moderately Affiliated* (Boston: The Susan and David Wilstein Institute, 1998), 37.

26 Glickman, "Jewish Education"; Steven M. Cohen, "The Impact of Varieties of Jewish Education upon Jewish Identity: An Intergenerational Perspective," *Contemporary Jewry* 16, no. 1 (1995): 68–96.

27 James Coleman, Thomas Hoffer, and Sally Kilgore, *High School Achievement: Public, Catholic, and Private Schools Compared* (New York: Basic Books, 1982).

28 Fred Genesee and Wallace. E. Lambert, "Trilingual Education for Majority Language Children," *Child Development* 54 (1983): 105–14.

29 Jimmy Bitton, "The Devaluation of Minority Experienced at Jewish Day Schools," *Canadian Jewish News*, 3 September 2015; Morton Weinfeld, *The System of Jewish Education in Montreal: An Overview of Current Conflicts and Challenges* (Montreal: Jewish Education Council, 1985). This theme emerged in my study of Jewish schooling in Montreal, and similar concerns apply to the situation in Toronto.

30 "What You Think about Jewish Days Schools in the GTA," *The Jewish Tribune*, 6 August 2013.

31 Paul Lungen, "Day School Fees Vary across Canada," *Canadian Jewish News*, 2 September 2014.

32 Shahar, *Jewish Life in Montreal.*

33 Allan Woods, "Ex-student of Ultra-orthodox Jewish School System in Quebec Wants Compensation for Poor Education," *The Star*, 28 November 2014; Jason Magder, "Quebec to Toughen Laws to Keep Better Track of Students: Proulx," *The Gazette*, 3 June 2016.

34 Morton Weinfeld and Phyllis Zelkowitz, "Reflections on the Jewish Polity and Jewish Education," in *The Jews in Canada*, ed. Robert J. Brym, William

Shaffir, and Morton Weinfeld (Toronto: Oxford University Press, 1993), 142–52.

35 Gerald J.J. Tulchinsky, *Branching Out: The Transformation of the Canadian Jewish Community (Toronto: Lester Publishing Co., 1990),* see chapter 2; Irving Abella, *A Coat of Many Colours: Two Centuries of Jewish Life in Canada (Toronto: Lester and Orpen Dennys, 1990),* 130–3; Stewart Rosenberg, *The Jewish Community in Canada,* vol. 2. (Toronto: McClelland and Stewart, 1971), 265–70.

36 For a review of the American Jewish community's attitudes towards the separation of church and state, see Alan Mittleman, Jonathan D. Sarna, and Robert Licht, eds., *Jews and the American Public Square: Debating Religion and Republic* (Lanham, MD: Rowman and Littlefield Publishers, 2002).

37 Judith R. Baskin, "Jewish Studies in North American Colleges and Universities: Yesterday, Today, and Tomorrow," *Shofar* 32, no. 4 (2014): 9–26.

38 Frances Kraft, "First Mainstream Canadian Seminary Opens Officially," *Canadian Jewish News,* 23 December 2011.

39 Jewish studies courses were found on over thirty-five Canadian campuses in 1998. For a review of the various programs available, and a summary of the evolution of the field in Canada, see Michael Brown, ed., *A Guide to the Study of Jewish Civilization in Canadian Universities* (Toronto and Jerusalem: Centre for Jewish Studies at York University and the International Center for University Teaching of Jewish Civilization, 1998). For more recent listings of Canadian Jewish courses and programs see Canadian-Universities.net, http://www.canadian-universities.net/ Universities/Programs/Jewish_and_Hebrew-Quebec.html.

40 Yechiel Glustein, personal communication, 15 October 1998.

41 For example, see Jonathan S. Woocher, "Jewish Education in the Age of Google," in *What We Now Know about Jewish Education: Perspective on Research for Practice,* ed. Roberta Louis Goodman, Paul A. Flexner, and Linda Dale Bloomberg (Los Angeles: Torah Aura Productions, 2008), 32–8.

42 Alan M. Dershowitz, *The Vanishing American Jew (New York: Little, Brown and Company, 1997),* 333.

CHAPTER NINE

1 Gerald de Maio and Louis Henri Bolce III, "Our Secularist Democratic Party," *The Public Interest* 149 (Fall 2002): 3–20.

2 Emma Green, "Are Democrats Losing the Jews?" *The Atlantic,* 13 November 2014; Kenneth D. Wald, "The Choosing People: Interpreting the Puzzling Politics of American Jewry," *Politics and Religion* 8 (2015): 4–35;

Josh Zeitz, "No, Jews Aren't Defecting to the GOP," *Politico*, 7 April 2015. Jewish voters were roughly 30 per cent more likely to vote Democrat than the general electorate between 1948 and 2008.

3 Irving Abella, *A Coat of Many Colours: Two Centuries of Jewish Life in Canada* (Toronto: Lester and Orpen Dennys, 1990), 221.

4 Donald Avery, *Dangerous Foreigners* (Toronto: McClelland and Stewart, 1979); Merrily Weisbord, *The Strangest Dream: Canadian Communism, the Spy Trials, and the Cold War* (Toronto: Lester and Orpen Dennys, 1983).

5 Jean Laponce, "Left or Centre: The Canadian Jewish Electorate, 1953–1983," in *The Jews in Canada*, ed. Robert J. Brym, William Shaffir, and Morton Weinfeld (Toronto: Oxford University Press, 1993), 270–92. This study is based on evidence from 235 national surveys from 1953 to 1983 which included questions about religion and party preference.

6 Jeffrey Simpson, "How the Political Shift among Jewish Voters Plays in Canada," *Globe and Mail*, 28 September 2011.

7 Harold Waller and Morton Weinfeld, "A *Viewpoints* Survey of Canadian Jewish Leadership Opinion," *Viewpoints* 15, no. 4 (8 October 1987).

8 The Canadian Jewish Congress, "Brian Mulroney's Speech on Antisemitism: Israel Is the New Jew," *National Post*, 10 February 2003.

9 *The Jewish Virtual Library,* "Jewish Voting Records: U.S. Presidential Elections," http://www.jewishvirtuallibrary.org/jsource/US-Israel/jewvote.html.

10 Gregory A. Smith and Jessica Martinez, "How the Faithful Voted: A Preliminary 2016 Analysis," *Fact Tank: Pew Research Center*, 9 November 2016; "AJC 2015 Survey of American Jewish Opinion," AJC, https://www.ajc.org/news/ajc-2015-survey-of-american-jewish-opinion; "2000 Annual Survey of American Jewish Opinion," AJC, 28 September 2000; Ron Csillag, "Canadian Jews Condemn Trump's Immigration Moves," *Canadian Jewish News*, 9 February 2017, 14.

11 Brent E. Sasley and Tami A. Jacoby, "Canada's Jewish and Arab Communities and Canadian Foreign Policy," in *Canada and the Middle East: In Theory and Practice*, ed. Paul Heinbecker (Waterloo: Wilfrid Laurier University Press, 2007), 185–204; Paul C. Merkley, "Reversing the Poles: How Pro-Israeli Policy of Canada's Conservative Government May Be Moving Jewish Voters from Left to Right," *Jewish Political Studies Review* 23 (13 April 2012): 1–2; Donald Barry, "Canada and the Middle East Today: Electoral Politics and Foreign Policy," *Arab Studies Quarterly* 32, no. 4 (2010): 191–217.

12 Morton Weinfeld, "If Canada and Israel Are at War, Who Gets My Support? Challenges of Competing Diaspora Loyalties: Marshall Sklare Award Lecture," *Contemporary Jewry* 34, no. 3 (2014): 167–87.

13 "Ignatieff Defends 'War Crime' Comments," CBC News, 13 October 2006.

14 Howard Adelman, "Why the Tories Are Winning the Jewish Vote," *Canadian Jewish News*, 9 September 2015; Michelle Collins, "How the Jewish Vote Swung from Red to Blue," *Embassy*, 11 February 2009.

15 Linda Diebel, "Ignatieff Apologizes for Israeli War Crime Comment," *The Star*, 14 April 2008.

16 Daniel Wolgelerenter, "Campaign Notebook: Four 'Jewish' Battleground Ridings to Watch," *Canadian Jewish News*, 10 August 2015.

17 Janice Arnold, "Most Jews in Riding Voted Tory, Cotler Concedes," *Canadian Jewish News*, 11 May 2011.

18 Simpson, "How the Political Shift among Jewish Voters Plays in Canada."

19 "Jew v. Jew v. Jew v. Jew v. Jew: Six Journalists Debate the Question of Why Shrill Partisanship Is Tearing Apart the Canadian Jewish Community," *The Walrus*, 1 September 2015; Benjamin Shinewald, "As Tories Press for Jewish Support, Jewish Voters Push Back," *Globe and Mail*, 9 October 2015.

20 Michael Taube, "Why Jews Will Continue to Support the Tories," *Canadian Jewish News*, 21 January 2016.

21 For a review of this issue, see Arthur Liebman, *Jews and the Left* (New York: J. Wiley, 1979).

22 Lawrence Fuchs, *The Political Behavior of American Jews* (Glencoe, IL: The Free Press, 1956).

23 Laponce, "Left or Centre," 284.

24 Gerald J.J. Tulchinsky, *Taking Root: The Origins of the Canadian Jewish Community* (Toronto: Lester Publishing Co., 1990), 25.

25 Howard Stanislawski, "Canadian Jewry and Foreign Policy in the Middle East," in *The Canadian Jewish Mosaic*, ed. Morton Weinfeld, William Shaffir, and Irwin Cotler (Toronto: John Wiley and Sons, 1981), 397–414.

26 For a review of this issue, see Charles Flicker, "Next Year in Jerusalem: Joe Clark and the Jerusalem Embassy Affair," *International Journal* 58, no. 1 (2002/03), 115–38.

27 Norman Spector, personal communication, 23 April 1998.

28 Ibid.

29 Morton Weinfeld, "Hugh Segal and the Ethnic Factor," *Globe and Mail*, 23 June 1998.

30 Peyton Lyon, personal communication, 23 June 1998.

31 "Passport Problem Solved: Axworthy," *The Gazette*, 11 October 1997. Two years later, reports began to circulate that Israel was using Canadian

passports to help their Lebanese Christian allies escape from Lebanon as
Israel withdrew its forces from South Lebanon.

32 See Yossi Shain, "The Role of Diasporas in Conflict Perpetuation or
Resolution," *SAIS Review* 22, no. 2 (2002): 115–44; Gabriel Sheffer,
"Transnationalism and Ethnonational Diasporism," *Diaspora* 15 (2006):
121–45.

33 Zvi Ganin, *An Uneasy Relationship: American Jewish Leadership and
Israel, 1948–57* (Syracuse, NY: Syracuse University Press, 2005).

34 Kalyani Thurairajah, "The Case of the Sri Lankan Tamil Diaspora and
Homeland: A Shared Ethnic Identity?" *Studies in Ethnicity and Nationalism* 17, no. 1 (2017): 115–32.

35 Morton Weinfeld, "Canadian Jews, Dual/Divided Loyalties, and the Tebbit
Cricket Test," *Canadian Ethnic Studies* 43, no. 3 (2011): 59–80.

36 Canadians for Justice and Peace in the Middle East, "2017 Survey: On
Israel-Palestine, Canadian Gov't Is Out of Touch," 16 February 2017,
www.cjpme.org/survey; David Zarnett and Jamie Levin, "Opinion: Survey
of Canadians' Views of Sanctions on Israel Flawed," *Canadian Jewish
News*, 4 April 2017.

37 Tulchinsky, *Taking Root*, 60.

38 Rufus Learsi, *The Jews in America: A History* (Cleveland: World Publishing Company, 1954), 202.

39 John Ibbitson, "Leadership Candidates Muddied in the Gutter," *Globe and
Mail*, 6 July 2000.

40 Henry Srebrnik, "Multiculturalism and the Politics of Ethnicity: Jews and
the Charlottetown Accord," in *Multiculturalism, Jews, and Identities in
Canada*, ed. Howard Adelman and John H. Simpson (Jerusalem: Magnes
Press, 1996), 102. But as mentioned earlier, Jewish political clout in the
postwar period does not mean that Jewish interests prevail in every policy
dispute.

41 Raymond Breton, *The Governance of Ethnic Communities* (New York:
Greenwood Press, 1991).

42 Michael Adams and Andrew Griffith, "Why Canada's Politicians Fixate on
the Ethnic Vote," *Globe and Mail*, 17 August 2015; Pieter Bevelander and
Ravi Pendakur, "Social Capital and Voting Participation of Immigrants
and Minorities in Canada," *Ethnic and Racial Studies* 32, no. 8 (2009):
1406–30; Kathy Megyery, ed., *Ethno-cultural Groups and Visible
Minorities in Canadian Politics: The Question of Access* (Ottawa: Royal
Commission on Electoral Reform and Supply and Services and Dundurn
Press, 1991). The mobilization of Sikhs to swell the membership rolls of
the BC NDP and elect Premier Dosanjh in early 2000 is a dramatic case.

43 Jonathan J. Goldberg, *Jewish Power: Inside the American Jewish Establishment* (Reading, MA: Addison-Wesley, 1996); John Mearsheimer and Stephen Walt, *The Israel Lobby* (New York: Farrar, Straus and Giroux, 2007).

44 Anya Ulinich, "Who the Jewish Billionaires Are Backing for 2016," *The Forward*, 21 May 2015; Nathan Guttman, "Meet the Jewish Billionaires Shaping the 2016 Presidential Election," *Haaretz*, 28 May 2015.

45 Paul Lungen, "Six Jewish MPs Head to Ottawa," *Canadian Jewish News*, 10 November 2015; "Jewish Members of U.S. Congress: 114th Congress," *The Jewish Virtual Library*, 2017.

46 The Centre for Israel and Jewish Affairs, http://www.cija.ca/.

47 See Stanislawski, "Canadian Jewry and Foreign Policy in the Middle East."

48 Pierre Anctil and Ira Robinson, eds., *Les communautés juives de Montréal: Histoire et enjeux contemporains* (Sillery, QC: Septentrion, 2010).

49 Morton Weinfeld and William Eaton, *A Survey of the Jewish Community of Montreal* (Montreal: Jewish Community Research Institute, 1979).

50 I attended one such meeting in the mid-1990s, where I first heard the term "deep Côte StLuc."

51 One such prominent group is Dialogue St-Urbain, which has involved Gerard Bouchard, brother of Lucien. Papers on French-Jewish relations in Quebec have been published in Pierre Anctil, Ira Robinson, and Gerard Bouchard's *Juifs et canadiens français dans la société québécoise* (Sillery, QC: Septentrion, 2000); Ira Robinson, "The Field of Canadian Jewish Studies and Its Importance for the Jewish Community of Canada," *Jewish Political Studies Review* 21, no. 3–4 (2009).

52 Mordecai Richler, *Oh Canada! Oh Quebec!* (New York: A.A. Knopf, 1992); Esther Delisle, *The Traitor and the Jew* (Montreal: Robert Davies Publishing, 1993); Esther Delisle, *Myth, Memories and Lies: Quebec's Intelligentsia and the Fascist Temptation, 1939–1960* (Westmount, QC: R. Davies Multimedia, 1998).

53 Victor C. Goldbloom, *Building Bridges* (Montreal: McGill-Queen's University Press, 2015).

54 "Jewish General Hospital Will Ignore Charter Values," *CTV Montreal News*, 14 November 2013; Ron Csillag, "Population Steady amid Tensions over Quebec Separatism and Proposed Kippah Ban," *The Forward*, 8 October 2013.

55 Charles Shahar, *Jewish Life in Montreal: A Survey of the Attitudes, Beliefs and Behaviours of Montreal's Jewish Community* (Montreal: Federation CJA, 2010).

56 Janice Arnold, "Caution, Relief Greet Vote," *Canadian Jewish News*, 10 December 1998.

57 Paul Lungen, "Synagogues Mobilize to Help Syrian Refugees," *Canadian Jewish News*, 12 November 2015; Joshua Ostroff, "Never Again: A Jewish Take on Anti-Syrian Refugee Sentiment," *The Huffington Post*, 17 November 2015; "Poll: 31% of Syrian Refugees Support ISIS – and Trudeau Is Importing 25,000 by Christmas," *The Rebel*, 14 November 2015.

58 David Taras and Morton Weinfeld, "Continuity and Criticism: North American Jews and Israel," in Brym, Shaffir, and Weinfeld, *The Jews in Canada*, 297.

59 Morton Weinfled, "The Distancing Debate," *Contemporary Jewry* 30 (2010): 279–81; Ron Miller and Arnold Deshefsky, "Brandeis v. Cohen et al.: The Distancing from Israel Debate," *Contemporary Jewry* 30 (2010): 155–64.

60 Theodore Sasson, *The New American Zionism* (New York: New York University Press, 2014).

61 Thomas Friedman, "Israel to American Jews: You Just Don't Matter," *New York Times*, 12 July 2017; Jewish Telegraphic Agency News Brief, "Head of US Conservative Synagogue Network Warns of 'Distancing' between Israeli, Diaspora Jews," 11 July 2017.

62 Zach Paikin, "Fear Is Dividing Canada's Jewish Community," *iPolitics*, 11 December 2012.

63 Mira Sucharov, "Values, Identity, and Israel Advocacy," *Foreign Policy Analysis* 7, no. 4 (2011): 361–80; Mira Sucharov, "Mideast Peace Can Only Be Based on Mutual Understanding," *Canadian Jewish News*, 28 January 2016.

64 Peter Beinart, *The Crisis of Zionism* (New York: Picador, 2012).

65 Jodie Shupac, "Two States Still Possible with Leadership, Panel Agrees," *Canadian Jewish News*, 3 February 2016.

66 Taras and Weinfeld, "Continuity and Criticism."

67 Shahar, *Jewish Life in Montreal.*

68 David Lazarus, "Condo Seeks Injunction," *Canadian Jewish News*, 6 November 1997.

69 Syndicat Northcrest v. Amselem, SCC 47 (2004), 2 S.C.R. 551, https://scc-csc.lexum.com/scc-csc/scc-csc/en/item/2161/index.do.

70 Margaret A. Somerville, *The Ethical Canary: Science, Society and the Human Spirit* (Toronto: Viking/Penguin Canada, 2000). See chapter 8, "Altering Baby Boys' Bodies: The Ethics of Infant Male Circumcision."

71 Yair Rosenberh, "Norway Passes Law Protecting Circumcision," *The Tablet*, 27 June 2014; M. Zuhdi Jasser and Thomas J. Reese, "Remember the Holocaust by Fighting Anti-Semitism," *USA Today*, 27 January 2016.

72 Brian J. Morris, Catherine A. Hankins, Aaron A.R. Tobian, John N. Krieger, and Jeffrey D. Klausner, "Does Male Circumcision Protect against

Sexually Transmitted Infections? Arguments and Meta-Analyses to the Contrary Fail to Withstand Scrutiny," *ISRN Urology* 2014, 2014.

73 Zosia Bielski, "Should Circumcision Be Outlawed? 'Intactivists' Think So," *Globe and Mail*, 13 January 2011.

74 Margaret Somerville, "Routine Circumcision of Baby Boys Is Wrong," *The Gazette*, 7 August 1998, B6; Margaret Somerville, "Respect in the Context of Infant Male Circumcision: Can Ethics and Law Provide Insights?," paper presented at the fifth International Symposium on Sexual Mutilations, Oxford University, 5–7 August 1998. Canadian media reports of the controversy proliferate. See Barbara Kay, "So This Is What Passes for Abuse," *National Post*, 13 February 2001, A18; Anne Marie Owens, "Tradition under the Knife," *National Post*, 20 February 2001, A13.

75 Louis Sandy Maisel and Ira N. Forman, *Jews in American Politics* (Lanham, MA: Roman and Littlefield Publishers, 2001).

76 See, for example, Gloria Galloway, "Nobel Laureate Joins Toronto Rabbi Group in Condemning Refugee Health Cuts," *Globe and Mail*, 7 July 2012; Ben Carniol, "Stephen Harper Is Out of Step with Jewish Values," *The Star*, 23 August 2015.

77 There are no studies of the size and impact of current Jewish giving to Canadian political parties and campaigns. Wealthy Jews have long been supporters of political parties, mainly the Liberals. While they do so as individuals, their involvement likely helps further the Jewish policy agenda described above.

78 Jim Walker, "The Jewish Phase in the Movement for Racial Equality in Canada," *Canadian Ethnic Studies* 34, no. 1 (2002): 1–29.

79 Michael Rosenberg and Jack Jedwab, "Institutional Completeness, Ethnic Organizational Style, and the Role of the State: The Jewish, Italian, and Greek Communities of Montreal," *Canadian Review of Sociology and Anthropology* 29, no. 3 (1992): 266–87; Henry Srebrnik, "Multiculturalism and the Politics of Ethnicity," in Adelman and Simpson, *Multiculturalism, Jews, and Identities in Canada*, 78–128.

80 "Parizeau Blames 'Money and the Ethnic Vote' for Referendum Loss," CBC Digital Archives, 30 October 1995, http://www.cbc.ca/archives/entry/quebec-referendum-reaction.

81 This section relies on Morton Weinfeld, "The Political-Demographic Environment of Canadian Jewry," in *Papers in Jewish Demography, 1989,* Jewish Population Studies 25, ed. U.O. Schmelz and S. DellaPergola (Jerusalem: Hebrew University of Jerusalem, Institute of Contemporary Jewry, 1993), 204–17.

82 JTA, "Black Lives Matter Endorses BDS: Israel Is 'Apartheid State,'" *Haaretz*, 4 August 2016; Emma Green, "Why Do Black Activists Care about Palestine?," *The Atlantic*, 18 August 2016.

83 Barry, "Canada and the Middle East Today."

84 Howard Adelman, "Blacks and Jews: Racism, Anti-Semitism, and *Showboat*," in Adelman and Simpson, *Multiculturalism, Jews, and Identities in Canada*, 128–78; Frances Henry, Carol Tator, Winston Mattis, and Tim Rees, *The Colour of Democracy* (Toronto: Harcourt Brace, 1995).

85 Harold Troper and Morton Weinfeld, *Old Wounds: Jews, Ukrainians, and the Hunt for Nazi War Criminals in Canada* (Markham, ON: Viking, 1988). See also Howard Margolian, *Unauthorized Entry: The Truth about Nazi War Criminals in Canada, 1946–56* (Toronto: University of Toronto Press, 1999).

86 Ron Csillag, "Complaints against Refugee Board Dismissed," *Canadian Jewish News*, 10 December 1998, 40. In September 1998, a former IRB member filed complaints about unprofessional conduct against three board members, one of which referred to a member making anti-Semitic and homophobic remarks. A report on the matter by Professor Ed Ratushny exonerated the first two and did not address the allegation which involved anti-Semitism, since the member was not reappointed to the board.

87 Brent Sasley, "Who Calls the Shots: An Inquiry into the Effect of Jewish and Arab Lobbies on Canadian Middle East Policy," *Literary Review of Canada* 19, no. 4 (May 2011); Harold M. Waller, "The Americas: Canada," in *American Jewish Year Book, 2008*, ed. David Singer and Lawrence Grossman (New York: American Jewish Committee, 2008), 305–37.

88 Jay Brodbar-Nemzer, Steven M. Cohen, Gary A. Tobin, Allan Reitzes, and Charles Shahar, "An Overview of the Canadian Jewish Community," in Brym, Shaffir, and Weinfeld, *The Jews in Canada*, 63.

89 Breton, "The Ethnic Group as a Political Resource

CHAPTER TEN

1 For a review of the basics of traditional Judaism as well as the more recent denominations, see George Robinson, *Essential Judaism: A Complete Guide to Beliefs, Customs and Rituals* (New York: Atria Books, 2016).

2 Ibid.

3 For an overview of the meaning of religion to Canadians, and the challenges facing organized religion, see Ronald Graham, *God's Dominion*

(Toronto: McClelland and Stewart, 1990). For a more quantitative analysis, see Reginald Bibby, *Unknown Gods: The Ongoing Story of Religion in Canada* (Toronto: Stoddart, 1993).

4 Erving Goffman, *The Presentation of Self in Everyday Life* (Garden City, NY: Anchor, 1959).

5 Samuel Heilman, *Synagogue Life: A Study in Symbolic Interaction* (Chicago: University of Chicago Press, 1976).

6 Luis Lugo, Alan Cooperman, Gregory A. Smith, Conrad Hackett, Cary Funk, Neha Sahgal, Phillip Connor, Jessica Hamar Martinez et al., *A Portrait of Jewish Americans: Findings from a Pew Research Center Survey of U.S. Jews* (Washington, DC: Pew Research Center's Religion and Public Life Project, 2013).

7 See Roger Kamenetz, *The Jew in the Lotus* (San Francisco: Harper, 1995); Celia Rothenberg and Anne Vallely, eds., *New Age Judaism* (Portland, OR: Valentine-Mitchell Publishers, 2008); Christopher Partridge, *New Religions, A Guide: New Religious Movements, Sects, and Alternative Spiritualties* (New York: Oxford University Press, 2004).

8 For a contemporary overview of the strengths and weaknesses of the denominations, see Jack Wertheimer, *A People Divided: Judaism in Contemporary America* (New York: Basic Books, 1993).

9 See Table 1 in Appendix.

10 Ibid.

11 Charles Shahar, *Jewish Life in Montreal: A Survey of the Attitudes, Beliefs and Behaviours of Montreal's Jewish Community* (Montreal: Federation CJA, 2010).

12 Ben Volman, Toronto director of Chosen People Ministries (Canada) Messianic Rabbi Kehillat Eytz Chaim, Tree of Life Congregation, personal communication, 2 May 2016.

13 Rabbi Lionel Moses, personal communication, 30 December 1998. The ad appeared in the 17 December 1998 issue of the *Canadian Jewish News*. Rabbi Harold Shulweis in Los Angeles has actively encouraged the "unchurched" to consider Judaism as an option.

14 Lugo et al., *A Portrait of Jewish Americans*; Shahar, *Jewish Life in Montreal*; Charles Shahar and Tina Rosenbaum, *Jewish Life in Greater Toronto: A Survey of the Attitudes and Behaviours of Greater Toronto's Jewish Community* (Toronto: UJA Federation, 2005).

15 Shahar, *Jewish Life in Montreal*.

16 Ibid.

17 Shahar and Rosenbaum, *Jewish Life in Greater Toronto*.

18 Ibid.
19 David E. Eagle, "Changing Patterns of Attendance at Religious Services in Canada," *Journal for the Scientific Study of Religion* 50, no. 1 (2011): 187–200; Reginald W. Bibby, "Continuing the Conversation on Canada: Changing Patterns of Religious Service Attendance," *Journal for the Scientific Study of Religion* 50, no. 4 (2011): 831–9.
20 Bibby, *Unknown Gods*, 6.
21 Frank Newport, "Three-Quarters of Americans Identify as Christian," *Gallup: Politics*, 24 December 2014.
22 Stephanie Nolen, "Give Them Jesus but Hold the Theology," *Globe and Mail*, 2 January 1999, A1, A5.
23 Statistics Canada, NHS Data Tables, Catalogue number 99-010-X2011037.
24 Katherine Blaze Carlson, "Organized Religion on the Decline? Growing Number of Canadians 'Spiritual but not Religious,'" *National Post*, 21 December 2012.
25 Stuart Macdonald, "Death of Christian Canada? Do Canadian Church Statistics Support Callum Brown's Theory of Church Decline?," *Historical Papers 2006: Canadian Society of Church History*, 135–56, http://historicalpapers.journals.yorku.ca/index.php/historicalpapers/article/viewFile/39195/35537; Bibby, *Unknown Gods*, 8; Carlson, "Organized Religion on the Decline?"; Richard Foot, "Falling Church Membership Drops Off Agenda," *National Post*, 26 June 2007; Richard Foot, "Decline in Anglican Membership Is Quickening: Extinction by 2061 Feared," *National Post*, 1 December 2005.
26 Shahar and Rosenbaum, *Jewish Life in Greater Toronto*.
27 Charles Silberman, *A Certain People* (New York: Summit Books, 1985), 260.
28 Charles Liebman, *The Ambivalent American Jew* (Philadelphia: The Jewish Publication Society, 1973).
29 Steven Cohen and Arnold Eisen, *The Jew Within: Self, Community, and Commitment among the Variety of Moderately Affiliated* (Boston: The Susan and David Wilstein Institute, 1998), 38.
30 See Marshall Sklare, ed., *The Jewish Community in America* (New York: Behrman House, 1974); Wertheimer, *A People Divided*.
31 Lugo et al., *A Portrait of Jewish Americans*; Shahar, *Jewish Life in Montreal*; Shahar and Rosenbaum, *Jewish Life in Greater Toronto*; Uriel Heilman, "Jewish School Enrollment Up 12 Percent, Fueled by Haredi Orthodox Growth," *Jewish Telegraph Agency*, 31 October 2014.

32 Louis Wirth, *The Ghetto* (Chicago: University of Chicago Press, 1928).

33 For an overview of the strengths and dangers of fundamentalism among the three monotheistic faiths, see Karen Armstrong, *The Battle for God* (New York: A.A. Knopf, 2000). For an understanding of the life of Orthodox Jews in Toronto suburbia, see Etan Diamond, *And I Will Dwell in Their Midst: Orthodox Jews in Suburbia* (Chapel Hill: University of North Carolina Press, 2000).

34 Simon Dein and Lorne L. Dawson, "The 'Scandal' of the Lubavitch Rebbe: Messianism as a Response to Failed Prophecy," *Journal of Contemporary Religion* 23, no. 2 (2008). 163–80.

35 M. Herbert Danzger, *Returning to Tradition: The Contemporary Revival of Orthodox Judaism* (New Haven: Yale University Press, 1989).

36 Arthur Magida, "The Aish Phenomenon," *Moment*, June 1998; aish.com, "About Us," http://www.aish.com/about/?s=nb.

37 Michael Meyer, *Response to Modernity: A History of the Reform Movement in Judaism* (New York: Oxford University Press, 1988).

38 Sheri Shefa, "Shul Offers Program for Intermarried Non-Jewish Women," *Canadian Jewish News*, 24 November 2011; Morgan Lowrie, "Teaching Non-Jewish Moms about Judaism," *Montreal Families*, last modified 2017, http://www.montrealfamilies.ca/Montreal-Families/February-2014/Teaching-non-Jewish-moms-about-Judaism/.

39 Marshall Sklare, *Conservative Judaism: An American Religious Movement*, rev. ed. (New York: Schocken, 1972).

40 "New Rabbi's Manual," *The Forward*, 23 October 1998, 3.

41 Daniel Gordis, "Conservative Judaism: A Requiem," *Jewish Review of Books*, Winter 2014, www.jewishreviewofbooks.com/articles/566/requiem-for-a-movement; Lila Sarick, "Feature: Does Conservative Judaism Need Saving?," *Canadian Jewish News*, 8 September 2014; Richard Menkis, "Conservative Judaism and Its Challenges from the Left (Reconstructionism and Renewal) and Right," in *Canada's Jews: In Time, Space and Spirit*, ed. Ira Robinson (Boston: Academic Press, 2013), 308–42.

42 Stuart Schoenfeld, "Canadian Judaism Today," in *The Canadian Jewish Mosaic*, ed. Morton Weinfeld, William Shaffir, and Irwin Cotler (Toronto: John Wiley and Sons, 1981), 129–50.

43 Elan Dresher, Norbert Hornstein, and Lipa Roth, "A Montrealer Seder," in *The Big Book of Jewish Humor*, ed. William Novak and Moshe Waldoks (New York: Harper and Row, 1981), 114–16.

44 Hillel Halkin, "You Don't Have to Be Orthodox to Cherish the Sabbath," *Jewish World Review*, 13 December 2002, www.jewishworldreview.com.

45 Rela M. Geffen, *Elaboration and Renewal: Rites of Passage in Judaism* (Philadelphia: Jewish Publication Society, 1993); Lugo et al., *A Portrait of Jewish Americans.*

46 Susan Weidman Schneider, *Jewish and Female* (New York: Simon and Schuster, 1984).

47 For a discussion of bar mitzvah, see Stuart Schoenfeld, "Some Aspects of the Social Significance of the Bar/Bat Mitzvah Celebration," in *Essays in the Social Scientific Study of Judaism and Jewish Society*, ed. Jack N. Lightstone, Stuart Schoenfeld, and Simcha Fishbane (Montreal: Department of Religion, Concordia University), 277–304, reprinted in *The Bar/Bat Mitzvah Handbook*, ed. Helen Lenneman (Denver: Alternatives in Religious Education, 1993). In a more lighthearted vein, see Nancy Berk, *Secrets of a Bar Mitzvah Mom* (Lincoln, NE: Iuniverse Inc, 2005).

48 Marshall Sklare, *America's Jews* (New York: Random House, 1971), 114–17.

49 Lugo et al., *A Portrait of Jewish Americans*; Shahar, *Jewish Life in Montreal*; Shahar and Rosenbaum, *Jewish Life in Greater Toronto.*

50 Jay Brodbar-Nemzer, Steven M. Cohen, Allan Reitzes, Charles Shahar, and Gary A. Tobin, "An Overview of the Canadian Jewish Community," in *The Jews in Canada*, ed. Robert J. Brym, William Shaffir, and Morton Weinfeld (Toronto: Oxford University Press, 1993), 54, 62.

51 *Canadian Jewish News*, 9 January 1999.

52 Alana Mitchell, "Mother Nature's Holy Alliance," *Globe and Mail*, 5 January 1999, A1, A8.

53 Wade Clark Roof and William McKinney, *American Mainline Religion: Its Changing Shape and Future* (New Brunswick, NJ: Rutgers University Press, 1987), 40.

54 Cohen and Eisen, *The Jew Within*. This is the kind of Judaism which Steven Cohen and Arnold Eisen found in their interviews with "moderately affiliated" Jews.

55 Rabbi Ron Aigen, personal communication, 26 January 1998; Rabbi Reuben Poupko, personal communication, 27 January 1998.

56 Rabbi Moshe Shulman, personal communication, 31 January 2001.

57 Rabbi Baruch Frydman-Kohl, personal communication, 9 February 2001; Rabbi John Moscowitz, personal communication, 2 February 2001.

58 Yair Ettinger, "Newly-Minted Female Orthodox Rabbis to Be Called Rabba," *Haaretz*, 12 June 2015; Norma B. Joseph, "Women in Orthodoxy: Conventional and Contentious," in *Women Remaking American Jewish Life*, ed. Riv-Ellen Prell (Detroit: Wayne State University Press, 2007), 181–210.

59 Jodie Shupac, "LGBTQ Inclusion: How Welcoming Are Conservative Shuls?," *Canadian Jewish News*, 23 June 2014.

60 Michael Lemberger, "Gay Synagogues' Uncertain Future," *Tabletmag.com*, 11 March 2013.

CHAPTER ELEVEN

1 Leonard Saxe, Theodore Sasson, Graham Wright, and Shahar Hecht, *Antisemitism and the College Campus: Perceptions and Realities* (Brandeis University, Cohen Center for Modern Jewish Studies, July 2015), https://bir.brandeis.edu/handle/10192/30810.

2 Irving Abella and Harold Troper, *None Is Too Many: Canada and the Jews of Europe, 1933–1948* (Toronto: Lester and Orpen Dennys, 1982); Ira Robinson, *A History of Antisemitism in Canada* (Waterloo: Wilfrid Laurier University Press, 2015).

3 Daniel J. Levinson, Else Frenkel-Brunswik, Theodor W. Adorno, and Nevitt Sanford, *The Authoritarian Personality* (New York: Harper, 1950); Gordon Allport, *The Nature of Prejudice* (New York: Addison-Wesley, 1954); Bruno Bettelheim and Morris Janowitz, *The Dynamics of Prejudice* (New York: Harper and Row, 1950).

4 For a review of these studies, see William Helmreich, "The Sociological Study of Anti-Semitism in the United States," in *Approaches to Anti-Semitism: Context and Curriculum*, ed. Michael Brown (New York: The American Jewish Committee, 1994), 134–41.

5 Louis Wirth, *The Ghetto* (Chicago: University of Chicago Press, 1928). For examples of the latter, see Herbert Gans, "The Origins of a Jewish Community in the Suburbs," in *The Jews: Social Patterns of an American Group*, ed. Marshall Sklare (Glencoe, IL: The Free Press, 1958), 204–48; Judith R. Kramer and Seymour Levantman, *Children of the Gilded Ghetto* (New Haven, CT: Yale University Press, 1961); Marshall Sklare and Joseph Greenblum, *Jewish Identity on the Suburban Frontier: A Study of Group Survival in an Open Society* (New York: Basic Books, 1967).

6 John Seeley, Alexander Sim, and Elizabeth W. Loosley, *Crestwood Heights* (Toronto: University of Toronto Press, 1956); Evelyn Kallen, *Spanning the Generations: A Study of Jewish Identity* (Toronto: Longmans, 1977).

7 Abella and Troper, *None Is Too Many*.

8 Steve Oney, *And the Dead Shall Rise: The Murder of Mary Phagan and the Lynching of Leo Frank* (New York: Anchor, 2003).

9 Charles Stember, *Jews in the Mind of America* (New York: Basic Books, 1966).

10 Irving Abella, *A Coat of Many Colours: Two Centuries of Jewish Life in Canada* (Toronto: Lester and Orpen Dennys, 1990), 181.

11 Many in the anti-racist community would disagree with this assessment. They would argue that our legal system, including laws and their implementation, serves to perpetuate racial inequalities and systemic racism in many ways. With the exception of First Nations in Canada, I disagree. There certainly is racism and anti-Semitism in Canada. But Canadian law and governance today – as opposed to the past – work to oppose those evils.

12 Harold Brackman, "Regents Beware: You Are Already Under Attack for Calling Out 'Anti-Zionism,'" *jewishjournal.com*, 11 June 2015.

13 Karen Brodkin, *How Jews Became White Folks and What That Says about Race in America* (New Brunswick, NJ: Rutgers University Press, 1998).

14 Richard Menkis, "Anti-Semitism and Anti-Judaism in Pre-Confederation Canada," in *Anti-Semitism in Canada: History and Interpretation*, ed. Alan Davies (Waterloo: Wilfrid Laurier University Press, 1992), 11–38; Robinson, *A History of Antisemitism in Canada*.

15 Michael Brown, "From Stereotype to Scapegoat: Anti-Jewish Sentiment in French Canada from Confederation to World War One," in Davies, *Anti-Semitism in Canada*, 239–66.

16 Gerald J.J. Tulchinsky, *Taking Root: The Origins of the Canadian Jewish Community* (Toronto: Lester Publishing Co., 1990), 61–80.

17 Menkis, "Anti-Semitism and Anti-Judaism in Pre-Confederation Canada," 26–7.

18 Gerald J.J. Tulchinsky, "Goldwin Smith: Victorian-Canadian Anti-Semite," in Davies, *Anti-Semitism in Canada*, 67–92.

19 Pierre Anctil, "Interlude of Hostility: Judeo-Christian Relations in Quebec in the Inter-War Period, 1919–1939," in Davies, *Anti-Semitism in Canada*, 135–66.

20 Phyllis Senese, "Anti-Semitic Dreyfusards: The Confused Western-Canadian Press," in Davies, *Anti-Semitism in Canada*, 93–112.

21 Cyril H. Levitt and William Shaffir, *The Riot at Christie Pits* (Toronto: Lester and Orpen Dennys, 1987).

22 Lita-Rose Betcherman, *The Swastika and the Maple Leaf* (Toronto: Fitzhenry and Whiteside, 1975).

23 Ibid., 123.

24 Marilyn Nefsky, "The Shadow of Evil: Nazism and Canadian Protestantism," in Davies, *Anti-Semitism in Canada*, 197–226.

25 Anctil, "Interlude of Hostility," 156.

26 Henry Milner and Sheilagh H. Milner, *The Decolonization of Quebec* (Toronto: McClelland and Stewart, 1973).

27 See Esther Delisle, *The Traitor and the Jew* (Montreal: Robert Davies Publishing, 1993). Anctil offers a more nuanced perspective in "Interlude of Hostility."

28 Nefsky, "The Shadow of Evil."

29 Abella, *A Coat of Many Colours*, 180; Anctil, "Interlude of Hostility," 148.

30 Betcherman, *The Swastika and the Maple Leaf*, 85–98.

31 Esther Delisle, *Myth, Memory, and Lies.*

32 See Betcherman, *The Swastika and the Maple Leaf: Quebec's Intelligentsia and the Fascist Temptation, 1939–1960* (Westmount, QC: R. Davies Multimedia, 1998).

33 Howard Palmer, "Politics, Religion, and Anti-Semitism in Alberta, 1880–1959," in Davies, *Anti-Semitism in Canada,* 167–96. See also Janine Stingel, *Social Discredit: Anti-Semitism, Social Credit, and the Jewish Response* (Montreal: McGill-Queen's University Press, 2000).

34 Robinson, *A History of Antisemitism in Canada,* 107.

35 Warren Kinsella, *Web of Hate* (Toronto: HarperCollins, 1994); One study in the 1980s identified 130 such organizations and 586 individual members of these organizations. See Stanley R. Barrett, *Is God a Racist? The Right Wing in Canada* (Toronto: University of Toronto Press, 1987).

36 For a review of the broad sweep and types of anti-Semitism, see Robert Wistrich, *A Lethal Obsession: Anti-Semitism from Antiquity to the Global Jihad* (New York: Random House, 2010).

37 See Joshua Trachtenberg, *The Devil and The Jews: The Medieval Conception of the Jews and Its Relation to Modern Antisemitism,* 2nd ed. (Philadelphia: Jewish Publication Society, 1983).

38 Adolf Hitler, *Mein Kampf* (Boston: Houghton Mifflin, 1943). For a detailed discussion of the "Protocols" and Jewish conspiracy, see Norman Cohn, *Warrant for Genocide: The Myth of the Jewish World Conspiracy and the Protocols of the Elders of Zion* (New York: Harper and Row, 1967).

39 Hitler, *Mein Kampf,* 307.

40 Ibid., 305–6.

41 Ibid., 314, 319.

42 Ibid., 309.

43 Ibid., 307.

44 Barrett, *Is God a Racist?,* 209–10

45 Steve Mertl and John Ward, *Keegstra* (Saskatoon: Western Producer Prairie Books, 1985), 5.

46 Deborah Lipstadt, *Denying the Holocaust: The Growing Assault on Truth and Memory* (New York: Plume, 1994).

47 Gabriel Weimann and Conrad Winn, *Hate on Trial: The Zündel Affair, the Media, and Public Opinion in Canada* (Oakville, ON: Mosaic Press, 1986), 105.

48 Jack Jedwab, "La connaissance de l'Holocauste et le désir d'action chez les Canadiens," presentation on the seventieth anniversary of Kristallnacht, Association for Canadian Studies, Montreal, 10 November 2008; Norma Greenaway, "Just 40% of Canadians Know How Many Jews Died in the Holocaust," *The Ottawa Citizen*, 24 January 2005.

49 Ryan Maloney, "Alex Johnstone, NDP Candidate, Says She Didn't Know Auschwitz was a Death Camp," *Huffington Post*, 23 September 2015.

50 Weimann and Winn, *Hate on Trial*, 124.

51 Ibid.

52 David Bercuson and Doug Wertheimer, *A Trust Betrayed: The Keegstra Affair* (Toronto: Doubleday, 1985); Mertl and Ward, *Keegstra*.

53 Judgements of the Supreme Court of Canada, Ross v. New Brunswick School District Np. 15, 1996, SCC Case Info 24002, http://scc-csc.lexum.com/scc-csc/scc-csc/en/item/1367/index.do.

54 For a review of the issues of hate speech and free speech as these relate to the case of British historian David Irving, see Lipstadt, *Denying the Holocaust*. Irving sued Lipstadt for libel in England because she referred to him as a holocaust denier. He lost.

55 Paul Lungen, "B'nai Brith Audit Finds Anti-Semitism Moving Online," *Canadian Jewish News*, 2 May 2016.

56 Peter Ward, *White Canada Forever* (Montreal: McGill-Queen's University Press, 1978).

57 Delisle, *The Traitor and the Jew*, 124–33.

58 Reasons for Decision, in the matter of the Human Rights Code RSBC 1996, c.210, tribunal member Nitya Iyer, 4 November 1997, 109.

59 Jeffrey Reitz and Raymond Breton, *The Illusion of Difference: Realities of Ethnicity in Canada and the United States* (Toronto: C.D. Howe Institute, 1994), 73. But that comparison could yield a very different conclusion if the authors had used the Jewish – not general – populations in the respective countries. There are close to sixteen times more American than Canadian Jews. Therefore, there should be a sixteen-to-one ratio. To find a ratio of ten-to-one meant that the per-capita number of anti-Semitic incidents in Canada was much higher than in the United States. So, Canadian Jews would in fact seem *more* likely to be victimized than American Jews. In relation to hate speech, there are two ways to interpret this. One is that Canadian Jews need more protection by hate speech legislation, since they are more vulnerable. The other is that American Jews have prospered

without such protections, so Canadians do not need them either. Either makes sense. Whether the lower than expected frequencies of anti-Semitic incidents in the United States is due to a regime of free speech or other factors is unclear.

60 "The 40 Worst Colleges for Jewish Students, 2016: The Algemeiner's 1st Annual List of the US and Canada's Worst Campuses for Jewish Students," *The Algemeiner*, https://www.algemeiner.com/the-40-worst-colleges-for-jewish-students-2016/.

61 Bernard Harrison, *The Resurgence of Anti-Semitism: Jews, Israel, and Liberal Opinion* (Landham, MD: Rowman and Littlefield Publishers, 2006); Pierre-André Taguieff, cited in ibid., 23; Tyler Levitan, "Criticizing Israel's Politics Isn't Anti-Semitism," *Huffington Post*, 14 August 2015; Mike Fegelman, "When Criticism of Israel Becomes Anti-Semitism," *Huffington Post*, 31 August 2015.

62 "B'nai Brith Audit Reveals Anti-Semitism in Canada Reaches an All-Time High," *The Edmonton Jewish News*, 11 June 2015.

63 B'nai Brith Canada, *2014 Annual Audit of Anti-Semitic Incidents* (League for Human Rights of B'nai Brith Canada, 2015).

64 League for Human Rights of B'nai Brith Canada, *2009 Audit of Antisemitic Incidents* (Downsview, ON: 2010).

65 Toronto Police Service, *2014 Annual Hate/Bias Crime Statistical Report*, http://antisemitism.org.il/article/95184/police-find-jews-most-targeted-hate-crimes.

66 Mary Allen, "Police-Reported Hate Crime in Canada, 2012," *Juristat* (Statistics Canada), 26 June 2014.

67 Saxe et al., *Antisemitism and the College Campus*.

68 Karen Seidman, "BDS Vote Stirs Up Hostility on McGill Campus," *The Gazette*, 25 February 2016.

69 Jack Jedwab, "Attitudes towards Jews and Muslims: Comparing Canada with the United States and Europe," *Association for Canadian Studies*, 19 September 2008. https://acs-aec.ca/pdf/polls/12218487649334.pdf.

70 John Geddes, "What Canadians Think of Sikhs, Jews, Christians, Muslims ..." *Maclean's*, 28 April 2009.

71 Anti-Defamation League, *ADL Global 100: 2014 Survey Results*, http://global100.adl.org/about.

72 Weimann and Winn, *Hate on Trial*, 144.

73 Geddes, "What Canadians Think of Sikhs, Jews, Christians, Muslims ..."

74 Taylor Buckner, "Attitudes toward Minorities: Seven Year Results and Analysis" (Montreal: League for Human Rights of B'nai Brith, 1991); Frank

Newport, "Americans Today Much More Accepting of a Woman, Black, Catholic, or Jew as President," *Gallup News Service*, 29 March 1999.
75 Anti-Defamation League, *ADL Global 100: 2014 Survey Results*. http://global100.adl.org/?_ga=1.216615312.720293156.1466017345#country/canada/2014.
76 Anti-Defamation League, *American Attitudes towards Jews in America* (Marttila Communications, October 2009), http://archive.adl.org/anti_semitism/poll_as_2009/anti-semitism poll 2009.pdf
77 Reginald Bibby, *The Bibby Report: Social Trends, Canadian Style* (Toronto: Stoddart, 1995).
78 Geddes, "What Canadians Think of Sikhs, Jews, Christians, Muslims ..."
79 Manuel Prutschi, personal communication, 30 January 2001; JTA, "Anti-Semitic Incidents in Canada Reach All Time High," *The Times of Israel*, 13 June 2015; M.J. Rosenberg, "Gaza War and Anti-Semitism," *The Huffington Post*, 29 July 2014; Morton Weinfeld, "Jewish Life in Montreal," in *Canada's Jews: In Time, Space and Spirit*, ed. Ira Robinson (Boston: Academic Press, 2013); Ira Robinson, "Reflections on Antisemitism in French Canada," *Canadian Jewish Studies* 21 (2013).
80 Peter Pineo, "The Social Standing of Ethnic and Racial Groupings," *Canadian Review of Sociology and Anthropology* 14 (May 1977): 147–57.
81 J.W. Berry and Rudolf Kalin, "Multicultural and Ethnic Attitudes in Canada: An Overview of the 1991 National Survey," *Canadian Journal of Behavioural Science* 27 (1995): 301–20.
82 Bibby, *The Bibby Report*, 57–8.
83 Charles Shahar and Tina Rosenbaum, *Jewish Life in Greater Toronto: A Survey of the Attitudes and Behaviours of Greater Toronto's Jewish Community* (Toronto: UJA Federation, 2005).
84 Weimann and Winn, *Hate on Trial*, 115, 152.
85 Geddes, "What Canadians Think of Sikhs, Jews, Christians, Muslims ..."
86 Gerard Bouchard, "Les Rapports avec la communauté juive: un test pour la nation québécoise," in *Juifs et canadiens français dans la société québécoise*, ed. Pierre Anctil, Ira Robinson, and Gérard Bouchard (Quebec, QC: Septentrion, 2000), 13–32. This is true even for outspoken condemnations of Quebec anti-Semitism. This essay by Gerard Bouchard is a case in point. It describes and condemns major incidents of anti-Semitism in Quebec history. But it focuses more on the 1920s rather than on the more significant 1930s. It ignores the conscription referendum, and includes the ritualistic denunciation of Richler and Delisle. For a popular discussion of the marginality of Jews in Quebec and related

anti-Semitism, see Joseph Rosen, "The Third Solitude," *Maisonneuve*, 23 July 2015.

87 Robinson, "Reflections on Antisemitism in French Canada."

88 Sol Littman, *Québec's Jews: Vital Citizens or Eternal Strangers: Analysis of Key Newspaper Coverage of Three Pertinent Incidents* (Simon Wiesenthal Center, 1991), 4.

89 Robinson, "Reflections on Antisemitism in French Canada."

90 Luis Lugo, Alan Cooperman, Gregory A. Smith, Conrad Hackett, Cary Funk, Neha Sahgal, Phillip Connor, Jessica Hamar Martinez et al., *A Portrait of Jewish Americans: Findings from a Pew Research Center Survey of U.S. Jews* (Washington, DC: Pew Research Center's Religion and Public Life Project, 2013).

91 Shahar and Rosenbaum, *Jewish Life in Greater Toronto.*

92 Robinson, *A History of Antisemitism in Canada.*

93 Shahar, *Jewish Life in Montreal;* Shahar and Rosenbaum, *Jewish Life in Greater Toronto.*

94 Norman Podhoretz, "The Case for Bombing Iran," in *The Jewish Condition: Challenges and Responses – 1938–2008*, ed. William B. Helmreich, Mark Rosenblum, and David Schimel (New Brunswick, NJ: Transaction Publishers, 2008), 45–56.

EPILOGUE

1 Richard Alba, "On the Sociological Significance of the American Jewish Experience: Boundary Blurring, Assimilation, and Pluralism," *Sociology of Religion* 67, no. 4 (2006): 347–58.

2 Sylvia Barack Fishman, *Jewish Life and American Culture* (Albany: State University of New York Press, 2000).

3 Carmen Lambert, Tsuneo Ayabe, Tsukuba Daigaku, and Rekishi Jinrui Gakukei, *Ethnicity and Multiculturalism in Canada: An Anthropological Study* (Ibaraki, Japan: Institute of History and Anthropology, University of Tsukuba, 1986); Tsuneo Ayabe, ed., *A Comparative Study of Multiculturalism and Assimilation in Canada, the United States, and Australia* (Chiba, Japan: Josai International University, March 2001).

APPENDIX ONE

1 Charles Shahar, *2011 National Household Survey: The Jewish Population of Canada, parts One and Two* (Toronto: Jewish Federation of Canada/ United Israel Appeal: 2014), Appendix 2.

APPENDIX TWO

1 Luis Lugo, Alan Cooperman, Gregory A. Smith, Conrad Hackett, Cary Funk, Neha Sahgal, Phillip Connor, Jessica Hamar Martinez et al., *A Portrait of Jewish Americans: Findings from a Pew Research Center Survey of U.S. Jews* (Washington, DC: Pew Research Center's Religion and Public Life Project, 2013). The main source for NJPS will be Sidney Goldstein, *Profile of American Jewry: Insights from the 1990 National Jewish Population Survey* (New York: American Jewish Yearbook, 1992), 77–173.

2 Charles Shahar, *2011 National Household Survey: The Jewish Population of Canada* (Toronto: Jewish Federation of Canada/United Israel Appeal: 2014); Charles Shahar, *2011 National Household Survey: The Jewish Community of Montreal* (Toronto: Jewish Federations of Canada/United Israel Appeal: 2015).

3 Charles Shahar, *Jewish Life in Montreal: A Survey of the Attitudes, Beliefs and Behaviours of Montreal's Jewish Community* (Montreal: Federation CJA, 2010); Charles Shahar and Tina Rosenbaum, *Jewish Life in Greater Toronto: A Survey of the Attitudes and Behaviours of Greater Toronto's Jewish Community* (Toronto: UJA Federation, 2005).

4 The results of that 1996 survey are found in two reports, both titled "A Survey of Jewish Life in Montreal" and published by the Federation of Jewish Community Services of Montreal. Part 1, by Charles Shahar, was released in December 1996; part 2, by Shahar and Randal F. Schnoor, was released in May 1997.

5 The results of this survey are summarized in Jay Brodbar-Nemzer, *A First Look: Greater Toronto Jewish Community Study* (Toronto: Toronto Jewish Congress and the Jewish Federation of Greater Toronto, June 1991).

6 The data from this survey are analyzed, and also compared to the NJPS data, in Jay Brodbar-Nemzer et al., "An Overview of the Canadian Jewish Community," in *The Jews in Canada*, ed. Robert J. Brym, William Shaffir, and Morton Weinfeld (Toronto: Oxford University Press, 1993).

7 Raymond Breton, Wsevolod W. Isajiw, Warren E. Kalbach, and Jeffrey G. Reitz, *Ethnic Identity and Equality: Varieties of Experience in a Canadian City* (Toronto: University of Toronto Press, 1990).

Index

Clark, Joe, 251, 272
Clarke, Austin, 213
class: conflict, 184, 268, 302, 318; and education, 229–30, 234; and identity, 180, 310; and the Jewish population, 5, 15, 76, 154, 158, 160–3; middle, 27, 95, 107, 111, 113, 124, 142–3, 183; mobility, 78, 92, 94; upper, 38; working, 59, 71–2, 86, 88–90, 103–4, 258. *See also* corporate elite; incomes; occupations
Clinton, Bill, 118
Clinton, Hillary, 245
clothing trade. *See* garment industry
cohanim, 24
Cohen, Harvey, 137
Cohen, Judith, 193
Cohen, Leonard, 76, 187, 193, 210, 313
Cohen, Matt, 193
Cohen, Maxwell, 95
Cohen, Nathan, 212
Cohon family, 102
Collins, Doug, 205, 321–5. *See also* hate speech; *North Shore News*
Combined Jewish Appeal (CJA) (Montreal). *See* Federation CJA
comedians, 31, 186–7, 211, 216–7. *See also* culture; entertainment industry; humour
commandments, 36, 218, 238, 275, 278, 296. See also *mitzvot*
common-law relationships, 127, 382n52
Communauté Sépharade Unifiée du Québec, 20, 182, 263
communism, 17, 19, 65, 249, 316, 320; anti-Semitism of, 318–19
Communist Party of Canada, 244

community life: divisions in, 50, 61, 154, 173, 184–5, 302–6; and the Holocaust, 60, 205, 210; and identity, 39–40, 53, 224–5, 291, 294, 297; and immigration, 56, 62, 66–71; importance of, 153–7; institutions of, 123, 129, 158, 160, 164–70, 175–8, 181, 198, 211, 221, 233–4, 240, 283; leaders of, 110–13, 183; participation in, 97, 101–2, 117, 137–45, 148–9; structure of, 78–9, 82–5, 88. *See also* American Judaism; demography; education; ethnicity; "inreach" programs; Jewish community centres; organizations
concentration camps. *See* death camps
Concordia University, 237, 261
Conference on Jewish Material Claims Against Germany, 205
Conservative Judaism, 19, 32, 276, 280, 283–4, 287–92; and education, 222, 239; and gender, 119, 139; religious practice of, 299, 301–6; social relations of, 160, 192, 303
Conservative Party of Canada, 246–7, 255, 264, 273
Conservative Rabbinical Assembly, 292
conspiracy theories, 215, 317, 319–20, 322–3
contraception, 43, 125, 131
conversion: Conservative, 283; contemporary, 32–3, 52, 291, 295; formal, 145–6; historical, 29; and intermarriage, 6, 145, 147, 150, 152, 281; of Jews,

302; and education, 220, 234–5,
311; and intermarriage, 151,
332; and Israel, 35; and philanthropy, 179, 391n45; and religious practice, 285–6; and sex,
125, 131. *See also* Catholicism;
Christianity
Protocols of the Elders of Zion,
320, 322
Proulx, Gilles, 335
Prutschi, Manuel, 332
public schools, 211, 220, 226,
228–9, 234–5, 242, 309
public service, 73, 91, 257–8
Purim, 130, 196, 294

Qana (Lebanon), 247
Quebec: anti-Semitism in, 310,
314–16, 326, 328, 331, 334–5,
419n86; culture of, 191; demography of, 47–8, 131, 285, 349;
education in, 221, 234; immigration to, 65, 69–70; and
Israel, 332; minorities in, 245;
National Assembly of, 256;
nationalism, 61, 263, 339;
Superior Court of, 266. *See also*
Charter of Values; Montreal;
Quebec Jewish Community;
Quiet Revolution; "reasonable
accommodation"
Quebec City, 56
Quebec-Israel Committee, 166
Quebec Jewish Community, 77,
99, 354–5; education, 189, 231,
234–5; francophone, 74; out-
migration of, 81; politics of, 61,
215, 249–50, 259, 263, 269–70;
press, 198; survival of, 260–3.
See also Communauté Sépharde

Unifiée de Québec; Montreal
Jewish Community
Quebec Theatre Guild, 191
Quiet Revolution, 108
Quinzaine Sépharade Festival, 20

rabbinate, 279; debates of, 17; in
Israel, 265; membership in, 65;
orthodox, 32, 124; training of,
293. *See also* rabbis
Rabbinical College of Canada, 238
Rabbinical Council (Montreal),
138
rabbis: and conversion, 147–8;
debates among/about, 109, 291–
2, 301–6; education of, 238,
267, 276, 293; and divorce,
131–2; ideal of, 115; and intermarriage, 151; jokes about, 14,
291; and LGBTQ Jews, 138–40;
politics of, 245, 264; roles of,
42, 107, 111, 119, 129, 182,
279–80, 288; women as, 120–1.
See also rabbinate
Rabbi's Manual, 292
Rabin, Yitzhak, 50, 303
Rabinovitch, Samuel, 316
race, 18, 22–23, 318, 320; in
Canada, 102; and Jewish identity, 29, 31; and hate speech,
321. *See also* class; ethnicity;
gender; genetics
racism: in Canada, 33, 59, 171,
234, 248, 317–18; and hate
speech, 321, 324–6; and intermarriage, 129, 150; in Israel, 21;
opposition to, 266, 269–70,
285, 308; policy based, 327,
415n11; study of, 309, 313;
toward Jews, 31, 74, 158, 271,

Vancouver, 79, 129

Vancouver Jewish community, 53, 81, 83, 96–7, 347; and education, 106, 122, 223; religious practices of, 300; social patterns of, 133, 143–4, 157, 306, 382n52

Van den Haag, Ernest, 10, 25

Vassanji, M.G., 213

Victoria, British Columbia, 79, 81, 347, 387n7

Vidal, Gore, 190, 212

Vilna Gaon, 231

Volman, Ben, 282

volunteerism, 60, 154, 179–81, 210

Waddington, Miriam, 193

Waldheim, Kurt, 182, 205

Wapella, Saskatchewan, 80

war crimes, 207

War Crimes Unit (Department of Justice), 272

Ward, The (Toronto), 78

"War on Christmas," 285

Wasserman, Dora, 191

Waxman, Al, 216

Wayne and Shuster, 186–7, 194, 216–17

Weber, Max, 15, 108, 361n18. See also *Protestant Ethic and the Spirit of Capitalism*

Weiner, Garry, 256, 258

Weinzweig, John, 194

welfare, 58, 74, 104; agencies, 101–2, 110, 169, 172; communal, 165. See also organizations; welfare state

welfare state, 4, 171, 184, 248–9, 268

West Bank, 141, 198, 214

Western Canada: anti-Semitism in, 314–16; Jewish population of, 58, 69, 77, 79–5, 157, 220, 250, 263, 269–70, 300. See also Jewish Colonization Association; Vancouver Jewish community; Winnipeg

Western Guard, 317, 320

Western Wall, 50, 202, 265

Wexner, Leslie, 176

white privilege, 313, 342

white supremacy, 317, 325

Who Owns Canada (Rosenberg), 91, 360n9

Wiesenthal Museum of Tolerance (Los Angeles), 209

Windsor, Ontario, 79, 81, 250, 347

Winnipeg, 58, 78, 83, 129; anti-Semitism in, 328–9; Jewish community of, 71, 80–1, 143, 178, 193, 256, 347; Jewish neighbourhoods of, 154, 157, 159; Jewish schools in, 223. See also Canadian Museum of Human Rights

Wirth, Louis, 44, 289, 309. See also *Ghetto, The*

Wiseman, Adele, 193, 212–13

Wisniewski, Bernard, 206

Wisse, Ruth, 237

Wolbromsky, Ruby and Linda, 201

Wolfe, Rose, 251

women, 119–24: and education, 95, 188, 222; elderly, 143–4; in employment, 90–1, 93, 105–6; Jewish identity of, 147; LGBTQ, 137–8, 140–1; and marriage, 133–5, 371n60, 385n92; in politics, 89; in religion, 182, 202,